BY THE HAND OF MORMON

By the Hand of Mormon

The American Scripture that Launched a New World Religion

Terryl L. Givens

OXFORD
UNIVERSITY PRESS
2002

OXFORD
UNIVERSITY PRESS

Oxford   New York
Auckland   Bangkok   Buenos Aires   Cape Town
Chennai   Dar es Salaam   Delhi   Hong Kong   Istanbul   Karachi
Kolkata   Kuala Lumpur   Madrid   Melbourne   Mexico City   Mumbai   Nairobi
São Paulo   Shanghai   Singapore   Taipei   Tokyo   Toronto

and associated companies in

Berlin

Copyright © 2002 by Terryl L. Givens

Published by Oxford University Press, Inc.,
198 Madison Avenue, New York, New York 10016

Oxford is a registered trademark of Oxford University Press

Library of Congress Cataloging-in-Publication Data

Givens, Terryl.
By the hand of Mormon : the American scripture that launched
a new world religion / Terryl L. Givens.
p.   cm.
Includes bibliographical references and index.
ISBN 0-19-513818-X (alk. paper)
1. Book of Mormon. I. Title.
BX8627 .G58 2002
289.3´22--dc21   2001053118

9 8 7 6 5 4 3 2 1

Printed in the United States of America
on acid-free paper

To Nathaniel, Jonathan, Rebecca, Rachael, Elisabeth, Andrew

And thou shalt be brought down, and shalt speak out of the ground, and thy speech shall be low out of the dust, and thy voice shall be, as of one that hath a familiar spirit, out of the ground, and thy speech shall whisper out of the dust.

—Isaiah 29:4

Acknowledgements

The University of Richmond has generously funded travel and research related to this project, for which I am grateful. In a study as wide-ranging as this one, I have necessarily relied on the knowledge and good will of a number of colleagues, forging and renewing some wonderful friendships in the process. William Slaughter at the Archives of the Church of Jesus Christ of Latter-day Saints, as usual, went beyond the call of duty in making suggestions and helping me obtain photographs. David Whittaker's command of Mormon history and its sources is immense, and he gave me especially useful guidance and advice. Richard Rust, a kind and outstanding scholar of the Book of Mormon, provided sound criticisms. Also contributing to the process were Larry Peer, Doug Winiarski, and Richard Ouellette.

I am indebted to Steve Harper for his steadfast support—as well as numerous leads and sources. Louis Schwartz provided insight and fresh perspectives. Anthony Russell, a true scholar and faithful friend, has made me work and think harder about all things religious. Richard Bushman, one of the great gentlemen and scholars of his generation, was generous enough to make useful suggestions along the way. My editor at Oxford, Cynthia Read, deserves special mention for the professionalism and kindness she has brought to all her dealings with me. As always, George Givens, my father and mentor, provided steady encouragement and rare source material. Finally, I thank my wife, Fiona, for making the long journey delightsome.

Author's Note

Historians working with miracle stories turn out something that is either periphrastic of the faith, indifferent to it, or merely silly.

—Jacob Neusner

In a history of a religiously controversial subject, of which the Book of Mormon is a premiere example, the disputability of the facts is too obvious to bear repeating on every page. I have therefore avoided constructions like "Joseph Smith's *alleged* vision," or "the *purported* visit of Moroni," as they would become tiresome and pedantic if repeated on every page. My focus in any case has not been on whether the Book of Mormon or the account of it given by Joseph Smith is true. Rather, I have tried to examine why the Book of Mormon has been taken seriously—for very different reasons—by generations of devoted believers and confirmed skeptics. But while those polarities are moved by its perceived divinity or sacrilege, indifference is becoming less of an option. As the resources of archaeology, literary analysis, evangelical polemics, and varieties of textual and cultural studies are increasingly brought to bear on this historically contentious and influential document, it has assumed a number of disputed identities: authentically ancient text, imaginative masterwork, nineteenth-century cultural product, and engine behind the growth of the next world religion. It would seem appropriate at this juncture in its tempestuous career to attempt an overview of what this "golden bible" has meant, and might conceivably yet come to mean, to its various readerships.

Contents

Introduction   3

ONE   "A Seer Shall the Lord My God Raise Up":
The Prophet and the Plates   8

TWO   "Out of the Dust":
The Book of Mormon Comes Forth   43

THREE   "A Marvelous Work and a Wonder":
The Book of Mormon as Sacred Sign   62

FOUR   "I, Nephi, Wrote This Record":
The Book of Mormon as Ancient History,
Part 1—The Search for a Mesoamerican Troy   89

FIVE   "I, Nephi, Wrote This Record":
The Book of Mormon as Ancient History,
Part 2—The Search for a Rational Belief   117

SIX   "Devices of the Devil":
The Book of Mormon as Cultural Product or
Sacred Fiction   155

SEVEN   "Plain and Precious Truths":
The Book of Mormon as New Theology,
Part 1—The Encounter with Biblical Christianity   185

EIGHT   "Plain and Precious Truths":
The Book of Mormon as New Theology,
Part 2—Dialogic Revelation   209

NINE   "A Standard Unto My People":
The Book of Mormon as Cultural Touchstone   240

Notes   247

Index   311

BY THE HAND OF MORMON

Introduction

[Mani] seem[s] to suggest that already in the third or fourth century the idea had got around, at least to perceptive minds, that religious movements have each a book, that a new religious movement must have a new written book.

—Wilfred Cantwell Smith

In 1842, four years after Governor Lilburn Boggs expelled all Mormons from the state of Missouri, and two years before his own martyrdom, Joseph Smith sent a now famous account of the new religious movement he had founded to the editor of a Chicago newspaper.[1] Included was a description of the golden plates delivered to him by the angel Moroni, which he had translated and published as the Book of Mormon in 1830.

These records were engraven on plates which had the appearance of gold. Each plate was six inches wide and eight inches long and not quite so thick as common tin. They were filled with engravings in Egyptian characters and bound together in a volume, as the leaves of a book with three rings running through the whole. The volume was something near six inches in thickness, a part of which was sealed. The characters on the unsealed part were small, and beautifully engraved. The whole book exhibited many marks of antiquity in its construction and much skill in the art of engraving.

The passage reads rather like a catalogue description penned by a connoisseur of fine books. It shows not just an eye for detail, but an aesthetic sensibility and an appreciative but restrained regard for the beauty and sheer craftsmanship of what was before him. There is something almost uncanny in the dispassion with which the prophet focuses on the pure physicality of the plates. Already, they had generated a legacy of cultural conflict and religious controversy that would culminate in both empire building and martyrdom. But Smith's eye is here focused on the plates as concrete, inert artifact. It all reminds one of the great impressionist painter Claude Monet's last painting of his beloved Camille; as she lay deceased upon her death bed, he was drawn to paint her one final time. Instead of seeing his dead wife, he wrote, he suddenly found himself "in the act of mechanically observing the succession . . . of fading colors which death was imposing on [her] immobile face."[2] Certainly the deceased may have coloring that intrigues us, and even the stone tablets of Moses, assuming they were real, must have had particular dimensions. Still, we do not generally think of holy artifacts or of departed loved ones in such terms as these.

Scripture is not an easy category to define. Religious scholar Miriam Levering describes three traditional approaches: We consider to be sacred texts those that have supernatural origins, those that are used to define our relationship to the sacred, or those that are simply treated as sacred. But Levering suggests that such categories do not do full justice to the multidimensional ways in which scripture can be experienced by a community. Consequently, she advocates "examining all of the ways in which individuals and communities *receive* these words and texts: the ways people respond to the texts, the uses they make of them, the contexts in which they turn to them, their understandings of what it is to read them or to understand them, and the roles they find such words and texts can have in their religious projects."[3] Shlomo Biderman agrees that "to understand scripture is to understand the conditions under which a group of texts has gained authority over the lives of people and has been incorporated into human activities of various important kinds."[4]

Since its publication, the Book of Mormon has been cast in a variety of roles that served the "religious projects" of both believers and detractors. Sign of the end times, litmus test of prophetic authority, Rosetta stone of Mesoamerican civilizations, barometer of public gullibility, prima facie evidence of blasphemy—these and other functions have characterized the record's tumultuous history. One astute—and generally objective—observer of Mormonism has remarked that "the tale of an unsophisticated farm boy who found some engraved metal plates and used 'magic spectacles' to translate therefrom a thousand years of pre-Columbian American history appears so incredible to many non-Mormons that they simply dismiss the prophet's visions as hallucinations, regard his 'golden bible' as a worthless document, and wonder how any intelligent person could ever accept it as true."[5]

This present work is an attempt to answer that question, among others, but in the context of a larger history of the reception and impact of a scripture that has hitherto received little critical investigation. From the day of its founding, Mormonism's name, doctrine, and image have been largely dependent on this book of scripture, transmitted to the boy-prophet Joseph Smith by an angel. After the Bible, this Book of Mormon is the most widely distributed religious book in America. By the new millennium, over fifteen thousand copies a day were being printed, in some 94 languages.[6] Long considered a sacred revelation by the faithful, a fraud by detractors, and ignored by non-Mormon scholars, the book in recent years has been undergoing significant reappraisal on all three fronts.

Within the Church of Jesus Christ of Latter-day Saints (LDS Church), discussion has emerged over the role and significance of the Book of Mormon in establishing early LDS doctrine, and recent years have seen both a repackaging of the sacred volume (newly subtitled, as of 1982, "Another Testament of Jesus Christ") and a dramatic reemphasis on its place in the lives of individual members. For the first century and more of the Book of Mormon's existence, its historicity was assumed by the faithful, but attempts to authenticate its antiquity were confined largely to amateurs. Increasingly sophisticated endeavors began by midcentury, and since 1980, several LDS scholars have worked under the aegis of the Foundation for Ancient Research and Mormon Studies to amass literary, anthropological, historical, and other support for an ancient origin for the Book of Mormon. Then in 1997, the Church officially took that institute under its wing, incorporating it into Brigham Young University in a move that represents a significant shift in the church's policy toward scientific approaches to the Book of Mormon.

Meanwhile, skeptics are forsaking the facile scenarios of the nineteenth century (that Smith plagiarized accounts by Ethan Smith or Solomon Spaulding) and are searching for new sources of and explanations behind the scripture. (John Brooke, for example, finds parallels with hermeticism,[7] and D. Michael Quinn and others build upon Fawn Brodie's early explanation that emphasized nineteenth-century environmental influences.[8]) On a different front, two scholars at a recent regional meeting of the Evangelical Theological Society praised the professionalism of Mormon apologetics, and reproached their religious colleagues for the dearth of scholarly, sophisticated, and informed critiques of the book.[9]

In the larger realm of religious studies, developments have been equally dramatic. Academics here have traditionally ignored Joseph Smith and his story of gold plates. But theologians and religious scholars of the first rank, from Jacob Neusner to James Charlesworth to (the more controversial) Harold Bloom, have been suggesting for a few years that it is time to take Smith's writings more seriously. Neusner calls the Book of Mormon "a fresh Christian expression" that has too often endured scholarly neglect.[10] Charlesworth and Krister Stendahl have presented papers that examine relations between the Book of Mormon and both pseudepigraphical and New Testament texts.

Harold Bloom refers to the profound and provocative parallels between kabbalistic texts and Smith's writings, and more recently has described the Book of Mormon and its "doctrine of angels" as being of "extraordinary interest."[11] In Europe, the late German theologian Ernst Wilhelm Benz and the Finn Heikki Raisanen have argued that Joseph Smith needs to be taken more seriously as a theologian.[12] Structuralist literary scholar Seth Kunin has written on the book, as has French critic Viola Sachs (who refers to the text as "the New World scripture").[13]

In spite of the book's unparalleled position in American religion and its changing meaning for apologists, critics, and theologians, no full-length study has attempted to present to the wider public a study of this book and its changing role in Mormonism and in American religion generally. In fact, as historian Nathan Hatch has written, "for all the attention given to the study of Mormonism, surprisingly little has been devoted to the Book of Mormon itself . . . . The pivotal document of the Mormon church, 'an extraordinary work of popular imagination,' still receives scant attention from cultural historians." He cites the opinion of sociologist and scholar of Mormonism Jan Shipps as well, that "historians need to return to the centrality of the 'gold bible,' Joseph Smith's original testament to the world, which certified the prophet's leadership and first attracted adherents to the movement."[14] "Whatever its source," Shipps writes elsewhere, the Book of Mormon "occupies a position of major importance in both the religious and intellectual history of the United States."[15]

Nevertheless, at the present time, available treatments are largely limited to apologetic or inspirational literature directed to the faithful, and vitriolic attacks shelved in the cult section of Christian bookstores.[16] The Book of Mormon is perhaps the most religiously influential, hotly contested, and, in the secular press at least, intellectually underinvestigated book in America. This study, then, will examine the initial shape and subsequent transformations of the Book of Mormon, how it has been understood, positioned, packaged, utilized, exploited, presented and represented, by its detractors and by its proponents. It will survey its shifting relationship to LDS doctrine and proselytizing, its changing status and reputation among theologians and scholars, and explore what impact its obtrusive presence may have on Christian conceptions of scripture, of revelation, and of the canon.

Principally, the Book of Mormon has been read in one of at least four ways by its various audiences: as sacred sign, or divine testament to the last days and Joseph's authorized role as modern day prophet and revelator; as ancient history, or a factual account of the pre-Columbian peopling of the Western hemisphere first by a small Old World exodus occurring in the era of Babel and later by groups from Jerusalem in the age of Jeremiah; as cultural production, the imaginative ravings of a rustic religion-maker more inspired by the winds of culture than the breath of God; and as a new American Bible or Fifth Gospel, displacing, supporting, or perverting the canonical word of God, according to the disposition of the reader.

That it was accounted a "marvelous work and a wonder" by all who observed its coming forth is not to be doubted. But it is useful to remember that while for many Christians that expression implied a mighty act of God prophesied by Isaiah, for an equally substantial number the famous definition posed by Samuel Johnson was more pertinent: "All wonder is the effect of novelty upon ignorance."

Joseph Smith, Jr. (1805–1844).
Prophet and founder of the Church of Jesus Christ of Latter-day Saints, and translator of the Book of Mormon. From Charles W. Carter's glass negative (© 1885) of original by an unknown artist.
(Courtesy LDS Church Historical Department)

ONE

"A Seer Shall the Lord My God Raise Up": The Prophet and the Plates

Be ready to receive whatever new truth God might reveal to you, for "the Lord hath more truth and light yet to break forth out of his holy word."

—Rev. John Robinson to the Pilgrims,
upon embarking for America

New York . . . is the theatre of humbugs; the chosen arena of itinerating mountebanks, whether they figure in philosophy, philanthropy, or religion. . . . Hence those who seek to make proselytes to any creed, however absurd, or to find believers in any pretensions, however incredible, or miraculous, may gather kindred spirits here, by "calling them from the vasty deep, and they will come." . . . And if they can make a pedantic show of learning, lay claims to the character of philosophers, deal in hieroglyphics and technicalities, and profess supernatural and miraculous powers . . . they will find here a great multitude of disciples.

—David Reese in 1838

It is both fitting and ironic that at a small crossroads in the town of Palmyra, New York, four churches occupy the four corner lots of the intersection. Fitting, because the four contiguous meeting houses with their four steeples that intermingle on the skyline aptly symbolize the hurly-burly of religious sects vigorously competing for new proselytes, as Joseph Smith described the Palmyra area at the time of the Second Great Awakening. Ironic, because the embarrassment of denominational riches suggested by the intersection was not enough to provide a spiritual home for 14-year-old Joseph Smith himself. His youthful quest for a "true church" to join led him to a momentous encounter

Four steeples in Palmyra, New York. In the early 1800s, the town was the scene of religious revivals that prompted Joseph Smith's spiritual awakening and led to both his first vision and a subsequent visitation from the angel Moroni, guardian of the gold plates. (Author's photograph)

with heavenly beings in which he learned that no church in Palmyra— or anywhere else—was the true church of God.[1]

Like many seekers of the Second Great Awakening, the young Smith found himself caught up in a scene of fervid revivalism and confused by the competing claims of ministers seeking converts. Deciding to pray for heavenly guidance, Smith had retired to the woods to ask God which church he should join. On that early spring morning in 1820, two person-ages, identifying themselves as God the Father and Jesus Christ, had ap-peared to the boy in a grove of trees on his father's homestead.[2] Though it may be true, as Mormon historian Richard Bushman writes, that in seek-ing such guidance "an answer for himself must be an answer for the en-tire world" and that with the vision "a new era in history began," the boy's initial reading was clearly less grandiose.[3] His personal quest for spiritual guidance may have precipitated an epiphany on the order of Paul's on the road to Damascus, but the important truths he learned were that his personal sins were forgiven and that he should hold himself aloof from the sects of his day. Although the timing and the naming of the event assign it absolute primacy in the founding of Mormonism, the vision was described by the young Joseph and apparently interpreted by him at the time as a private experience with no greater implications for the world at

large or for Christian believers generally. In returning from the divine
visitation, his understated remark to his mother was simply, "I have
learned for myself that Presbyterianism is not true."[4]

In fact, so far was Smith at this point from universalizing his private
revelation that his own mother continued *her* affiliation with the Presbyterian church for another several years. Apparently Smith did share his
experience with at least a few persons outside the family circle, for he
later said that he was chastised by the clergy and ridiculed by neighbors
for his claims.[5] It was not until 1832 that he actually recorded the event,
and he withheld publishing a version until 1842, just two years before his
death.[6] Accordingly, neither Smith nor Mormon missionaries made much
mention of the vision in the early years of Mormonism.[7] Even in the 1830
"Revelation on Church Organization and Government," a kind of manifesto that heralded the church's formal founding, the vision received no
more than a passing, cryptic allusion to a time when "it was truly manifested unto this first elder [Joseph Smith] that he had received a remission of his sins."[8] Clearly, the experience was understood at the time, and
even scripturally portrayed, as part of a personal conversion narrative,
not the opening scene in a new gospel dispensation.

Joseph and Lucy Smiths' farm, home of Joseph Smith, Jr.,
at the time of his first vision. (Anderson collection, 1907;
Courtesy LDS Church Historical Department)

So the young Joseph Smith bided his time until the fall of 1823. By then, he was 17 years old; some three and a half uneventful years had passed since the experience Mormons now refer to as the "First Vision."

Visitation from Moroni

Now on the night of September 21, 1823, the 17-year-old Smith was once again engaged in a private spiritual quest. Nothing in particular seems to have been the catalyst behind his petition that night, other than a sense that the absolution of sin granted him as a youth of 14 was in need of renewal. He was merely seeking once again "forgiveness of all my sins and follies," in his words. And yet, Smith at the same time recorded that he prayed this night with "full confidence in obtaining a divine manifestation, as I previously had one" (JS-H 1:29). His expectation was fully satisfied when his room erupted with brilliant light and an angel who identified himself as Moroni appeared at Joseph's bedside. And this time, before the night was over, the young man would no longer be able to doubt that he was caught up in events of world-shaking importance.

After stating his own name and his divine commission, the messenger told Smith that "God had a work for [him] to do; and that [his] name should be had for good and evil among all nations." The nature of that work was hinted at in the words that followed immediately: "He said there was a book deposited, written upon gold plates, giving an account of the former inhabitants of this continent, and the source from whence they sprang. He also said that the fulness of the everlasting Gospel was contained in it, as delivered by the Savior to the ancient inhabitants" (JS-H 1:33-34).

This book "written upon gold plates" would forever alter the life and reputation of the young farmboy, and would serve as the principal catalyst behind the rise of a worldwide church. More than any other factor, it would come to ground Joseph's reputation as seer and charlatan, beloved prophet and reviled blasphemer, as disturber of the peace and empire builder. At the present day, over one hundred million copies of this "gold bible" have been printed and distributed throughout the world,[9] and the religion it helped to found stands on the threshold, according to one researcher, "of becoming the first major faith to appear on earth since the Prophet Mohammed rode out of the desert."[10]

If we seek an explanation behind the staggering success of a document so controversial that it has been called everything from the origin of modern America's "creeping nincompoopism"[11] to the product of "an authentic religious genius,"[12] we might do well to begin by looking closely at Moroni's prologue to the great religious drama about to unfold. With those few words spoken to Joseph Smith, the angel managed to convey something of the complexity and variability of the roles this "golden bible" would play. First, Moroni emphasized the rootedness of this new revelation from Heaven in artifactual reality. Referring to a book actually "deposited" in the earth, and consisting of a physical, tangible medium—actual gold plates—lifts the revelatory experience beyond the nebulous stuff of visions and alters the whole dynamic of the religious claims Smith would be making. It shifts the debate—at least partly—from the realm of interiority and subjectivity toward that of empiricism and objectivity.

Second, the angel characterized the book as an account of America's "former inhabitants," thus setting in motion a pattern that both Joseph and subsequent Mormons would adopt. Moroni, in fact, revealed to Joseph that he was one of those inhabitants of ancient America, the last prophet of his people, chronicler of their history, and keeper of their sacred plates. Grounding the text in a history that is proximate and verifiable proves a keenly double-edged sword, subjecting the record as it does to the exacting gaze of scholarly verification. Its claim to reveal *this* continent's history gives it an appealing relevance at the same time it raises expectations of confirmatory evidence.

Third, the angel reported that the "fulness of the everlasting Gospel" was contained in the plates, but added the enigmatic clause, "as delivered by the Savior to the ancient [American] inhabitants." Such a formulation seems almost calculated to combine shocking novelty with a kind of wry nonchalance. He might as well have said the record affirmed those same ten commandments that God delivered to Atlantis. The angel's perplexing description foreshadows the paradoxical charges soon to come: that the Book of Mormon is both clichéd and heretical, pedestrian and preposterous. And the description raises as many questions as it answers: does the record reiterate canonical scripture, extend canonical scripture, or replace canonical scripture?

Accompanying the plates, the angel had said, were "two stones in silver bows" that would be used for translating the plates. That he, Joseph, would be that translator was never explicitly stated by the angel, but seemed indicated in Moroni's promise that, at some subsequent time, Joseph could retrieve the record from a nearby hillside where it had, apparently, lain buried for 1,400 years.

Following Moroni's description of the plates and relics, the angel quoted several verses of scripture that Smith recognized as coming from both the Old and the New Testaments (though some were altered)— verses that had clear millennialist import for him and his contemporaries.[13] The angel repeated Malachi's ominous predictions of apocalypse, to be ushered in by the coming of the Lord's "messenger, [who] shall prepare the way before me: [after which] the Lord, whom ye seek, shall suddenly come" (Mal. 3:1); he recited Isaiah's prophecy that an "ensign for the nations" would be set up in the context of a "second" gathering of his people, and Moses' prophecy (quoted by Peter) that "a prophet shall the Lord your God raise up unto you of your brethren, like unto me; him shall ye hear in all things whatsoever he shall say unto you" (Isa. 11; Deut. 18:15; Acts 3:22). Moroni identified this prophet as Christ, but he went on to quote Joel's reference to the Lord pouring out his spirit upon all flesh in a new Pentecostal era, at which point "your young men shall see visions" (Joel 2:28).[14] Additionally, Moroni "quoted many other passages of scripture," at least one of which was Daniel's prophecy of the "stone cut out of the mountain without hands" (JS-H 1:41; Dan. 2:44).[15]

To what extent Joseph then saw himself in the allusions to Moses' prophet, Joel's young men, or Malachi's messenger is difficult to say. (Apparently, in spite of Moroni's clarification, many Latter-day Saints persisted in seeing in Moses' words an allusion to Joseph Smith. One member complained to the editor of the church newspaper that among his brethren, "many . . . are in error concerning the prophet of whom Moses spake."[16]) Neither do we know if he then had intimations of the role in which he would later cast himself—"to be one of the instruments in setting up the kingdom of Daniel."[17] But Moroni had made clear that an era of history-changing turmoil was now dawning, that the end time was near, and that spiritual forces were being unleashed while the wicked would soon "burn as stubble." At the center of it all, soon to emerge from obscurity into both defamation and renown, was young Joseph himself. And the instrument through which these cataclysms would be made manifest and propagated was a fantastic set of golden plates, to which subject the angel now returned.

Smith learned that the actual "time that [the plates] should be obtained was not yet fulfilled," although "the vision was opened to my mind that I could see the place where the plates were deposited." He was warned that the plates were not to be shown to any person, and then the angel "ascended till he entirely disappeared, and the room was left as it had been before." Shortly thereafter the angel reappeared, rehearsed the entire message with additional words of "great judgments which were coming upon the earth," and disappeared as before. Then, yet a third time the scene was repeated. On this occasion, the angel cautioned the boy that Satan would tempt him to obtain the plates "for the purpose of getting rich." Thus, in deflating counterweight to the grandiose role being thrust upon the young Smith, the angel had warned him against the twin temptations he would face: to aggrandize himself spiritually or materially by misusing the plates. He was neither to exhibit the plates to anyone nor to think of alleviating his family's acute impoverishment by selling them.

Hill Cumorah. This hillside in Manchester, New York,
three miles south of the Smith farm, was where Joseph Smith
first viewed the gold plates in September of 1823.
(Anderson collection, 1907; Courtesy LDS Church Historical Department)

The morning after the heavenly messenger's three visits, he appeared
a fourth time. In a field where the fatigued Smith fainted while returning home early from chores, Moroni rehearsed the entirety of his teachings, warnings, and commands, and then instructed Joseph to relate all
that he had experienced to his father. Joseph immediately did so, and
his father encouraged him to visit the hill to see the miraculous artifacts. So on that morning of September 22, 1823, Joseph Smith left the
field and walked down the Palmyra-Canandaigua road, turning off to
the left about halfway to the village of Manchester when he recognized,
a few hundred feet in the distance, the hill Moroni had shown him in
the vision the night before. Owing to "the distinctness of the vision" he
had had, he knew by which side to approach, and nearing the top, he
stopped and removed a large stone. Underneath, like a New World counterpart to the lost ark of the covenant, Smith found a large stone box
with the sacred relics of an ancient civilization inside: the gold plates,
the "interpreters," as well as the breastplate the angel had described.
According to some accounts, the box contained two other artifacts: the
sword of Laban, which an early writer in the Book of Mormon had taken
from a Jewish ruler and which served in subsequent Book of Mormon
history as both a model for other weapons and as an important article

in the royal regalia, and a spherical brass instrument (the "Liahona") that functioned as a miraculous compass belonging to the principal group of Jewish exiles who left the Old World and whose story opens the Book of Mormon.

Apparently, in his excitement at beholding the concrete objects of his vision, Smith forgot the angel's words that the time for obtaining the objects was yet distant; according to his 1842 account, he tried to retrieve the plates, "and was again informed that the time for bringing them forth had not yet arrived" (JS-H 1:42, 53). In his 1832 version of the episode, Smith is more frankly self-critical: "I had been tempted of the advisary [sic] and saught [sic] the Plates to obtain riches . . . therefore I was chastened."[18] The angel had warned him against a susceptibility to selfishness; now, looking down at the treasures and contemplating the potential value of such curiosities, his greed apparently tainted his motives. In addition to angelic reprimand, Smith's mother, Lucy Mack, recorded that by some divine agency Smith was actually "hurled to the ground with great violence" as was Uzzah for steadying the ark.[19]

Joseph Smith's friend and scribe Oliver Cowdery, who would most likely have had his information from Joseph himself, confirmed Smith's lapse and its painful consequence in an account he wrote for church members in 1835. By the time of Smith's arrival at the hill, Cowdery wrote, "the certainty of wealth and ease in this life, had so powerfully wrought upon him" that the angel's injunction "had entirely gone from his recollection." As a consequence, "On attempting to take possession of the record a shock was produced upon his system, by an invisible power which deprived him, in a measure, of his natural strength."[20]

Limbo

What followed Smith's first visit to the hill was in effect an imposed probation of four years.[21] During that interim, Smith was required to report to the same place on each yearly anniversary, to be tutored by the angel Moroni in the mission he was charged to perform. Smith recorded little of those unusual meetings, except to say that he "received instruction and intelligence . . . respecting what the Lord was going to do and how and in what manner his kingdom was to be conducted in the last days" (JS-H 1:54). His mother filled in a few more details: "From this time forth Joseph continued to receive instructions from time to time, and every evening we gathered our children together and gave our time up to discussion of those things which he instructed to us." Apparently, Joseph was learning more from the angel than principles of salvation. His mother recorded that these "amusing recitals" included an overview of the customs, wars, religion, and even architecture of the ancient Americans.[22]

Neither Smith nor his mother recorded many details of the next few years. We know he had been quick to share his first vision with residents of his community. Now, however, Lucy Mack recorded a warning from the angel Moroni that Joseph passed on to his family: "Father and Mother, the angel of the Lord says that we must be careful not to proclaim these things or to mention them abroad." So, other than his immediate relatives, it does not appear that Smith shared his experience with outsiders—at least initially. And even conversations within the family circle about Moroni and his record ended several weeks after that first visit. In November of 1823, Joseph's eldest brother, Alvin, died tragically from medical mistreatment. Lucy Mack recorded that Alvin had "manifested a greater zeal and anxiety" about the record than the rest of the family. With him gone, "we could not endure to hear or say one word upon that subject, for the moment that Joseph spoke of the record it would immediately bring Alvin to our minds. . . ."[23]

For the next two years, we hear nothing more of angelic ministrations or ancient records. Smith continued to help with the grueling work of the family farm, occasionally hiring himself out to help with the annual payments on their property. Defensively responding to rumors that the Smith family had all been slackers, another of Joseph's brothers, William Smith, later reminisced about a daily routine that was grim, even by the standards of nineteenth-century farmsteaders: "Neither did my fathers family spend their time or any portion of their time in idle habbits. Such was the prevailing Sircumstancies of the family, Connected with the want of money and the scarcity of provisions that nesessaty made an imperative demand upon evrey energy, nerve or member of the family for boath economy and labour which this demant had to be met with the strictest kind of endustry [sic]."[24] Then, in October of 1825, an opportunity arose that would contribute a decisive element to both Smith's personal life and public reputation. Josiah Stowell, an affluent farmer from South Bainbridge, New York, believed he possessed a map identifying the location of a lost silver mine near the town of Harmony, which was just across the Pennsylvania border along the Susquehanna River. He had come to Palmyra with a friend, Joseph Knight, to buy grain. While in the area, he heard reports that the young Smith boy "possessed certain means by which he could discern things invisible to the natural eye."[25] Most likely, those "means" referred to a seer stone, or "peep stone," that Smith discovered while digging a well with one Willard Chase, the year before Moroni's visit.[26] Stowell offered good wages if Joseph and his father would travel back to Harmony with him to assist in the search.

Money hole near Cortland, New York. Called "Winchell holes"
by the locals, these are the purported traces left by a money-digger of that
name from Vermont, who may have been a passing associate of
Oliver Cowdery's father, William. (Author's photograph)

In recent years, an abundant literature has sprung up describing the
pervasiveness of a nineteenth-century folk culture that had no difficulty
reconciling Protestant religiosity with excursions into the magical and
superstitious.[27] That culture, combined with ubiquitous reports of lost
mines and buried treasure, fueled a practice of "money-digging" that
all classes except the most intellectually progressive seem to have engaged in.[28] Around this author's own birthplace in Cortland County,
New York, some farmlands exhibit to this day the occasional manmade
depressions that old locals still refer to as "Winchell holes," the purported traces of searches carried out by a nineteenth-century money-
digger from Vermont.[29]

The line between angels and guardian spirits, buried plates and buried treasure is a matter of scholarly contention and negotiation. Skeptics then and now have found in the prevailing cultural climate a
causative explanation for the abundant supernaturalism of the religion
soon to emerge from upstate New York. Certainly Joseph himself was
aware of the possibilities for disastrous contamination of the one by the
other, but he seems to have come to a full recognition of their distinctness only with time. The stone he found in the well, for example, he
considered to be truly endowed with special powers.[30] Neighbors later
hostile to him would testify that he had used the object to participate in

Money hole in Harmony, Pennsylvania, where Joseph Smith
reportedly helped Josiah Stowell dig for silver in 1825.
(Anderson collection, 1907; Courtesy LDS Church Historical Department)

nocturnal rituals aimed at retrieving buried gold and silver. Most affidavits do not mention Joseph as being actually present on these occasions but as being the "eyes" behind the operation. In at least some of this retrospective animosity, we can clearly discern the feelings of embarrassment about what was wasted time at best and exploitation at worst; at least one participant lost a "large fat sheep" in trying to placate spirits guarding the treasure.[31] Joseph did not deny his engagement as a money-digger (he even specified his wages for it in the church newspaper[32]), but he did insist that he engaged in the pursuit sporadically, reluctantly, and temporarily.

In that October of 1825, however, the entreaties of the wealthy farmer Josiah Stowell, together with the Smith family's poverty, led him to accept the offer of employment. Together with his father and several neighbors, Joseph set out on the 135-mile journey to Harmony, Pennsylvania. Although they only persisted in their efforts for a month or so, the experience was important for two reasons. First, while he worked near Harmony, Joseph boarded at the home of Isaac Hale. One of Hale's daughters was a tall and attractive 21-year-old named Emma. She and Joseph soon fell in love and, over her father's strenuous objections, married a little more than a year later. Second, Joseph's engagement as a treasure-seeker was at this point public and formal; he even signed a contract. He and his mother would both complain in later years that this brief employment by Josiah Stowell was the real source of Joseph's reputation as a money-digger.

Several circumstances now converged to change the direction of Smith's life, and prepare him for the next stage in the Book of Mormon's appearance. First, the Stowell silver mine project was a failure. Joseph's and Lucy Mack's accounts both cast Joseph in the role of enlightened skeptic, persuading Stowell to give up his costly effort by mid-November. Evidence exists that shortly thereafter, in March of 1826, a nephew of Stowell named Peter Bridgeman filed a complaint against Joseph for disorderly conduct—apparently related to his occult practices. Joseph had earlier confided to Martin Harris that the angel Moroni had told him "he must quit the company of the money diggers."[33] Now, in the trial provoked by Bridgeman, it became clear even to hostile observers that Joseph was "mortified" to see his gift clamored after "only in search of filthy lucre."[34] Finally, there was the matter of Joseph's interest in Emma Hale. When his fellow Palmyrans returned home in the wake of the silver mine fiasco, Joseph had stayed on to work for both Josiah Stowell and Joseph Knight (in nearby Colesville) and to court Emma. When Isaac Hale refused permission to the couple, they waited until a Sunday while he was at church and rode to the home of Squire Tarbill who married them on January 18, 1827. The pair located in Manchester, but Emma wrote home the next summer requesting permission to come collect some belongings. Peter Ingersoll was hired to assist them, and both he and Isaac Hale recorded the exchange that occurred when Joseph was confronted by his angry father-in-law. It was bad enough for Joseph not to have much in the way of prospects. But those pursuits in which he *was* engaged were not calculated to warm the heart of a father-in-law concerned for the welfare and reputation of his bright and talented daughter. Although differing in some details, the two accounts both have Joseph promising "to give up his old habits of digging for money and looking into stones."[35] Joseph was sincere, no doubt. His money-digging days were now firmly behind him. But gold and seer stones were still very much in his future.

The Gold Plates

Moroni had first come in September of 1823. Lucy recorded that Joseph revisited the location that would be known as Hill Cumorah in September of 1824, but for the second time returned without the plates. Neither she nor Joseph made any mention of his annual visit to the hill in 1825—which presumably occurred just before he left in search of Josiah Stowell's silver mine. His fourth visit would have occurred while he was living in Harmony, working and courting Emma. With the promised delivery date now just a year away, and having apparently decided about this time to resist all appeals to engage in conjuring, his interests began to return to the angel's message. He does not record at what point he was released from his vow of silence, but his father seems to have broken it on at least one occasion. Lucy Mack wrote that in 1825 or 1826, Joseph Sr. shared the story of the plates with Martin Harris, a family friend. No one else, she insisted, was in on the secret.[36] But somehow, at least one neighbor and member of the money-digging circle, Samuel Lawrence, learned of the plates and the annual visits to Cumorah as well.[37]

It is possible that Joseph was by this time sharing his story with a slowly expanding circle of intimates. If he had been testing the waters of public acceptance of his message in any large-scale fashion, we might expect the vociferous response to the Book of Mormon to have begun earlier than it did. As it is, hardly a mention is made of the plates by outside sources before 1827. Not until 1829 does a local paper mention reports of the "golden bible," "an ancient record, of a religious and divine nature and origin" found "through supernatural means," though it does remark such speculation had existed "for some time past."[38]

On the other hand, given the prevalence of gold-diggers, treasure-hunters, and mine-seekers at this place and time, it is possible that rumors of one more buried hoard, even in the form of a gold bible, were not distinctive enough to warrant much attention. That was certainly the case with at least one neighbor. Thomas Taylor did not believe that Joseph was a prophet or that the Book of Mormon was scripture—but he thought the story of recovered plates to be not especially incredible: "Why not he find something as well as anybody else. Right over here, in Illinois and Ohio, in mounds there, they have discovered copper plates."[39] Similarly, Martin Harris recorded that upon first hearing the story of the gold plates, he presumed that "the money-diggers had probably dug up an old brass kettle, or something of the kind. I thought no more about it."[40] In all likelihood, the scattered reports of the buried record that did make the rounds were received with equal nonchalance.

At any rate, shortly after his most recent visit to the hill, Joseph Smith himself, apparently in excited anticipation of the end of his period of probation and imposed silence, at last was beginning to share the details of his visions with intimates. He first divulged his mission to the family for whom he was then working, the Knights. The son recorded later that in November of 1826, Joseph "made known to my father and I, that he had seen a vision, that a personage had appeared to him and told him where there was a gold book of ancient date buried. . . . My Father and I believed what he told us."[41]

Joseph Knight, Jr., and his father, who accepted his story without hesitation, may thus be considered the first outside his family to respond positively to Joseph Smith's visionary claims. The senior Knight also remembered that Joseph said at this time that the angel had informed him that he would deliver the plates to Joseph on the next anniversary of his visit to the hill, provided "he would Do right according to the will of God."[42]

The next visit from the angel came shortly after Joseph and Emma returned to Palmyra from Pennsylvania (either after their January wedding in 1827, or following their Pennsylvania trip to retrieve Emma's belongings in August of that year[43]). On a business errand for his father in nearby Manchester, Joseph was unusually late returning home. When he at last arrived, in one of his not uncommon public acknowledgments of his own shortcomings, Joseph revealed that he had just experienced at the hands of the angel Moroni "the severest chastisement I ever had in my life," well deserved because of his neglect of spiritual things, he explained. He then went on to reassure his parents that he was back on course, and that, according to the angel's words, "the time [had] now come when the record should be brought forth."[44]

Years later, when Joseph dated the commencement of his labors in the great cause of the Restoration, he would not refer back to his first vision, or even the visit of the angel Moroni. September of 1827, he told the church, was the month of his enlistment.[45] By the time September 21 of that year rolled around at last, a small group of family and intimates had made simple preparations. Joseph Knight, Smith's good friend and supporter from Colesville, was aware of the day on which Joseph expected to retrieve the plates from the hill and planned his business travel so as to be in Palmyra at that time, bringing along Josiah Stowell of the silver mine adventure. Fearing interference from the meddling Samuel Lawrence, Joseph asked his father to reconnoiter Lawrence's farm on the afternoon of the 21st. The elder Smith reported no unusual activity. After the family's guests had retired to bed, around midnight, Joseph asked his mother if she had a chest with lock and key. She panicked when she was unable to provide one, but Joseph reassured her that he could do without. Then, with Emma dressed in riding gear, they borrowed Knight's horse and wagon and headed for Hill Cumorah.[46]

Although the hill was only a few short miles from the Smith home, Joseph and his wife were away from shortly after midnight of the 22nd until sometime after the household had arisen that next morning. When they returned, both Knight and Lucy describe a kind of mock solemnity with which Joseph tormented his expectant audience. (That Joseph could show levity at a time such as this reveals an irrepressible playfulness that he could never quite shake off. It would recurrently expose him to charges of undignified, unprophetlike comportment—and suggests as well the possibility that perhaps some of his involvement with money-digging and sheep-sacrificing involved bemused detachment as well as earnest engagement.[47]) Knight remembered that on seeing the young man that momentous morning, Joseph at first said nothing. Only after breakfast did he call Knight aside to break the spell: "He set his foot on the Bed and leaned his head on his hand and says, 'Well I am Dissopinted.' 'Well,' says I, 'I am sorry.' 'Well,' says he, 'I am grateley Dissopinted; it is ten times Better than I expected'" [sic].[48]

Lucy also suggested that at first he misleadingly conveyed a sense of failure, by saying nothing at the time of his return from the hill. After she left the room in apparent distress, he quickly followed her with words of reassurance. "'Mother,' said he, 'Do not be uneasy. All is right. See here,' said he, 'I have got a key.'" What follows is one of the first in a remarkable catalogue of eyewitness testimonies describing firsthand experience of golden plates, ancient breastplates, "directors," and "interpreters." Together they constitute perhaps the most extensive and yet contentious body of evidence in support of the tactile reality of supernaturally conveyed artifacts that we have in the modern age.

"I . . . took the article in my hands," Lucy records, "and, examining it with no covering but a silk handkerchief, found that it consisted of two smooth three-cornered diamonds set in glass, and the glasses were set in silver bows connected with each other in much the same way that old-fashioned spectacles are made."[49] Joseph's brother William, who was 16 at the time, gave an even fuller description of the instrument many years later, in 1890: "A silver bow ran over one stone, under the other, arround [sic] over that one and under the first in the shape of a horizontal figure 8. . . . [T]hey were much too large for Joseph and he could only see through one at a time using sometimes one and sometimes the other." These stones, he continued, "were attached to the breastplate by a rod which was fastened at the outer shoulde[r] edge of the breastplate and to the edge of the silver bow."[50]

Others who worked with Joseph on the translation also testified to the real existence—if not physical particulars—of this mysterious instrument. Oliver Cowdery would later affirm that he had seen with his own eyes (and handled with his own hands, according to one version[51]) the "Holy Interpreters." Martin Harris saw them along with the breastplate and the sword of Laban, in the presence of the angel who revealed them.[52]

The Urim and Thummim, as Joseph came to call the instrument, means "lights and perfections" in Hebrew,[53] and are first mentioned in Exodus in the set of instructions pertaining to Aaron's priestly garments. There, too, the terms are associated with a breastplate (the "breastplate of judgment"). Although the specifications for most of Aaron's accoutrements are quite detailed, the Urim and Thummim are not described.

They are instead introduced as an already familiar given: "thou shalt put in the breastplate of judgment the Urim and Thummim" (Exod. 28:30). In Numbers, they are mentioned in connection with Joshua's elevation to the leadership of Israel, though again somewhat cryptically. The high priest, it is indicated, shall use them in receiving heavenly guidance for Joshua: "the priest . . . shall ask counsel for him after the judgment of Urim before the Lord" (Num. 27:21). A reference in 1 Samuel more clearly establishes their connection to seership. Saul's famous encounter with the witch of En-dor, we learn, is the result of his failure to obtain revelation by "dreams, prophets, or Urim" (1 Sam. 28:6). Nevertheless, these and a few other scattered references reveal little concerning the puzzling origin, description, or operation of the ancient oracles. Adam Clarke, an older contemporary of Joseph Smith, discusses the mysterious Urim and Thummim in his magisterial commentary first published in 1810:

> What these were has, I believe, never yet been discovered. 1. They are nowhere described. 2. There is no direction given to Moses or any other *how to make them.* 3. Whatever they were, they do not appear to have been *made* on *this* [their first mentioned] occasion. 4. If they were the work of man at all, they must have been the articles in the ancient tabernacle, matters used by the *patriarchs*, and not here particularly described, because well known.[54]

A modern critic has written that "Smith obviously did not use the type of instrument referred to in the Old Testament as Urim and Thummim, which biblical scholars conclude, was a device for casting lots to determine the will of God."[55] In actual fact, the consensus he alleges among "biblical scholars" just doesn't exist. As one full-length study by Cornelius van Dam concludes, "there is simply not sufficient biblical evidence to endorse the lot mode of revelation as an explanation for the [Urim and Thummim.]" More likely, he continues, the instrument "consisted of a single gem." Also consistent with Smith's description and employment of the artifact are van Dam's belief in "the phenomenon of a (supernatural) light in close conjunction with the [Urim and Thummim]," and his view that "priesthood and prophecy" are more closely connected to each other and to the Urim and Thummim "than biblical scholarship has recognized since the early nineteenth century."[56]

At what point Joseph identified the instrument he received from Moroni with the Urim and Thummim of the Old Testament is not known. Joseph initially referred to it by the same term the Book of Mormon itself uses, "interpreters." W. W. Phelps, editor of the church's *The Evening and the Morning Star*, was apparently the first to use the biblical term, though not until 1833.[57] Still, Joseph had been told by the angel Moroni that the device was "what constituted *Seers* in ancient or former times" (JS-H 1:35), so he apparently knew that he was thereby connected with a venerable tradition of seership. The very indeterminateness of such an ancient allusion is the kind of occasion that calls for prophetic intervention. In this case, it is precisely this circumstance of a sacred artifact apparently known anciently but no longer, of the survival in the scriptural record of tantalizing hints and shadows of ampler realities and contexts no longer present that helped define the particular prophetic role Joseph set about enacting. Restoration, as he comes to understand the process, always builds upon the fragmentary remains of eternal truths, and thus diminishes the sense of historical and conceptual distance that separates one biblical dispensation from another. The golden plates were a remarkable relic—but one without any biblical or historical precedent.[58] The Urim and Thummim, on the other hand, were gradually understood to be the actual embodiment of a connection to specific canonical scriptures, to vaguely understood but divinely sanctioned oracular practices, and to remote but recognizable moments of the past. Significantly, in the initial euphoria of his first successful return from Hill Cumorah, Joseph seems to have forgotten the plates altogether in his excitement over the interpreters. Both chroniclers of that morning's events agree on that point. Lucy Mack recorded that on that historic morning Joseph showed her the (thinly veiled) instrument, "but did not tell me anything of the record."[59] And Knight, describing his closeted conversation with Joseph about the visit to the hill, concluded that "he seamed to think more of the glasses or the urim and thummem then he did of the plates [*sic*]."[60]

Joseph had not forgotten the plates, of course, but neither had he returned home with them. Lucy Mack wrote that he had secreted them in an old birch log, about three miles from home. The next day, September 23, he found work in nearby Macedon. He hoped to use the money earned for a chest in which to secure the plates. While he was away, a neighbor approached the senior Smith with questions about the "gold bible." Martin Harris having learned of it two or three years earlier (according to Lucy), and Joseph Knight knowing even the date of anticipated delivery, rumors had apparently spread. Harris would later state that the money-diggers Joseph had earlier associated with (in the Stowell silver mine affair or elsewhere) "claimed that they had as much right to the plates as Joseph had, as they were in company together. They claimed that Joseph had been a traitor, and had appropriated to himself that which belonged to them."[61] Similarly, David Whitmer reported "conversations with several young men who said that Joseph Smith had certainly gold plates, and that before he attained them he had promised to share with them."[62] The exact connection of two of these young men to Joseph is not clear, but both now bore him grudges. Willard Chase would continue to insist that Joseph's seer stone, which he would use along-side the interpreters as a medium of translation, had in fact been stolen from him. And Samuel Lawrence, who had somehow learned even of the hillside where the plates were buried, had been threatened by Joseph for continuing to intrude into the whole business.[63]

Now, aided by a conjuror they recruited from sixty miles away, a group of a dozen or so conspired to learn where the plates were hidden and take them by force. The morning of September 24, Joseph Sr. recon-noitered the neighborhood, discovered Chase, Lawrence, the conjuror, and others, and overheard their plans. He returned home to warn the family. Emma rode off to Macedon, explained matters to Joseph, and the two of them came back at once, meeting his worried, pacing father a mile from their farm. Once home, Joseph calmly arranged for his brother Hyrum to find a lockable chest, then set off alone on a three-mile walk to retrieve the plates. He took them from their hiding place in the birch log (oak tree, according to Harris), wrapped them in his frock, and cut through the woods to avoid pursuers or the merely curious. But by now, apparently, the Chase gang was on to him. Three separate times armed individuals ambushed him before he made his way home, frightened, bruised, exhausted, and suffering a dislocated thumb. He asked his mother to send word for his father and their two houseguests, Stowell and Knight, to scout the area and make sure his pursuers were gone. They returned without seeing anyone.

As the plates lay on the table, veiled in the linen frock and awaiting Hyrum and the cherry chest into which they would shortly be secured, several of those present in the room examined them. Josiah Stowell would claim that he was "the first person that took the Plates out of your [Joseph's] hands the morning you brought them in."[64] Family mem-bers remembered being allowed to handle them, although without re-moving their frock covering. Lucy is reported to have said that she "hefted and handled" the plates, without actually seeing them.[65] Will-iam, the prophet's younger brother, told an interviewer that "he had hefted the plates as they lay on the table wrapped in an old frock or jacket in which Joseph had brought them home. That he had thum[b]ed them through the cloth and ascertained that they were thin sheets of some kind of metal."[66] Katharine, 14 or 15 at the time, told her grandson that she, also, was present "when her brother, Joseph Smith, came in nearly exhausted, carrying the package of gold plates. . . . She told me Joseph allowed her to 'heft' the package but not to see the gold plates." She also reported, in words very like William's, that on another occa-sion she "rippled her fingers up the edge of the plates and felt that they were separate metal plates and heard the tinkle of sound that they made."[67] Emma's later testimony was to the same effect.[68]

After the violence and commotion of Joseph's flight from his attackers, and with even the children in the household aware of the treasure their family owned, word spread quickly. In the next days, Chase and Lawrence and others effectively declared war on what became a besieged Smith household. Joseph hid the plates under the family hearthstone, then moved them to the loft of his father's cooper shop. The mob ransacked the building but found only a decoy box, nailed shut and buried in the shop floor. By now, Joseph knew his situation—and the security of the plates—was precarious. He also knew that if he was to proceed with a translation of the ancient record, he could only do so under circumstances of greater calm and security than he was likely to find in Palmyra anytime soon.

The Translation

A short distance north of the village of Palmyra lived a prosperous and respected farmer, Martin Harris. Lucy described him as a "confidential friend" of Joseph Smith, Sr. The young Joseph had worked for him as a boy, and the kindly Harris had even bought him a new suit of clothes when Joseph was wooing Emma and trying to impress her father.[69] Now, in his present distress, Joseph turned to him again, sending his mother to request that he come at once. It happened that Harris had been in Palmyra a few days earlier and had listened to the simmering controversy regarding Joseph's alleged discovery of a gold bible. He was preparing to visit the Smiths to learn the details for himself, he said, when Lucy arrived on her errand. He assured her he would soon visit young Joseph and sent his wife and daughter on ahead of him. They returned with a report of having hefted the plates as the others had, though Mrs. Harris was disgruntled at not being permitted, as a potential supporter, a full and unobstructed view of the plates. A few days later Harris himself made the trip, interviewed Emma and the rest of the family, and finally Joseph himself. Harris then felt the weight of the veiled object of so much controversy for himself, was satisfied that it was either lead or gold, and since the Smith's "had not credit enough to buy so much lead"—let alone gold—he was intrigued enough to make his support for the endeavor a subject of personal prayer. That night, he felt "by the still small voice spoken in [his] soul" that Joseph's story was true. Henceforth, he wrote, "I was satisfied that it was the Lord's work, and I was under a covenant to bring it forth."[70]

As an outsider to the family, Harris heard rumors that made him even more acutely aware than Joseph of the dangers now facing the Smiths, and he urged that Joseph and Emma move to Harmony to be with her family,[71] even supplying them with a $50 gift to pay off debts and cover

Joseph and Emma Smith home, Harmony, Pennsylvania.
The center part of the structure was the Smiths' residence and
the place where Joseph translated much of Book of Mormon from
December of 1827 to June of 1829. (Anderson Collection, 1907;
Courtesy LDS Church Historical Department)

traveling expenses. And so, in December of 1827, Joseph and his pregnant wife hid the plates in a barrel of beans, loaded their wagon, and
began their 135-mile trip, leaving three days earlier than their announced
departure date to throw off any enemies with designs on the plates.

Isaac Hale may have been happy to see his daughter again, but he
cannot have been happy to learn the reasons for their flight from Palmyra.
Only the previous summer, Joseph had promised Isaac "to give up his
old habits of digging for money and looking into stones." To add to his
father-in-law's contempt, Joseph now claimed to have the plates in his
possession, essentially asked for asylum as a result of the attendant persecution, yet refused Isaac's request for a glimpse of the plates. In an
apparent compromise, Joseph was reduced to hiding the plates in the
woods, and moved into a small house on the Hale property.

Even with respite from aggressively curious neighbors and critics,
Joseph did not begin translation of the plates immediately. He claimed
to have the Urim and Thummim, or interpreters, true enough, but ini-

Martin Harris (1783–1875).
An early supporter of
Joseph Smith and the financial
backer of the Book of Mormon's
publication, Harris was one of the
three witnesses who testified that
"an angel of God came down from
heaven" and showed him the gold
plates. (Courtesy LDS Church
Historical Department)

tially he did not seem to have had any clear idea of exactly how they were to be used or how the actual process of translation would come about. In February of 1828, a few months after the Smiths had settled in, Martin Harris arrived in Harmony to pursue an earlier plan to have Joseph's account of the strange engravings authenticated by an eastern scholar.[72] As usually depicted, the journey was primarily for Harris's peace of mind as a prospective investor in the translation project. That is most likely, but it is also possible that, failing in his initial efforts at translation, Joseph hoped to procure a simplified lexicon of the characters to use as a key for translating. That seemed to be Joseph Knight's understanding: "He now Began to be anxious to git them translated. He therefore with his wife Drew of[f] the Caricters exactley like the ancient and sent Martin Harris to see if he Could git them Translated."[73] Joseph Smith recorded that Harris went at the behest of the Lord, who "had shown him that he must go to New York City with some of the caracters [sic],"[74] but he shed no further light on the purpose of the journey. Since Joseph wrote that prior to Harris's departure, he used the Urim and Thummim to translate some of those characters,[75] it is also possible that he wanted an appraisal of his own accuracy.

In February of 1828, Harris set out for New York City, initiating one of the more disputed episodes in the early history of the Book of Mormon. Since it is known that he consulted with a Reverend John Clark in Palmyra, he probably got from him recommendations for what scholars he might visit in New York.[76] Apparently, he stopped along the way in Albany to see one Luther Bradish, who had some familiarity with Egypt and antiquities.[77] Going on to the city, he first visited Dr. Samuel L. Mitchell, referred to by his colleagues as the "Magnus Apollo" of the day.[78] Mitchell, not able to speak authoritatively on the subject of Egyptian, referred Harris to Charles Anthon, a professor of ancient languages at Columbia University. For what happened next, we have three versions: one by Harris, and two, sometimes conflicting accounts, by Anthon.

Harris reported that he visited the "celebrated" Professor Anthon, showed him the transcribed characters (called "Reformed Egyptian" in the plates themselves) together with their translation, and was assured that "the translation was correct, more so than any he had before seen translated from the Egyptian." Anthon gave him a signed statement to that effect, then took it back and tore it up when informed that the characters came from gold plates delivered up by an angel of God.[79]

In 1834, Anthon wrote a very different account of the visit for E. D. Howe, who was collecting affidavits to discredit Smith and his work. Anthon told Howe that "a simple-hearted farmer" called on him with a paper on which were "all kinds of crooked characters disposed in columns." He immediately perceived it was trick or hoax, and warned Harris accordingly. Harris asked for a written statement, "which of course I declined giving."[80]

A few years later, in a letter to T. W. Coit, Anthon claimed he had never before addressed the subject of the Harris visit in writing. He repeated his assertion that he saw the bogus nature of the characters right

Anthon Transcript. This is the probable transcript of Book of Mormon characters copied out by Joseph Smith and taken by Martin Harris to Columbia University professor Charles Anthon for authentication in early 1828. (Courtesy Library-Archives, Reorganized Church of Jesus Christ of Latter Day Saints, Independence, Missouri) away, and that he advised Harris he was probably the intended victim of a fraud, and when asked for a written statement to that effect, "did so without hesitation."[81]

The two men had very different interests at stake in telling their respective versions. For Anthon, writing a few years after Mormonism was established, his intellectual reputation could be irreparably harmed if he were connected to this gold bible and what he called the "wretched fanatics" associated with it. Harris had a good name as well, but he had not yet devoted either his financial resources or his allegiance to the project. In attempting to reconcile the discrepancies, some have proposed a compromise, suggesting that Harris misheard Anthon, confusing "correct transcription" with "correct translation."[82] That doesn't work, however, first, because in Harris's version he makes clear his recognition of the distinction between "the translation" and the characters "not yet translated," *both* of which he says Anthon authenticates at distinct moments in their interview, and second, because Anthon describes the characters themselves as spurious in both his accounts. In any event, one thing stands out as certain. In spite of Anthon's claim that the enlightened Harris left Anthon's office declaring "that he would in no shape part with his farm or embark in the speculation of printing the golden book,"[83] the farmer went on to do just that. Obviously energized by his interpretation of the Anthon interview, he "went home to Palmyra, arranged his affairs, and returned again to [Joseph's] house about the 12th of April, 1828 and commenced writing for [him] while [he] translated from the plates."[84]

In the weeks before the new arrangement, Emma had been doing the initial scribal work for Joseph. But it was with Harris's participation, six and a half months after Joseph received the plates, that the process of translation really got underway. As for the particulars of how Joseph produced his translation, we know some details but not others. Several witnesses to the actual process left descriptions that are fully consistent on several counts. That the process involved dictation—hence the need for Emma or Harris to serve as scribe—is affirmed by all who viewed or participated in any phase of it and appears to be substantiated by textual evidence as well.

Emma told an interviewer years later that "when my husband was translating the Book of Mormon, I wrote a part of it, as he dictated each sentence, word for word, and when he came to proper names he could not pronounce, or long words, he spelled them out. . . . When he stopped for any purpose at any time he would, when he commenced again, begin where he left off without any hesitation."[85] Similarly, "Father" Whitmer "who was present very frequently during the writing of this manuscript affirms that Joseph Smith had no book or manuscript before him from which he could have read as is asserted by some that he

Martin Harris farm. After his visit to Charles Anthon, Harris mortgaged
the farm (and later sold most of it) to pay the cost of printing the
Book of Mormon. (Courtesy LDS Church Historical Department)

did, he (Whitmer) having every opportunity to know."[86] Oliver Cowdery,
who took the vast majority of the dictation, affirmed that he "wrote with
[his] own pen the entire book of Mormon (save a few pages) as it fell
from the lips of the prophet."[87]

The resultant manuscript was effectively a stream of dictation, with
no interruption from first page to last. John H. Gilbert, the principal
compositor at E. B. Grandin's shop where the book was printed, described the first 24 pages of manuscript delivered by Joseph's brother
Hyrum as "closely written and legible, but not a punctuation mark from
beginning to end."[88] Milton Backman, Stan Larson, and Royal Skousen
have written on other textual evidence for a dictated manuscript, citing
homophonic miscues, or errors of the ear (e.g., "no" corrected to read
"know"), scribal anticipation errors (cross-outs that appear before in-
tervening dictation), and the general lack of revisions in the text.[89] Those
extensive portions that largely parallel the King James Version of Isaiah
2-14 and 48-54 and Matthew 5-7 seem, even to at least one Mormon
scholar, prima facie evidence that Joseph simply used an open copy of
the King James Bible, at least for those portions.[90] If so, that would con-

travene both the testimony of eyewitnesses and textual hints that Joseph was dictating extemporaneously. (For example, as Royal Skousen has shown, Joseph's thematic divisions of Isaiah are inconsistent with the KJV chapter groupings. Also, Cowdery's spellings in these sections mimic the spelling he used in other portions of the Book of Mormon, not King James spelling, showing the relevant passages were the product of dictation rather than scribal copying.[91])

In what manner or form those words came to Joseph is less clear. In the first phase of translation, he employed the interpreters, the two clear stones set in rims, that he received on the same night as the plates. Only one description of how he used them exists, and it is problematic.[92] But at some point in the two months Harris wrote for him, from mid-April to mid-June, Smith apparently took to using a seer stone interchangeably with the interpreters. Several witnesses *did* describe the seer stone and its employment. The stone was egg shaped, but flatter, and dark brown. Joseph would place it in the bottom of a hat, and place his face in the hat so as to exclude the light, then dictate.

This procedure has led some critics to the rather imaginative speculation that, since all witnesses confirm the absence of source texts, Joseph must have concealed notes in the bottom of the hat, which he then dictated to Cowdery.[93] (Asked pointedly if it were possible that he could have used a concealed book or manuscript in the process, Emma insisted that "if he had anything of the kind he could not have concealed it from me."[94]) Harris had his own recurrent doubts about the whole process. He admitted that on one occasion he tested the validity of the seer stone by surreptitiously placing a substitute in its place. Upon next resuming the translating, "The Prophet remained silent, unusually and intently gazing in darkness, no traces of the usual sentences appearing. Much surprised, Joseph exclaimed, 'Martin! What is the matter? All is dark as Egypt!'"[95]

Of all those closely involved with the process, Harris gave the most specific information about Joseph's translation method: "By aid of the seer stone, sentences would appear and were read by the Prophet and written by Martin, and when finished he would say, 'Written,' and if correctly written, that sentence would disappear and another appear in its place, but if not written correctly it remained until corrected."[96] Harris was here writing more than 50 years after the events he described, and may have exaggerated the mechanical nature of the process.[97] Later, when Cowdery attempted to translate, he failed, and was chastised in a revelation for presuming to merely ask rather than to "study it out in [his] mind" (Doctrine and Covenants 9:7-8). So clearly something more than visual observation was involved. Joseph himself was reluctant to say much about the actual process of translation. In response to a question from his own brother Hyrum, Joseph said in an October 1831 conference of the church, "that it was not intended to tell the world all the particulars of the coming forth of the Book of Mormon; and also said that it was not expedient for him to relate these things."[98]

For two months, then, using sometimes the ancient spectacles and sometimes the seer stone, Joseph dictated while Harris wrote. Eventually, they had a manuscript of over 116 pages including the account Joseph called "the Book of Lehi." Then, disaster struck. Harris's wife Lucy had been bitterly resentful of her husband's involvement in the whole Book of Mormon affair. It didn't help that when she desired to accompany her husband on his fact-finding mission in February of 1828, he had sneaked off to Harmony without her. Such subterfuge both enraged her and confirmed her suspicions that a religious imposter was about to exploit her good-natured and gullible husband. When, back from New York, Martin informed her he was throwing his support into the project, she journeyed back to Harmony with him. Once there, she demanded a view of the plates, and when refused, she ransacked the home of Joseph and Emma trying to find them. Humiliated and thwarted in all her efforts, she began to spread rumors of Joseph's fraudulent designs and returned to Palmyra, where she theatrically dispersed her linens and furniture among neighbors, ostensibly to keep them safe from Joseph and his family.[99]

Martin was caught between loyalty to his wife and his firm conviction that he was an essential player in a momentous work of God about to come forth. Attempting to mediate between the two, he asked Joseph if he could show Lucy the dictated manuscript to allay her suspicions and win her support. Joseph prayed for permission but was refused. Martin persisted in his pleas, so Joseph inquired once more, but with the same response. His scribe was relentless in his nagging. "After much solicitation I again enquired of the Lord and permission was granted him to have the writings on certain conditions,"[100] Joseph recorded. These conditions were that Harris show them only to his wife and four other family members.

Martin bound himself by solemn oath to these conditions, then set out happily for his home with the only copy of the manuscript on June 14. The next day, Emma gave birth to a boy in a harrowing delivery that left her near death. The baby died some hours later. Joseph waited anxiously for Harris while he nursed Emma slowly back to health. Two weeks later, Harris had still not returned, and a worried Joseph set out for Palmyra after him. Harris had not returned for the simple reason that he had lost the manuscript, and fear and shame had kept him from his appointment. Now in the greatest distress, he confessed to Joseph that he had broken his covenant. He had shown the manuscript to all and sundry who had inquired, and on the morning of Joseph's arrival, he found the bureau in which he kept it was empty. Joseph and his family were devastated by the calamity; in retrospect it was a painful passage in Joseph's maturation as a prophet and leader. At the time, it appeared a permanent, tragic end to his work and calling, a catastrophe for which he assumed full blame, as his mother remembered: "Oh, my God, my God," she reported Joseph lamenting, "All is lost, is lost! What shall I do. I have sinned. It is I who tempted the wrath of God by asking him for that which I had no right to ask." She recalled, "Our sobs and groans and the most bitter lamentations filled the house."[101]

Exactly what happened to the manuscript has never been ascertained. Suspicion immediately fell on the unpopular Lucy Harris, and a subsequent revelation to Joseph interpreted the theft of the pages as part of a plot: "Wicked men have taken them from you . . . And . . . because they have altered the words, they read contrary from that which you translated and caused to be written; And, on this wise . . . they may say they have caught you in the words which you have pretended to translate" (D&C 10:8-13). Others believed that Lucy burned either all or part of the manuscript.[102]

The day after the terrible news, Joseph returned to Harmony, not knowing if he would ever translate again. Pleading with the Lord for forgiveness, Joseph was visited by an angel who required that he "suffer the consequences of his indiscretion, and . . . give back the Urim and Thummim into his . . . hands"—but with a promise that he would receive them again.[103]

A short while later, Joseph wrote, he received them back, but only long enough to obtain through their means a revelation. Ironically, the communication he received, which became the earliest revelation actually written down by the prophet, was a stinging indictment of his own failings as a prophet: "[A]lthough a man may have many revelations, and have power to do many mighty works, yet if he boasts in his own strength, and sets at naught the counsels of God, and follows after the dictates of his own will and carnal desires, he must fall and incur the vengeance of a just God upon him. . . . And behold, how oft you have transgressed the commandments of God . . ." (D&C 3:4, 6). He was also enjoined to further repentance, assured of the Lord's mercy, and again deprived of the sacred oracles.

A few months later, on September 22, 1828, the plates and the Urim and Thummim were given to him again.[104] Emma, however, recorded that Joseph made use of the Urim and Thummim, meaning the interpreters, only for the 116 pages of the Harris manuscript. "After that he used a small stone, not exactly black, but was rather a dark color."[105] David Whitmer confirmed her version, saying that after Joseph's repentance, Moroni gave him the seer stone but did not return the interpreters.[106]

One year to the day had passed since Joseph retrieved the plates from Cumorah. One year, and virtually nothing to show for it.[107] The euphoria of recent months, as he and Harris had grown into the rhythm of producing several pages a week, bringing to light ancient voices and buried civilizations, was replaced by betrayal, remorse, chastisement, and loss. For a while, at least, he seems to have lost both the means and the will to continue. After receiving back from the angel both the plates and permission to renew translation work, he recorded curtly, "I did not, however, go immediately to translating, but went to laboring with my hands upon a small farm which I had purchased of my wife's father."[108] So, except for a few sporadic efforts, with his wife Emma reprising her role as scribe,[109] Joseph spent that fall and winter struggling to support his family. The unsympathetic Hale family offered no assistance, and Joseph was reduced to begging provisions from his hard-pressed friend Joseph Knight, who gave him "some few things out of the Store a pair of shoes and three Dollars."[110]

Through that winter and into the spring, Joseph continued to struggle to eke out a living while the gold plates lay largely neglected. Finally, in March of 1829, the Lord directed Joseph in a revelation to cease his translation efforts, insubstantial as they apparently were, "and stand still until I command thee, and I will provide means whereby thou mayest accomplish the thing which I have commanded thee" (D&C 5:34). Help came soon thereafter in the form of a young schoolteacher by the name of Oliver Cowdery.

Cowdery, then 22, had been boarding with the Smith family while he taught at the district school in Palmyra. He had heard the story of the golden bible from another Palmyra resident, David Whitmer, and now had plenty of opportunity to hear the particulars from Lucy Mack and Joseph Sr. By the time Joseph's younger brother Samuel Smith set out for Harmony in early April to spend the spring with Joseph, Oliver had decided he had a role to play in the remarkable events that were unfolding around the prophet. He arrived in Harmony with Samuel on the fifth of April. His providential arrival and immediate immersion in the project must have been an exhilarating lift for Joseph. But Joseph simply recorded, "two days after the arrival of Mr. Cowdery . . . I commenced to translate the Book of Mormon, and he began to write for me."[111] A year earlier, Martin Harris and Joseph had done well to produce 116 pages in a little over two months. Cowdery may have been a more efficient scribe, but Joseph had progressed as a translator as well. Working laboriously from the plates in the initial stages, with a blanket suspended to hide them from view (according to some accounts), Joseph now relied upon the seer stone alone, with the plates apparently covered and laid aside while he worked. So casual and natural a process had it become that Emma said Oliver Cowdery and her husband translated while she was at work in the same room.[112] Cowdery's future wife, Elizabeth Ann Whitmer, and the skeptical Isaac Hale's son-in-law, Michael Morse, both were frequently present while the work was underway, and said they watched as Joseph dictated word after word to his scribe.

Joseph must have wondered what to do about the sections that had been translated and lost. In a revelation received in May of 1829, he was told of a conspiracy to doctor the stolen manuscript and was advised to not retranslate the lost portion. Instead, he was told to substitute an alternate account that occupied a later section of the plates, one that gave "a more particular account" of early Nephite history (D&C 10:39).[113] So Joseph and Oliver began with the Book of Mosiah and continued forward.[114] Shortly thereafter, on the 15th of the month, they neared the end of 3 Nephi. Questions arose about the references to baptism and remission of sins "that we found mentioned in the translation of the plates." Accordingly, they

> went into the woods to pray and inquire of the Lord. While we were thus employed, praying and calling upon the Lord, a messenger from heaven descended in a cloud of light, and having laid his hands upon us, he ordained us, saying: Upon you my fellow servants, in the name of Messiah I confer the Priesthood of Aaron, which holds the keys of the ministering of angels, and of the Gospel of repentance, and of baptism by immersion for the remission of sins.[115]

Joseph recorded that this messenger, who was John the Baptist, said "that I should be called the first Elder of the Church, and he (Oliver Cowdery) the second."

This mention of a church—and the ordination of its first two officers—was a significant development in the career of a prophet who as yet had no flock, no ministry, and no doctrine to teach. At just what point Joseph envisioned the formal organization of a church is not clear. (Formal organization would occur on April 6, 1830, just days after the Book of Mormon came off the press.) The first, somewhat vague, allusion to a church had apparently occurred a few months previous, in a March revelation wherein the Lord promised his people to "work a reformation among them, and . . . establish my church, like unto the church which was taught by my disciples in the days of old."[116] Then, around the time of John the Baptist's appearance, the Lord reiterated his promise that "if this generation harden not their hearts, I will establish my church among them" (D&C 10:53).

Now, officially designated an elder in the impending organization of the church by an angelic messenger, Joseph may have first realized that he was to be much more than a translator of ancient scripture and that the Book of Mormon itself was but a prelude to a greater work about to unfold. From this point on, the Book of Mormon would inescapably be charged with new meaning, insofar as it was coming to be wedded to the rise of a new religion and, soon, the ushering in of a new dispensation altogether.

Given the interruptions to seek occasional employment to buy necessities, Joseph's ongoing family responsibilities, and the need to address doctrinal questions that arose, Joseph and Oliver managed a truly prodigious rate of translation during the months of April and May—over 3,500 original words a day essentially set down indelibly as they went.[117] Meanwhile, the old Palmyra hostilities now caught up with them in the Harmony area. Fortunately for Joseph, the Hales had at last grown supportive—or they may have simply disapproved of bigotry more than they disapproved of delusion. In any event, Joseph recorded that they "had become very friendly to me, and . . . were opposed to the mobs."[118] Still, "the spirit of persecution which had already manifested itself in the neighborhood" led Joseph to ask Oliver to request safer lodging with his friend David Whitmer. David's parents agreed, and in early June the pair relocated, along with Emma, to the Whitmer home in the town of Fayette, situated back across the state border in the heart of the Finger Lakes region of New York, about 25 miles southeast of Palmyra.[119]

There Joseph found hospitable lodgings, plenty of assistance with the translation, and, for the first time ever, a friendly, receptive neighborhood. In addition to Cowdery's continuing help, Emma, Christian Whitmer, and John Whitmer all took turns transcribing. As the translation process drew to a close in the next weeks, Joseph's heavy, prophetic burden continued to be dispersed as he learned that the record would not need to go before the world on the strength of his word alone.

The Witnesses

The message of the Book of Mormon was and continues to be inseparable from the story of its origins—a story involving angels, seer stones, and golden plates. Given the fact that epiphanies, dreams, and visions are entirely subjective experiences, and that supernatural trappings are generally more of an impediment than invitation to belief, one might expect that Smith would have emphasized content over context, or at least allowed himself and his audience the leisure of some flexibility in interpreting his experiences. One finds in his language only the merest hint that the phenomenology of the First Vision was at least somewhat indeterminate and mysterious. "When I came to myself again," he wrote in the 1838 version, "I found myself lying on my back" (JS-H 1:20). Was it a literal visitation? Was it a dream? Was he in a trance? Was the experience transmitted to his mind directly, or was he "carried away in the spirit" like an Ezekiel or John? The public reception of such experiences reported by a Smith or a Swedenborg can always be somewhat tamed or muted if the inherent vagueness of these categories and designations is exploited to move interpretation away from the objectively real and verifiable toward the subjectively real and privately experiential. In the case of visionary Charles Finney, for example, one writer describes how he actually forestalled the charges of blasphemy or egomania by just such a semantic retreat: even though he claimed to be visited by Jesus himself, "he would later qualify the objective reality of the event: 'It did not occur to me then, nor did it for some time afterward, that it was wholly a mental state.'" This same scholar goes on to contrast such caution with Joseph Smith's more radical gesture: "But although Finney de-emphasized the literality of his experience, Smith did just the opposite. In his unpublished history, he reported that when the angel first came to tell him of the plates, he thought it was a dream but later changed his mind."[120] Smith's rhetoric regarding his visions and visitations, in other words, consistently resisted the domesticating strategy of reducing them to an inner experience. "I had actually seen a light," he would write of his first vision, "and in the midst of that light I saw two Personages, and they did in reality speak to me" (JS-H 1:25).

When it came to the Book of Mormon, the case was driven home with even more resistance to hedging or equivocation. "Blessed are they that have not seen, and yet have believed," said Jesus to the doubting Thomas (John 20:29). Nevertheless, the ancient Israelites kept the tablets of Moses in the sacred ark, as a perpetual witness that their law was truly written by the hand of God himself. And though Joseph was not allowed to preserve the golden plates for posterity's edification, he was allowed to summon witnesses who left signed affidavits testifying to their contact with actual plates of gold.

Throughout the trying process of safeguarding and translating the ancient record, ever-besieged by family, friends, and skeptics alike, Joseph had been obedient to Moroni's directive not to share a view of the plates with anyone. Even his ill-advised permission for Martin Harris to publicly share the translated manuscript had been a catastrophe. That had been in June of 1828. Now, in March of the following year, Harris was shamelessly importuning the prophet once again for renewed confirmation that the nearly complete translation was based on real plates. He wanted to see them for himself. Given the fact that he had provided material assistance, was older than Joseph, was better known in the area, and had lost the good will of his wife over the whole matter, he doubtless felt entitled to at least that much. In a revelation Joseph received that month, Harris learned that three special witnesses would soon be given "power that they may behold and view these things as they are." If he humbled himself sufficiently, he was promised, he would be granted "a view of the things which he desires to see" (D&C 5:11-13, 24).

In June, the final month of translation at the Whitmer home, Joseph learned that the record provided ancient confirmation of that promise: Moroni wrote that the plates would be "shown by the power of God" unto three "who shall assist to bring forth this work" (Ether 5:2-3),[121] and Nephi made a similar prediction. As his inner circle of three close associates—David Whitmer, Oliver Cowdery, and Martin Harris—participated in and monitored the progress of translation, they became excited at the prospect of fulfilling both ancient prophecy and their own longings to see for themselves the mysterious, holy relics. After repeated entreaties to Joseph, he confirmed through the Urim and Thummim that they could indeed receive "a view of the plates, and also of the breastplate, the sword of Laban, the Urim and Thummim . . . and the miraculous directors which were given to Lehi" (D&C 17:1). The promise was followed by a command that they bear testimony to the world of that which they would have the privilege of seeing.

A few days later, Joseph felt the time had come. According to his account, he gathered his three companions and they retired to the nearby woods "to try to obtain, by fervent and humble prayer, the fulfillment of the promises given." Each one prayed in turn, but without effect. Harris, feeling in his faithlessness that he was an impediment to a heavenly manifestation, retired from the group. Minutes later, in Joseph's words, "we beheld a light above us in the air, of exceeding brightness; and behold, an angel stood before us. In his hands he held the plates which we had been praying to have a view of. He turned over the leaves one by one, so that we could see them, and discern the engravings thereon distinctly." There followed a voice out of the bright light, saying, "These plates have been revealed by the power of God, and they have been translated by the power of God."[122] On a nearby table, the other sacred relics lay exposed to their view.

With the miraculous witness now secured by the other two, Joseph left to seek out the distressed Harris. He found him, and together they continued to supplicate the Lord. Soon the same vision the three had experienced previously was granted to Harris as well. An exuberant Harris burst out, "'Tis enough 'tis enough; mine eyes have beheld; mine eyes have beheld." It is hard to say who was more relieved, Harris from his years of nagging doubts, or Joseph from having no one to help diffuse the weight of a world's skepticism and trust his story unreservedly. His mother recalled that upon returning from the woods, Joseph threw himself on the bed, crying "Father! Mother! You do not know how happy I am. . . . I do feel as though I was relieved of a dreadful burden which was almost too much for me to endure."[123]

Joseph had taken note when Nephi spoke of three witnesses who would testify of the Book of Mormon. But Nephi had mentioned yet "more witnesses" in addition to the special three (2 Nephi 11:3). A few days after the manifestation experienced by the three, most of the

Whitmer family accompanied Joseph and Oliver to Palmyra to finalize printing arrangements. At that time, Joseph invited the five males in the Whitmer clan (including one son-in-law), along with his father and brothers Hyrum and Samuel, to accompany him to a family prayer spot in the woods. There, without heavenly manifestations or angelic voices, Joseph matter-of-factly displayed to them the golden plates. They handled them, turned over the leaves, and examined the engravings.

In their published testimony, appended to the first published Book of Mormon (but prefacing modern editions), the first three witnesses describe an encounter that is orchestrated and supervised by heavenly agents. They see the plates "through the grace of God." They know the translation is true, because the voice of God "declared it unto" them. The plates themselves were brought and laid before their eyes by "an angel of God [who] came down from heaven." Although they were close enough to the relics to see "the engravings thereon," as they twice tell us, they neither touched nor handled them for themselves.

On the other hand, the testimony of the eight, likewise included in every edition of the Book of Mormon, is lacking in any traces of supernaturalism. Joseph Smith simply showed them the plates, allowing them to make their own examination and draw their own conclusions. Their verdict, being freely drawn, is thus more compelling even as it is more qualified. The plates, they write, do indeed have "the appearance of gold," the engravings have "the appearance of an ancient work," and as for the translation itself, they mention it without testifying to its truthfulness. What emerges as alone indisputable is the fact that Joseph Smith does possess a set of metal plates: "[W]e did handle [them] with our hands," they affirm; "[W]e have seen and hefted, and know of a surety that the said Smith has got the plates of which we have spoken."

Oliver Cowdery (1806–1850). "I wrote with my own pen the entire Book of Mormon (save a few pages) as it fell from the lips of the Prophet Joseph Smith. . . . I beheld with my eyes and handled with my hands, the gold plates from which it was transcribed." (Courtesy LDS Church Historical Department)

Taken together, the two experiences seemed calculated to provide an evidentiary spectrum, satisfying a range of criteria for belief. The reality of the plates was now confirmed by both proclamation from heaven and by empirical observation, through a supernatural vision and by simple, tactile experience, by the testimony of passive witnesses to a divine demonstration and by the testimony of a group of men actively engaging in their own unhampered examination of the evidence.

It is certainly true that none of the witnesses were disinterested observers. All were close supporters and friends of Smith or actual family members. On the other hand, all of the first three witnesses eventually fell out with the prophet. Cowdery, who in 1834 would ascend to the rank of assistant president of the church, was excommunicated for apostasy in April of 1838. There is no record of him ever retracting his testimony, and in 1848 he rejoined the church, affirming at that time that "I wrote with my own pen the entire Book of Mormon (save a few pages) as it fell from the lips of the Prophet Joseph Smith, as he translated it by the gift and power of God, by the means of the Urim and Thummim. . . . I beheld with my eyes and handled with my hands, the gold plates from which it was transcribed."[124]

David Whitmer also left the church during the turbulent year of 1838.[125] Unlike Cowdery, he never reconciled with the church, believing until his death in 1888 that Smith drifted into error after publishing the Book of Mormon. The most frequently interviewed of all the witnesses, he affirmed to the end that "I have never at any time denied that testimony or any part thereof, which has so long since been published with that Book, as one of the three witnesses."[126]

Martin Harris was excommunicated during the same wave of apostasy that carried away Whitmer and Cowdery. Like Cowdery, he was rebaptized a few years later, and steadfastly affirmed throughout his life his Book of Mormon testimony. At least one historian has written of Martin Harris's alleged equivocation about his vision, pointing out that he claimed to have seen the plates with his "spiritual eyes," rather than his natural ones, and thus that he "repeatedly admitted the internal, subjective nature of his visionary experience."[127] It is not clear, however, that visionaries in any age have acquiesced to such facile dichotomies. Working with several eighteenth-century accounts of visionary experience surrounding the Cambuslang Revival, one historian has noted how frequently editing ministers made insertions and deletions in the documents in order to impose rigid distinctions between "the Eye of faith" and "bodily eyes." He concludes, "to the ministers, though not the laity, the distinction was clearly critical."[128] To similar effect, Ned Landsman cites the case of one Catherine Jack-

David Whitmer (1805–1888). Like Martin Harris and Oliver Cowdery, Whitmer was one of three witnesses who published their testimony that the gold plates were shown them "by the power of God, and not of man." All three would later grow disaffected from the prophet Joseph, but none ever retracted his testimony. (Courtesy LDS Church Historical Department)

son, who converted during this same revival. A church elder brought her to the Seceder minister James Fisher as evidence of the authenticity of the Cambuslang conversions. The plan backfired when she described her vision of Christ as occurring through her "'bodily eyes,' a phrasing Fisher seized upon to discredit the revival."[129]

Paul himself referred to one of his own experiences as being "in the body, or out of the body, I cannot tell" (2 Cor. 12:3). He obviously considered such a distinction irrelevant to the validity of his experience and the reality of what he saw. It is hard to imagine a precedent more like Harris's own versions in which he emphatically asserts until the day of his death the actuality of the angel who "came down from heaven" and who "brought and laid [the plates] before our eyes, that we beheld and saw," while also reporting, according to others, that he "never claimed to have seen them with his natural eyes, only with spiritual vision."[130]

In the case of the Book of Mormon, the distinction is ultimately irrelevant. Why, one can fairly ask, should it be necessary to spiritualize what are, in essence, presented as archaeological artifacts? Dream-visions may be in the mind of the beholder, but gold plates are not subject to such facile psychologizing. They were, in the angel's words, buried in a nearby hillside, not in Joseph's psyche or religious unconscious, and they chronicle a history of *this* hemisphere, not a heavenly city to come. As such, the claims and experiences of the prophet are thrust irretrievably into the public sphere, no longer subject to his private acts of interpretation alone. It is this fact, the intrusion of Joseph's message into the realm of the concrete, historical, and empirical, that dramatically alters the terms by which the public will engage this new religious phenomenon.

TWO

"Out of the Dust":
The Book of Mormon Comes Forth

Which Book was given by inspiration, and is called The Book of Mormon and is confirmed to others by the ministering of angels, and declared unto the world by them.

—from first issue of the church's
Messenger and Advocate (June 1832)

Mother Goose's Melodies. The only Pure Edition. Containing all that have ever come to light of her memorable writings, together with those which have been discovered among the mss. of Herculaneum, likewise every one recently found in the same stone box which held the golden plates of the Book of Mormon.

—title page of *Mother Goose's Melodies*, 1835

In his old age, the patriarch Jacob "called unto his sons, and said, Gather yourselves together, that I may tell you that which shall befall you in the last days." Coming to his favorite, he prophetically likened Joseph to "a fruitful bough, even a fruitful bough by a well; whose branches run over the wall." Choice blessings, he promised, would follow him "unto the utmost bound of the everlasting hills" (Gen. 49:1, 22, 26). Few ancient Jews or modern readers have taken that overrun well to refer to the Pacific Ocean or the everlasting hills to evoke images of Utah's Wasatch Mountains. But to many Latter-day Saints, the Book of Mormon story that begins in Jerusalem and ends in the Western Hemisphere fulfills that very prophecy of Jacob. In this version, the long odyssey foretold by the patriarch begins in the time of Jeremiah and King Zedekiah, around 600 B.C. The Babylonians under

Nebuchadnezzar have besieged the royal city Jerusalem, inhabited for the most part by the tribes of Judah and Benjamin. Scattered among those Israelites who still inhabited the land of Judah at this time, and were soon to be carried into a Babylonian exile, lived remnants of the other ten tribes that had disappeared into Assyrian captivity over a century earlier. One such man is named Lehi, who traced his genealogy to "Joseph; yea, even that Joseph who was the son of Jacob, who was sold into Egypt" (1 Nephi 5:14).

In these years of growing panic and distress, while Jerusalem's fate awaited the verdict of empires clashing on every side, while Egyptians and Assyrians and Babylonians fought for supremacy, Jewish prophets once again took up the mantra of crying repentance to a threatened kingdom. Jeremiah is one of those figures, and his life, warnings, and lamentations are chronicled in several books of the Old Testament. But Lehi is another such prophet, though he is never mentioned in the biblical record. It is his story that founds the Book of Mormon. Swept up in a series of visions, he begins to declare to his people "their wickedness and abominations," as well as "the coming of a Messiah and also the redemption of the world" (1 Nephi 1:19). After incurring resentment and then persecution, he is warned in a vision to gather his immediate family and depart into the wilderness. Sending his four sons back once to recover important Jewish records engraved on plates of brass, and then again to enlist a family with marriageable daughters (as well as some sons), Lehi finally departs southward through the Arabian peninsula.

After a wilderness sojourn of eight years, Lehi's righteous son Nephi is told in a vision to build a ship, and the group makes preparations for a lengthy voyage. Then Lehi launches into the Indian Ocean with his wife and a company of about two dozen. If he followed the sea lanes used by later voyagers, he would have "touched India and ultimately the Malayan peninsula. From that point [his] ship likely threaded through the islands of the western Pacific, then across the open reaches north of the equator to landfall around 14 degrees north latitude," on the west coast of Central America.[1]

Soon after landing, Lehi dies and conflict breaks out between Nephi, Lehi's successor as prophet, leader, and record-keeper, and his brothers Laman and Lemuel. Nephi leads his people inland several days' journey, where they become established as a righteous, prosperous people. They build a temple, engage in metalworking and agriculture, and call themselves "Nephites." Meanwhile, their rivals, soon known by the name "Lamanites" and cursed with darkness, become "an idle people, full of mischief and subtlety" and "a scourge unto [Nephi's] seed" (2 Nephi 5:24-25). Thus is established the pattern that will dominate much of the millennium-long history to follow, as chronicled by Nephi and other keepers of the sacred records. When recurrent cycles of Nephite prosperity and complacency lead to spiritual blight, wars with the Lamanites intensify, accompanied by prophetic chastisement and repentance. Toward the end of the Nephite record especially, accounts of internal dissension and government corruption multiply, along with detailed narratives of civil war, treacherous defections, and the rise of great robber armies. Brilliant generalship, spiritual reform, and stirring heroism provide brief moments of respite from the advancing tide of cataclysmic destruction.

What prevents the record from falling into a faceless, Calvinist morality play, emphasizing human recalcitrance and the inevitable degeneration of human empires, is the emphatic insistence of Mormon, fourth-century abridger of the Nephite records, that individual choice produces cataclysmic consequences. "Either something or nothing must depend on individual choices," writes C. S. Lewis,[2] and Mormon, writing at the end of his people's existence around A.D. 340, embraces the first option. He illustrates the point by describing a period of fragile and hard-won peace during in the first century B.C., in which a single malcontent aspires to kingship. Inciting both spiritual apostasy and political dissent, Amalickiah succeeds in provoking a rebellion that soon engulfs the whole face of the land in years of bitter warfare. "Yea, and we also see," moralizes Mormon, "the great wickedness one very wicked man can cause to take place among the children of men" (Alma 46:9).

The hero who emerges as national savior is the young captain Moroni (namesake of the man of angelic fame). Through force of charisma and inspired leadership, he eventually succeeds in quelling the civil war and restoring peace. Moroni, in Mormon's eyes, serves not as a convenient instrument of a nation's predestined salvation, but as an instance of a species of man himself capable of upsetting the very balance of good and evil in the universe. In fact, writes Mormon, "if all men had been, and were, and ever would be, like unto Moroni, behold, the very powers of heaven would have been shaken forever; yea, the devil would never have power over the hearts of the children of men" (Alma 48:17).

Book of Mormon Christology

The earliest writers of the Book of Mormon, Nephi and Jacob, ground their prophetic worldview in the writings of Isaiah, which were contained in the brass plates brought from Jerusalem and partially copied onto the gold plates (of Isaiah's 66 chapters, 21 appear in their entirety and a few others in part). Through their midrashic interpretations of Isaiah, the Nephites see themselves as a scattered remnant of Israel and live in the firm expectation of a coming Messiah and with the understanding that their new home is for them a "land of promise, a land which is choice above all other lands; a land which the Lord God hath covenanted . . . should be a land for the inheritance of [their] seed" (2 Nephi 1:5).

This orientation explains an otherwise puzzling feature of the Book of Mormon—its pervasive references to Jesus Christ. Interspersed with the historical narrative are not only predictions of his coming, but sermons by Nephite missionaries, kings, and priests on a host of related subjects, including Christ's atonement, faith, resurrection, the plan of salvation, mercy and justice, infant baptism, and the purpose of life. Most prominent of all is the story that serves as historical and doctrinal fulcrum of the narrative, a story suggestive of both plagiarism and daring innovation at one and the same time. Five years before the crucifixion of Christ in Palestine, a Lamanite missionary appears in the Nephite land of Zarahemla with a momentous message. He prophesies that in five years' time miraculous signs will herald the coming of the Son of God himself into the world. His message is greeted with disbelief for the most part. Some voice the criticism that "it is not reasonable that such a being as a Christ shall come; if so, and he be the Son of God, the Father of heaven and of earth, as it has been spoken, why will he not show himself unto us as well as unto them who shall be at Jerusalem? Yea, why will he not show himself in this land as well as in the land of Jerusalem?" (Hel. 16:18-19).

The question, of course, is implicit in the very structure and existence of the Book of Mormon. We have already been presented with New World Israelites, a New World Promised Land, and a New World Scripture. A New World appearance by the resurrected Christ would seem to follow naturally. And it does. This appearance of the risen Savior in the New World is the center of the Book of Mormon, historically and thematically. It is also the dramatic, quintessential example of Joseph Smith's restorationism.

This centeredness on Christ, the Messiah, in a document purporting to have been written by New World Israelites over a period from the six centuries *before* Christ to A.D. 421 is certainly one of the more remarkable—and daring—features of the Book of Mormon, theologically. Not only foreknowledge of Christ—the Bible has its messianic moments— but the very concept of a fall and the need for both salvation and a savior as taught in the Book of Mormon are, of course, absent from Israelite religion as generally believed to exist at the time of the Exile. So while Mormon scholars emphasize the Book of Mormon's Hebrew connections, ultimately Stephen Robinson seems right to concede that the Book of Mormon culture would have to be, to a remarkable degree, "idiosyncratic," "a unique culture which, through revelation accepted only by it, held sophisticated Christian beliefs in a pre-Christian era."[3] As Nephi's brother Jacob explains, writing near the beginning of that era, "We knew of Christ and we had a hope of his glory many hundred years before his coming, and not only we ourselves had a hope of his glory but also all the holy prophets which were before us" (Jacob 4:4). The Book of Mormon, to put it simply, is, at least in part, a history of pre-Christian Christians, who "talk of Christ, . . . rejoice in Christ, . . . prophesy of Christ" centuries before his coming (2 Nephi 25:26).

Such seeming anachronism is not entirely inconsistent with early Christian traditions or with canons of both the Old and New Testament. Referring to Adam's transgression, an impressive number of biblical scholars, Howard N. Wallace and Umberto Cassuto to name only two, conclude "that distinct formulated traditions about the fall existed before the Pentateuch," and Robert Gordis complains that translating the Hebrew term 'ādām as "man" when it should be read as the proper name "Adam" obscures a number of biblical allusions to the fall. "In view of the vast interest in Adam in post-biblical thought," he writes, "we cannot understand the endeavor to ignore such references to him in the OT."[4]

Regarding pre-Christian messianic expectations, two second-century Fathers, Justin Martyr and Irenaeus, as well as the medieval *Book of the Bee* and *4 Baruch*, cite currently unknown passages from Jeremiah that predict details of the Messiah's birth, ministry, and resurrection.[5] In addition, a number of Dead Sea Scrolls reveal that "at least some Jews of that time expected a Messiah who would be a divine savior, performing many miracles, and bringing the resurrection."[6] Margaret Barker uses canonical and deuterocanonical as well as rabbinical and Qumran material to argue that Christ's New Testament titles, "Son of God, Lord and Messiah," were *not* the result of "creative theologizing" of the first Christians," but were already present "in the expectations and traditions of first-century Palestine." They simply "fitted Jesus into an existing pattern of belief."[7]

Finally, Paul's reading of the Old Testament as prefiguring Christ is, of course, the basis of all Christian typology. The author of Hebrews went so far as to suggest that the gospel "was first preached" to the children of Israel; Peter claimed that "all" the prophets testified "that Christ should suffer," uncertain only "what, or what manner of time the Spirit of Christ which was in them did signify, when it testified beforehand the sufferings of Christ" (Heb. 4:6; Acts 3:18; 1 Peter 1:10-11). And as for his actual appearing to the inhabitants of the Western Hemisphere, Latter-day Saints are fond of pointing out his cryptic remark to the Jews, that "other sheep I have, which are not of this fold: them also I must bring, and they shall hear my voice; and there shall be one fold, and one shepherd" (John 10:16).

Obviously, such passages are less than persuasive as evidence of a comprehensive knowledge of Christ and of his gospel being prevalent among the Jews going back all the way to Moses. And there is certainly little in the New Testament to support the even bolder contention of Joseph Smith, which he would maintain in a subsequent scriptural production, that Adam himself was taught faith in Christ, was baptized in water, and then "with fire, and with the Holy Ghost."[8] But that is precisely the point. It would be entirely inaccurate to consider Joseph's account of Christ among the Nephites as a gloss on those few biblical passages that hint of such a possibility, or to see it as a mere elaboration or extrapolation.

Again and again in Joseph's career we see this same pattern. The temple of Solomon contained a large "molten sea" of brass, and Paul makes a single enigmatic allusion, still confounding to all scholars and commentators, to "baptism for the dead" (1 Cor. 15:29). Joseph Smith inaugurates Temple building, and in Nauvoo, a large font resting on the backs of 12 oxen is dedicated where Mormons will be baptized vicariously for the deceased. Malachi mentions Elijah, who will "turn the heart of the children to their fathers" (Mal. 4:5-6). Joseph preaches the eternity of the family unit, and a Latter-day Saint preoccupation with ancestors and genealogy begins that continues, famously, to the present day. Jeremiah is told that before he was in the belly, God knew him and ordained him a prophet (Jer. 1:5). Joseph fleshes out a concept of premortal existence that encompasses man, fallen angels, Jesus Christ, and Lucifer. In none of these cases, or a dozen others that could be mentioned, could one make a reasonable, theological defense of Joseph's ampler enactment of these principles and practices on the basis of the few paltry biblical allusions that exist. Their insufficiency, their incompleteness is very much to Joseph's purposes. They are the feeble fragments that point to an insoluble absence, to frustrating gaps in the historical record, to the poverty and corruption of a text that leaves us in a state of bewildered spiritual deprivation. Joseph Smith is no Luther, poring over the scriptures to provide revisionist interpretations of Christian doctrine, or a King Josiah, rediscovering neglected scrolls of scripture. He is Moses, bringing down utterly new tablets from the mount, to a people still possessed of shadowy recollections of a former, fuller knowledge of Jehovah.

And so we find, in the book of Third Nephi, an account both familiar and audacious. A voice from heaven announces the risen Lord, like the voice of God at Christ's baptism as described in the synoptic gospels. Next, a postascension Jesus descends from heaven and invites the assembled Nephite multitudes to "feel the prints of the nails in his hands and in his feet," as he had invited Thomas earlier. Then, in language often identical to—but often differing significantly from—the King James Version, he delivers a discourse at their temple very like the Sermon on the Mount. Over the next eighteen chapters, he chooses disciples, institutes the Lord's supper, heals the sick, teaches and prays, blesses little children, and then, following the New Testament pattern, ascends to heaven. But he shortly returns, and awards not one but three apostles the gift of tarrying in the flesh until his second coming, before finally ascending again.

Some overlap with the gospels of the New Testament notwithstanding, the effect of this whole episode is to explode the historical particularity, the utterly unique and unrepeatable fact of Christ's eruption into human time. This account, so blatantly familiar that it almost begs to be labeled (and often has been) facile plagiarism,[9] seems calculated to emphasize the iterability of Christ's operations in the human sphere. As if to reinforce that point, Christ tells the Nephites before he leaves, "ye are they of whom I said: Other sheep I have which are not of this fold." But the doubling of one hemispheric manifestation to two is in turn transformed into several, perhaps endless visitations: "And verily, verily, I say unto you that I have other sheep, which are not of this land, neither of the land of Jerusalem, neither in any parts of that land round about whither I have been to minister" (3 Nephi 15:21; 16:1).

To multiply Christ's earthly manifestations in this way is clearly to challenge conventional understanding of the incarnation, God's embodiment and subsequent ministry and resurrection in Palestine, as the supreme miracle of Christianity. The Book of Mormon may not challenge the primacy of his birth, crucifixion, and resurrection in the Old World, but it does dilute the singularity of his Palestinian ministry, miracles, and manifestations (during and after his life) with a plethora of other contexts in which he has operated. This multiplication of "interventions" cannot avoid being read as an assault on the way the "supreme miracle" of the universe has always been constituted—as *the* supreme miracle.

And just as the solitary instance of Christ's earthly appearing proliferates into several manifestations, so does the scriptural record of his incarnation multiply into a potentially endless series of revelations:

> For behold, I shall speak unto the Jews and they shall write it; and I shall also speak unto the Nephites and they shall write it; and I shall also speak unto the other tribes of the house of Israel, which I have led away, and they shall write it; and I shall also speak unto all nations of the earth and they shall write it. And it shall come to pass that the Jews shall have the words of the Nephites, and the Nephites shall have the words of the Jews; and the Nephites and the Jews shall have the words of the lost tribes of Israel; and the lost tribes of Israel shall have the words of the Nephites and the Jews. (2 Nephi 29:12-13)

So insistent is the Book of Mormon on this theme, that it even plays itself out within the book itself. A few centuries into their American history, the descendents of Lehi encounter another displaced people "who were called the people of Zarahemla" and "were brought by the hand of the Lord across the great waters" from Jerusalem at the time of King Zedekiah's captivity, about 587 B.C. (Omni 15-16). The two groups unite, and subsequently discover records of yet a third civilization, followers of one Jared who departed the Old World at the time of the tower of Babel. Their exodus, dealings with the Lord (including even a vision of the pre-existent Christ), migration to the Western Hemisphere, and subsequent contentious history and extermination are all chronicled in the Book of Ether, which comprises most of the last 50 pages of the Book of Mormon.

This doubling and redoubling of providential history, divine activity, gospel content, and even gospel record—both described and enacted within the Book of Mormon—may go far to explain a history of the book's reception that began with the charge of "BLASPHEMY" first trumpeted by the *Rochester Daily Advertiser*.[10] It is a radical reconceptualization of the way Christian myth and Christian history are supposed to operate. Instead of a cardinal eruption of the divine into the human, spawning a spate of mythic reverberations, we have a proliferation of historical iterations, which themselves collectively become the ongoing substance rather than the shadow of God's past dealings in the universe.

Following Christ's ministry to the Nephites, then, the Book of Mormon narrative draws painfully and tragically to its close. After a utopian interlude of some two hundred years following Christ's visit, the Nephites return to their vain and prideful ways. Divisions and dissensions ensue, and war follows soon after. But this time, the wars are unprecedented in their scope and ferocity. They are in fact genocidal, wars of total annihilation, and for the Nephites, more favored and enlightened in righteousness and therefore more chastened and damned in their apostasy, the centuries-old conflict will end at a hill called Cumorah. Mormon, the last great Nephite commander, survives just long enough to see the extinction of his once mighty people. Looking out upon a quarter-million of his own dead, he records his pathetic farewell:

> And my soul was rent with anguish, because of the slain of my people, and I cried: O ye fair ones, how could ye have departed from the ways of the Lord! O ye fair ones, how could ye have rejected that Jesus, who stood with open arms to receive you! . . . O ye fair sons and daughters, ye fathers and mothers, ye husbands and wives, ye fair ones, how is it that ye could have fallen! But behold, ye are gone, and my sorrows cannot bring your return. (Morm. 6:16-20)

The curtain closes, and with this final scene of appalling loss and carnage still echoing like a Greek tragedy, the reader is immediately subjected to another version of this catastrophic history, only the players this time are the Jaredites. Their journey from blessedness to oblivion takes about twice as long as the Nephites (the third millennium B.C. to sometime between 600 and 300 B.C.), but only 30 pages to narrate. This compactly abridged account, following as it does upon the prayer of Moroni (son of Mormon), that his posterity will "learn to be more wise than we have been" (Morm. 9:31), has the effect of recasting the Book of Mormon as a morality tale of epic scope.

Herein lies just one of the major differences between the Bible and the Book of Mormon. The former is a collection of writings from different authors working in perhaps a dozen genres, lacking any one editor or compiler of the whole. The Book of Mormon, on the other hand, takes its name from its primary editor, Mormon, who from the perspective of a man who has witnessed the obliteration of his family, his people, and his civilization abridges a thousand years of records to produce a single coherent narrative for future generations.

It is important to distinguish narrative—in this case an epic story with actors, a plot, and recurrent themes and motifs—from history, if by that we mean a methodical, sequential record of important or public events.[11] Given the very focused preoccupations of Nephi at one end of the volume and Mormon at the other, and the huge disproportion between chronological time and textual volume, the Book of Mormon is clearly "history" in a very qualified sense. As John Sorenson points out, for example, "sixty-two percent of the entire Book of Mormon deals with one particular 160-year period (130 B.C.–A.D. 30), while the following three centuries take up only four pages. . . . Surely we could not label such a concise volume 'the story of the American Indian.' Even for 'the people of Nephi' it can barely be considered a history."[12]

Structure of the Book of Mormon

The actual manuscript history of the records, as told by the various Nephite compilers, is fairly complex, involves several distinct sets of plates, with multiple authors and editors, and further accounts for the polyphonic structure of the Book of Mormon. The more comprehensive set of plates was known as "the large plates of Nephi." The first of these were hand-fashioned by the prophet of that name after his arrival in the New World, and were envisioned as a secular record of Lehi's posterity, chronicling "the reign of the kings and the wars and contentions of my people" (1 Nephi 9:4). Since Nephi and his successors all the way down to Moroni recorded over ten centuries of unabridged history on these "large plates," the term may well describe a category of records rather than one particular set fashioned by Nephi. It was intended that they be kept under the stewardship of Nephite rulers, but that did not turn out to be what happened.

In the reign of Mosiah II, the Nephites experience a crisis of rapid growth and secularization. The original tribal unit of Lehi and his posterity, for whom religion is part of the familial and cultural fabric, is now represented as having become a diverse society in which believers are "persecuted." One response to the situation is the establishment of the "church" as an independent institution around 120 B.C. (Mos. 25). Shortly thereafter, about halfway through Nephite history, King Mosiah transfers the records to Alma the Younger, high priest of the Nephites and founder of the church. Consequently, Alma's account reads more like the Book of Acts than Kings or Chronicles, detailing missionary journeys, the growth of the church, and miraculous conversion stories. Thereafter, secular and religious elements alternate and intermingle in the records. When warrior prophets like Helaman or Mormon inherit the plates, the record reads more like the book of Joshua, with detailed accounts of military campaigns and protracted warfare.

About A.D. 385, even as he continues faithfully recording on the plates of Nephi a "full account" of his people's "wickedness and abominations" (Morm. 2:18), the prophet Mormon creates a new record of his own, "yea, a small record of that which hath taken place from the time that Lehi left Jerusalem, even down unto the present time. Therefore, I do make my record from the accounts which have been given by those who were before me" (3 Nephi 5:15-16). This abridgment, made on the plates of Mormon, was his edited version of his people's history, drawn from one thousand years of writings recorded on the "large plates" of Nephi, that culminates in his people's annihilation. So the history of the Nephites that Joseph translates is actually Mormon's abridgment of the writings of Nephi, Jacob, Mosiah, Alma, Helaman, and the rest of the chroniclers (hence the title, Book of Mormon). The first 116 pages of the translation of that abridgment, covering the period from Lehi's ministry to about 130 B.C., were those pages lost by Martin Harris.[13]

In addition to the large primary plates of Nephi that Mormon abridged, there was a second, overlapping set called "the small plates of Nephi," on which Nephi recorded "the more part of the ministry" of his people. Largely first person narratives of spiritual conversion and testimony, they begin with Nephi's abridgment of his father Lehi's record, which Nephi mentions in 1 Nephi 1:16. Nephi also incorporates substantial portions of the writings of Isaiah, which he said were contained in a set of brass plates that he stole from their former, wicked steward, one Laban of Jerusalem. Because, as John Welch points out, the brass plates contained the book of Deuteronomy, which was probably the book of the law discovered by Josiah around 625 B.C., the plates of brass may have been royal records, compiled between 625 and 610 B.C., and in the keeping of a high-ranking military officer associated with the King.[14] Other textual evidence suggests they were a lineage record, "privately held and controlled," with Northern Kingdom characteristics that are remarkably consistent in their similarity to the biblical E source.[15]

Nephi's small set of plates, passed on to spiritual rather than political successors, dealt with the religious life of the Nephites from 600 up to 130 B.C.; it covered, then, the same time frame as that described by the lost 116 pages. Unlike the large plates, the small plates of Nephi were not subjected to Mormon's abridging; they were a set that Mormon appended in their entirety to the large plates. They were translated last by Joseph Smith, but were inserted by him in their proper chronological place; they thus occupy the first 143 pages of the modern English edition of the Book of Mormon.

The text of the Book of Mormon as we have it, then, contains an episodic lineage history of the Nephites, although the first quarter, coming from the small plates of Nephi, is dominated by Isaiah's prophecies and sermons by Nephi and his brother Jacob. Relatively little in these pages gives us a glimpse of an unfolding Nephite history or of a larger world outside their own. A scant dozen times in the course of almost five centuries do the writers even indicate a year in which they are writing (using their departure from Jerusalem as the reference point). Nephi's introductory remarks, made in the context of his family's escape from Jerusalem's imminent destruction, and of his father's escape from murderous critics, set a tone for optimism in the face of providential design: "But behold, I, Nephi, will show unto you that the tender mercies of the Lord are over all those whom he hath chosen, because of their faith, to make them mighty even unto the power of deliverance" (1 Nephi 1:20). The "land of promise," hopeful moniker of their new found home, is an expression that appears 27 times in his small plates. The morals that Nephi draws from his own perspective as New World Joshua are unstintingly celebratory of God's faithfulness. Editorializing about the miraculous compass provided them by God, which directs them to a supply of food when they are at the point of starvation, he draws the simple precept: "And thus we see that by small means the Lord can bring about great things." Later observing how raw meat sufficed to nourish and sustain his people in the wilderness, he lectures us in the same didactic vein: "And thus we see . . . if it so be that the children of men keep the commandments of God he doth nourish them, and strengthen them, and provide means whereby they can accomplish the thing which he has commanded them" (1 Nephi 16:29; 17:3).

By contrast, much of the balance of the record, written mostly in the third person and mediated as it is by Mormon's perspective from the side of apocalyptic destruction rather than of hopeful exile, is marked by the somber lessons of lived history.[16] No land of promise for him; he uses the expression five times, twice referring to the Old World, and the other three times looking back to the glory days of the first settlement

("Oh, that I could have had my days in the days when my father Nephi first came out of the land of Jerusalem, that I could have joyed with him in the promised land").[17] From the "reign of the judges" on (established 92 B.C.), we hear frequent, consistent reference to the historical time frame. Thus, the vast bulk of the ascertainable dates (some two hundred) fall within the second half of the millennium-long principal history of the Book of Mormon. Given Mormon's tragic narrative position, the methodical invocation of each passing year tolls like a grim countdown to his people's inevitable annihilation: "In the seventy and second year of the reign of the judges . . . the contentions did increase"; "And thus in the commencement of this, the thirtieth year, they were in a state of awful wickedness"; "And now it came to pass in the two hundred and thirty and first year, there was a great division among the people"; "And it came to pass in the three hundred and forty and sixth year they began to come upon us again" (Hel. 11:1; 3 Nephi 6:17; 4 Nephi 1:36; Morm. 2:22). When he reverts to the didactic formula first employed by Nephi, it is more often to sing God's justice than his mercy. Describing one of the recurrent cycles of Nephite apostasy, he writes: "And thus we see that except the Lord doth chasten his people with many afflictions, yea, except he doth visit them with death and with terror, and with famine and with all manner of pestilence, they will not remember him." And in his subsequent commentary on the Jaredite wars of extinction, he sadly concludes for us, "And thus we see that the Lord did visit them in the fulness of his wrath, and their wickedness and abominations had prepared a way for their everlasting destruction" (Hel. 12:3; Ether 14:25).

After Mormon completes his abridgment and appends the small plates of Nephi, he turns them over to his son Moroni. Moroni includes a poignant explanation for the brevity of his own comments: "After the great and tremendous battle of Cumorah, behold, the Nephites who had escaped into the country southward were hunted by the Lamanites, until they were all destroyed. And my father also was killed by them, and I remain alone to write the sad tale of the destruction of my people. . . . And behold, I would write [more] also if I had room upon the plates, but I have not, and ore I have none, for I am alone" (Morm. 8:2-5). Several years later, Moroni apparently adds a few more plates on which he writes, from memory, an abridgment of another set of plates, the 24 plates of Ether, which were discovered by a Nephite group around 121 B.C. and which chronicle the history of the Jaredite people. Finally, some twenty years later, Moroni finds himself still alive with more to say. He writes briefly on topics such as priesthood authority, administering the Lord's supper, church government, and infant baptism. He testifies to the truthfulness of his writings, invites all to come to Christ, then seals up the sacred record.

Despite the widespread assumption that Moroni deposited the plates in the Hill Cumorah mentioned by Mormon, scene of the cataclysmic final battle, the record suggests he did *not* bury the plates in a hill of that name. Mormon writes that he "hid up in the hill Cumorah all the records which had been entrusted to me by the hand of the Lord, *save it were these few plates* [the Book of Mormon] *which I gave to my son Moroni*" (Morm. 6: 6, emphasis mine). When Moroni eventually comes to bid posterity farewell and entombs the record, some 35 years of wandering have passed. The modern designation of the New York site of discovery as Hill Cumorah was first made by Oliver Cowdery in 1835. Joseph Smith did, however, accept the popular name for the place by 1842, as apparent in a "Letter to the Church," in which he referred to Moroni's message to him as "Glad tidings from Cumorah!" (D&C 128: 20). The perseverance of that identification (as well as the church's official designation of the upstate New York mount as "Hill Cumorah") led to a common belief among many Mormons—and their critics—that Nephite geography and history must encompass New York state.[18]

Publication and Circulation

With the translation essentially complete, and affidavits from eleven witnesses, Smith was now ready to seek a publisher for the record. Finding the local bookseller and printer Egbert B. Grandin reluctant, Joseph and Martin Harris traveled to Rochester to find another publisher. Realizing the work would proceed anyway, Grandin apparently overcame his scruples or his reservations and agreed to publish the work in Palmyra, though he demanded a security of $3,000 before proceeding. Fulfilling his wife's worst fears, Harris now agreed to mortgage his farm for the required amount, promising to pay the printing cost within 18 months.[19] Late that summer of 1829, printing work on the Book of Mormon began in Grandin's second-floor establishment.

The popular Mormon perception of the order of events would have Joseph, aided by a small circle of intimates, working in virtual solitude to finish the translation. Then upon publication, he assembles six elders together to organize the church on April 6, 1830, whereupon his brother Samuel Smith fills a rucksack with copies of the new scripture and sets out as the first missionary of the new dispensation. This version misses the importance of the long drawn-out printing process as a time when the story of the Book of Mormon began to filter out to the public and the first bands of converts began to align themselves with the new work. In actual fact, the commencement of the translation process, not the book's publication, was the first catalyst to active proselytizing for the new faith. When the six elders, in compliance with New York state law, gathered for the church's formal incorporation, they were surrounded by about 40 or 50 other members, the nucleus of an already steadily growing group of believers.[20]

Many who aligned themselves with these "Mormonites" in those formative months were personal correspondents and relatives of those involved in or close to the translation process. Shortly after being engaged as Joseph's scribe in the spring of 1829, Oliver Cowdery wrote his friend David Whitmer in Fayette, New York, describing the work he was assisting in and even sending along portions of the translation. Whitmer, in turn, shared the letters and translation with his family.[21]

As we have seen, by the time Joseph and Oliver had relocated to the Whitmer home, they had already received the Aaronic Priesthood, been baptized, and made aware of an impending church to be restored. From that point, the forthcoming Book of Mormon was inevitably cast in a new role. Assent to the truthfulness of the gold plates would now entail assent to a proper church, signified by the ordinance of baptism. And neither the preaching nor the baptizing needed to wait upon legal formalities.

Joseph recorded that in the area of the Whitmer neighborhood, people were "disposed to enquire into the truth of these strange matters which now began to be noised abroad. . . . We met with many from time to time who were willing to hear us. . . . From this time forth many became believers, and some were baptized whilst we continued to instruct and persuade as many as applied for information."[22]

Once the manuscript was delivered to the printer, Joseph recorded in his history, "we still continued to bear testimony and give information."[23] Unwilling to wait for the finished volumes, Christian Whitmer, David's brother, "copied from the manuscript the teachings and the doctrine of Christ, being the things which we were commanded to preach." Similarly anxious, others took signatures as they came off the press in the fall of 1829 and used them in preaching or distributed them to the curious. Thomas Marsh journeyed from Lyons, New York, to inquire about the "Golden Book." He "found Martin Harris at the printing office, in Palmyra, where the first sixteen pages of the Book of Mormon had just been struck off, the proof sheet of which I obtained from the printer and took with me. . . . After staying there two days I started for Charleston, Mass., highly pleased with the information I had obtained concerning the new found book."

(*Facing page*)   Portion of original Book of Mormon manuscript corresponding to 1 Nephi 4:38–5:14 in current editions. The scribe has not been identified. (© by Intellectual Reserve, Inc. Courtesy Family and Church History Department. Used by permission)

Lehi searches the Records

this it came to pass that we took the plates of brass & the
servant of Laban & departed into the wilderness and journied
unto the tent of our father & it came to pass that after we
came down into the wilderness unto our father behold
he was filled with joy and also my mother Sariah was exceeding glad for she truly had mourned because of us
for she had supposed that we had perished in the wilderness and she also had complained against my father
telling him that he was a visionary man saying behold
thou hast led us forth from the land of our inheritance & my sons are no more and we perish in the
wilderness and after this manner of language had my
Mother complained against my father and it had came
to pass that my father spake unto her saying i know
that i am a visionary man for if i had not seen the things of god in a vission i should not have known the
goodness of god but had tarried at jerusalem and had
perished with my brethren but behold i have obtain
a land of promises in the which things i do rejoice
yea and i know that the lord will deliver my sons
out of the hands of Laban and bring them down again
unto us in the wilderness and after this manner of language
My father Lehi comfort my mother Sariah concerning
us while we journied in the wilderness up to the
land of jerusalem to obtain the record of the jews and
when we had returned to the tent of my father behold
their joy was full and my mother was comforted and
spake saying now i know of a surity that the lord hath
commanded my husband to flee into the wilderness
yea and also know of a surity that the lord hath protected
my sons and delivered them out of the hands of Laban
and gave them power whereby they could accomplish
the thing which the lord hath commanded them and after
this manner of language did she speak and it came to pass
that they did rejoice exceedingly and did offer sacrifice
and burnt offerings unto the lord and they gave thanks
unto the god of israel and after that they had given thanks
unto the god of israel my father Lehi took the records
which were engraven upon the plates of brass and
he did search them from the beginning and he beheld
that they did contain the five books of moses which
gave an account of the creation of the world and also of adam
and eve which was our first parents and also a record of the jews
from the beginning even down to the commencement of
the reign of Zedekiah king of judea and also the prophecies
of the holy prophets from the beginning even down to the
commencement of the reign of Zedekiah and also many prophecies which have been spoken by the mouth of jeremiah
and it came to pass that my father Lehi also found upon the
plates of brass a genealogy of his fathers wherefore he knew that
he was a descendant of joseph yea even that joseph which
was the son of jacob which was sold into egypt and which
was preserved by the hand of the lord that he might

Another visitor from Lyons, Solomon Chamberlain, had had a vision in 1816 of "a book to come forth, like unto the Bible." Hyrum took Chamberlain to the printing office and gave him not one but four 16-page signatures. Convinced he had found the book of his vision, Chamberlain "took them with their leave and pursued my journey to Canada, and I preached all that I knew concerning Mormonism, to all both high and low, rich and poor, and thus you see this was the first that ever printed Mormonism was preached to this generation."[24]

Oliver Cowdery and Joseph Smith also took loose sheets from the printing to share with their own relatives. From Joseph's perspective, the value of the previews was not so much as preaching guides or distillations of gospel truths, but rather as tangible evidence that his disputed claims about a magnificent record were about to be realized: "There begins to be a great call for our books in this country," he wrote in October of 1829. "The minds of the people are very much excited when they find that there is a copyright obtained and that there is really a book about to be produced."[25]

Joseph's optimism proved to be misplaced. Indeed, citizens in the area around Palmyra, alerted to the reality of the impending publication, *were* excited—but not exactly in the way Joseph had hoped. Fifteen days after his application for copyright on June 11, even before the manuscript was completed, the *Wayne Sentinel*, a local Palmyra paper, reprinted the title page Joseph had filed with that application. In the accompanying article, the writer seemed hopeful that reports of the imminent publication would prove groundless ("it is pretended that it will soon be published").[26] As printing proceeded, the skepticism gave way to hostility. At the end of August, the *Palmyra Freeman* called the book "the greatest piece of superstition that has come to our knowledge."[27]

On September 2, Abner Cole began a weekly called the *Palmyra Reflector*. In the first issue, he made sarcastic reference to Joseph Smith and his "gold bible," then by December he progressed from mockery to pirating. Because he used Grandin's press, Cole had access to those pages in the shop that were already printed. He reprinted excerpts in December and January editions of the weekly, before Joseph's threats of legal action caused him to stop. But the alarmists and satirists had had their effect. In January of the new year, residents organized a boycott of the offending book.[28] They even sent a deputation to Grandin, who panicked and sus-

---

(*Facing page*)   Two first editions of the Book of Mormon. The annotations in the copy opened to 1 Nephi 4 (current chapter system), are by LDS Seventy and Book of Mormon scholar B. H. Roberts, who owned it. (Photographs by Bradley Sheppard. George Givens Collection)

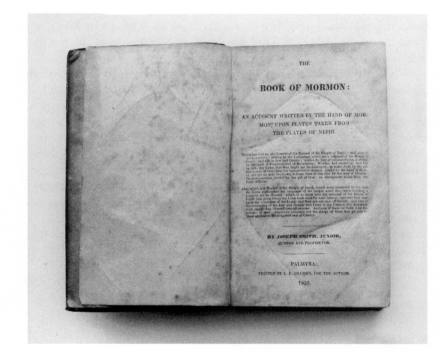

pended publication until Joseph managed to allay his fears. Work resumed, and on March 26, 1830, the Book of Mormon was offered for sale in the Palmyra Bookstore of E. B. Grandin.

Now it was Harris, rather than Grandin, who bore fully the financial pressures of publication. Clearly he believed in the work, but with his farm now hostage to sales, he had additional incentive to move copies of the book. Accordingly, wrote one source, he "gave up his entire time to advertising the Bible to his neighbors and the public generally in the vicinity of Palmyra. He would call public meetings and address them himself."[29] Joseph Knight, who along with the prophet, encountered him loaded down with unsold copies, recorded the famous result of his efforts: "The books will not sell for no Body wants them," the farmer lamented.[30]

Samuel Smith, brother of the prophet and generally considered the first missionary of the new church, was equally unsuccessful in trying to market the book farther from home. His mother recorded that

John Gilbert (1802–1895).
Principal typesetter for the
Book of Mormon,
Gilbert, standing here with
Book of Mormon signatures,
described the manuscript he
worked with as "closely
written and legible, but
not a punctuation mark
from beginning to end."
Photograph ca. 1890.
(Courtesy LDS Church
Historical Department)

on the thirtieth of June, Samuel started on the mission to which he had been set apart by Joseph, and in travelling twenty-five miles, which was his first day's journey, he stopped at a number of places in order to sell his books, but was turned out of doors as soon as he declared his principles. When evening came on, he was faint and almost discouraged, but coming to an inn, which was surrounded by every appearance of plenty, he called to see if the landlord would buy one of his books. On going in, Samuel inquired of him, if he did not wish to purchase a history of the origin of the Indians. "I do not know," replied the host, "how did you get hold of it?" "It was translated," rejoined Samuel, "by my brother, from some gold plates that he found buried in the earth." "You d—d liar!" cried the landlord, "get out of my house—you shan't stay one minute with your books."[31]

Samuel found a few of the curious willing to accept the book if it was gratis. But none would pay for the privilege of reading it. Pomeroy Tucker confirmed that "the book . . . fell dead before the public. . . . It found no buyers, or but very few."[32]

Little more than a decade after the book was made public, a Mormon in Philadelphia assessed the results: "No sooner had the Book of Mormon made its appearance, than priests and professors began to rage, Madam Rumour began with her poisonous tongues; epithet upon epithet, calumny upon calumny, was heaped upon the few that were first engaged in the cause; mobs raged, and . . . a general hue and cry was raised."[33] If Joseph was disappointed by the book's reception, he did not show it. He recorded with typical understatement that, "as the ancient prophet had predicted of it, 'it was accounted as a strange thing.' No small stir was created by its appearance."[34] In any event, it is remarkable but true that almost from the instant of its publication, the Book of Mormon ceased to be the focus of Joseph's attention. It now assumed its role as herald of something far greater than itself: a new church, a new dispensation, and a new American prophet.

THREE

"A Marvelous Work and a Wonder": The Book of Mormon as Sacred Sign

Signs function, then, not through their intrinsic value but through their relative position. . . . The idea . . . that a sign contains is of less importance than the other signs that surround it.

—Ferdinand de Saussure

Joseph Smith's vision for the church and kingdom he was called to found, and the destiny of the people he led, was nothing if not ambitious. By 1842, when he sent a "Historical Sketch" of the rise and progress of the church to John Wentworth, the Saints, as its members were called,[1] had already endured persecutions, mobbings, and expulsion from Missouri. In the midst of physical and financial adversity, missionaries had already fanned out across the states and across the ocean. As converts streamed into the church's new city-state of Nauvoo, Illinois, under more gathering clouds, Joseph defiantly predicted to Wentworth that "no unhallowed hand can stop the work from progressing, persecutions may rage, mobs may combine, armies may assemble, calumny may defame, but the truth of God will go forth boldly, nobly, and independent till it has penetrated every continent, visited every clime, swept every country, and sounded in every ear, till the purposes of God shall be accomplished and the great Jehovah shall say the work is done."[2]

Joseph and his brethren found biblical evidence for this confidence in Nebuchadnezzar's dream of a stone "cut out without hands, which . . . became a great mountain, and filled the whole earth." Daniel's interpretation of the dream, Joseph believed, was even now in process of fulfillment: "And in the days of these kings shall the God of heaven set up a kingdom, which shall never be destroyed: and the kingdom shall not be left to other people, but it shall break in pieces and consume all these kingdoms, and it shall stand for ever" (Dan. 2:34-35, 44). Early Mormons turned to this imagery of Daniel in song, sermon, and writings to understand and to proclaim their historic role and destiny.[3] And they early recognized the pivotal role the Book of Mormon would play in this everlasting kingdom. W. W. Phelps, for example, wrote in 1835 that "there began the church of Christ in 1830; yea, there the stone cut out of the mountain without hands, as foretold by Daniel, commenced rolling to fill the earth, and may it continue, in a moral sense, in dreadful splendor, till it fills the whole, and wickedness is ended. So much for Hill Cumorah."[4]

Then in December of 1835, a month much given over to studying Hebrew, entertaining visitors, and showing off the church's recently acquired Egyptian mummies, Joseph took time out to write an article on "the important subject of the gathering," concentrating on the parables of Matthew 13. Turning to the parable of the mustard seed, he found there another powerful image for the events unfolding around him: "we can discover plainly that this figure is given to represent the Church as it shall come forth in the last days." More specifically, he continued, we can understand the parable as follows:

> Let us take the Book of Mormon, which a man took and hid in his field, securing it by his faith, to spring up in the last days, or in due time; let us behold it coming forth out of the ground, which is indeed accounted the least of all seeds, but behold it branching forth, yea, even towering, with lofty branches, and God-like majesty, until it, like the mustard seed, becomes the greatest of all herbs. And it is truth, and it has sprouted and come forth out of the earth, and righteousness begins to look down from heaven, and God is sending down his powers, gifts, and angels, to lodge in the branches thereof.[5]

This is stirring imagery, designating the Book of Mormon a herald, or portent, of other magnificent events to come. The spectacle of its "springing up," "coming forth," and "branching" out, and its consequent role as a locus of heavenly manifestations and angelic activity, seem to suggest that what it signifies as event may be more important than what it actually says.

Popular opinion may have it, in the words of one distinguished religious historian, that "the Book of Mormon, [is] one of the bases for unique Mormon teachings."[6] Even the LDS *Encyclopedia of Mormonism* seems to agree, contending that "the Book of Mormon forms the doctrinal foundation of the Church."[7] However, looking at the Book of Mormon in terms of its early uses and reception, it becomes clear that this American scripture has exerted influence within the church and reaction outside the church not primarily by virtue of its substance, but rather its manner of appearing, not on the merits of what it *says*, but what it *enacts*. Put slightly differently, the history of the Book of Mormon's place in Mormonism and American religion generally has always been more connected to its status as *signifier* than *signified*,[8] or its role as a sacred sign rather than its function as persuasive theology. The Book of Mormon is preeminently a concrete manifestation of sacred utterance, and thus an evidence of divine presence, before it is a repository of theological claims.

Ensign to the Nations

On the night that Moroni visited the boy-prophet for the first time, he quoted the eleventh chapter of Isaiah, "saying that it was about to be fulfilled."[9] Referring to a "second" gathering of scattered Israel, this millennialist prophecy declares that the Lord "shall set up an ensign for the nations, and shall assemble the outcasts of Israel, and gather together the dispersed of Judah from the four corners of the earth" (Isa. 11:12). To Latter-day Saints, language of a gathering and Israel's redemption was much more than spiritual metaphor. Indeed, literal gathering became one of the most distinctive and historically determinative characteristics of the new movement. Missionaries fanned out in all directions before the ink was even dry on the first edition of the Book of Mormon. In December, the very year of the church's organization, a revelation directed the Saints to "assemble together at the Ohio" (Doctrine and Covenants 37:3). As the assembly point shifted westward and converts poured in, even Charles Dickens took notice: "It sounds strange to hear of a church having a 'location.' But a 'location' was the term they applied to their place of settlement . . . in Jackson County, Missouri."[10]

Initially, the church itself was likened to this "ensign" or battle standard, around which spiritual Israel was called to literally assemble from the nations of the earth. As the first issue of the church newspaper reminded readers, "It is the duty of the Church of Christ, in Zion, to stand as an ensign to all nations, that the Lord hath set his hand the second time to restore the House of Israel to the lands of their inheritance,"[11] and a year later, in 1833, Joseph referred to the "Elders of Zion" as "an Ensign to the Nations."[12] The problem, as many scholars of Mormonism have pointed out, is that the church did not readily stand out in a crowded field.[13] Their seeming peculiarities notwithstanding, Jan Shipps agrees that "the Saints sometimes had difficulty in differentiating themselves from other Christians who were in the field at the same time."[14] In an age described by one editor as a "paradise of heterodoxy,"[15] it was hard to startle or impress anymore. One historian has alleged that in such a crowded field, Mormons found it necessary to actually risk their own "destruction by straining to advertise Mormon deviance."[16] What the Mormons did have in their favor was a new book of scripture and a remarkable story to go with it. As Shipps writes, "the existence of the Book of Mormon is what initially set LDS preaching apart from the exhortations of the 'sectarians.'"[17] Gradually, as the most visible component of the new religion, the Book of Mormon came to share the designation of "ensign to the nations" with the church itself.

In 1835, Joseph referred to the publication of the Book of Mormon as one of three signs that the work of the last days had commenced.[18] He had actually recognized that connection years earlier, as it had been made explicit in the Book of Mormon itself. In his appearance to the Nephites shortly after his resurrection, Christ declared, "I give unto you a sign, that ye may know the time when . . . I shall gather in, from their long dispersion, my people, O house of Israel." That gathering would take place, he promised, "when these works and the works which shall be wrought among you hereafter shall come forth from the Gentiles, unto your seed." Accordingly, Joseph Smith had sent a party of four on a mission to descendants of those Nephites and Lamanites months after the publication of the Book of Mormon. Leading elder Oliver Cowdery and his companions traveled some 1,500 miles, first preaching to the Cattaraugus in Buffalo before journeying on to the Wyandots in Ohio, and then crossing the Missouri frontier to proselytize the Shawnee and Delaware tribes. Oliver Cowdery claimed their listeners were encouragingly receptive, but the missionaries were expelled from the Indian country by government agents before long. Still, by preaching the Book of Mormon to these Indian tribes, early missionaries had begun the work of conveying to the "seed" of that New World multitude described in 3 Nephi the record of their own forefathers, fulfilling prophecy, and confirming the advent of the end times.[19]

Pursuing this connection between the Book of Mormon and Israel's final gathering, Charles Thompson published in 1841 the first major work on the Book of Mormon by a church member, his 256-page study of *Evidences in Proof of the Book of Mormon*, in order to "correct the public mind in reference to its real intent and character." This intent and character were embodied in the fact that heavenly angels had "brought to light the Book of Mormon, and set it as a sign among the people and lifted it up as an ensign on the mountains of nations."[20] "This ensign, standard, and sign," he continued, would serve to announce the imminent gathering of Israel, "the literal seed of Jacob, from all nations, unto their own land." Almost at once, the church's *Times and Seasons* picked up the refrain, commending Thompson's book and echoing his references to the new scripture as "a sign to Israel, that the time of their redemption had come," "an ensign for the nations," "an ensign upon the mountains, and . . . sign among the people for the purpose of gathering and uniting the whole house of Israel."[21]

In one of the church's first extended treatments of the Book of Mormon, Benjamin Winchester helped establish the same theme: "Nothing could be more plain, and explicit from the Bible, than that God has one of the most powerful, and majestic works to do in these latter-days, that he has ever done; and if the prophecies are true, miracles and revelations will be given." The Book of Mormon, he continues, is just such a revelation, calculated by its appearance to alert the world that "the Lord is nigh.—Israel gathered, Zion built, and, in a word, the way prepared for the appearance, or second advent of the Messiah."[22] Indeed, the Book of Mormon had proclaimed its own importance in this very regard:

> And now behold, I say unto you that when the Lord shall see fit, in his wisdom, that these sayings shall come unto the Gentiles according to his word, then ye may know that the covenant which the Father hath made with the children of Israel . . . is already beginning to be fulfilled. And ye may know that the words of the Lord . . . shall all be fulfilled; and ye need not say that the Lord delays his coming unto the children of Israel. . . . And when ye shall see these sayings coming forth among you, then ye need not any longer spurn at the doings of the Lord. (3 Nephi 29:1-4)

Isaiah too had prophesied of words that would come forth at a future time, in a scriptural context that early Mormons found to be so rich in prophetic specificity as to proclaim its undeniable fulfillment in their day. After speaking of a voice, "as of one that hath a familiar spirit," whispering out of the dust, the prophet had invoked the image of a sealed book delivered to a learned man. He acknowledges his inability to read a sealed book, whereupon "the book is delivered to him that is not learned." The man's weakness notwithstanding, the Lord promises to bring to pass "a marvellous work among this people, even a marvellous work and a wonder" (Isa. 29:4-14). To early converts, the plates buried in the earth, Harris's experience with the erudite Charles Anthon, and Smith, the untutored farmboy and instrument of God who ushered in the "fulness of the gospel," were convincing counterparts of Isaiah's inspired prediction. The Book of Mormon was the element that fulfilled prophecy even as it alerted the world to the imminence of momentous events at last unfolding.

This vital role for the Book of Mormon was seized upon enthusiastically by the early Saints and was responded to avidly by numerous converts. Mormons shared with a host of other nineteenth-century Christians intensely millenarian anticipations, and, as Marvin Hill comments, Mormonism's "'primitive gospel' orientation has long been recognized."[23] Of the 1830s especially, it has been written that "never in the history of Western society had the millennium seemed so imminent;

never before had people looked so longingly and hopefully for its advent. It was expected that twenty years or less would see the dawn of that peaceful era."[24] Of the very year in which the Book of Mormon was published, another historian wrote, "The ardor of religious awakening resulting from the new discoveries in the gospel was very much increased about the year 1830, by the hope that the millennium had now dawned, and that the long expected day of gospel glory would very soon be ushered in."[25] Alexander Campbell, cofounder of the Disciples of Christ, typified the belief of many "primitivists" and "restorationists" that a return to early Christian purity of belief and practice would usher in a period of divine blessing. At the same time, he anticipated divine participation in this process: "Do not the experiences of all the religions—the observations of the intelligent—the practical result of all creeds, reformations, and improvements—and the expectations and longings of society—warrant the conclusion that either some new revelation, or some new development of the revelation of God must be made, before the hopes and expectations of all true Christians can be realized . . . ?"[26]

Campbell saw signs of the approaching end all around in the social and religious conditions of his day. William Miller, who would inspire a vast following as well, relied upon his reading of Revelation to ascertain an exact date for Christ's return in 1843. But Mormons were now empowered to go beyond the skills of personal observation and scriptural exegesis alone. They had in their possession a recovered record whose very existence was seen as prophetic proof that the final dispensation was truly arrived. Even before its first page was opened, the Book of Mormon by its miraculous provenance proclaimed that mighty preparations were afoot. And when readers *did* study its message, what they found was confirmation of its outward meaning. Actual invocation and interpretation of Book of Mormon passages by early church writers was relatively uncommon. Surprisingly uncommon, in fact. But in those instances where official church publications do quote and comment on selected passages, "what stands out in bold relief . . . is the thematic preeminence of . . . the restoration of Israel."[27] When the Book of Mormon was cited or described, it was to teach the doctrine of gathering and an imminent second coming.

In the Mormon view, this gathering to precede the second coming was part and parcel of another event about to unfold, the establishment of a New World Zion. As the prophet would later phrase the connection, "We believe in the literal gathering of Israel and in the restoration of the Ten Tribes; that Zion will be built upon this continent; that Christ will reign personally upon the earth; and, that the earth will be renewed and receive its paradisiacal glory."[28] In support of this view, perhaps the most quoted Book of Mormon passage in early church publications was Ether 13:4-8:

> Behold, Ether saw the days of Christ, and he spake concerning a New Jerusalem upon this land. And he spake also concerning the house of Israel, and the Jerusalem from whence Lehi should come—after it should be destroyed it should be built up again, a holy city unto the Lord; wherefore, it could not be a new Jerusalem for it had been in time of old; but it should be built up again, and become a holy city of the Lord; and it should be built unto the house of Israel. And that a New Jerusalem should be built upon this land, unto the remnant of the seed of Joseph, for which things there has been a type. . . . Wherefore, the remnant of the house of Joseph shall be built upon this land; and it shall be a land of their inheritance; and they shall build up a holy city unto the Lord, like unto the Jerusalem of old.

Here, then, was confirmation that we are in the last days, that the great work of gathering—a literal gathering—has commenced, and that the American Indians ("the remnant of the seed of Joseph") along with the Latter-day Saints adopted into the house of Israel together share in the promises made to Abraham. (Mormons paid more than passing notice to their belief that the American Indians were to play a central role in the gathering. In addition to the mission of 1830, the church's public teachings were pronounced enough in this regard that Missouri persecutors would later formally cite, as one reason for expelling Mormons from Clay County, their tendency to declare, "even from the pulpit, that the Indians are a part of God's chosen people, and are destined by Heaven to inherit this land, in common with themselves."[29])

The plans of the Saints to establish themselves in Jackson County, Missouri, where they had hoped to build their American Zion, were thwarted by persecution. Throughout the summer of 1833 came farm burnings, lootings, mobbings, and the destruction of the church printing press. In July, a group including Edward Partridge, bishop of the church, were whipped, tarred and feathered. Partridge watched as "Charles Allen was next stripped and tarred and feathered, because he would not agree to leave the country, or deny the Book of Mormon."[30]

By the fall, a general expulsion of the Saints had been forced. On November 7, "the shores of the Missouri river began to be lined on both sides of the ferry, with men, women, and children," the first waves of several hundred exiles.[31] A journalist reported the judgment of one of the locals: "'The people of Jackson can stand any thing but men who profess to have seen angels, and to believe the book of Mormon,' said an elderly man, who is a very self-pretending righteous one, while the mob were leading up their objects of hatred on whom they thirsted to spill their blood."[32] Months later, church leaders published a public "Appeal" in order to document the persecutions and to provide a rationale for their settlement there to begin with. "The Book of Mormon,

"Joseph Smith . . . addressing the chiefs and braves of several tribes of
Indians in the City of Nauvoo." The 1907 lithograph is by John McGahey.
(Courtesy LDS Church Historical Department)

which we hold equally sacred with the Bible, says, 'that a New Jerusalem should be built upon this land,'" they wrote simply.[33]

This assertion was singled out by Alexander Campbell as one of the
internal evidences in proof of the Book of Mormon's profane origins:
"This ignorant and impudent liar, in the next place, makes the God of
Abraham, Isaac, and Jacob, violate his covenants with Israel and Judah
concerning the land of Canaan, by promising a new land to the pious
Jew."[34] Indeed, Mormons were unique, as Grant Underwood has pointed
out, in rereading Old Testament references to Jerusalem and Zion through
this Book of Mormon prism, finding in them so many allusions to a pair
of holy cities that would be built in opposite hemispheres.[35] True, as
long ago as the revolutionary era, Timothy Dwight, instrumental in inaugurating the Second Great Awakening, preached that America was
"both a new Eden and a latter-day Zion," and "echoed a universal sentiment of his countrymen when he declared that this luxuriant Eden is
indeed 'the favorite land of heaven.'"[36] But the Latter-day Saints were
relentless in literalizing the forecast of an American Zion, where both
literal and figurative Israel, the descendants of Lehi and the spiritually
elect, would congregate. And the Book of Mormon, by both its descrip-

tion of that Zion and its miraculous appearance as herald of that coming city, gave special force and reality to that prophecy.

At least as pertains to the way the scripture was cited and invoked, it seems that Underwood is correct that the Book of Mormon's "earliest uses were primarily eschatological and reflected as well as reinforced a millenarian world view."[37] It is important to recognize, however, that the book was more important, even in this regard, as a sign than as a theological document. By way of illustration, one important source of information on early Mormon proselytizing comes from the journals of William McLellin, Joseph Smith's one-time secretary and one of the original twelve Latter-day Saint apostles (the highest governing body in the church after the prophet and his two counselors, or First Presidency). Active on several proselytizing missions, and an avid record-keeper, McLellin is one of the best sources available for the nature and content of early Mormon missionary activity. Jan Shipps points out the surprising fact that McLellin's extensive account of six years of preaching includes only three mentions of the Book of Mormon as a source for sermons. "For all that," she writes, "the Book of Mormon was critically important. . . . LDS preachers seem to have pointed primarily to the *fact* of the book, . . . to its coming forth as the opening event in the dispensation that was serving as the 'winding-up scene' before the curtain rose on the *eschaton*. The Book of Mormon was therefore presented as the ultimate sign of the times."[38]

This role of the new scripture was especially in evidence during the church's first phenomenally successful missionary effort that was launched a few months after its organization. In the fall of 1830, as we saw, witnesses Oliver Cowdery and Peter Whitmer, Jr., along with Parley P. Pratt and Ziba Peterson, embarked on the first missionary journey of the church to the west, heading for the Indian territory that bordered Missouri. Recruitment of American Indians was unsuccessful, but within a few weeks they had baptized 130 converts in northeastern Ohio, a number equal to the entire eastern membership at that time. Many of these early converts, like future Mormon stalwart Sidney Rigdon, were Campbellite restorationists. One of Campbell's associates, Walter Scott, had inadvertently paved the way for Mormon missionaries when he "contended ably for the restoration of the true, original apostolic order which would restore to the church the ancient gospel as preached by the apostles. The interest became an excitement; All tongues were set loose in investigation, in defense, or in opposition. . . . The air was thick with rumors of a 'new Religion,' a 'new Bible.'"[39] And Campbell himself chose as the epigraph for his new *Millennial Harbinger* that same passage of scripture that Mormons believed was fulfilled in the angel Moroni's visit to Joseph: "I saw another messenger flying through the midst of heaven, having everlasting good news to proclaim to the inhabitants of the earth, even to every nation and tribe, and tongue and people—saying with a loud voice, Fear God and give glory to Him, for the hour of His judgment is come."[40]

So, when he told a crowd in Mayfield, Ohio, "that there must be something sent from God in order to prepare the people for the glorious reign of Christ,"[41] Parley P. Pratt was striking a resonant chord. And the Book of Mormon he presented by way of such a sign from God had a receptive audience. As a Campbellite minister living near Kirtland, Ohio, in the fall of 1830, John Murdock also anticipated a restoration of primitive Christianity. When missionaries presented him with the Book of Mormon as evidence the restoration had been accomplished, he "did not ask a sign of them by working a miracle. . . . For I did not believe that the spirit would attend their ministration if the Book of Mormon was not true." As for the Book of Mormon's message, it went without saying that he *expected* it to "contain the same plan of salvation as the Bible."[42] Its most vital message, in other words, was in what it pointed to.

Also in Mayfield lived Lyman Wight, who with Isaac Morley and eight other families had emulated an early Christian pattern by entering into a covenant to hold all things in common. So satisfied were they with the effort that "we truly began to feel as if the millennium was close at hand." Once again, the message of the four missionaries was especially appealing in these circumstances. As Wight recorded further, "I shall therefore content myself by saying that they brought the Book of Mormon to bear upon us, and the whole of the common stock family was baptized."[43] In the same vein, Donna Hill writes that future Mormon leader Sidney Rigdon also was converted through the Book of Mormon, finding that it "affirmed his own beliefs in a literal gathering and an imminent millennium."[44]

A few years later, a journalist reporting on missionary efforts in Iowa got the same message. He reported that the traveling elder gave "a brief history of the Book of Mormon," and that he portrayed it as "an event intended to prepare for the great work, the second appearance of Christ, when he shall stand on the Mount of Olives, attended by Abraham and all the Saints, to reign on the Earth for the space of a thousand years."[45]

While millenarianism would prime a generation of converts to welcome the shape and content of this new revelation from heaven, subsequent generations would lose some of their eschatological ardor. So "even though an apocalyptic scenario of the last days is still a central Mormon doctrine, it is no longer enunciated . . . with anything like the emphatic fervor of nineteenth-century leaders."[46] Such a development makes all the more plausible Gordon Wood's assessment of the timely fit between the Book of Mormon's publication and its cultural context: "Its timing in 1830 was providential. It appeared at precisely the right moment in American history; much earlier or later and the Church might not have taken hold."[47]

My Servant Joseph

While the Book of Mormon was consciously invoked to support the claim that Israel's restoration had begun, its miraculous coming forth was evidence of something else as well—that the man who assisted in the effort was an anointed prophet of God. Many prophetic figures throughout history have laid claim to divine authority or inspiration. Visions and visitations were nothing new, even to a post-Enlightenment world. By 1760, for example, the Swedish mystic and scientist Emanuel Swedenborg was widely known to have experienced multiple visions; not only was he visited by entities from the realm of spirits, he was soon comfortable making repeated visits there himself, virtually at will. In the United States and a few years later lived Jemima Wilkinson. While suffering a fever probably from typhus, she experienced the first of several visions: "The heavens were open'd," she later recorded, "And She saw two Archangels descending from the east, with golden crowns upon their heads, clothed in long white Robes, down to the feet; Bringing a sealed Pardon from the living God."[48]

Additional examples, as Donna Hill points out, include Lorenzo Dow, who had a dream vision of God and Jesus in 1791; Charles Finney and Elias Smith had visions of Christ preceding their ministries; John Samuel Taylor, a Palmyra neighbor of the Smiths, heard Christ call him to a public ministry in a dream; and in the same year Moroni appeared to Joseph Smith, Asa Wild received one of several revelations confirming Joseph's information that all Christianity had gone astray.[49] Richard Bushman has found over 32 pamphlets relating personal visions in the period 1783 to 1815—and those are just the published ones.[50]

The forces that determine the fate and posthumous reputation of mystics and prophets[51] like Joan of Arc, Menocchio, the sixteenth-century miller,[52] and Joseph Smith are a complex mix of institutional power, political interests, and cultural factors. Sometimes, in the post-Enlightenment especially, the court of public opinion achieves eventual consensus about the merits of religious founders and their teachings, virtually unaided by the arbiters of orthodoxy. Such was the case, for example, with Jemima Wilkinson, a native of upstate New York like so many American prophets of the nineteenth century. Her typhus-induced vision was followed by other heavenly manifestations, which became the substance of her Sunday sermons throughout the area. Soon she was renowned as a prophetess, interpreter of dreams, and possibly the very Christ himself returned in female form. She garnered enthusiastic support initially, and a society of followers built a community that lasted for decades. Eventually, however, her influence waned as quietly and unspectacularly as her unorthodox career had begun years before. As her most sympathetic biographer opined, her fading from religious history was the result of a failure "to develop any real organization or doctrine that would be distinctive enough to retain the loyalty of her followers when her physical energies and the force of her personality began to decline."[53]

In the case of the American prophet Joseph Smith, a violent death only set in motion an era of church consolidation and expansion that continues unabated to the present. While his betrayal by state officials and murder at the hands of a painted mob lent him a martyr's aura, his reputation before and after his death crystallized around the Book of Mormon, a particularly durable expression of religious doctrine. Fawn Brodie's psychobiography of Joseph Smith opens with the remark that Smith was rash enough "to found a new religion in the age of printing."[54] Certainly a hostile popular press would aggravate the Saints' difficulties; a particularly vehement attack in the *Nauvoo Expositor*, followed by the Saints' imprudent destruction of the press, would be the immediate precipitating factors in the Carthage tragedy.[55] At the same time, of course, the legacy that Smith left in print ensured that neither he nor his band of followers would suffer the oblivion of a Jemima Wilkinson. As his canonized eulogy explains, "in the short space of twenty years, he has brought forth and translated the Book of Mormon, which he translated by the gift and power of God, and has been the means of publishing it on two continents; . . . [and] has brought forth the revelations and commandments which compose this book of Doctrine and Covenants, and many other wise documents and instructions for the benefit of the children of men" (D&C 135:3).

Other figures in the visionary tradition left behind published visions and revelations, but often to far different reception than Joseph Smith's. Jacob Boehme (1675–1724), a shoemaker from Bremen, produced extensive accounts of his otherworldy experience. Stephen Hobhouse calls him "the greatest mystic produced by any of the Churches of the Reformation"; both William Law and Nicolas Berdyaev regarded Boehme as "one of the greatest mystics of all time." W. R. Inge compares his works to "a mine, in which precious metal is embedded."[56] Emanuel Swedenborg (1688–1772) was in some ways the most visible and highly respected visionary of the Enlightenment period, and his voluminous writings have appeared extensively in anthologies. He was lauded by Immanuel Kant, quoted by Ralph Waldo Emerson, and approvingly cited and imitated by the young William Blake. Boehme, Swedenborg, and other visionaries could have their detractors as well, but a stark difference from Joseph Smith remains. With both Boehme and Swedenborg, their writings did not serve to impose on the authors only the extreme labeling options of prophet or fraud with quite the same forcefulness as the Book of Mormon did to Joseph Smith. In fact, what many appreciative treatments of the earlier figures reveal is the ease with which visionary writings may be cut adrift from their authors, as it were, and made presentable for public consumption by editorial intrusion. By contrast, the Book of Mormon reveals itself to be inseparably connected to the Mormon prophet. Its origin and mode of translation make his revelatory production—like his prophetic status itself—resistant to selective or qualified acceptance.

In the case of Boehme, it is surprising to observe the ease with which an editor like Hobhouse, so manifestly in awe of his subject yet without any compunction whatsoever, blithely assumes the burden of protecting Boehme from himself:

> I have left out . . . subjects dealt with by Boehme . . . which are to us today [1949] so incredible and fantastic as to be out of place in serious reading; e.g., imaginary details of the life of the angels and of Adam in paradise, Adam's sexual nature, and the geography of Heaven and of Hell. These must, in my judgment, be described as "false" mythology without that symbolic value or relevance to reality possessed by all true "myths" (like those of Plato and Genesis).

A little later, Hobhouse expresses the hope that his readers "will find a substantial residue of truth in the theology and psychology of this book, while enjoying the imaginative poetry and charm of such parts as they can only regard as pleasant mythology, quite divorced from reality."[57] So while Boehme may be awarded the laurels of a great mystic, it does not follow that his revelations are revered in their totality as divine pronouncement. In fact, the very possibility of such selective appreciation is part and parcel of what enables his—or any mystic's—elevation to the spiritual pantheon.

Two factors in the editor's treatment of Boehme play apparent roles in the process by which Boehme's writings are validated as legitimate mystical experience, i.e., epiphanies of a sort that are reconcilable—or at least nonthreatening—to orthodoxy. Though most starkly evident in Boehme's case, we will see these factors at work elsewhere as well. We will also see that they are utterly lacking in the case of Joseph Smith. The first is the susceptibility of the discourse itself to creative refashioning, or editorial intervention; in this case, some portions of Boehme's writings submit to the category of "true mythology" with "symbolic value." What doesn't, is simply "left out" by the author, unproblematically. The writing must be of a kind that one feels free to read, assess, selectively appreciate, or censure, according to its perceived plausibility or inherent merits.

Second, the language employed must reaffirm its own limitedness, its own inability to accurately reveal the divine mystery it approaches but can never capture. Note that the editor dismisses Boehme to the extent that his works cannot be related to reality "symbolically," or "mythically." That they should be read as simple *reflection* of reality is apparently deemed too absurd to consider. If we can decipher some kind of hidden meaning from a revelation about the "geography of heaven and hell," for example, then we stand to benefit accordingly. But if we are being offered a map of the celestial world's physical terrain, then it all seems to be just so much silliness.

From the Middle Ages to the present, theologians have proposed numerous theories, exegetical and linguistic, to produce models of meaning more appropriate to religious discourse than such simple one-to-one correspondence. St. Augustine, for example, pities those who interpret Genesis 1:1 ("In the beginning God made Heaven and Earth") as referring simply to His fashioning of the visible universe. That, Augustine reasons, is to limit God's work to the "intelligible and corporeal creation." By the time he finishes his reading of the Bible's opening words, the first verse contains the mystery of the Trinity, describes the heavenly Jerusalem, and foreshadows the formation and growth of the Church.[58]

The insistence of Augustine and his successors that we go beyond the "surface" of scriptural texts to their "stupendous depth, [wherein] we shudder to peer deep"[59] is tied, then to a belief that God and his operations cannot adequately be captured in normal language. The very distinction between the sacred and the mundane, the spiritual and the physical, or what Augustine calls "heaven and earth," that "visible and invisible nature"[60] would collapse if language could simply and straightforwardly refer to either realm on the same terms. That is what Samuel Taylor Coleridge means when he explains what is at stake in this kind of dualism: "The very ground of all Miracle," he proclaimed, is "the heterogeneity of Spirit and Matter."[61] The ineffable, in other words, must remain forever demarcated from the material. To collapse the two into one would signal the collapse of the sacred itself.

This dualism is reaffirmed and sustained in Western religious culture by means of all-pervasive linguistic practices. There must always remain that realm in the face of which language admits its insufficiency, its limitations. Because to articulate in human terms, to subject to concrete utterance is to assimilate to a human universe. By the same token, any insufficiency we find in language would serve as guarantor of the transcendent, just as surely as the transcendent affirms the insufficiency of language. Language *must* come up against its own limitations, or how can the ineffable find place in the universe? In other words, to contain the power of language to refer, to name, is to assure the survival of a realm beyond the human one. Or the illusion of one, in any case. As William James so astutely observed, for some religious persons "*richness* is the supreme imaginative requirement. When one's mind is of this type," he continues, one's inner needs include "at every stage objects for adjectives of mystery and splendor, derived in the last resort from the Godhead."[62] The impression or sensation of something beyond language, in other words, suggests something sublime and worthy of worship.

The whole history of mysticism is, by and large, a prolonged exercise in exploring this incommensurability of human speech and human encounter with the divine. Scholar of mysticism Evelyn Underhill refers to the mystical communion as experience of "a nescience, a Divine Dark." "To see Him is to enter the Darkness."[63] In fact, as she points out, "It has become a commonplace with writers on mysticism to say, that all contemplatives took from Dionysius this idea of 'Divine Darkness.' . . . If, therefore, they persist—and they do persist—in using this simile of 'darkness' to describe their experience of contemplation, it can only be because it fits the facts. . . . What, then, do those who use this image of the 'dark' really mean by it? They mean this: that God in his absolute Reality is unknowable—is dark—to man's intellect."[64] As we will see, a prophet like Joseph Smith whose language does not reinforce this feeling of linguistic despair in the face of the nameless is censured accordingly.

Like Boehme's, Swedenborg's writings appear at first to be susceptible to the same kind of selective appreciation that made him a notable mystic if not theologian. But his endorsement by the respectable establishment, like Boehme's, depends entirely on the degree to which his writing yields to the sifting of "enlightened" editors. As Emerson explains in putting the mystic through his own idea-mill: "The world has a sure chemistry, by which it extracts what is excellent in its children and lets fall the infirmities and limitations of the grandest mind."[65]

When Swedenborg's writing yields to the kind of figurative or allegorical reading that Augustine employed on Genesis, he fares well. Whatever is found to have the kind of "mythology" or "symbolic value" that Boehme's editor sought may remain. What doesn't is summarily rejected, as happens with Swedenborg's treatment of celestial marriage: "Perhaps the true subject of the 'Conjugal Love,'" writes Emerson, "is Conversation, whose laws are profoundly set forth. It is false, if literally applied to marriage. . . . Heaven is not the pairing of two, but the communion of all souls."[66] In other words, we can accept Swedenborg's visionary writings on marriage as long as we can read them as mere metaphor.

In the final analysis, Swedenborg's contemporary fame and prodigious output, his endorsement by the philosopher Kant, his extensive body of published writings, all suggest an impact out of all proportion to what turned out to be a relatively insubstantial role in the history of religious thought.[67] The reason is not hard to fathom. One historian of mysticism writes that "his books are . . . so much in the nature of realistic reports, replete with physical detail, so lacking alike in divine imagination and mystic illumination, that the seers in the line from Plotinus and Boehme, though grateful to the Swedish visionary for, so to speak, shaking up Christianity, parted from him upon mature test of his 'system.'"[68] Or as a recent writer summarizes, the heaven exemplified by Swedenborg's visions is considered by moderns "as absurd, crude, materialistic, or sheer nonsense."[69]

Too much detail, and not enough poetry. Or, as Emerson sums up his appraisal of Swedenborg: "In his profuse and *accurate* imagery is no pleasure, for there is no beauty."[70] Too many particulars, and not enough parables, it would seem. For Swedenborg's mysticism was of the unabashedly material variety: the realms he visited and the personages he encountered were to him as real and tangible as anything on the streets of Stockholm. As he stated matter-of-factly, "[I]t has been granted me to associate with angels and to talk with them as one man with another; and also to see what exists in the heavens and in the hells, and this for thirteen years; and to describe them from the evidence of my own eyes and ears in the hope that ignorance may be enlightened, and unbelief dispelled. Such direct revelation is now made."[71] In fact, to the detriment of his status as a mystic, Swedenborg absolutely disallowed the allegorizing of these revelations, the reading of his descriptions as earthly shadows of heavenly realities.[72] On the contrary, as one critic writes, Swedenborg had "a profound respect for physical reality. Therefore, his awakening perceptions of spiritual reality did not bring him to a radical subordination of matter, nor even a dualistic construct, but rather produced a vastly enlarged whole of reality. This holistic approach to traditional spirit/matter and mind/body dichotomies is one of Swedenborg's major contributions . . . [and leads to] a comprehensive view of reality as a whole."[73] So we are left in the case of Swedenborg with an unapologetic description of spiritual realities that uncomfortably impinge on the concrete and the familiar.

Swedenborg's rejection of the Trinity, in this light, is at the same time an attack on the pretentiousness of theological language, its insistent gestures toward otherworldliness intimated by linguistic self-contradiction, the whole august tradition of the *via negativa*, and the hand-wringing despair of verbal inadequacy:

> [The angels] said also that members of the church who come from the world entertaining an idea of three Divine Persons cannot be admitted into heaven, because their thought wanders from one Person to another; and that it is not allowable there to think of three and speak of one, because in heaven every one speaks from his thought; speech being there from thought itself or thought speaking. . . . For in heaven there is a general communication of thought, so that if any one should enter there thinking of three and speaking of one, he would be instantly discovered and rejected.[74]

In such mocking terms does Swedenborg dispense with religious language that refuses to sully itself with concrete particularity and clarity. Thus we have Emerson's famous criticism, in which he condemns the mystic for a style of writing that—unlike the Christian creeds on the one hand and poetry on the other—does not allow the reader the freedom of his own wide-ranging interpretations or a comfortable kind of linguistic vagueness:

> For the anomalous pretension of Revelations of the other world,—only his probity and genius can entitle it to any serious regard. His revelations destroy their credit by running into detail. . . . I reply that the Spirit which is holy is reserved, taciturn, and deals in laws. . . . The teachings of the high Spirit are abstemious, and, in regard to particulars, negative. . . . Strictly speaking, Swedenborg's revelation is a confounding of planes,—a capital offense in so learned a categorist. This is to carry the law of surface into the plane of substance, to carry individualism and its fopperies into the realm of essences and generals,—which is dislocation and chaos.[75]

Or as a more modern theological formulation has it, "one must especially beware of arbitrary imaginative representations: excess of this kind is a major cause of the difficulties that Christian faith often encounters."[76] In concluding his study of *The Varieties of Religious Experience,* William James assesses a similar disposition on the part of scientific moderns to purify the religious imagination of anthropomorphic images: "The less we mix the private with the cosmic, the more we dwell in universal and impersonal terms, the truer heirs of science we become." The problem, James finds, is that "so long as we deal with the cosmic and the general, we deal only with the symbols of reality, but *as soon as we deal with private and personal phenomena as such, we deal with realities in the completest sense of the term*" (emphasis his).[77]

But to deal with realities "in the completest sense," to threaten full disclosure of the universe, or reduce the universal to the particular, is to compromise the status and value of the transcendent, the ineffable. This is precisely what orthodoxy resists in a mystic like Swedenborg (or Joseph Smith). As Emerson stubbornly insists, rather too anxiously: "The secret of heaven is kept from age to age. No imprudent, no sociable angel ever dropt an early syllable to answer the longings of saints, the fears of mortals."[78] Only slightly earlier than Emerson, Edmund Burke had given a revealing, romantic twist to this same brand of theological obscurantism: "It is our ignorance of things that causes all our admiration and chiefly excites our passions. . . . A clear idea," he goes so far as to say, "is another name for a little idea."[79]

The preservation of the miraculous, then, whether it takes the form of a creedal Christian God (or Rudolf Otto's "mysterium tremendum" or "wholly other") or of Edmund Burke's sublime, is inseparable from a wounded language, one that retreats from an unhampered power to name. Conventional notions of the sacred, in other words, require a sacred language that reveals the impossibility of describing the very things to which that language refers. And to the extent that mystics resist such a linguistic paradigm, they are especially likely to be censured by the orthodox.

It is clear that Joseph Smith, like Swedenborg, described his visions and revelations with unprecedented detail and specificity. From his sketch of Moroni ("above the common size of men, garment without seam") to his description of the plates ("six inches wide and eight inches long and not quite so thick as common tin"), Joseph's language was anything but a reveling in metaphor and obscurity. [80] The question that remains is, why could not the revelations of Joseph Smith, Book of Mormon included, be read as creatively, metaphorically, or selectively as those of other mystics, visionaries, or prophets? (I have focused on Swedenborg and Boehme as two most prominent examples of sanitized visionaries, but a host of lesser lights have been subjected to the same process. The Pentecostal outpourings of the 1742 Cambuslang, Scotland, revival, for instance, were meticulously documented and celebrated as a "vindication of [Presbyterian] worship." At the same time, one historian remarks that "those who edited the Cambuslang manuscripts were especially concerned to . . . reaffirm the rational and scriptural soundness of evangelical spirituality." In this case, that entailed "cut[ting] out almost all mention of ecstatic religious experience, such as visions, voices, and trances." Another scholar notes the excision from those same accounts of language that refers to "the voice of Christ," the Lord "telling directly," or God making covenants "in person."[81])

At least one critic has advocated subjecting the Book of Mormon to the same filter that made Boehme's and Swedenborg's revelations more palatable to the spiritually sophisticated. "The literary study and analysis of the Book of Mormon, when it is seriously undertaken in our time, will of necessity have a decidedly mythic orientation." This is not, he insists, in disregard for the religious value of the scripture. On the contrary, by way of analogy he claims it is only "possible for modern readers to take Blake's religious vision" seriously "through the instrumentality of myth. . . . The actual effect of the development of myth criticism has been to force students to take the writings of prophets, seers, and revelators *more* seriously than they had previously."[82]

Joseph Smith and his revelations, however, simply do not cooperate in such a project. The explanation is largely a matter of the way in which the Book of Mormon in particular came forth, making it highly resistant to interpretive negotiation. Boehme's writings could be selectively appreciated, with those embarrassing references to hell's geography conveniently ignored or turned into metaphor. So too, for Swedenborg's descriptions of celestial sex, or his overly specific descriptions of heavenly architecture. Guardians of poetic decorum like Emerson felt free to censure his mystic excursions when too many details began to taint the divine with the concrete and to threaten a lapse from the sacred into the silly.

Those who want to salvage Joseph Smith's prophetic role, on the other hand, by avoiding what they see as the embarrassing ramifications of his naked prose or the fragility of the book's historical claims are hard-pressed to devise nonliteral readings of his discourse in order to recapture a little mystery and terror.[83] The problem, of course, is that Joseph's prophetic writings were grounded in artifactual reality, not the world of psychic meanderings. It is hard to allegorize—and profoundly presumptuous to edit down—a sacred record that purports to be a transcription of tangible records hand-delivered by an angel.

The Russian critic Mikhail Bakhtin has suggested a framework that may be useful in clarifying some of these distinctions we have suggested, as well as the manner in which the Book of Mormon established a particular kind of prophetic authority. Bakhtin argues that there are two modes of language by which we are influenced: *authoritative discourse* and *internally persuasive discourse.* The latter category is any language that makes its claim upon us on the basis of its logic, rhetorical appeal, compelling argument, or emotional sway. "The authoritative word," on the other hand, "demands that we acknowledge it, that we make it our own; it binds us, *quite independent of any power it might have to persuade us internally; we encounter it with its authority already fused to it*" (emphasis mine).[84] Some language, in other words, is so wedded to an authoritative source that we find it difficult or impossible to assess the content as content. We cannot analyze, negotiate, critique, or selectively assimilate it.

An example of how such language operates in the case of a charismatic figure like Joseph Smith is provided by his longest extant pronouncement on the Book of Mormon—which turns out to be a philological, not doctrinal exposition. In a letter to the editor of *The Times and Seasons*, he puts to rest false accounts of the etymology of "Mormon":

> The error I speak of is the definition of the word "Mormon." It has been stated that this word was derived from the Greek word mormo. This is not the case. There was no Greek or Latin upon the plates from which I, through the grace of the Lord, translated the Book of Mormon. Let the language of the book speak for itself. On the 523rd page of the fourth edition, it reads: "And now, behold we have written this record according to our knowledge in the characters which are called among us the Reformed Egyptian, being handed down and altered by us, according to our manner of speech. . . . But the Lord knoweth the things which we have written, and also that none other people knoweth our language; therefore He hath prepared means for the interpretation thereof."

Here, then, the subject is put to silence; for "none other people knoweth our language;" therefore the Lord, and not man, had to interpret, after the people were all dead. And as Paul said, "The world by wisdom know not God;" so the world by speculation are destitute of revelation; . . . I may safely say that the word "Mormon" stands independent of the wisdom and learning of this generation.

Then, after rehearsing some useful but insufficient etymologies, Joseph asserts with no more authority than "the grace of the Lord" that "we have the word MORMON; which means, literally, more good. Yours, JOSEPH SMITH."[85]

Here a rather arcane—and theologically irrelevant—piece of philological trivia becomes an occasion for Smith to emphasize his prophetic authority. Unlike his treatment of textual themes in the Bible, where he invoked his limited Hebrew skills to engage the theologians on their own ground ("The word create came from the [Hebrew] word *baurau* which does not mean to create out of nothing"[86]), Smith here emphatically refuses to argue as linguist, theologian, or textual critic. He lists several cognates for "good" ("the Saxon, good; the Dane, god; the Latin, bonus; the Greek, kalos; the Hebrew, tob; and the Egyptian, mon"), thereby revealing his linguistic prowess, sure enough. But it is here displayed so that we may see the learning alone of the world *or* of a prophet is insufficient to resolve the mystery before him. "The word 'Mormon' [like the text itself] stands independent of the wisdom and learning of this generation." There can be no satisfactory synthesis of "worldly speculation" about meaning (it is "destitute"), and the divinely derived power to translate ("he hath prepared means for interpretation"). Outweighing learned theories of meaning and derivation, we have the simple and unequivocal declaration—"it means more good"—juxtaposed with the legitimizing signature of a prophet.

As Bakhtin explains, "Authoritative discourse may organize around itself great masses of other types of discourse . . . , but the authoritative discourse itself does not merge with these (by means of, say, gradual transitions); it remains sharply demarcated, compact, and inert."[87] In this case, Smith opposes in stark contrast what he calls "the speculation" of the world to "the spirit of revelation" that he embodies. His words are thus validated by the authority to which they are fused—not by linguistic analysis, scholarly opinion, rhetorical charm, or anything else. The resistance of Joseph's prophetic language to general criteria of persuasiveness is again echoed by Bakhtin's analysis: an authoritative text, he writes, "enters our verbal consciousness as a compact and indivisible mass; one must either totally affirm it, or totally reject it. It is indissolubly fused with its authority—with political power, an institution, a person—and it stands and falls together with that authority."[88]

This description is the key to understanding the Book of Mormon's primary role in the new dispensation, as a sign of Joseph Smith's divine calling. The book's role in heralding divine activity and reinforcing millenarian expectations was certainly profound, but it was not durable (millenarianism is no longer as pronounced in Mormonism). The wedding of sacred record to prophetic authority was even more profound, and it has been a connection that lasts to the present day. LDS writer (and later apostle) Bruce R. McConkie gave canonical utterance to the logic of LDS testimony that continues to be a feature of member and missionary expression alike: "The Book of Mormon . . . stands as a witness to all the world that Joseph Smith was the Lord's anointed through whom the foundation was laid for the great latter-day work of restoration."[89]

As a result, and unlike the mystical outpourings of a Boehme or a Swedenborg, the Book of Mormon was seldom presented—or received by the appreciative—in terms of its claims, arguments, or doctrines. Its prior incarnation as sacred history inscribed in gold, together with the aura of supernatural origins that always framed its mention, far overshadowed and even displaced whatever internal persuasiveness it might have had. And just as Joseph's prophetic authority was guarantor of the text's sacred status, so the very presence of this voice speaking "out of the dust," predicted by scripture and verified by the voice of angels and human witnesses alike, was guarantor that Joseph was indeed a prophet of God.

The particular model of seership that Smith exemplified and the authoritative nature of the text he produced were powerfully shaped by the nature of the translation process itself. In translating the gold plates, Joseph reinvented a prophetic role modeled more closely on Moses than on Paul. Where the tablets of Moses were written upon by the finger of God, the epistles of Paul captured all the frailties of one who knew when he "spoke as a man." In the absence of sacred relics marking the unbroken connection between the Creator and his creature, it was only a matter of time before Paul's explicit authorship, rather than God's, made possible the kind of interpretive negotiation typified by Crawford Howell Toy, a nineteenth-century American minister. Charged with heresy for a position that has since become mainstream, he argued that the writers of scripture operate "under purely free, human conditions. The inspired man speaks his own language, not another man's, and writes under the conditions of his own age, not under those of some other age."[90]

The advantage of such a model of inspiration, whether in the Bible or applied to a mystic like Boehme, as we have seen, is that it renders sacred discourse more elastic. Editorial and exegetical intrusion alike can be seen in those models as correctives in a human process, not profane meddling with a tottering ark. By not just emulating but actually invoking Old Testament modes of seership, Joseph Smith firmly precluded any such tampering at the same time that he foreshadowed a radically new paradigm for revelation and inspiration generally, one which would be fully fleshed out in the text he produced. True enough, the Lord indicated to Joseph that his commandments "were given unto my servants in their weakness, after the manner of their language" (D&C 1:24). But as prophet, Joseph's revelatory stance and range of expression are anything but "purely free."

The Urim and Thummim, the (principal) means by which Smith translated the gold plates, played at least three important roles in the shaping of the Book of Mormon's status as the kind of "authoritative discourse" that could not be sundered from the prophet who produced it or selectively appreciated with the editorial abandon of a Stephen Hobhouse.[91] First, the sacred instruments obviously established the Book of Mormon's claim to a scriptural status not just equivalent to the Bible but reminiscent of the sacred tablets themselves. As the very sign of prophetic authority, the Urim and Thummim Joseph claimed to possess connected him both to Moses and Aaron, as prophet and high priest, respectively. While Bible commentators continue to debate the exact nature of the Urim and Thummim, they share a consensus that "they were associated with the priestly office and were used when people came to seek divine consultation."[92]

Second, though they will disappear as certainly as did the ark and its contents, these interpreters by their palpability, divine provenance, and miraculous powers intrude themselves so conspicuously into the whole process as to violently polarize the Book of Mormon's reception around the issue of authenticity rather than theological merit. Like the spittle and clay with which Jesus healed the blind man, the sacred oracles serve as a physical conduit for the working of divine power, signaling that supernatural, rather than natural, processes are at work. With Joseph Smith serving as translator rather than author, a comfortable middle ground—that the record is a human product perhaps meriting some divine approbation—is well-nigh impossible. Bypassing fifteen hundred years of textual history, canonicity issues, disputations about manuscript provenance, and the role of human copyists, relatively few mediating factors are left to mitigate the record's uncompromising status as the "Word of God."

Third, the Urim and Thummim, because of their oracular function in revealing God's will anciently, are associated in Smith's case with a translation that is virtually unimpeachable. As signs of priestly authority, the interpreters make Joseph a holy medium rather than human source of the record. Any text's status as mere "inspirational literature" is precluded by these dramatic signs of the divine's role in both the origin *and* the translation of the text. The particular powers the prophet imputed to the sacred stones thus serve powerfully to redefine the limits and workings of inspiration. Smith himself said very little about the mechanisms of the translation process, but secondhand accounts provide us with a fairly clear picture. Though they differ in specifics, most scholars agree that Joseph did not work on the basis of impressions or speculation that he hoped was inspired. The Urim and Thummim, in other words, produced a translation precisely in accord with the original plates—no approximation or near-hits.

Steven Harper has written that "those who became Mormons were almost always first contemplative Bible believers who were skeptical of false prophets."[93] ("If you start a church with a prophet in it, every body will [be] against you, as they were against Ann Lee, Joanna Southcoate, and old Jemima Wilkinson," complained Mormon editor W. W. Phelps.[94]) In any assessment of Joseph's prophetic stature, the first and greatest evidence in his favor was the Book of Mormon he so miraculously obtained and translated. His role and authority as prophet and seer rested firmly on the validity of those claims. Joseph's own persistent emphasis on the record's origins over its content reinforced the book's role as sign and symbol rather than embodiment of new theology. Typical of this distinction was an 1838 newspaper article by the prophet, in which he published answers to a series of questions that he said were "daily and hourly asked by all classes of people." Of his list of a dozen or so popular queries, the only question pertaining to the new scripture was, "How and where did you obtain the Book of Mormon?" It seems rather remarkable that public interest in its message or doctrine was apparently not sufficient to make the list. (On the other hand, Mormon leaders and missionaries were fully complicit in shaping interest around the transmission rather than content of the record.) On the occasion in question, Joseph's by now familiar answer rehearsed the most important details: that it came from Moroni and was translated by divine gift.[95] The story of Joseph's first vision may have taken years to make the transition from personal conversion narrative to publicly proclaimed portent of the new gospel dispensation. But from the very first, Moroni's visit to the boy prophet was exhibit A in the case for Mormonism.

With regard to the prima facie implausibility of the book's origins, Klaus Hansen has written that "once having accepted its message, believers found it easy to accept the manner of its origin."[96] But in a very essential way, that formulation misses the point: the "message" of the Book of Mormon *was* its manner of origin. In the telling phrase so often found among early proselytizers, one elder, Wandle Mace, recorded in his journal that "we discoursed upon the first principles of the gospel and of the coming forth of the Book of Mormon. This was a favorite subject with me."[97] William McLellin, as we saw, placed little emphasis on the doctrinal content of the Book of Mormon, making prophecies of its coming forth, evidences of its truthfulness, and testimony of its worth "by far the most frequent topic in his sermons."[98] So central was it to his message that he complained of his companion John F. Boynton that in an otherwise "fine discourse," he "never mentioned the book of mormon once." Yet when McLellin himself mentioned it, the following treatment was typical: "I then arose and read the testimony of the three witnesses and reasoned upon the power and force of it."[99] The reality of the plates and their angelic courier, in other words, not the cogency of Nephi's writing, was the point.

Joseph apparently also believed the message *was* the manner of its coming forth or he would have spent *some* time writing or preaching about the Book of Mormon's content, instead of repeatedly talking about how he produced it. In an 1834 conference of elders, for example, he "gave a relation of obtaining and translating the Book of Mormon"— but if he said anything of its content, we have no record.[100] During the seven years of the church's Nauvoo period, when Joseph was preaching in public on a regular basis, the hundreds of recorded pages of his sermons contain only a handful of brief allusions to the Book of Mormon— and none of them involve sustained discussion of doctrine or any other content.[101] Of his trip to Washington during that period, a reporter captured what seemed to be a typical pattern: "He took good care . . . to say but little about the 'Book of Mormon.' He averred, however that nobody wrote it but him."[102] In 1831, Daniel Tyler heard Samuel Smith and Orson Hyde preach. He, too, was struck by the unexpected way in which the Book of Mormon featured in Mormon proselytizing: "Elder Smith read the 29th chapter of Isaiah at the first meeting and delineated the circumstances of the coming forth of the Book of Mormon, of which he said he was a witness. He knew his brother Joseph had the plates, for the prophet had shown them to him, and he had handled them and seen the engravings thereon. His speech was more a narrative than a sermon."[103] Reviewing almost 2000 articles and publications on the Book of Mormon going back to 1830, two researchers affirm this "tendency on the part of many speakers and writers merely to mention the Book of Mormon without entering into . . . meaningful discussion."[104]

Critics were just as intent as the Saints on focusing on the book's existence and circumstances rather than its teachings. Ann Taves has written of the richly suggestive fact that when Robert Burton, in his seventeenth-century *Anatomy of Melancholy*, defined religious enthusiasm as "madness or pathological religious despair," he thereby "recast the problem of religious dissent in terms of mental illness rather than heresy. By associating that which was problematic—indeed that which had produced regicide and republic—with false inspiration rather than false doctrine, enthusiasm could be explained in scientific rather than theological terms. Recast as delusion or madness, political and religious radicalism was more easily contained."[105]

In similar fashion, by emphasizing the medium rather than the content of Mormonism's new revelation, missionaries achieved a focus that detractors were quite happy to emphasize as well. When Charles Thompson undertook the first book-length defense of the Book of Mormon in 1841, he listed what he considered to be all "the objections commonly urged against it." Of the six he addressed, none pertained to what the Book *said*. It was criticized because (1) it was an "imposition" to claim to be a revelation from God; (2) God would "never give any more revelations to man after the [Bible]"; (3) "the Bible is full and complete"; (4) "God has imperatively forbidden any addition"; (5) the Book of Mormon is seen as an attempt "to do away" with the New Testament"; and finally, (6) it was actually written by Solomon Spaulding and Sidney Rigdon.[106]

The response of a Baptist *Religious Herald* editorialist when asked for information on the Mormons was therefore not so illogical as it may appear. He wrote to a reader in 1840, "We have never seen a copy of the book of Mormon, nor any abstract of their creed upon which we could fully rely, as a fair exposition of their opinions." Nevertheless, he confidently adjudges without any sense of irony, "The book of Mormon is a bungling and stupid production. . . . It contains some trite, moral maxims, but the phraseology . . . frequently violates every principle and rule of grammar. We have no hesitation in saying the whole system is erroneous."[107] As historian-sociologist Thomas O'Dea humorously—but accurately—summarizes: "The Book of Mormon has not been universally considered by its critics as one of those books that must be read in order to have an opinion of it."[108] Certainly there may be an element of blind prejudice in this. But it is important to realize that, even for the book's adherents, it has not always been deemed imperative to read it before having an opinion of it. Its strength as a pillar in Joseph's claim to be a prophet, just like its status as a blasphemous imposition, depends upon one's acceptance to or rejection of the story of its miraculous coming forth, more than on an analysis of its theological coherence.

All of this is not to suggest that the Book of Mormon is lacking in internally persuasive power, or that it doesn't articulate important theological claims, or that readers were not and are not attuned to the beauty or elegance or logic or appeal of the message—or to the lack of any of these. When the past LDS president Ezra Taft Benson, for instance, proclaims that the purpose of the Book of Mormon is to bring men to Christ,[109] he is doubtless sincere. One might indeed argue that the purpose of the Book of Mormon, like the Bible, is to "reveal . . . Jesus Christ." Still, there can be little doubt that the vast Mormon missionary effort and the pivotal role of the Book of Mormon itself would hardly be deemed successful if public response to the Book of Mormon were a blithe acceptance of the scripture's testimony of Christ but indifference to the prophetic claims of its translator.

What *distinguishes* the Book of Mormon as a religious document, in other words, has little to do with its internal claims. In this regard, the Book of Mormon well exemplifies the principle laid down by Wilfred Cantwell Smith and William A. Graham, and endorsed by Shlomo Biderman: "the element of content is not the major factor in establishing scripture. . . . Because of the enormous diversity of what is said in scripture, it cannot be defined or characterized by its content."[110] Joseph succeeded, in a way no other modern religious figure ever had (or ever tried), in welding the book to the demands of authoritative discourse so powerfully that the internally persuasive power of the message was rendered *relatively* moot. This contention is substantiated through a variety of personal conversion accounts, in Joseph's presentation of the Book of Mormon story (in which angels and interpreters function more prominently than synopsis or themes), in the rhetoric of critics ("We have never seen a copy of the Book of Mormon, nevertheless . . . ") and in the history of Mormonism's own rhetoric about the Book of Mormon.

This signlike function of the scripture is even affirmed to Joseph Smith by revelation. The "means" and "inspiration" of its translation as well as the "ministering angels" that attend its appearance in the world, the Lord declares, "prov[e] to the world that . . . God does inspire men and call them to his holy work in this age and generation, as well as in generations of old" (D&C 20:11).

Even those disaffected members who came to repudiate the prophet could not escape the logic of his connection to the Book of Mormon— which they generally refused to renounce. The three witnesses, all of whom broke with him sooner or later, were unwavering in their belief that the record he produced was unimpeachable proof that, at the time of its translating, he held the keys of the kingdom as God's holy prophet.[111] William McLellin, one of the twelve original Latter-day Saint apostles, similarly grew disillusioned with Joseph Smith's leadership and was cut off from the church not once but twice, the second time permanently. In 1880, one James T. Cobb, hoping to discredit the Book of Mormon, wrote letters to those he thought might provide telling testimony. He had good reason to believe McLellin would lend his support to his project, and must have been surprised by the response: "I have set to my seal that the Book of Mormon is a true, divine record and it will require more evidence than I have ever seen to ever shake me relative to its purity. I have read many 'Exposes.' I have seen all their arguments. But my evidences are above them all!" Lest Cobb misunderstand, McLellin made clear his words brooked no recent change of heart. "I have no faith in Mormonism," he wrote, "no confidence that the church organized by J. Smith and O. Cowdery was set up or established as it ought to have been. . . . But when a man goes at the Book of M[ormon] he touches the apple of my eye."[112]

Even the publishers of the *Nauvoo Expositor*, whose fierce denunciations of Joseph Smith's "abominations and whoredoms" precipitated the press's destruction and the prophet's murder, had this to say in the "Preamble" of the paper's first and only issue:

> We all verily believe, and many of us know of a surety, that the religion of the Latter Day Saints, as originally taught by Joseph Smith, which is contained in the Old and New Testaments, Book of Covenants, and Book of Mormon, is verily true; and that the pure principles set forth in those books are the immutable and eternal principles of Heaven, and speaks a language which, when spoken in truth and virtue, sinks deep into the heart of every honest man.—Its precepts are invigorating, and in every sense of the word, tend to dignify and ennoble man's conceptions of God and his attributes. It speaks a language which is heard amidst the roar of artillery, as well as in the silence of midnight.[113]

If Joseph Smith turned traitor to God, it took nothing from the privileged status he once held as mouthpiece of a sacred revelation from the dust. Fallen prophets, like fallen angels, could not be denied their prior glory, even by the faithless.

FOUR

"I, Nephi, Wrote This Record": The Book of Mormon as Ancient History, Part 1—The Search for a Mesoamerican Troy

One hundred years ago in Mesopotamia it was discovered that history lies behind the Old Testament.

—A. Parrot

The Book of Mormon account actually did take place *some*where.

—John Sorenson

I n 1990, two miles short of the Temple Mount in Jerusalem, workers building a water park broke through the ceiling of a hidden burial chamber. Archaeologists called to the scene discovered a dozen limestone ossuaries in the cavern, which dated to the first Christian century; one of the sarcophagi held the remains of a 60-year-old man and exhibited an amazing inscription on the lid: "Yehosef bar Qayafa"——"Joseph, son of Caiaphas."[1] Apparently, they had stumbled across the physical remains of the Jewish high priest who interrogated that Jesus we read of in the Gospels. It would be hard to imagine a more dramatic and unanticipated encounter between the mythic and the historic, between the timeless truths of faith and the gritty rubble of science.

An event such as this and the larger, increasing success and sophistication of archaeological investigations of biblical history call into question the provocative assessment proffered by the great religious scholar, Wilfred Cantwell Smith:

With the relatively recent rise in Western consciousness, culminating in the nineteenth and early twentieth centuries, of the new sense of history, and the (consequent?) careful and rigorous distinction between history and myth, something major happened. . . . When a sharp discrimination between these two was pressed in Western intellectual life, what happened by and large was that the West opted for history and rejected myth. . . . Might one almost make symbolic of this development, the moment (eighteenth century) when Bishop Ussher's date of 4004 B.C. was bestowed on the first chapter of Genesis? Later, the Church agonized over the fact that that date for creation was wrong. We may recognize now that the problem was not that particular date, but any date at all, the giving of a date; the notion that one is dealing here with historical time, rather than mythical time.[2]

Wilfred Cantwell Smith laments time-lining the days of creation as a misapplication of historical models to mythic constructs.[3] Such romantic nostalgia for pre-modern, mythic ways of apprehending the world may itself be an error worthy of Rousseau and a naïve dichotomy. In any case, the rise of archaeology and kindred sciences has made it increasingly impossible to preserve mythic realms and mythic texts free from the "contaminations" of historicizing.

So we have it that in contemporary Christianity, then, a canonical text with sacred status, a compendium of religiously significant myths, is increasingly appreciated as historically relevant, maybe historically valid, and even historically useful. (As one archaeologist says, to give but one particular example, "we didn't even know there were Philistines until we read about them in the Old Testament."[4]) In the case of the Book of Mormon, the process, initially at least, tended rather toward the reverse.

Returning to Joseph Smith's letter to Chicago editor John Wentworth, for example, we find the prophet representing the Book of Mormon as a historical record almost to the exclusion of other considerations and in a way that parallels his own introduction to the work. In this version of Moroni's first visitation, Smith writes that the angel—himself a historic, ancient American personage—began by rehearsing to him the entire history of the American continent: "I was also informed concerning the aboriginal inhabitants of this country, and shown who they were, and from whence they came; a brief sketch of their origin, progress, civilization, laws, governments, of their righteousness and iniquity, and the blessings of God being finally withdrawn from them as a people was made known unto me."[5] The plates are only mentioned *after* this narrative; they thus appear initially in the capacity of fleshing out or corroborating the ancient history recited by the angel. And indeed, after describing the plates and their translation, Smith returns to their content, paraphrasing Moroni's words to him:

In this important and interesting book the history of ancient America is unfolded, from its first settlement by a colony that came from the Tower of Babel, at the confusion of languages to the beginning of the fifth century of the Christian Era. We are informed by these records that America in ancient times has been inhabited by two distinct races of people. The first were called Jaredites and came directly from the tower of Babel. The second race came directly from the city of Jerusalem, about six hundred years before Christ.[6]

After giving a brief description of their religious organization, wars, and eventual destruction, he concludes: "For a more particular account I would refer to the Book of Mormon, which can be purchased at Nauvoo, or from any of our traveling elders."

Nowhere, in this context at least, does Joseph intimate that the record has any inherent religious or theological value. The plates are not remarkable for new truths, teachings, or gospel insights. Both he and the angel have described them as, essentially, ancient history. Joseph's fascination with this historical dimension to the ancient records clearly was traceable to his earliest contacts with the angel Moroni and appeared at times to overshadow other roles the plates would play. During his probationary period, as we have seen, he seemed more excited about the historic than the heavenly vistas opened to him by Moroni. As Lucy recalled, "In the course of our evening conversations, Joseph gave us some of the most amusing recitals which could be imagined. He would describe the ancient inhabitants of this continent, their dress, their manner of dwelling, the animals which they rode, the cities that they built, and the structure of their buildings with every particular, their mode of warfare, and their religious worship as specifically as though he had spent his life with them."[7]

Years later, Lucy was still regaling listeners with her memories of how "our sons would endeavor to get through their work as early as possible, and say, 'Mother, have supper early, so we can have a long evening to listen to Joseph.' Sometimes Joseph would describe the appearance of the Nephites, their mode of dress and warfare, their implements of husbandry, etc, and many things he had seen in vision."[8]

"Ancient America" in Nineteenth-Century Culture

As Joseph finished his translation of the plates and made preparations for the book's distribution, he needed to decide how the book would be presented to a public that had already heard much by way of rumor and innuendo. At first, he simply let the record speak for itself. Thus, on March 26, 1830, the village newspaper of Palmyra printed an advertisement under the head, *"The Book of Mormon."* It consisted of the reproduced title page from the book, followed by the simple announcement:

"The above work, containing about 600 pages, large Duodecimo, is now for sale, whole-sale and retail, at the Palmyra Bookstore, by HOWARD & GRANDIN."[9] The first formal, public announcement of Joseph Smith's work, then, was made in words taken from the Book of Mormon itself, as follows:

> The *Book of Mormon*: an account written by the hand of Mormon, upon plates, taken from the plates of Nephi. —
> Wherefore it is an abridgment of the record of the people of Nephi, and also of the Lamanites—Written to the Lamanites, who are a remnant of the house of Israel; and also to Jew and Gentile—Written by way of command-ment, and also by the spirit of prophecy and of revelation—Written and sealed up, and hid up unto the Lord, that they might not be destroyed—To come forth by the gift and power of God unto the interpretation thereof—Sealed by the hand of Moroni, and hid up unto the Lord, to come forth in due time by way of the Gentile—The interpretation thereof by the gift of God: an abridgment taken from the Book of Ether.
> Also, which is a record of the people of Jared, which were scattered at the time the Lord confounded the language of the people, when they were building a tower to get to heaven; which is to show unto the remnant of the House of Israel how great things the Lord hath done for their fathers; and that they may know the covenants of the Lord, that they are not cast off forever; and also to the convincing of the Jew and Gentile that Jesus is the Christ, the Eternal God, manifesting himself unto all nations. And now, if there be fault, it be the mistake of men: wherefore condemn not the things of God, that ye may be found spotless at the judgment seat of Christ.
> By Joseph Smith, Junior, Author and Proprietor[10]

Early press accounts of the Book of Mormon were obliging enough to reprint the same title page in their stories. In fact, the first such article had alerted the public to the book's impending publication exactly nine months earlier. On June 26, 1829, the *Wayne Sentinel*, after making mock-ing reference to reports of the "golden bible," had reprinted the title page "as a curiosity."[11]

To the general reader, the striking feature of these media reports could not have been the novelty of the golden bible's religious claims; they were not the issue.[12] True enough, the title page blurb contained refer-ences to "Jew and Gentile," "the spirit of prophecy," "the gift and power of God," and "the judgment seat of Christ," enough such language to substantiate the rumored "religious nature" of the text. But surely they would strike most readers as no more than a light overlay of familiar Christian rhetoric. Much more noteworthy would be its description as "an abridgement of the record of the people of Nephi, and also of the Lamanites," as well as "a record of the people of Jared, which were scat-tered at the time the Lord confounded the language of the people, when they were building a tower." The exotic names of peoples and ancient American figures it introduced: Ether, Nephi, Mormon, Lamanites, Nephites, and Jaredites—these constituted the initial strangeness of the book. A major appeal of the text itself, to both the historically curious and the flippantly cynical, was its claim to tell the public something about the people whose burial mounds lie scattered across the prairies of the Old Northwest, whose bones and artifacts emerged from the dust with provocative regularity. Various theories to account for the people of the mounds and kindred American Indians had been propounded back in Puritan times and earlier. Daniel Gookin, Indian superinten- dent for Massachusetts Bay Colony, mentioned in his encyclopedic work Israelites, Tartars, Scythians, and Moors as possible ancestors, before concluding that "there is nothing of certainty to be concluded. . . . The full determination [of the matter] must be left until the day when all secret and hidden things shall be manifested to the glory of God."[13]

But few were content to defer speculation until all of the facts—or revealed truths—were in. Stuart J. Fiedel describes the widespread hy- pothesis-mongering going on in the early Republic: "Jefferson tentatively concluded that the Indians' ancestors had raised the mounds and bur- ied their dead in them. However, others attributed the mounds to a van- ished civilized race, who had been exterminated by the Indians. The discovery of mounds in the Ohio and Mississippi valleys, which were larger and more complex than those previously known in the east, in- tensified the debate over the mound-builders' identity, and the mounds became the focus of a wildly imaginative literature in the early nine- teenth century."[14]

The Book of Mormon's explicit self-presentation as a solution to the enigma was reinforced by a history—a proximate, *this*-hemispheric his- tory—that threatened to prove as historically sprawling, as impressive, and as meticulously chronicled as the history of the descendants of Judah. This specificity and concreteness could prompt both ridicule and inter- est. Remarked one sarcastic author of an Illinois gazetteer in 1834:

> Those who are particularly desirous of information concerning the mil- lions of warriors, and the bloody battles in which more were slain than ever fell in all the wars of Alexander, Caesar, or Napoleon, with a particu- lar description of their military works, would do well to read the "*Book of Mormon*," made out of the "golden plates" of that distinguished antiquar- ian Joe Smith! It is far superior to some modern productions on western antiquities, because it furnishes us with the names and biography of the principal men who were concerned in these enterprises, with many of the particulars of their wars for several centuries. But seriously. . . . [15]

On the other hand, popular sentiment was certainly ripe for such an approach to marketing the Book of Mormon by 1830. The Reverend Ethan

Smith had published his *View of the Hebrews; or the Tribes of Israel in America* in 1823. A mere two years later, he published a second edition, explaining that "the importance of the question, *Where are the Ten Tribes of Israel?*; the speedy sale of the first edition of the work; and the obtaining considerable additional evidence relative to the origin of the American Indians" made another edition necessary.[16] Ethan Smith's was but one in a long line of tracts and treatises that placed the American Indian into the history of the tribes of Israel. This connection was suggested as early as the sixteenth century by the Dominican friar Diego Duran and saw print by 1607 in Gregorio Garcia's *Origin of the Indians of the New World*. The first English publication on the subject was probably Thomas Thorowgood's *Jews in America, or Probabilities That the Americans are of that Race* (1650), which influenced the Puritan John Eliot. More influential was James Adair's later *History of the American Indians* (London, 1775). Elias Boudinot (*A Star in the West*, 1816) and Josiah Priest (*The Wonders of Nature and Providence*, 1825) argued the same point to large readerships.[17]

Not that other theories for the settling of this hemisphere didn't continue to compete. Nineteenth-century explorer John Lloyd Stephens wasn't exaggerating when, expanding upon the candidates mentioned by Gookin, he asserted that "under the broad range allowed by a descent from the sons of Noah, the Jews, the Canaanites, the Phoenicians, the Carthaginians, the Greeks, the Scythians in ancient times; the Chinese, the Swedes, the Norwegians, the Welsh, and the Spaniards in modern, have had ascribed to them the honour of peopling America."[18] But in general, believers and skeptics were coming to agree that "the idea . . . that the Indians are descendents of the Jews . . . is generally entertained among the learned."[19] So the pitch of Samuel Smith and fellow missionaries ("[do you] wish to purchase a history of the origin of the Indians?") was an appeal to the familiar, not to the novel.

Abner Cole, who perhaps did as much to inflame and shape public reaction to the Book of Mormon as any (hostile) person of his generation, was quick to see the potential for ridicule in any effort to establish a concrete synthesis of ancient Hebrew roots and contemporary American Indian realities. While the Book of Mormon was in press, he had pirated portions and published them in his short lived *Palmyra Reflector*. Pressured at last into desisting in January of 1830, he exacted revenge as soon as the book was available by publishing two satires in June and July. He facetiously blends elements of the Book of Mormon ("Nephites" and biblical diction) with American Indian caricatures, Middle East-gravitas with frontier-absurd. Thus, we get not the Book of Nephi but the Book of Pukei, no resurrected prophets but a "spirit of the money-diggers"—complete with "Egyptian raiment, . . . Indian blanket and moccasins."[20] Cole's parodies thus served to solidify popular perceptions of the work as a pseudohistory, providing as it did fabricated grounds for seeing the work as an obvious mélange of contemporary influences. Such a challenge to the book's plausibility was unavoidable, given the church's early and emphatic casting of the book in terms of its historical value. Writing to a newspaper editor in 1833, Joseph asserted, quite simply, that "The Book of Mormon is a record of the forefathers of our western tribes of Indian. . . . By it we learn that our western tribes of Indians are descendants from that Joseph which was sold into Egypt."[21] His scribe was in agreement. Writing in 1835, Oliver Cowdery explained Moroni's mission as the commissioning of a translation of "the history of the aborigines of this country."[22] So the Book of Mormon virtually asked to be evaluated as ancient American history, and mockers like Cole were happy to comply.

Joseph and his fellow leaders actually did all they could to strengthen the Book of Mormon's position as a Rosetta stone to vanished American civilizations, as if both ancient history and modern religion would benefit by the connection. The very first issue of the church's newspaper, *The Evening and the Morning Star*, suggested in 1832 that "honest enquiring persons, who wish to learn the truth of the Book of Mormon" should look at Genesis 49, Ezekiel 37, and Isaiah 29, with their references to the descendents of Joseph, a "stick of Ephraim," and "a marvelous work and a wonder" in the latter days.

(Like Isaiah's reference to a sealed book, Ezekiel's prophecy was taken by Mormons to refer specifically to the record translated by Joseph Smith. "Take thee one stick," the Lord had commanded Ezekiel, "and write upon it, For Judah, and for the children of Israel his companions: then take another stick, and write upon it, For Joseph, the stick of Ephraim, and for all the house of Israel his companions." Jews and Christians have largely seen the imagery, which culminates in the two sticks being joined in the hand of the Lord, as a reference to the eventual gathering of a scattered Israel. But Latter-day Saints read the prophecy more literally, believing that the writing on the two sticks corresponds to the respective histories kept of Judah, or the Bible, and of Joseph's posterity through the lineage of Lehi, or the Book of Mormon.)

Knowing, however, the insufficiency of proof-texts alone, the editor went on to say, "Independent of Bible proof on the subject before us, we have the remains of towns, cities, forts &c., which silently declare to the beholder: We were built by a civilized people."[23] This statement is the first in what becomes a pattern in early LDS publications. In his study of the Book of Mormon in early Mormonism, Grant Underwood found that among pamphlets, journals, and periodicals, passages are cited from that work more often in their connection to ancient history than in reference to any single religious theme.[24]

Once the Book of Mormon is cast in these terms, by angels, prophets, editors, and satirists, the historical approach becomes double-edged, an irresistible tool of apologists and detractors alike. As one enthusiastic believer has claimed—perhaps with some overstatement, "The Book of Mormon is the only revelation from God in the history of the world that can possibly be tested by scientific physical evidence. . . . To confirm Book of Mormon history through archaeological discoveries is to confirm revelation to the modern world."[25] On the other hand, as LDS defender Hugh Nibley argues, archaeology may be better suited to unveiling fraud than establishing truth: "We can never prove absolutely that the Book of Mormon is what it claims to be; but any serious proven fault in the work would at once condemn it."[26]

Nevertheless, with the same ebullient optimism that would lead Heinrich Schliemann to unearth the historical reality behind Homer's Troy a generation later, Joseph Smith and his contemporaries confidently looked to establish concrete connections between their revealed text and physical remains of the ancients. But if Smith was to make his scriptural record a viable contender in this theory-mongering, his evidence would have to extend far beyond copper kettles and a few burial mounds. Abner Cole's parodies notwithstanding, the Book of Mormon didn't describe early native Americans in canoes and moccasins, but highly developed civilizations with "mighty cities" (Ether 9:23), temples (3 Nephi 11:1), "spacious palaces" (Mos. 11:9), and "many elegant and spacious buildings . . . ornamented with fine work . . . and all manner of precious things" (Mos. 11:8). In addition, writers of the plates described ship building, synagogues, and sanctuaries (Hel. 3:14). Initially, only a vivid imagination could see shadows of such opulence and greatness in the vast American wilderness, as did the editor of an 1832 descriptive essay published in *The Evening and the Morning Star* on "The far west, as the section of country from the Mississippi to the Rocky Mountains may justly be styled." "There is something ancient as well as grand about it, too," the editor opines, and suggests that it all takes the mind "back to the day, when the Jaredites were in their glory upon this choice land above all others, and comes on till they, and even the Nephites, were destroyed for their wickedness." But the editor, through the prism of the Book of Mormon, sees the land in terms of a glorious future as well as a tragic past. "The world will never value the land of Desolation, as it is called in the book of Mormon, for any thing more than hunting ground, for want of timber and mill-seats: The Lord to the contrary notwithstanding, declares it to be the land of Zion which is the land of Joseph, blessed by him. . . . where the saints of the living God are to be gathered together and sanctified for the second coming of the Lord Jesus."[27]

Just a short month later, developments on two fronts fueled the fires of enthusiasm. In 1833, Josiah Priest published his *American Antiquities and Discoveries in the West*. It may well be, as John Sorenson has written, that this "credulous mishmash of opinions and excerpts" reveals "the generally low level of public information and chaotic jumble of 'fact' on 'pre-Indian' settlers of America that prevailed in Joseph Smith's day."[28] But it prevailed among Joseph Smith's followers in particular. Priest's book was referenced or excerpted five times in the church's *Times and Seasons*,[29] and eight years later it contributed to the first sustained attempt to connect the Book of Mormon to North American antiquities, Charles Thompson's 1841 *Evidences in Proof of the Book of Mormon*. The work borrowed extensively from Priest's accounts of ruins in Ohio and Tennessee and juxtaposed them with descriptions of Nephite fortifications and defenses. The parallels were, to Thompson's mind, "sufficient to show to the public that the people whose history is contained in the Book of Mormon, are the authors of these works."[30]

Then, in the same year Priest published his *Antiquities*, the Saints received news that was interpreted as spectacular, independent vindication of their faith that the Book of Mormon was a window on past glories that dwarfed anything the mound builders left behind. "DISCOVERY OF ANCIENT RUINS IN CENTRAL AMERICA" ran a headline in the February 1833 issue of *The Evening and the Morning Star*:

> A LATE number of the London Literary Gazette, contains a letter from Lieut, Col: [Juan] Galindo, at Peten, in Central America, giving some idea of those antiquities which rescue ancient America from the charge of barbarism. These ruins extend for more than twenty miles, and must anciently have embraced a city and its suburbs. The principal edifice is supposed to have been a palace, formed of two rows of galleries, eight feet wide, separated by walls a yard thick; the height of the walls to the eaves is nine feet, and thence three yards more to the top. The stones of which all the edifices are built, are about eighteen inches long, nine broad and two thick, cemented by mortar. The front of the palace contained five lofty and wide doors. . . . A place of religious worship and a prison, complete the list of buildings enumerated by Col. G.
>
> "The whole of the ruins," says Col. G. "are buried in a thick forest, and months might be delightfully employed in exploring them. I have seen sufficient to ascertain the high civilization of the former inhabitants, and that they possessed the art of representing sounds by signs, with which I have hitherto believed no Americans previous to the conquest were acquainted."—"The neighboring country for many leagues distant, contains remains of the ancient labors of its people, bridges, reservoirs, monumental inscriptions, subterraneous edifices, &c." "Every thing bears testimony that these surprising people were not physically dissimilar from the present Indians; but their civilization far surpassed that of the Mexicans and Peruvians; they must have existed long prior to the fourteenth century."

What partisan of the Book of Mormon wouldn't rejoice, as the editor does, seeing in this timely exploration the providential beginning of a new era: "We are glad to see the proof begin to come, of the original or ancient inhabitants of this continent. It is good testimony in favor of the book of Mormon, and the book of Mormon is good testimony that such things as cities and civilization, 'prior to the fourteenth century,' existed in America."[31]

So even as the Galindo exploration intensified Mormon interest in the evidences of archaeology and introduced Central American civilizations into the equation, all remains, from plains mounds to Guatemalan ruins, were still encompassed within a panhemispheric concept of Indians that emphasized the essential continuity of their history as a whole and its connectedness with the Book of Mormon.

In particular, since the plates were found in New York, Joseph Smith would himself continue to find evidence and make connections from Panama to the Hill Cumorah. Shortly after the publication of the Book of Mormon and the organization of the church, converts became established in two places of gathering. The first was Kirtland, Ohio, where early missionary success followed by a revelation in December of 1830 led Joseph to assemble the Saints. Soon thereafter, in July of 1831, a revelation designated Jackson County, Missouri their true "land of promise," "appointed and consecrated for the gathering of the saints" (D&C 37; 57:1-2). By early 1834, the Saints in Missouri were suffering persecution and expulsion, and the prophet mounted a relief expedition called Zion's Camp, which departed on May 1 and soon provided fodder for the church's first amateur archaeologists.

Wilford Woodruff, one of the camp members, recorded in his journal that

During our travels we visited many mounds thrown up by the ancient inhabitants, the Nephites and Lamanites. This morning, June 3rd, we went on to a high mound near the river. . . . On the summit of the mound were stones which presented the appearance of three altars, they having been erected, one above the other, according to the ancient order of things. Human bones were seen upon the ground. Brother Joseph requested us to dig into the mound; we did so; and in about one foot we came to the skeleton of a man, almost entire, with an arrow sticking in his backbone. . . . Brother Joseph feeling anxious to learn something of this man, asked the Lord, and received an open vision. The man's name was Zelph. He was a white Lamanite, the curse having been removed because of his righteousness. He was a great warrior, and fought for the Nephites under the direction of the Prophet Onandagus. The latter had charge of the Nephite armies from the Eastern sea to the Rocky Mountains. Although the Book of Mormon does not mention Onandagus, he was a great warrior, leader, general, and prophet. Zelph had his thigh bone broken by a stone thrown from a sling, but was killed by the arrow found sticking in his backbone. There was a great slaughter at that time. The bodies were heaped upon the earth, and buried in the mound, which is nearly three hundred feet in height.[32]

Joseph himself, in a letter to Emma, referred to the area of the discovery as "the plains of the Nephites," [33] and a few years later, in 1838, named a place north of Far West, Missouri, Tower Hill, "a name I gave the place in consequence of the remains of an old Nephite altar or tower that stood there."[34] Several revelations received from 1828 through 1831 had referred to the American Indians as Lamanites, and to Missouri as the land of the Lamanites, thereby reinforcing the habit of considering North America as Book of Mormon territory (D&C 3, 10, 19, 28, 30, 32, 49, 54).

The mental map that Joseph must have been forming for Book of Mormon history apparently encompassed both north and south American continents. Two virtually identical maps exist, allegedly produced by Joseph himself, entitled "A chart, and description of Moroni's travels through this country."[35] The map locates the Book of Mormon's "land Bountifull [sic]" in "Sentral [sic] America, has the words "starting point" below the reference to Central America, and identifies Salt Lake, Independence, Missouri, and Nauvoo, Illinois. Also noted is "Commorre [Cumorah] N.Y." In the right-hand margin are the words, "Moroni's Travels starting from Sentral America to the Sand hills Arizona then to Salt Lake U[tah], T[erritory], then to Adam on Diammon Mo, then to Nauvoo, Ill, then to Independence Mo, then to Kirtland Ohio then to Cumorah NY."

As developments unfolded in the southern hemisphere, however, the efforts of Joseph and his brethren to identify Book of Mormon lands would increasingly focus southward—far southward. Actual Book of Mormon descriptions of geography give readers little to go on by way of absolute location. Most prominent is probably the oft-repeated reference to a "narrow neck of land" that separates "the land northward" from "the land southward." Placing this "neck" in Panama seemed the obvious place to start, and with the news of great Central American civilizations newly discovered, the landing site of Lehi's people seemed clear. Joseph was alleged to have learned by revelation that Lehi landed at 30 degrees south latitude, in Chile, but the facts are unclear.[36]

If the discoveries of Col. Galindo reported in 1833 hadn't been evidence enough, subsequent explorations that came to national notice in the summer of 1841 were even more decisive. In that year, flush with the discoveries and writings of Josiah Priest and the Prussian explorer and scientist Alexander von Humboldt, Benjamin Winchester wrote that the ruins of North and South America provided "sufficient evidence both circumstantial, and scriptural, to establish the authenticity of the Book of Mormon."[37] But even as he wrote, the famous explorer and travel writer John Lloyd Stephens and the architectural artist Frederick Catherwood returned from Central America and were presenting lectures on their discoveries to enthusiastic audiences in New York. The public saw illustrations and heard descriptions of temple complexes, palaces, massive hieroglyphic-emblazoned tablets, and stone towers, columns, and statuary at Palenque, Copan, and six other ancient cities buried deep in the central American jungles, which journalists compared to the monuments of Egypt, Greece, and Rome. The Nauvoo church paper, in the June 15 issue, reprinted the report from the *New York Weekly Herald* with the banner, "AMERICAN ANTIQUITIES—MORE PROOFS OF THE BOOK OF MORMON."

Illustrations by Frederick Catherwood from the 1841 edition *of Incidents of Travel in Central America, Chiapas, and Yucatan* by John Lloyd Stephens. This book was the major catalyst that moved Joseph Smith and others to consider Mesoamerica as the seat of Book of Mormon civilization. (Courtesy L. Tom Perry Special Collections, Harold B. Lee Library, Brigham Young University, Provo, Utah)

A few months later, in September of 1841, John M. Bernhisel sent Joseph a copy of Stephens's freshly published *Incidents of Travel in Central America, Chiapas, and Yucatan*, the first English-language account of the Mayan civilization and an immediate bestseller (12 printings and 20,000 copies in three months).[38] This landmark event in the history of American archaeology was also a defining moment in the history of the Book of Mormon. Over the next several months, Joseph, in his correspondence and editorials (which he wrote or supervised), evinced a confident sense that the Book of Mormon was actually now emerging as even more significant, historically, than he had at first recognized.

The Book of Mormon originally appeared on a crowded stage with several speculative histories espousing the Indian-Israel connection. The problem, of course, was that the monuments left behind by the ancients had little apparent connection with the current Native American peoples. A similar disconnect became blatantly evident in Joseph's gold bible; nothing in the book rang familiar to those conversant with the language, customs, or culture of the Iroquois or the Wyandots. Abner Cole's parody of Jewish Indians wearing moccasins and speaking Egyptian was simply a comic presentation of a real difficulty: how to make the Book of Mormon—with all its exoticism—credible as a history of familiar peoples.

Now, with the developments ushered in by Stephens and company, it became both possible and desirable to cast the Book of Mormon as an ancient American history of a very different order than those represented by other pseudogenealogies of the American Indian. Not just because the Book of Mormon claimed a divine origin, but because it was *not* a history of the North American Indians then extant. Rather, it could declare itself a history of civilizations only then, in the 1830s and 1840s, coming to light. Upon arriving in the ancient city of Copan, Stephens's very first observation was of the disconnectedness of past and present, of the insufficiency of traditional histories and explanations to account for what he beheld in the jungle vastness:

> We came to the bank of a river, and saw directly opposite a stone wall, perhaps a hundred feet high, with furze growing out of the top, running north and south along the river, in some places fallen, but in others entire. It had more the character of a structure than any we had ever seen ascribed to the aborigines of America, and formed part of the wall of Copan, an ancient city on whose history books throw but little light. I am entering abruptly upon new ground.[39]

The disconnect first parodied by Abner Cole, and verified by Stephens and others, now actually qualified the Book of Mormon to fill a niche no other history could. As Karl Ackerman describes the situation, the Stephens book dramatically intensified a conundrum first created by the vague reports that began to filter northward about "ancient ruined cities in the Americas" in the 1820s. Beginning with Alexander Humboldt's account of his 1804 visit to Mexican ruins, then the writings of Antonio del Rio and Guillermo Dupaix describing their exploration of Palenque, scholars went in two directions. They "either dismissed outright the suggestion that a great culture might once have flourished in these tropical jungles or speculated without evidence that the ruins must have been built by settlers from the Old World."[40]

Now Stephens's enthusiastic presentation narrowed the debate but intensified the mystery. Following lavish descriptions of elaborate "architecture, sculpture, and . . . all the arts which . . . had flourished in this overgrown forest," he asks:

> Who were the people that built this city? America, say historians, was peopled by savages. But savages never reared these structures, savages never carved these stones. . . . Books, the record of knowledge, are silent on this theme. The city was desolate. No remnant of this race hangs around the ruins. . . . It lay before us like a shattered bark in the midst of the ocean, her masts gone, her name effaced, her crew perished, and none to tell whence she came, to whom she belonged, how long on her voyage, or what caused her destruction; her lost people, . . . perhaps, never to be known at all. . . . All was mystery, dark, impenetrable mystery, and every circumstance increased it.[41]

Joseph was quick to see how the Book of Mormon had arrived on the scene of this mystery with impeccable timing. Responding immediately to the Stephens account, Joseph wrote back to Bernhisel, thanking him for the "kind present" and ecstatically declaring that it "corresponds with & supports the testimony of the Book of Mormon." "Of all histories that have been written pertaining to the antiquities of this country," he continued, "it is the most correct luminous & comprihensive [sic]."[42] Picking up the thread of Stephens's remarks, he wrote (or sanctioned) these remarks in a subsequent article: "Some have supposed that all the great works of the west, of which we have been treating, belong to our present race of Indians; but from continued wars with each other, have driven themselves from agricultural pursuits, and . . . were reduced to savagism. But this is answered by the Antiquarian Society, as follows. . . ."[43]

What follows is an enumeration of accomplishments from metallurgy to walled cities to highly developed statuary and ceramics that have never, the writer insists, been attributed to "our present race of Indians." Most dramatically unaccountable of all, he concludes, are "the stupendous ruins, the elegant sculpture, and the magnificence of the ruins" discovered by Stephens and Catherwood. Unaccountable, that is, except by reference to the Book of Mormon.

Elaborating this view in that same *Times and Seasons* article, the author writes, "If men, in their researches into the history of this country, in noticing the mounds, fortifications, statues, architecture, implements of war, of husbandry, and ornaments of silver, brass, &c.—were to examine the Book of Mormon, their conjectures would be removed, and their opinions altered; uncertainty and doubt would be changed into certainty and facts; and they would find that those things that they are anxiously prying into were matters of history, unfolded in that book. . . . Their ruins speak of their greatness; the Book of Mormon unfolds their history." As Stephens had written, one day in Copan, one look at the stonework and stele, was sufficient to convince him that they were viewing no monuments from early Native Americans, but "the remains of an unknown people," indecipherable hieroglyphics, and "written records of a lost people."[44]

In this context, Joseph could both see and present the Book of Mormon not as a text in search of evidence, not as a supernatural mystery seeking corroboration—but as *itself* the evidence the scholars needed to solve *their* mysteries. Joseph thereby firmly and decisively thrust the Book of Mormon into a role from which it has never fully extricated itself. Truth, as pertaining to this holy record, is forever connected in the Mormon conception with historical truth. When Orson Pratt, one of the book's first devoted apologists, emphatically declared that "the Book of Mormon must be either true or false," he was not referring to its message or teachings.[45] He meant the record is all that it claims to be: a history recorded by ancient American prophets, hidden in the ground by the warrior-prophet Moroni, and revealed anew and translated by the gift and power of God. From its earliest appellation as "a history of the American Indians" to the suggestive photographs of Mayan ruins included in recent missionary editions (full color echoes of Catherwood's beautiful sketches), the book's "truthfulness," we are reminded, is rooted in its *historical* facticity.

The same Orson Pratt emphasizes this dimension with all the zeal and attention to detail of a hardened archaeologist. In his *Remarkable Visions* (which first presented Joseph's First Vision to the world), Pratt quotes Oliver Cowdery's description of the resting place of the gold plates:

> How far below the surface these records were anciently placed, I am unable to say; but from the fact that they had been some fourteen hundred years buried, and that too, on the side of a hill so steep, one is ready to conclude that they were some feet below, as the earth would naturally wear, more or less, in that length of time. . . . But suffice to say, a hole of sufficient depth was dug. At the bottom of this was laid a large quantity of cement, and into this cement, at the four edges of this stone, were placed four others, their bottom edges resting in the cement . . . .

Pratt continues to describe the stone repository of the plates, and then their discovery by Joseph: "A little exertion in removing the soil from the edges of the top of the box, and a light lever, brought to his natural vision its contents. While viewing and contemplating this sacred treasure with wonder and astonishment, behold! The angel of the Lord, who had previously visited him, again stood in his presence."[46]

Again we see the familiar pattern, the striking juxtaposition of realms: The sacred relics are heralded by and connected with manifestations of a heavenly order. But that cannot diminish the plain truth that the plates are material artifacts, as real, tangible, and rooted in history as any shards of pottery, and they are seen with "natural vision." Perhaps most striking in this regard, because so utterly divorced from any encounter with the divine or angelic bystanders, was David Whitmer's view of the stone box in which the plates were buried. Decades after his own apostasy and Joseph's martyrdom, Whitmer related to a *Chicago Times* reporter that "three times has he been at the hill Cumorah and seen the casket that contained the tablets, and the seer-stone. Eventually the casket had been washed down to the foot of the hill, but it was to be seen when he last visited the historic place."[47] Shorn of celestial glory or visionary residue, the durable container remained, to Whitmer's mind at least, as unimpeachably real as the upstate New York countryside.

With the Stephens publication of 1841, as far as some of the leaders in Nauvoo were concerned, matters seemed now clearly settled. "Even the most credulous cannot doubt," the editor of the *Times and Seasons* wrote. "These wonderful ruins of *Palenque* are among the mighty works of the Nephites—and the mystery is solved." From a concrete connection between the Book of Mormon and ancient ruins, it was but a small step to making positive correlations between Nephite place names and their Mesoamerican counterparts. In this same issue, for example, it was affirmed that "Lehi . . . landed a little south of the Isthmus of Darien (Panama)."[48]

And a few weeks later, the editor confidently asserted, "We are not agoing to declare positively that the ruins of Quirigua [in Guatemala] are those of Zarahemla, but when the land and the stones, and the books tell the story so plain, we are of opinion, that it would require more proof than the Jews could bring to prove the disciples stole the body of Jesus from the tomb, to prove that the ruins of the city in question, are not one of those referred to in the Book of Mormon."[49]

In the years when archaeology was in its infancy and Mesoamerican ruins still the province of self-styled adventurers in safari hats, few critical objections could be raised to partisans of the Book of Mormon's historicity. The identification of Book of Mormon places with geographical counterparts, begun by the editorialist of the *Times and Seasons* in the 1840s, continued to be a practice with official sanction. Two years after the release of Stephens's book the explorer published a second volume that *Times and Seasons* heralded as "a work that ought to be in the hands of every Latter-day Saint; corroborating, as it does the history of the Book of Mormon. . . . [T]he Book of Mormon unfolds . . . accounts of a people, and of cities that bear a striking resemblance to those mentioned by Mr. Stephens, both in regard to magnificence and location."[50]

Joseph's enthusiasm for the service that antiquities could render the cause of Book of Mormon historicity was likely part of the motivation behind an announcement in the city newspaper that carried the full weight of heavenly decree: "According to a Revelation, received not long since, it appears to be the duty of the members of the Church of Jesus Christ of Latter-day Saints, to bring to Nauvoo, their precious things, such as antiquities, . . . as well as inscriptions and hieroglyphics, for the purpose of establishing a Museum of the great things of God, and the inventions of men, at Nauvoo." The collection of "ancient records, manuscripts, paintings and hieroglyphics,"[51] along with the city library, was to be housed in the Seventies Hall. Later, the City Council of Nauvoo went so far as to stipulate that the librarian could receive, "in payment for stock in the association," not only books but "antiquities" and other items of interest.[52]

Sometimes, early church leaders were precipitous in their search for confirming artifacts, as in the case of the Kinderhook incident. In April 1843, six bell-shaped brass plates with ancient-looking inscriptions were excavated near Kinderhook, in Pike County, Illinois. The plates caused a stir in Nauvoo, and John Taylor editorialized exuberantly that "circumstances are daily transpiring which give additional testimony to the authenticity of the Book of Mormon."[53] There is sketchy evidence that Joseph said he could translate them, although the plates soon disappeared and nothing further developed until 1879, when two of those involved in the discovery claimed the episode was a hoax designed to entrap the prophet.[54] Tests conducted in 1980 verified the nineteenth-century origin of the plates. Since the trap was not sprung in Joseph's lifetime, it would appear that, not taking the bait, he could not be definitively linked to claims about their authenticity or that he quickly distanced himself from the whole affair.

After the death of Joseph, Orson Pratt became the most vocal defender of the Book of Mormon, as well as the foremost exponent of its geographical correlations. Still trumpeting the Stephens volume, he declared in an 1848 pamphlet that "a careful reader of [the Book of Mormon] can trace the relative bearings, and distances of many of these cities from each other; and if acquainted with the present geographical features of the country, he can, by the descriptions given in that book, determine, very nearly, the precise spot of ground they once occupied."[55]

In spite of his sustained enthusiasm for Stephens's account (he would publish extensive extracts of volume two as editor of the *Millennial Star* in 1866), Pratt was at this time shifting Book of Mormon history a few thousand miles to the south. In accordance with Joseph's original (re-puted) statement, he again had Lehi landing in "Chili," with the Nephites residing "in the northwestern portions of South America."[56] In 1879, Pratt prepared a historic edition of the Book of Mormon. It was distinctive for its being the first version organized into chapters and verses. But it was also significant for its incorporation of some 75 geographical comments and identifications into the footnotes. In these, he situated Lehi's landing on the coast of Chile, equated the River Sidon with the River Magdalena in Colombia, and the Waters of Ripliancum with Lake Ontario. The Jaredites, on the other hand, were brought by the Lord "upon the western coast of North America," "probably South of the Gulf of California." By the time of their destruction, noted Pratt, pertinent locales included "Lake Ontario" and "the shore of the New England States."[57]

For the time being, it appears, Mormons valued the Book of Mormon as faithful history of their own continent, secure in the belief that its historical validity was amply confirmed by the abundant ruins so gen-eral throughout the lands of Mesoamerica.

B. H. Roberts

At the turn of the century, after the travails of Missouri and martyrdom in the East, and then migration and colonization in the West, Mormon-ism entered what E. E. Ericksen referred to as Mormonism's third era— one of internal conflict and intellectual adjustment that required, in the words of Sterling McMurrin, "constructing a rational philosophy in the light of modern scientific thought."[58] During these years, two classi-cally trained Mormon scholars, George Reynolds and Janne M. Sjodahl, began the first systematic assemblage of external evidence from both the Old and New Worlds for Book of Mormon authenticity. They worked to construct a coherent internal geography, to correlate Book of Mor-mon names with Middle Eastern or South American counterparts, and to establish cultural parallels between textual elements and the ancient world. But most of their research would not be collected and published as a seven-volume commentary until many years after their deaths.[59]

The truly dominant Mormon intellectual of the era, scholars are unani-mous in declaring, was B. H. Roberts (1857–1933). From his first experi-ence debating a Campbellite minister on the Book of Mormon in 1881, Roberts was devoted to defending the Mormon scripture. While in En-gland as a church mission president in 1887 and 1888, he studied in the Picton Library, collecting notes on American archaeology that could serve as external evidence in support of the Book of Mormon.[60] The three vol-umes of the work that resulted, *New Witnesses for God*, appeared in 1895, 1909, and 1911. One noteworthy contribution of his was to differentiate efforts to establish the book's authenticity as an ancient record, which he thought was possible, from efforts to establish Book of Mormon geography and archaeology, which he thought was not. The latter was doomed to fail according to the Book of Mormon itself, he reasoned, since the cataclysmic upheavals in the Western Hemisphere accompanying the death of Christ, as described in 3 Nephi, would render modern-day identification of Nephite monuments and places impossible.

Nevertheless, turning to his study of "American antiquities," and what he saw as the dearth of sources available to Joseph Smith, Roberts felt the circumstantial evidence was strongly in favor of an ancient origin to the record. Nothing that had to this point been advanced by scholars, he was convinced, "conflicted with the claims of the Book of Mormon and . . . much of their work supported the story."[61] By this time, the few historical criticisms being raised did not amount to serious objections, in Roberts's view, such as lack of evidence for Nephite use of iron and steel and for horses, cows, and other domestic animals mentioned in the Book of Mormon. Roberts believed he had dealt successfully—though not definitively—with the threats to Book of Mormon authenticity. He concluded the volumes by expressing confidence that "a little more time, a little more research" would provide "the data necessary for a complete and satisfactory solution of all the difficulties which objectors now emphasize."[62] Though flawed and not even entirely self-convincing, Roberts's work "was the most effective defense of the Book of Mormon that had been produced" to that time.[63]

Meanwhile, Benjamin Cluff, Jr., president of Brigham Young Academy (University after 1903), persuaded the church to officially sanction the first actual foray into Book of Mormon archaeology.[64] Under Cluff, who was trained in pedagogy and mathematics, a ragtag group made up mostly of students began an audacious expedition to South America in 1900. Although they hoped to amass all manner of scientific data, the main purpose was to discover the Nephite capital of Zarahemla, believed to lie along the banks of the Magdalena River in Colombia. With the preclassic civilizations of Mesoamerica (dating from 2000 B.C. to A.D. 450, contemporary with Book of Mormon civilizations) yet to be discovered, this first effort to authenticate the New World scripture was premature by any standard. Delays at the Mexican border led to breakdown of morale and discipline, and soon the members' inexperience and poor organization caused the church to rescind its support. A few continued on, hungry and ill-equipped. They arrived in Colombia at last, only to find that internal chaos made further travel into the interior unthinkable. The six remaining explorers returned home after almost two years on the road. Cluff insisted that the effort succeeded in stimulating interest in the Book of Mormon and Mesoamerican antiquities, though it failed in its primary purpose. But the church's abrupt withdrawal of its endorsement was the first sign of a dawning recognition that optimism

The Cluff Expedition. The ambitious but unsuccessful attempt to locate
evidence of Book of Mormon civilization in Colombia was launched in 1900,
headed by Benjamin Cluff, President of Brigham Young Academy.
(Courtesy L. Tom Perry Special Collections, Harold B. Lee Library,
Brigham Young University, Provo, Utah)

might need to be tempered with more prudence. A new spirit of intellectual caution would become the rule in Book of Mormon archaeology
for many years to come.[65]

In 1890, a series of small relics and artifacts had been found in
Montcalm County, Michigan, marked with hieroglyphics. By 1908, other
finds included copper plates with depictions of the flood and other Old
Testament material. Several of these "Michigan relics" ended up in the
collection of Daniel Soper and Father James Savage, who believed "they
were dealing with remains relevant to the descendants of the Lost Tribes
of Israel."[66] Recognizing the potential relevance to Book of Mormon historicity, the LDS Deseret Museum sent James E. Talmage, geologist and
future apostle, to investigate. In spite of the relics' potential, in Talmage's
words, to confirm "much of the history in the Book of Mormon," he
examined the evidence and dismissed them as patent forgeries.[67]

Then in 1920, the church convened a committee to prepare a new
edition of the Book of Mormon. As part of their work, they examined

the footnotes throughout the 1879 version. After evaluating the bases on which geographical correlations were made, they decided to delete every reference to every modern-day country, river, and geographical feature.[68] Henceforth, in its canonical form at least, the Book of Mormon was disburdened of any *particular* geographical claims. The new spirit of caution would prove well timed.

On August 22, 1921, a young member wrote a letter to church apostle James E. Talmage that would shake up the world of Mormon apologetics and dramatically refocus Roberts's own intellectual engagement with Mormonism. The brief letter sounded routine enough. "Dear Dr. Talmage," wrote W. E. Riter, "During the past few years I have associated and had some religious discussions with some non-'Mormons.' Mr. Couch of Washington, D.C., has been studying the Book of Mormon and submits the enclosed questions concerning his studies. Would you kindly answer them and send them to me."[69] The five questions were not entirely original objections to the Book of Mormon; Couch wanted to know:

1. How to explain the immense diversity of Indian languages if all are supposed to be relatively recent descendents of Lamanite origin?
2. How can the Book of Mormon mention the horse if it was not introduced until the time of the Conquest?
3. How can Nephi mention having a bow of steel before such metal was known to the Jews?
4. How can the Book of Mormon mention "cimiters" before the rise of Mohammedan power?
5. How could the Nephites possess "silk" if it was unknown to America at that time?

Talmage asked Roberts to provide answers to the questions, a task to which his three volumes should have well suited him. Several weeks later, Roberts still had not responded to the request. In late December, he wrote the president of the church, explaining the delay and asking for more time:

> While knowing that some parts of my [previous] treatment of Book of Mormon problems . . . had not been altogether as convincing as I would like to have seen them, I still believed that reasonable explanations could be made that would keep us in advantageous possession of the field. As I proceeded with my recent investigations, however, and more especially in the, to me, new field of language problems, I found the difficulties more serious than I had thought for; and the more I investigated the more difficult I found the formulation of an answer to Mr. Couch's inquiries to be.[70]

This honest, and apparently surprising, recognition that Book of Mormon apologetics required more than passing reference to a few

Guatemalan ruins, marked a turning point for both Roberts personally and the church generally. Roberts would spend the remainder of his life wrestling with the critics, the evidence, and his own questions, struggling to stay "in advantageous possession of the field." At the same time, Roberts worked to alert the leadership of the church to the need for a sophisticated, critically informed approach to Book of Mormon studies. He had justified his interest in the rational foundations of belief in his 1909 publications: "While desiring to make it clear that our chief reliance for evidence to the truth of the Book of Mormon must ever be the witness of the Holy Spirit, . . . I would not have it thought that the evidence and argument presented . . . are unimportant, much less unnecessary. Secondary evidences in support of truth, like secondary causes in natural phenomena, may be of firstrate importance, and mighty factors in the achievement of God's purposes."[71]

Now, in light of his own concerns about the "evidence and argument" behind the Book of Mormon, he petitioned the First Presidency of the church for permission to present his concerns to the leadership. In two marathon sessions, on January 4 and 5, 1922, he did just that, presenting a 141-page report on "Book of Mormon Difficulties." His survey of the relevant scholarship left him much less sanguine about the future than he had felt in 1909. "These questions are put by me . . . to bring to the consciousness of myself and my brethren that we face grave difficulties in all these matters. . . . I am sure that neither an appeal to the books written by men, nor even to the books of scripture now in our possession, will solve our present difficulties."[72] Nevertheless, at least some of the brethren were unfazed by Roberts's concerns. Even the Quorum's leading intellectual, James E. Talmage, a scientist by training, wrote in his journal following the meetings: "many of the 'difficulties,' or objections as opposing critics would urge, are after all but negative in their nature. The Book of Mormon states that Lehi and his colony found horses upon this continent when they arrived; and therefore horses were here at that time."[73] Finding those and a few subsequent meetings unsatisfactory, Roberts departed soon thereafter to preside over a mission in the eastern states.

At some point in his studies, Roberts had found other grounds for concern as well when he examined parallels between the Book of Mormon and the work of a nineteenth-century minister, the Reverend Ethan Smith. Smith's *View of the Hebrews*, published in 1823 and again in 1825, was a compendium of evidence for the Hebraic origins of the American Indian. Roberts never published his resulting treatise, "A Book of Mormon Study," but it provides an elaborate case for the possibility that Smith's *Views* could have furnished Joseph with a "ground plan" for his own work. Roberts publicly and privately affirmed his belief in the divine origins of the Book of Mormon until his death in 1933, but a lively debate has emerged over whether his personal conviction really remained intact in the aftermath of his academic investigations.[74] It seems most plausible that Roberts's unflinching intellectual integrity led him to articulate the most probing critique he could of the Book of Mormon, and he found himself incapable of solving the dilemmas he uncovered. But neither did he find his doubts sufficient to overpower his faith. As he wrote to church leaders in 1923, "Let me say once and for all, so as to avoid what might otherwise call for repeated explanation, that what is herein set forth does not represent any conclusions of mine. . . . It may be of great importance since it represents what may be used by some opponent in criticism of the Book of Mormon. I am taking the position that our faith is not only unshaken but unshakable in the Book of Mormon, and therefore we can look without fear upon all that can be said against it."[75]

In the decades that followed Roberts's presentation in church headquarters, leaders would from time to time express their continued optimism about the contributions of archaeology to the Book of Mormon's historicity, while others shunned such an approach. Elder Rey Pratt, for example, returned from presiding over the Mexican missions to report in the church's General Conference in April 1923: "It has been my good fortune to travel somewhat in fields rich in archaeology, in this country, and I bear you my testimony that not one spade of earth has been overturned that has revealed a single thing except what is corroborative of the Book of Mormon and its being a divine record."[76]

Church apostle John A. Widtsoe concurred in his October 1927 remarks. Although he felt the truest witness "lies within the work itself," he harbored no doubt that

> within the next few years [the Book of Mormon] will be corroborated by all manner of discoveries. Men are digging in the earth; things are found that we did not dream of a few years ago. A man voiced the opinion a few days ago—a visiting Englishman—that every new discovery in American archaeology tends to confirm the truth of the Book of Mormon. We shall use such finds and discoveries for the establishment in the hearts of seekers after truth, of the correctness of the Book of Mormon.[77]

And in the October conference of 1928, Elder Levi Edgar Young expressed his confidence that "What archaeologists have done for the Holy Bible in the Holy Land, archaeologists will do for the Book of Mormon in this land of America." He admitted that "not yet have scholars found definite remains or ruins that coincide with Book of Mormon history." But he expressed confidence that such discoveries "in the not far distant future may be clearly related to Book of Mormon history, [and] Semitic origins will be found in this land, and the institutions so well described in the Book of Mormon will be made clearer by archaeologists, as they have done in Mesopotamia, Palestine, and Egypt."[78] Six months later, Elder James H. Moyle presented in the same forum scattered evidence from archaeology to support the case.

But many in the church leadership resisted the allure of scientific efforts at corroboration and urged the caution or skepticism advocated by Roberts. Antoine Ivins, on the First Council of Seventy (seven officials just under the twelve apostles in the LDS hierarchy), was one such leader. "Can we get [a testimony] by studying the archaeology of America and reasoning from that point of view that the Book of Mormon tells a true story, and that consequently the Prophet Joseph Smith was a true prophet?" he asked.

> As I grow older I like to dig into the archaeology and the ethnology of America somewhat, mainly with a view of getting things to tell other people that might help them along this line. But I find that there is in the minds of people who have studied these things such great confusion that you can hardly bring any uniform interpretation out of their studies and their reports. One man reads the inscriptions on the ruins of Mexico as far as he can, or looks at them and tries to interpret them. Another man does exactly the same thing, and they write quite divergent reports about them. What good is it then as a testimony to the Book of Mormon?[79]

The New World Archaeological Foundation

New winds began to blow in 1945, when the new president of Brigham Young University created a chair of archaeology and filled the post with M. Wells Jakeman, one of the first Mormons formally trained as an archaeologist.[80] Three years later, the new Department of Archaeology sponsored its first field work in southeastern Mexico. Then, in the 1950s, an amateur scholar named Thomas Ferguson (present on that first 1948 dig) tried to nudge the church further into a new era of engagement with Book of Mormon archaeology. Until now, church leaders and intellectuals from Joseph Smith to B. H. Roberts had waited upon the external evidence for the Book of Mormon as it gradually materialized—or, in some cases, failed to materialize. Ferguson advocated vigorous efforts to uncover dramatic proof he was sure could be found. Born in 1915, Ferguson studied political science and later received a law degree. But his real passion, if never supported by training or qualification, was to verify the Book of Mormon through field work in the ruins of Mesoamerica. He traveled to Mexico and Guatemala in 1946, visiting museums and ruins, identifying Book of Mormon cities, and filming voraciously. Upon returning, he and his traveling companion, J. Willard

Marriott, shared their films and experiences with John A. Widtsoe of the Quorum of the Twelve. Widtsoe responded enthusiastically to the presentation.

Soon Ferguson was publishing articles and a study of Book of Mormon geography. He made more trips to Central America and found an important collaborator in Milton R. Hunter, a member of the First Council of Seventy. Together they published *Ancient America and the Book of Mormon* in 1950. Ferguson, whose overzealousness may be suggested by his desire at one point to rent a helicopter and look for the Cave of Ether (mentioned in the Book of Mormon), felt that he and Hunter had already made archaeological history with this publication: "We believe it is probably the first book containing concrete and factual evidence, archaeological and historical, establishing the actual and physical resurrection of Christ."[81] Overconfident he may have been. But Alfred V. Kidder, a leading American archaeologist and past head of archaeology work for the Carnegie Institution of Washington, reviewed the copy that Ferguson sent him and gave the young enthusiast encouragement. More importantly, he helped Ferguson draft a proposal in April of 1951 asking the church to fund an ambitious project of archaeological investigations, aiming to solve "the paramount problem of origins of the great civilizations of Middle America."[82] Several months later, the church denied the request for the five-year, $150,000 plan.[83]

Undeterred, by June of 1952 Ferguson had raised private funds sufficient to organize the Middle American Archaeological Foundation—later changed to the New World Archaeological Foundation (NWAF)—and to sponsor the first year of excavations in Mexico at those sites Ferguson tentatively identified as Nephite lands. Board members included church leaders Widtsoe and Hunter, and the advisory panel of prominent non-Mormon scholars included Alfred V. Kidder, Gordon F. Ekholm (of the American Museum of Natural History), and Gordon R. Willey (of Harvard). Esteemed biblical archaeologist W. F. Albright offered his congratulations and support, and Thor Heyerdahl wrote Ferguson that his own recent work confirmed that "there was a white people in Southern Mexico and Guatemala many centuries before Columbus."[84]

The foundation was expressly commissioned, in the words of Kidder, to test three theories about the origin of the advanced civilizations of Mesoamerica: "(1) That they were autochthonous; (2) That, as set forth in the Book of Mormon, they were derived from ancient Israel; (3) That their rise was due to stimuli from some Asiatic source."[85] The fact that archaeologists from Harvard, Carnegie, and the American Museum of Natural History were apparently willing to consider the Book of Mormon as constituting a serious theory of Mesoamerican peopling to be tested alongside their competing theories could be interpreted by some as a dramatic coming of age for Book of Mormon studies. An NWAF editor and eminent archaeologist, J. Alden Mason, insisted that the organization was not in the business of confirming scriptural accounts of antiquity, that the purpose of the foundation was "*not* to seek corroboration of the Book of Mormon account."[86] Still, even if the approach was scientifically objective and the whole enterprise not just archaeology in the service of apologetics, the prestige of those endorsing the project had lent powerful support to the credibility of the Book of Mormon. The text was clearly a viable player on the field of Mesoamerican studies. Non-Mormon scholars had just indicated as much, and in print.

In 1952, Mexico granted a five-year concession (subsequently renewed) to excavate in the basin of the Grijalva River in southern Mexico, and field work began under the direction of Mexican archaeologist Pedro Armillas that winter. Over the next several years (and with church funding from 1955 on[87]), the NWAF conducted successful field work, excavated several ruins, and published numerous papers and findings. Excavations shed enormous light on a range of occupations that span a period both preceding and postdating Nephite history. They unearthed pottery, figurines, codices, tombs, and canal works— but without discovering anything as conclusive as Nephi's tomb. The most impressive find, in Ferguson's opinion, was a set of tiny cylinder seals with markings, apparently dating between 400 and 700 B.C. The biblical archaeologist W. F. Albright identified the markings on one as "degenerate cartouches of Mediterranean inspiration."[88] In a subsequent book, Ferguson listed some 300 cultural elements that he argued parallel Middle Eastern culture.[89] His enthusiasm was such that he was soon discussing a documentary film project with Twentieth Century-Fox and a Book of Mormon museum, filled with his discoveries, with hotelier Willard Mar-

The Tlatilco seal. The markings on this cylinder seal (ca. 700–400 B.C.), found at Tlatilco, Mexico, have been controversially described by F. W. Albright, a biblical archaeologist, as "degenerate cartouches of Mediterranean inspiration." (Courtesy Milwaukee Public Museum)

riott.[90] Though his lasting influence upon Book of Mormon scholarship was negligible, Ferguson did much at the time to raise the visibility of Book of Mormon research.

Throughout much of the LDS community, exuberant optimism continued to erupt in a series of publications by LDS amateur archaeologists, often criticized by serious scholars within the church for doing more harm than good to the cause of Book of Mormon apologetics. Titles like *Book of Mormon Evidences in Ancient America* (1953), *The Book of Mormon on Trial* (1963), *These Early Americans: External Evidences of the Book of Mormon* (1974), trumpeted a number of archaeological artifacts and correlations that, to the uninitiated, seemed to make a watertight case for the Book of Mormon as ancient history. The church endorsed such evidence through distribution of a popular proselytizing film, "Ancient America Speaks," written, produced, and narrated by Paul R. Cheesman. While stopping short of making definitive claims, the film lent a considerable air of scholarly credibility to Book of Mormon archaeology by suggesting the historical plausibility of the Book of Mormon in light of Mesoamerican ruins.

In spite of recurrent efforts at a Book of Mormon archaeology, it has certainly been far from the case that archaeologists by and large consider the Book of Mormon worth their serious attention. When rumors surfaced as early as 1951, for example, that Smithsonian archaeologists were relying upon the Book of Mormon as a guide for field work, the Institution was quick to distance itself from such allegations. In a prepared statement from the National Museum of Natural History, authorities set the record straight in terms that delighted Book of Mormon critics, who have reprinted the statement in numerous contexts. A revised statement, released in 1979 (but later drastically modified again), makes nine points:

1. The Smithsonian Institution has never used the Book of Mormon in any way as a scientific guide. Smithsonian archaeologists see no direct connection between the archeology of the New World and the subject matter of the book.
2. The physical type of the American Indian is basically Mongoloid, being most closely related to that of the peoples of eastern, central, and northeastern Asia. Archaeological evidence indicates that the ancestors of the present Indians came into the New World—probably over a land bridge known to have existed in the Bering Strait region during the last Ice Age—in a continuing series of small migrations beginning from about 25,000 to 30,000 years ago.
3. Present evidence indicates that the first people to reach this continent from the East were the Norsemen who briefly visited the northeastern part of North America around A.D. 1000 and then settled in Greenland. There is nothing to show that they reached Mexico or Central America.

4. ... None of the principal Old World domesticated food, plants or animals (except the dog) occurred in the New World in pre-Columbian times. American Indians had no wheat, barley, oats, millet, rice, cattle, pigs, chickens, horses, donkeys, camels, before 1492. (Camels and horses were in the Americas, along with the bison, mammoth, and mastodon, but all these animals became extinct around 10,000 B.C. at the time the early big game hunters spread across the Americas.)

5. Iron, steel, glass, and silk were not used in the New World before 1492 (except for occasional use of unsmelted meteoric iron). . . . True metallurgy was limited to southern Mexico and the Andean region, . . . [and did not include] iron.

6. ... Certainly there were no [interhemispheric] contacts with the ancient Egyptians, Hebrews, or other peoples of Western Asia and the Near East.

7. No reputable Egyptologist or other specialist on Old World archaeology, and no expert on New World prehistory, has discovered or confirmed any relationship between archaeological remains in Mexico and archaeological remains in Egypt.

8. ... No inscriptions using Old World forms of writing have been shown to have occurred in any part of the Americas before 1492 except for a few Norse runes which have been found in Greenland.

9. There are copies of the Book of Mormon in the library of the National Museum of Natural History, Smithsonian Institution."[91]

Yet even as the Smithsonian attempted to suppress unwarranted rumors and conclusions about Book of Mormon historicity, another front had been opened that would inject new vigor into the debate and launch a new era of LDS apologetics.

FIVE

"I, Nephi, Wrote This Record": The Book of Mormon as Ancient History, Part 2—The Search for a Rational Belief

It necessarily follows from the supposition of our rational faculties being *limited*, that there is *room* for our being instructed by revelation. . . . However upon supposition of such a revelation, we must be supposed to be able to see the evidence of its being such. It is the proper office of reason to determine whether what is proposed to us under the notion of a revelation from God, be attended with suitable attestations and credentials, or not. So that even in this case, we may *of ourselves judge what is right*.

—Jonathan Mayhew, 1748

Underlying the debate about the intellectual credibility of sacred texts, or their historical verifiability, is a larger question that has to do with the relationship between faith and reason. *Can* "spiritual" truths be proved? Is rational validation of religious belief *desirable*? Mormons have in some ways eluded at least some formulations of the problem. Collapsing the spiritual and earthly realms, affirming the corporeality of God, insisting that "all matter is spirit," claiming, as does Orson Pratt, that angels ministered to Joseph even as he looked upon the plates "with natural vision"—these are all so many echoes of a thoroughgoing Mormon monism that cannot help but attach to the word "faith" a theologically idiosyncratic value.

More specifically, the Mormon doctrine of faith, founded on the Book of Mormon's own teaching, is that it is only *"at first"* that one cannot know truthfulness with surety, only initially that "faith is not a certain knowledge." After one acts upon a seed of faith, "knowledge [may become] perfect," and "faith [become] dormant." This process of enlightenment, says Alma, is "real . . . because it is light; and whatsoever is light, is good, because it is discernible" (Alma 32:26-35). Not unrelated to all this, we find a typical feature of Mormon religious practice is the monthly affirmation in "testimony meetings" that the individual "knows" the church is true, that Joseph Smith is a prophet, and so forth. Faith, in other words, is the presumptive prelude to knowledge; the two conditions differ in degree rather than kind.

On the other hand, the kind of knowledge to which Mormons aspire is not one that can be obtained independently of the role of the Holy Ghost, the testator of all truth. For it is "by the power of the Holy Ghost," Moroni affirms, that "ye may know the truth of all things" (Moro. 10:5). Still, even as Mormon scholars affirm on the one hand that no amount of scientific evidence can prove the Book of Mormon true, it is hard to shake the heritage of Joseph Smith's famous claim that "the Lord has a hand in bringing to pass his strange act, and proving the Book of Mormon true in the eyes of all the people. . . . Surely 'facts are stubborn things.' It will be and ever has been, the world will prove Joseph Smith a true prophet by circumstantial evidence, *in experimentis*, as they did Moses and Elijah."[1]

So, reluctant to "rely upon the arm of flesh" on the one hand, but unwilling to forego the resources of scholarship in shoring up the Book of Mormon's historicity on the other, church leaders have taken to embracing the position of Austin Farrer: "Though argument does not create conviction, lack of it destroys belief. What seems to be proved may not be embraced; but what no one shows the ability to defend is quickly abandoned. Rational argument does not create belief, but it maintains a climate in which belief may flourish."[2]

Hugh Nibley

No one in the history of Mormon scholarship has done more to establish rational grounds for belief in the Book of Mormon than Hugh Nibley. Acquiring impressive scholarly credentials (summa cum laude from UCLA and a Berkeley Ph.D. dissertation written in three weeks in 1938) before heading off to war, Nibley's serious engagement with the Book of Mormon began at Normandy on the appropriately named Utah Beach on June 6, 1944. It was then and there, he recalls, "that it really hit me—how astonishing the Book of Mormon truly is. It had never hit me before, but all I could think of that day was how wonderful this Book of Mormon was."[3]

After the war, his first work on the subject was a 1948 piece "The Book of Mormon as a Mirror of the East." That article, and the position it articulates, grew over the next few years to become three lengthy serials: "Lehi in the Desert," "The World of the Jaredites," and "There Were Jaredites." As the title of his first article suggests, Nibley believes the aim of Book of Mormon scholarship is not a particular, stupendous find on the order of Tutankhamen's tomb, but rather an evaluation of the totality of the Book of Mormon text as an ancient document. Referring to the story of Lehi, for example, Nibley later asks:

> does it correctly reflect "the cultural horizon and religious and social ideas and practices of the time"? Does it have authentic historical and geographical background? Is the mise-en-scène mythical, highly imaginative, or extravagantly improbable? Is its local color correct, and are its proper names convincing? Until recent years men were asking the same questions of the book of Exodus, and scholars were stolidly turning thumbs down until evidence accumulating in its favor began to turn the scales. As one student described it, the problem "is rather to prove, by innumerable small coincidences, that which Ebers has so well called the `Egypticity' of the Pentateuch, than to establish any particular historical point by external and monumental evidence." Just so the problem of 1 Nephi is to establish both its "Egypticity" and its "Arabicity" by like innumerable coincidences.[4]

This emphasis on the book's rootedness in Middle Eastern rather than Mesoamerican culture has been typical of Nibley's approach. As he has insisted, "If you want proof of the Book of Mormon, you must go to the Old World. You won't find it in the New World."[5] Accordingly, as his editor explains, "Dr. Nibley's broad knowledge of the ancient Near East . . . allowed him to reconstruct the probable cultural backgrounds of men like Lehi and Nephi and to read between the lines in the Book of Mormon to identify evidences of their cultural world."[6]

Like Marcel Proust's *petite madeleine*, the first forty pages of the Book of Mormon engender under Nibley's analysis a rich tapestry of linguistic, political, geographic, religious, and historical threads that are convincingly sixth century B.C. Middle Eastern. Palestine's cultural and economic ties to Egypt at this time are reflected in Nephi's instruction in "the language of the Egyptians" (1 Nephi 1:2). The "reformed Egyptian" of the plates finds a parallel in period names that combine "Egyptian and Hebrew in a process of fusion for which a great deal of evidence now exists."[7] Nibley compares the Book of Mormon "Hermounts" (a wild country of the borderlands) with the Egyptian "Hermonthis," (the land of Month, god of wild places and things), and points out the "bull's-eyes" of the Book of Mormon characters Paanchi, Korihor, and Pahoran. Paankhi turns out to be an Egyptian name in the seventh century B.C, and Korihor turns up in both Egyptian and Asiatic derivatives.[8] In this regard, it is well worth noting that William Foxwell Albright, doyen of

American ancient Near Eastern studies, wrote to a critic seeking to de-
bunk Smith's writings that "when the Book of Mormon was written,
Egyptian had just begun to be deciphered and it is all the more surprising that there are two Egyptian names, Paanch[i] and Pahor[an] which
appear together in the Book of Mormon in close connection with a reference to the original language as being 'Reformed Egyptian.'"[9]

When Lehi leads his band of exiles into the desert south of Jerusalem, he took "what we *now* know to have been the only possible way
out. . . . Only the south desert, the one land where Israel's traders and
merchants had felt at home through the centuries, remained open—even
after Jerusalem fell this was so."[10] At their first camp, Lehi follows the
now recognized Middle Eastern practice ("which no Bedouin would
dream of transgressing," says one scholar), of naming both rivers and
valleys found along the journey after family members.[11] Subsequently,
the band buries Ishmael at a place *not* named by them—"[it] was called
Nahom," and there the women "did mourn exceedingly" (1 Nephi 16:34).
The Arabic root NHM means "to sigh or moan," and the related Hebrew *Nahum* means "comfort," Nibley informs us.[12] In 1978, an eighteenth-century map was noticed indicating a place name "Nehhm" in
that region, but it was not until the early 1990s that ancient evidence of
that name's authenticity surfaced. In that era, a German archaeology
team discovered a carved altar a few dozen miles east of modern San'a
in Yemen, inscribed with a reference to the tribe of Nihm, and another
with a like inscription has since been found from that area.[13] Found in
the very area where Nephi's record locates Nahom, these altars may
thus be said to constitute the first actual archaeological evidence for the
historicity of the Book of Mormon.

When Lehi admonishes his faltering sons, Nibley points out, it is in
the poetic rhythms and structure peculiar to the oldest Arabic poetry of
the desert (the *qasida*):

> And when my father saw that the waters of the river emptied into the
> fountain of the Red Sea, he spake unto Laman, saying: O that thou mightest
> be like unto this river, continually running into the fountain of all righ-
> teousness!
> And he spake also unto Lemuel: O that thou mightest be like unto this
> valley, firm and steadfast, and immovable in keeping the commandments
> of the Lord! (1 Nephi 2:9-10)

Here we find impressive congruence with a series of characterizations
particular to these *qasidas* and the earliest Semitic verse, known as the
saj^c: they are what German scholars have called *Quellenlieder*, songs inspired by running water; they are addressed to one or more traveling
companions; they are hortatory, urging the hearer to be like the thing he

Altar from near San'a, Yemen. The most impressive find to date corroborating Book of Mormon historicity, this is one of two known altars with inscriptions referring to the tribe of *NHM*, corresponding to the place name referred to by Nephi ("Nahom") when his party passed through what would become modern-day Yemen. (Courtesy Lehi's Trail Foundation)

beholds; each couplet is followed by a perfectly matched "brother"; they are recited extempore.[14]

As for the actual medium on which Lehi's clan history is inscribed, Nibley cites parallels to Nephi's gold plates that include the gold and silver plates of Darius, "sacred history deposited in a special stone box

Two examples of ancient writing on metal plates.
Left: The Copper Scroll 3Q15 from Qumran,
25–100 C.E. (Photograph by Bruce and
Kenneth Zuckerman, West Semitic Research,
Courtesy Department of Antiquities, Jordan)
Below: The Plates of Darius II, a set of gold and
silver plates from Persia, fourth century B.C.
(Courtesy L. Tom Perry Special Collections,
Harold B. Lee Library,
Brigham Young University, Provo, Utah)

by a near contemporary of Lehi"; the Copper Scroll from the Dead Sea caves, whose message "about the recording and storing of bronze and gold plates, should give pause to the most skeptical critic of the Book of Mormon," and over a hundred other examples of ancient writing on metal plates.[15]

In subsequent studies, Nibley moved beyond the writings of Nephi to explore other evidence of ancient origins in cultural practices described throughout the Book of Mormon. The rites of execution practiced on two Book of Mormon villains, he finds, suggest Jewish traditions concerning the angel Shamhozai; Moroni's "standard of liberty" and other battle practices are strikingly similar to descriptions on the so-called Battle Scroll found in Qumran. Finally, "of all the possible ties between the Book of Mormon and the Old World, by far the most impressive," he writes, "is the exact and full description of the long coronation rite described in the book of Mosiah with the 'standard' Near Eastern coronation ceremonies as they have been worked out through the years by the 'patternists' of Cambridge."[16]

The coronation he refers to occurs at the temple in Zarahemla, when King Benjamin addresses multitudes of people who have gathered together to witness his bestowal of the kingdom on his son, Mosiah. The ceremony includes a number of elements that Nibley finds paralleled in a tenth-century account of the coronation of the Prince of the Captivity (or Exilarch) in Babylon, made by Nathan the Babylonian.[17] According to Nathan, it was customary for all to bring precious gifts to the ceremony (which Benjamin, explicitly contrasting himself to others in that role, expressly forbids). In Babylon, a speaker's tower ten feet high was constructed to make the king viewable by all. Similarly, Benjamin "caused a tower to be erected, that thereby his people might hear the words which he should speak unto them" (Mos. 2:7).

In both cases, a lengthy address is part of the proceedings. The new year's greeting described by Nathan finds echo in Benjamin's casting of the occasion as a day of rebirth and new beginning. In compliance with the festival's main purpose of reaffirming national obedience to the Law, the Exilarch then reads to the people from the Book of the Law. In the case of Benjamin, he likewise reviews the moral code ("that ye should [not] murder, or plunder, or steal, or commit adultery"), exhorts his people to "keep the commandments of my son, or the commandments of God which shall be delivered unto you by him," and reminds them that "there are not any among you, except it be your little children that have not been taught concerning these things" (Mos. 2:13, 32, 34). Additionally, Nathan observed the participants engage in choral responses to the king, just as Benjamin's people "all cried aloud with one voice," reciting more than fifty words collectively at a critical juncture in the ceremony. In sum, Nibley writes, "the knowledge of the Year Drama and the Great Assembly has been brought forth piece by piece in the present generation. One by one the thirty-odd details ... have been brought to light and are now attested in every country of the ancient world. There is no better description of the event in any single ritual text than is found in the Book of Mosiah."[18]

Following Nibley's lead, a number of LDS scholars have further explicated the Mosiah coronation as an ancient Israelite festival. John A. Tvedtnes explored its relationship to the Israelite Feast of Tabernacles.[19] Terrence L. Szink and John W. Welch, for instance, argue that "Benjamin's speech contains numerous elements pertinent to the New Year holy day, the Day of Atonement observances, the Feast of Tabernacles, and the sabbatical or jubilee year. These elements," they conclude, "account for the vast majority of themes or topics found in Benjamin's speech."[20] Stephen D. Ricks finds the treatment of kingship in Mosiah, the coronation ceremony itself, the treaty-covenant pattern evident in this section, and a cluster of concepts common to Israelite religion (rising from the dust, enthronement, kingship, and resurrection) offer further support for placing the episode in the same ritual setting "as the covenant renewal festivals and coronation assemblies in the Old Testament."[21]

Nibley has said of his method that he simply wishes "to give the Book of Mormon the benefit of the doubt."[22] Still, Nibley's legendary erudition, fluency across a spectrum of languages, and prodigious output (appearing in a wide range of scholarly publications from the *Classical Journal* and *Encyclopedia Judaica* to *Church History* and *Revue de Qumran*) have lent his work a weight that is unprecedented in Mormon studies.

Praised by the likes of non-LDS scholars Raphael Patai, Jacob Neusner, James Charlesworth, Cyrus Gordon, Jacob Milgrom, and former Harvard Divinity School dean George MacRae ("it is obscene for a man to know that much," he grumbled, hearing him lecture), Nibley has done more than any Mormon of his era to further the intellectual credibility of the Book of Mormon.[23] Inspired in large measure by his work, a more recent generation of LDS researchers brings a range of impressive scholarly credentials to serious Book of Mormon scholarship.[24]

The Foundation for Ancient Research and Mormon Studies (FARMS)

Attorney and classical scholar John Welch inaugurated a new era in Book of Mormon studies with the incorporation of FARMS—the Foundation for Ancient Research and Mormon Studies—in 1979, the same year that the Smithsonian publicly dismissed claims of their reliance on the Book of Mormon for field work. Unlike the New World Archaeological Foundation (NWAF), Welch's organization never approached the Book of

Mormon as a document of merely potential authenticity. Rather, the foundation unabashedly operates on the assumption that the Book of Mormon presents us with a historical record; at the same time, its members maintain a high standard of scholarly sophistication and a healthy dose of cautiousness. Perhaps learning from the frenzied optimism of Ferguson and others, Welch conveys a more muted approach: "While many current discoveries present sensational opportunities for us, we must be extremely careful not to overstate our position."[25]

The research strategy at FARMS is also a dramatic departure from the archaeological obsessiveness of the NWAF and its predecessors. Though not himself affiliated with FARMS, Hugh Nibley provides a kind of intellectual rationale for its orientation, and his voluminous works became one of FARMS's most ambitious editing projects. Like Nibley, researchers at FARMS have focused on internal evidence in the book, emphasizing Old World parallels rather than New World ruins. Recognition of one such Old World parallel in particular launched Welch's own career as a Book of Mormon scholar and apologist. As a young missionary in Germany in 1967, he attended a lecture at a theological seminary on the subject of chiasmus—a Hebraic literary device also used in Greek and other ancient literary texts, noted in the New Testament by J. A. Bengel in the eighteenth century but not studied with great depth until the twentieth. John Jebb, one of the earliest to investigate the form in the Bible, defined this "introverted parallelism" as follows: "There are stanzas so constructed, that, whatever be the number of lines, the first shall be parallel with the last; the second with the penultimate; and so throughout, in order that looks inward."[26] Sometimes these patterns operate fairly evidently at the sentence level, but they can involve much larger textual structures of great complexity and subtlety. Some days after hearing the German lecture, awakened by the idea that evidence of Hebrew style apparent in the Bible should be apparent in the Book of Mormon as well, Welch searched there for examples. Almost immediately, he found an instance in Mosiah 5:10-12:

> (a) And now . . . whosoever shall not take upon them **the name** of Christ
>   (b) must **be called** by some other name;
>   (c) therefore, he findeth himself on the **left hand of God**.
>   (d) And I would that ye should **remember** also, that this is **the name** . . .
>   (e) that never should be **blotted out**,
>   (f) except it be through **transgress**ion; therefore,
>   (f') take heed that ye do not **transgress,**
>   (e') that the name be not **blotted out** of your hearts . . . .
>   (d') I would that ye should **remember** to retain **the name** . . .
>   (c') that ye are not found on the **left hand of God**,
>   (b') but that ye hear and know the voice by which ye shall **be called**,
> (a') and also, **the name** by which he shall call you.[27]

The experience shaped Welch's view—embraced by his colleagues at FARMS—that "the Book of Mormon should be studied with literary, linguistic, historical, religious, political, military, legal, social, economic, and just basic textual concerns in mind," to find if "aspects of the book reflect ancient culture, language, law and history."[28]

FARMS now serves largely to coordinate and facilitate Book of Mormon scholarship. It is not, in the words of one of its directors, "a monolithic 'think tank.'" They publish a monthly bulletin of updates on Book of Mormon research (*Insights*), a semiannual *Journal of Book of Mormon Studies*, an annual *Review of Books on the Book of Mormon*, and books with titles like *Isaiah in the Book of Mormon*, *Book of Mormon Authorship: The Case for Ancient Origins*, and *Finding Biblical Hebrew and Other Ancient Literary Forms in the Book of Mormon*.

Other publication projects on the Book of Mormon do exist. The Foundation for Research in Ancient America of the Reorganized Church of Jesus Christ of Latter Day Saints (descended from a group of Mormons who rejected Brigham Young's succession to leadership) publishes *The Witness*, and the same church's Zarahemla Foundation publishes *Glyph Notes*. *Qumran Quest* is a newsletter using Dead Sea Scrolls evidence to support the Book of Mormon, and the Ancient America Foundation publishes their own newsletter. The now-defunct *Newsletter and Proceedings of the Society for Early Historic Archaeology* was also dedicated largely to Book of Mormon research. However, it is fair to say that none of these efforts have had the audience, resources, or scope of the Foundation for Ancient Research and Mormon Studies.

John Sorenson and Book of Mormon Geography

For most Latter-day Saints, the point of departure for all historical investigation of the Book of Mormon is the position expressed by Brigham Young University professor of anthropology John Sorenson: "the Book of Mormon account actually did take place *some*where. We who believe the book is authentically ancient are confident that there were indeed real places where real Nephis and Almas did the things the volume says they did." Nevertheless, there is something startling in the leap this distinguished sociocultural anthropologist makes into plausible specificity. The Nephite lands are likely "the territory between Guatemala City and the city of Veracruz, Mexico," he writes. In his works, we see photographs of places like Tehuantepec Pass captioned: "where Nephite and Lamanite armies . . . often marched up and down this defile." And in an oversized coffee-table book with glossy photos inviting us to "visualize Book of Mormon life," we see figurines, architecture, and monuments that he presents in order to construct plausible pictures of actual Book of Mormon civilizations. [29]

As we have seen, Mormons have speculated about Book of Mormon geography from the Palmyra period to the present. At one time or another, proffered candidates for a Nephite homeland have included the North and/or South American continents, Central America on either side of the isthmus, Michigan, and other places. As recently as 1980, skeptics were confident that LDS scholars had learned—or should have learned—reticence and restraint in such efforts. Referring to attempts by LDS scholars to pin down Book of Mormon geography, one writer objects:

> I do not think that this area of history will presently provide any results for two reasons: first, because of lack of material. The Book of Mormon provides us with an approximate idea of the *relative* position of many of its cities, the narrow neck of land, and other geographical landmarks. But no archaeologist has been able to locate a single Nephite text or city. We cannot even locate the approximate areas of the Nephite or Lamanite civilizations. There are at least seven current theories attempting to locate these civilizations in different areas on the American continent. But even a recent church editorial has described these attempts as useless speculation.[30]

Useless or not, speculation has continued and is moving toward a consensus among Mormon scholars. In the early years following publication of the Book of Mormon, proffered theories placed the Nephites and Lamanites over the entire hemisphere, with Panama as the "narrow neck" dividing the dominions into lands northward and southward. The publication of Stephens's *Incidents of Travel* seems to have moved the presumed site of landing from Chile to Central America, but Orson Pratt moved it back to Chile in 1868, and reaffirmed the hemispheric nature of Book of Mormon civilization. By the 1920s, the problems inherent in such a vast model were becoming apparent, but even B. H. Roberts was reluctant to challenge it. Then in 1927, Janne Sjodahl published a series of competing models, one of which (Willard Young's) limited the Nephites and Lamanites to El Salvador, Honduras, Guatemala, and Belize. In the same book, he wrote that "students should be cautioned against the error of supposing that all the American Indians are the descendants of Lehi, Mulek, and their companions," and in 1938 a Church Department of Education study guide for the Book of Mormon told students that "the Book of Mormon deals only with the history and expansion of three small colonies which came to America and it does not deny or disprove the possibility of other immigrations, which probably would be unknown to its writers."[31] Although at the popular level the old model persisted, since the 1960s Mormon scholars have been zeroing in on the lands of Mesoamerica as the stage on which Book of Mormon history unfolded. Sidney Sperry at Brigham Young University, its archaeology department, and various Book of Mormon related societies (the Society for Historic Early Archaeology; the Ancient America Foundation; and the Foundation for Research in Ancient America) all operated on that assumption.[32]

So when, in 1984, Sorenson summarized the results of 45 years of research into Book of Mormon geography and culture in the church's *Ensign*, and then published a full-blown study the next year as *An Ancient American Setting for the Book of Mormon*, he was not introducing a new thesis.[33] Still, his is by far the most thoroughly researched and meticulously argued foray into the field; his book both presents a credible case for a real-world setting and renders moot a great many criticisms of the Book of Mormon's plausibility.[34] This is because he argues for a principal Book of Mormon geography that encompasses an area approximately 500 miles long and perhaps 200 miles wide. (By comparison, he points out, 95 percent of Old Testament events took place in an area even smaller: 150 miles by less than 75.)[35]

Notwithstanding such modest dimensions—not to mention the absence of Book of Mormon pronouncements to the contrary—critics continue to expend immense effort gleefully attacking the red herring of the Book of Mormon as hemispheric history. Brigham D. Madsen, for instance, musters contemporary statements about "present knowledge concerning the origins of native races in the New World," then asks triumphantly, "how LDS church members today reconcile the Book of Mormon narrative of New World settlement" with conventional theories of American Indian ancestry.[36]

So given the persistent misunderstanding—both within and outside the church—of the Book of Mormon's limited claims about Book of Mormon populations and lands, Sorenson may well be correct that "many Latter-day Saints will have to change their thinking markedly to adjust to the dimensions we have discussed."[37] But so will many critics. It will be remembered that some of the serious objections to the Book of Mormon that B. H. Roberts found difficult to counter were also predicated on the assumption that the gold plates chronicled the history of an entire hemisphere.[38] The first, and most troubling problem presented him by the church leadership, was how to explain the immense diversity of Indian languages if all are relatively recent descendents of Lamanite origin. Indeed, church leaders and members alike have always referred to modern Native Americans as "Lamanites," thus perpetuating the assumption that all aboriginal tribes and groups from the Inuit to the Patagonians share a common history and ancestry rooted in the Book of Mormon.

In actual fact, not only does the text of the Book of Mormon not argue exclusive possession of the hemisphere, it intimates the presence of other groups on several occasions.[39] Sorenson convincingly shifts the scene of debate from two entire continents to a couple of valleys and riverbanks, and the Book of Mormon is transformed from a sweeping saga of semiglobal proportions to local or clan history. He thus gives opponents a vastly reduced target to aim at, but one that is very specific:

> The narrow neck of land [a pivotal Book of Mormon feature] is the Isthmus of Tehuantepec. The east sea is the Gulf of Mexico or its component, the Gulf of Campeche. The west sea is the Pacific Ocean to the west of Mexico and Guatemala. The land southward comprises . . . mainly the states of Chiapas and Tabasco, together with highland and coastal Guatemala and possibly part of El Salvador. The land northward consists of part of Mexico west and north of the Isthmus of Tehuantepec. . . . The river Sidon was the Grijalva River. The city of Zarahemla lay on the west bank of this river and could well have been the archaeological site of Santa Rosa. . . . The final battleground where both Jaredite and Nephite peoples met their end was around the Tuxtla Mountains of south-central Veracruz.

These correlations, he insists, are "now known with a high degree of probability." Sorenson does admit that "a few statements in the Book of Mormon cannot yet be squared with what we know today about the

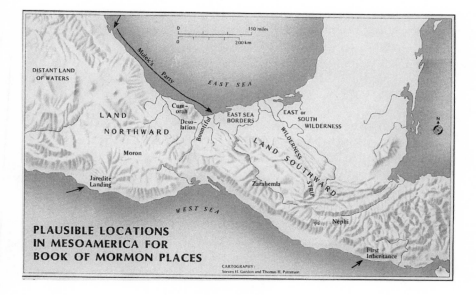

Map of Mesoamerica (southernmost Mexico to Honduras and El Salvador) with superimposed Book of Mormon sites, as proposed by anthropologist John Sorenson. (Cartography: Steven H. Gordon and Thomas H. Patterson; © Foundation for Ancient Research and Mormon Studies)

Mesoamerican area. . . . More research is needed on those points. But none of the problems is, in my view, a serious one."[40]

It may well be that no definite connection between archaeology and Book of Mormon geography or peoples has ever been demonstrated. Book of Mormon archaeology—if there is such a thing—may be no more established today as a legitimate science than it was in 1834 when Joseph identified the remains of Zelph, the white Lamanite. On the other hand, Mesoamerican studies in general are not much farther along today either, at least when it comes to solving the big mysteries. W. Krickeberg's assessment penned in 1966 is essentially unchallenged still:

> Present evidence is *totally inadequate* to explain how these advanced cultures arose. . . . Apparently without *roots*, without any preparation, the earliest American civilizations appear ready on the scene: in Mesoamerica the Olmec, in the Andean lands the Chavin. These remarkable phenomena can perhaps only be explained satisfactorily by assuming one or more drives influencing ancient American from the *outside*. Otherwise it is difficult to understand *how primitive conditions* which varied little during 15,000 to 20,000 years of persistence *could suddenly experience* a violent surge of progress, passing through the whole scale of advancing culture to a full blown civilization. Such a thing is utterly out of the question in the case of the two oldest American civilizations: *All of a sudden they are simply there*" [emphasis his].[41]

The Smithsonian Statement

Three years before the 1985 publication of his study of Book of Mormon geography, Sorenson had entered the Book of Mormon wars with a point by point response to the famous 1979 Smithsonian statement.[42] Whereas the Smithsonian Institute holds that "the physical type of the American Indian is basically Mongoloid," Sorenson cites a number of scholars who posit a biologically heterogeneous group, including the possibility of Near Eastern or Mediterranean components.[43] As for the status of the Bering Strait land bridge theory, Sorenson points to a number of anomalous archaeological sites in Chile, Brazil, and the eastern United States, not to mention the Norse settlement in Greenland, that E. James Dixon uses to illustrate the contention that "various groups of humans could have attempted colonization of the American continents . . . only to subsequently disappear," while "evidence of their passing would be extremely difficult to detect in the archaeological record."[44] Other studies suggest Asian settlement of Washington state and a late Siberian migration to central California.[45]

Similarly, Sorenson faults as outdated the Smithsonian Institute's insistence that the Norse were the first people to make a transoceanic voyage. The annotated bibliography of *Pre-Columbian Contact with the America Across the Oceans*, published in 1990, lists some 5,600 entries on the contested subject. The editors, of which Sorenson is one, conclude that the literature makes it "both plausible and probable that numerous voyages did cross the oceans and in several places."[46]

While conceding that many Old World crops and animals were not present in America before the Spaniards, Sorenson illustrates why lack of diffusion cannot be construed as lack of contact. (The Romans had contact with India, but did not adopt rice as a crop, for example.)

One of the more frequent criticisms of the Book of Mormon, cited by the Smithsonian and addressed by Sorenson, involves the mention of materials in this hemisphere for which there is insufficient evidence: iron, steel, glass, and silk. Resolving these problems, it turns out, may depend more on issues of translation rather than archaeology per se. Translators have long recognized the appropriateness of substituting comparable terms when no lexical counterpart exists for a word. For example, peoples from ancient Greece to ancient Mexico used fibers from wild moths, the pod of the ceiba tree, and silkworms that have no connection to Far Eastern varieties to produce fine fabrics that have been designated "silk" by travelers and chroniclers.[47]

Glass does not actually appear in any New World context in the Book of Mormon, so it is not a valid point of controversy. Steel, on the other hand, is mentioned a smattering of times in the Book of Mormon. The Jaredites fashion swords of steel, Nephi possesses a bow of steel, and he teaches his people to work with steel (as well as copper and brass). On this subject of ancient metallurgy, the Smithsonian Institute has chosen to disregard both linguistic and archaeological evidence that would support the Book of Mormon's plausible use of these terms. First, a standard handbook points out that "steel" in the King James version, which language Joseph seemed to adopt, "should often be read 'bronze' or 'copper.'"[48] But Nephi and Mormon may well have intended something closer to the word's normal meaning. In that case, meteoric nickel-iron, found extensively in Mesoamerica, has been termed a "type of steel"[49] and may well have been the source for Nephite weapons manufacture.

Next, Sorenson notes that the Smithsonian's dismissal of pre-Columbian Egyptian-Mexican contacts is curious in and of itself, since the connection is nowhere claimed in the Book of Mormon. Finally, he turns to the question of Old World writings in the pre-Columbian New World. The Smithsonian asserts that except for Norse runes, "No inscriptions using Old World forms of writing have been shown to have occurred in any part of the Americas before 1492." Quite right, says Sorenson, with a few possible exceptions.[50] But also not surprising, since the Book of Mormon writing system was unique to a small and geographically confined people.

Sorenson's rebuttal included the proposal that the Smithsonian issue a revised statement incorporating the positions and findings he documented. Following receipt of Sorenson's 1995 revision of his paper and follow-up meetings with FARMS officers, the Smithsonian in 1998 began issuing a very different response to queries about the Book of Mormon. The form letter now reads simply, "Your recent inquiry concerning the Smithsonian's alleged use of the Book of Mormon as a scientific guide has been received in the Office of Communications. The Book of Mormon is a religious document and not a scientific guide. The Smithsonian Institution has never used it in archeological research and any information that you may have received to the contrary is incorrect."[51]

Clearly, the Smithsonian is no longer willing to claim discrepancies exist between the Book of Mormon and the current state of American archaeology (though this is in all likelihood a product of controversy-avoidance rather than Sorenson's scholarly suasion). Meanwhile, Nibley, Sorenson, and the researchers at BYU and FARMS continue their work at a blistering pace. A comprehensive review of even the most recent work done on the Book of Mormon would be impossible. *A Comprehensive Annotated Book of Mormon Bibliography* lists over 6,500 entries through 1995.[52] Even discounting the vast numbers of nonacademic essays in church publications, the amount of scholarly research that has emerged in the last few decades especially is considerable. Still, we might take a representative sampling of some of the topics that FARMS researchers and other Mormon scholars have addressed in the ongoing Book of Mormon wars: Book of Mormon language, Biblical plagiarism, population problems, proper names, and anachronisms and general implausibilities.

The State of the Debate

Language and Form

Nephi began his account with an explanation that he was writing "in the language of my father, which consists of the learning of the Jews and the language of the Egyptians" (1 Nephi 1:2). Later, the last chronicler, Moroni, adds his note that "we have written this record according to our knowledge, in the characters which are called among us the reformed Egyptian, being handed down and altered by us, according to our manner of speech" (Morm. 9:32).

Mormon scholars take this to suggest the possibility that the writers used modified Egyptian symbols to represent Hebrew words ("Hebrew words, idioms, and syntax written in Egyptian cursive script"[53]), certainly a bizarre idea for a nineteenth-century audience. Now, as John

Tvedtnes points out, "the use of Egyptian symbols to transliterate Hebrew words and vice versa, is known from sixth century B.C. texts discovered at Arad and Kadesh-Barnea."[54] Papyrus Amherst 63, for example, "contains a scriptural text in a Northwest Semitic tongue written in an Egyptian script."[55]

Physical evidence for the unique script is limited to the purported transcription of characters taken from the plates and shown by Martin Harris in 1828 to Professor Charles Anthon.[56] They consist of seven horizontal rows of unusual markings, that have been variously described as everything from Phoenician writing to Mayan script to occult symbols, from "a Nubian corruption of Egyptian" to secret masonic code.

Though the expression "reformed Egyptian" garnered no small amount of ridicule at the time and since ("deformed English" rather than "reformed Egyptian," sniffed Charles Shook in 1910, after looking at the Anthon Transcript[57]), scholars now generally recognize that "Demotic Egyptian, of origin not long before Lehi's Exodus, is certainly a 'reformed Egyptian,' as are other well-known and less-known variations."[58] Nibley points out that Meroitic, "a baffling and still largely undeciphered Egyptian script which developed out of Demotic under circumstances remarkably paralleling the purported development of the Nephite writing, has the most striking affinities to the characters on the so-called Anthon Transcript."[59] William J. Hamblin notes other examples of "mixing a Semitic language with modified Egyptian hieroglyphic characters," such as the Byblos Syllabic texts of Phoenicia, Cretan hieroglyphics, and Proto-Sinaitic inscriptions of ancient Syria and Palestine.[60]

If the root language of the Book of Mormon is actually Hebrew, then Egyptian script notwithstanding, one would expect it to reflect Hebrew linguistic and literary patterns. As we saw, John Welch discovered the presence of chiastic patterns in the book in the late 1960s.[61] Since then, Welch and others have analyzed numerous instances besides the Mosiah example. In an unusually extended and complex example, Alma recounts his miraculous conversion in a 1,200 word narrative, in the course of which 18 word groups are unfolded, then repeated in 18 mirror images with absolutely perfect symmetry (Alma 36). The fulcrum on which the chiasm rests is the word "atone," nestled between a recollection "of one Jesus Christ, a son of God" and a cry of his heart to "Jesus, thou Son of God." On the fallen side of the chiasm, for example, we find attacks on the church, physical paralysis, fear of God's presence, and the pains of a damned soul. On the redeemed side of the chiasm we have joy "as exceeding as was my pain," longing for God's presence, physical restoration, and missionary labors. Even the syntactical patterns of one side mirror or develop those of the other, as "Do as I have done" of verse 2 becomes "Know as I do know," of verse 30, and "their trials and their troubles and their afflictions" of verse 3 becomes "trials and troubles of every kind, and in all manner of affliction" of verse 27.

Of course, not all the language of the Book of Mormon is elegant or rhetorically polished. The *Baptist Herald*, we noted, objected in 1840 that "the phraseology . . . [of the Book of Mormon] frequently violates every principle and rule of grammar." Mark Twain famously considered the book to be "chloroform in print,"[62] and I. Woodbridge Riley complained at the turn of the century that "barbarisms and solecisms abound, due to what Smith called his 'lack of fluency according to the *literati.*' Over and above these are unique expressions, which well deserve the name of 'Smithisms.'" [63]

Some defenders believe that apparent solecisms are actually evidence of Hebraic backgrounds. For example, one perennial Mormon critic mocks the seeming illogic of Alma 46:19, where in the 1830 edition Moroni is depicted as going "forth among the people, waving the rent of his garment in the air, that all might see the writing which he had written upon the rent." [64] As John Tvedtnes explains,

> the unlikely usage of "rent" in English as a noun no doubt contributed to the fact that, in subsequent editions of the Book of Mormon, it was changed to read "rent part" (Alma 46:19). But the Hebrew would, in this instance, use but one word, *qera'*, "rent (part)," coming from *qara'*, "he rent, tore," for nouns, in Hebrew, are derived from roots—as are Hebrew verbs—by the addition of certain vowel patterns that distinguish them from other parts of speech.[65]

Other examples of Hebraisms that Tvedtnes discusses include the absence of a "Heaven" in the singular (in the Hebrew "samayim" has only a dual form), pronominal suffixes, such as in Jacob 5:2 ("hear the words of me" instead of "my words"), and more than a dozen instances of the "construct state," where two nouns are linked by "of" rather than using one as an adjective. For example, we find "plates of brass" (or "gold"), "rod of iron," "altar of stones," and "words of plainness," but never "brass plates," "iron rod," "stone altar," or "plain words."

Additionally, there are several instances of the "cognate accusative." In English, one would say, "I had a dream"; in Semitic languages, "I dreamed a dream" would be a common construction. We find that particular formulation in the Book of Mormon (1 Nephi 3:2), as well as "cursed with a sore cursing" (Jacob 3:3), "work all manner of fine work" (Mos. 11:10), and "judge righteous judgments" (Mos. 29:43).[66]

Royal Skousen, a Book of Mormon textual scholar, also notes the prevalence of a particular Hebraic "if-and" construction, that sounds oddly ungrammatical when transposed into English where an "if-then" form would be expected. The author of the Book of Helaman uses it seven times in just one single passage:

Yea and if he saith unto the earth, Move, and it is moved; yea, if he saith unto the earth, Thou shalt go back, that it lengthen out the day for many hours, and it is done . . . . And behold, also, if he saith unto the waters of the great deep, Be thou dried up, and it is done. Behold, if he saith unto this mountain, Be thou raised up, and come over and fall upon that city, that it be buried up, and behold it is done . . . and if the Lord shall say, Be thou accursed that no man shall find thee from this time henceforth and forever, and behold, no man getteth it henceforth and forever. And behold, if the Lord shall say unto a man, Because of thine iniquities thou shalt be accursed forever, and it shall be done. And if the Lord shall say, Because of thine iniquities, thou shalt be cut off from my presence, and he will cause that it shall be so. (Hel. p. 440 of 1830 edition)

Skousen notes that this non-English pattern occurs at least 14 times in the original version. [67] Of course, the real question is whether such patterns are *unique* to Hebrew or at least nonexistent in Joseph Smith's other writings. In a seemingly impressive article, skeptic Edward H. Ashment scours Joseph's revelations recorded in the 1833 Book of Commandments for these Hebraic constructions. And indeed, he does find examples of most (the cognate accusative, for instance). But in two cases (extrapositional nouns and pronouns, and naming conventions), he finds none. And twice he claims to find parallels, only to blunder badly. No valid instance of either a pronominal suffix or an "if-and" construction occurs in the other writings of Joseph Smith that Ashment examines.[68] His inability to locate a single comparable instance of those Hebraic forms outside the Book of Mormon becomes, ironically, evidence that strengthens the claims of Skousen and Tvedtnes.

The American Sermon on the Mount and the Isaiah Problem

It was apparent from the first that much in Joseph Smith's golden bible sounded baldly familiar. Early critics like Abner Cole sometimes dismissed the whole Book of Mormon as either simple plagiarism or slightly more elaborate reworking of borrowed biblicisms:

If the critical reader will examine the "Book of Mormon," he will directly perceive, that in many instances, the style of the Bible, from which it is chiefly copied, has been entirely altered for the worse. In many instances it has been copied *upwards*, without reference to chapter or verse, . . . and that the old and new Testament, have been promiscuously intermingled, with the simple alteration of names, &c. with some interpolations, which may easily be discovered, by the want of grammatical arrangement.[69]

A contemporary authority on Christian religion claims that "about 27,000 words of the Book of Mormon were borrowed from [the King

James Bible.]" Philip Barlow argues that even that dramatic estimate is shy by "well over 50 percent,"[70] lending apparent weight to the accusation that "the whole work is a mosaic of Old Testament allusions and New Testament proof-texts."[71]

The borrowing from Isaiah is unashamedly explicit. After Lehi and his party flee Jerusalem, they are commanded to return in order to retrieve "the record of the Jews . . . engraven upon plates of brass" (1 Nephi 3:3) and possessed by one Laban, apparently a Jewish elder of some authority. With considerable difficulty, Nephi and his brothers secure the plates and deliver them to Lehi. After reading the records, he pronounces them to contain "the five books of Moses," "a record of the Jews from the beginning" to the reign of Zedekiah, genealogies, and "many prophecies" of Isaiah and Jeremiah, as well as of nonbiblical prophets Zenock, Neum, and Zenos (1 Nephi 5:11-14, 19:10, 21).

Thereafter, Nephi elects to read to his brethren (and transcribe on his plates) many of the prophecies of Isaiah, for "there are many things which have been spoken by Isaiah which may be likened unto you, because ye are of the house of Israel" (1 Nephi 6:5). Indeed, when Nephi says his "soul delighteth in the words of Isaiah," he means it. Even with the space of his plates limited, and in spite of the "difficulty of engraving," he uses over 40 percent of his allotted room to quote, paraphrase, or explicate the prophet (almost 50 of 117 pages in the 1981 edition).

Given the notorious authorship questions that touch on Isaiah scholarship, Joseph's situating of Isaiah passages in a Jewish canon purporting to date to 600 B.C. would seem to bear telling evidence today of either fraud or inspiration. Isaiah, once taken to be a single historical prophet living and writing in eighth-century Jerusalem, has splintered into two and perhaps three or more authors (shades of Homer!). Consensus in this area has reached the point that the *Oxford Dictionary of the Christian Church* asserts, "critics are now generally agreed that everything after chapter 36, as well as considerable portions of the earlier chapters, have no real claim to be his."[72] Because the Book of Mormon's Isaiah portions—including extensive parts of Isaiah 40-55—allegedly derive from brass plates that predate 600 B.C., they could not have been written by the postexilic "Deutero-Isaiah" of conventional wisdom.

Ironically, those who have historically been most critical of Book of Mormon claims, biblical fundamentalists, cannot use an argument that would undermine their own view of Isaiah's authorship. (This same problem cropped up in 1853, much to the consternation of the author of the first anti-Mormon novel: "The secret enemies of the Christian religion, . . . in assailing [Mormon] claims to working miracles and other professions, . . . leveled many a blow, safely, that bore equally hard upon the miracles of Scriptures."[73]) Looking elsewhere for evidence of fraudulent composition, Stan Larson believes Joseph produced the Isaiah passages by simply reworking those verses with italics in the King James Version.[74] He claims that "about half" of the Isaiah passages are identical to the KJV, and most of the rest differ "at the very point where the KJV has italics."[75] That is not exactly accurate. As Royal Skousen demonstrates, only 29 percent of the 516 changes Joseph incorporated can be correlated with those translator interpolations red-flagged by italics, and of almost 400 Book of Mormon passages marked by italics in the KJV, Joseph only altered 150, or 38 percent. In other words, in most cases he did not dictate changes where italics did occur, and most of the changes he did dictate were to unitalicized passages.

Given the number of ancient Isaiah variants now available, scholars are in a position to compare them to Joseph's revisions in order to debate the authenticity of those changes he made to the KJV. In the most comprehensive study to date, John Tvedtnes compares those variant Isaiah passages in the Book of Mormon to a number of other variants, including versions of the Masoretic text, two Isaiah scrolls from Qumran, and early Aramaic and Syriac translations (Targumim and Peshitta). He finds 89 instances where variants "lend evidence to [the Book of Mormon's] authenticity as a translation from an ancient document, often with indications that it was older than the Hebrew text of Isaiah from which the KJV was derived."[76] On the other hand, in over 40 cases, Book of Mormon variants have no support from the earliest documents available.

One variant reading of Isaiah deserves special notice. In Isaiah 2:16, the prophet writes (in the King James version and all other early English versions save Coverdale's[77]), "And upon all the ships of Tarshish, and upon all pleasant pictures." The Septuagint version of Isaiah reads, "And upon all the ships of the sea, and upon all pleasant pictures." Nephi's version incorporates both: "And upon all the ships of the sea, and upon all the ships of Tarshish, and upon all pleasant pictures" (2 Nephi 12:16). Unless Joseph had access to both versions, which seems unlikely, one reasonable implication of such variations is that the Book of Mormon version predates the other two, each of which dropped a different phrase over time.

But it is the Sermon on the Mount, according to John Welch, that "since the 1830s . . . has been considered by critics to be the Achilles heel of the Book of Mormon."[78] The pivotal episode of the Book of Mormon is the visit of the resurrected Christ at the Temple Bountiful to those who survived the three-day apocalypse at the time of his death.[79] After the land has been wracked with earthquake, fire, and impenetrable darkness, a voice from heaven announces him, and he descends to display the wounds in his side, hands, and feet. He calls and commissions a Nephite Twelve and delivers a sermon very like the famous version recorded in Matthew.

New Testament scholar Krister Stendahl, one of few non-Mormon academics to look closely at LDS scripture, has studied 3 Nephi and concluded that "the Book of Mormon belongs to and shows many of the signs of the Targums and the pseudepigraphic recasting of biblical material."[80] While not discounting its sacred status or origins ("they may be overtly revelatory"), he clearly sees the text as a nineteenth-century expansion and application of ancient material. Specifically, he believes that unlike Matthew's Jesus, a "teacher of righteousness," 3 Nephi's character is a "Johannine Jesus, the revealed revealer who points to himself and to faith in and obedience to him as the message."[81]

Comparing 3 Nephi to the King James text rather than to John, Stan Larson again finds the textual evidence reflects poorly on 3 Nephi's historicity. Focusing on eight passages from Matthew that "a wide range of authorities agree" are inauthentically rendered in the KJV, Larson finds the Book of Mormon mimics the "errors of the KJV" when it should, if inspired, have more in common with "the most original Matthean texts."[82] Defenders claim that the "range of authorities" is actually a narrowly defined interpretive school,[83] and that the "differences are insignificant from the standpoint of translation."[84]

This is not to say there are no variations that, on the other hand, suggest an ancient origin for the temple sermon. John Welch considers the counterpart of Matthew 5:22 deserving of recognition. Matthew's Jesus warns that "whosoever is angry with his brother without a cause shall be in danger of the judgment." Third Nephi's Jesus omits the qualification, "without a cause." So, Welch points out, "do many of the better early manuscripts."[85]

Given the abundance of early manuscripts found since 1830, he concludes, "this high degree of confirmation of the received Greek [texts] speaks generally in favor of the [Book of Mormon's] Sermon at the Temple, for one could not have gambled wisely on such confirmation a century and a half ago, before the earliest Greek New Testament manuscripts had been discovered."[86]

But Welch goes well beyond a defensive posture on the sermon issue, noting the inadequacies of all scholarly efforts to adequately understand the Sermon on the Mount itself (its organization seems unclear and its parts torn out of context to a host of critics). He argues that the venue of the New World sermon—a Temple—provides a basis for a plausible, unifying interpretation of the Sermon as a "temple text," by which he means, "one that contains allusions to the most sacred teachings and ordinances of the plan of salvation, . . . [that] ordain or otherwise convey divine powers through symbolic means, presented together with commandments that are or will be received by sacred oaths that allow the recipient to stand ritually in the presence of God."[87]

Population

When Lehi's group arrives in the New World, they comprise an extended clan of at least two, perhaps three dozen people.[88] Three of them are elderly and at least 14 are couples probably capable of reproduction. Out of this small pool of populators rather large numbers soon emerge. Within a mere 40 years of settlement, the colony has fractured in two, Nephi is offered a kingship, and "wars and contentions" have taken place. Clearly, what the record calls wars and kings might more appropriately be called, from our perspective, feuds and clan leaders. Such problems of terminology do not seriously impugn Book of Mormon historicity. Hard numbers that are more difficult to explain away do not appear until well along in the narrative. Exactly four centuries after settlement, a small colony of Nephites is attacked by Lamanites. Three thousand forty-three Lamanites die in the battle (Mos. 9:18). A hundred years later, 87 B.C., over nineteen thousand Nephites and Lamanites perish in a bloody engagement. And by the end of Nephite history, A.D. 385, almost a quarter million Nephite soldiers perish in the final slaughter of their people.

As long ago as 1887 M. T. Lamb disputed the plausibility of such growth and of the rapid acquisition of all the trappings of civilization (metallurgy, temple construction, large scale husbandry) from such meager resources.[89] Of the first of the above figures in particular, one modern critic, John C. Kunich, writes that "even to produce a total population as large as the fatality figures for this one day [over three thousand] would have required an annual growth rate of 1.2 percent during the preceding four centuries."[90] In the present age, those figures are not hard to achieve. Growth rates in Mesoamerica—presumptive setting for the Book of Mormon—are currently well above 2 percent (they range from 2.4 percent in Mexico to 3.1 percent in Belize, Honduras, and Guatemala).[91] The same critic insists that such a rate—in fact anything above a growth rate of 1.2 percent—"was never achieved on a global basis or in the industrialized regions of the world as a whole until C.E. 1950–60 and was not reached in the developing regions as a whole until the 1930s."[92] But as John Tvedtnes and James Smith point out, statistics for pre-industrial growth rates are notoriously conjectural (though certainly marked by sporadic eruptions), and in any case, it is likely that Book of Mormon populations would include any number of annexed groups as well, throwing all statistical projections into irrelevance.[93]

(On the other hand, it requires neither annexation nor enormous variation from the most conservative figures to accommodate the Book of Mormon numbers. It would only require that the people of the Book of Mormon were as exceptional in their fecundity as the Mormon people today are in their longevity! Compared to American mortality tables as a whole, Mormon rates are eight to eleven years longer.[94]) In the absence of statistical evidence, chroniclers from Nephi to Mormon can only record their own surprised observation that their people "did multiply and prosper exceedingly," that they "did multiply exceedingly fast," or that "they did multiply and spread, . . . insomuch that they began to cover the face of the whole earth" (Mos. 23:20; 4 Nephi 1:10; Hel. 3:8. See also 2 Nephi 5:13; Mos. 9:9; 23:20; Alma 50:18; 62:48; Hel. 6:12; 11:20).

5/6 Hev 44 Bar Kokhba, Roman period, 132–135 c.e. This land deed found near the Dead Sea refers to one "Alma ['lm'] son of Yehudah." Two Nephite prophets in the Book of Mormon bear the same name. (Collection of the Israel Antiquities Authority. Photo © The Israel Museum, Jerusalem)

Book of Mormon Names

We have mentioned Nibley's discussion, seconded by Albright, of Paanchi, Pahoran, and Korihor as Egyptian. Recent work by FARMS researchers has revealed an impressive number of other proper names unknown in the Bible, present in the Book of Mormon, and now attested by ancient Middle Eastern sources. Sariah (S´ryh in Hebrew), for example, appears frequently in the Bible as a male name, transliterated Seraiah (2 Samuel 8:17; 2 Kings 25:23; 1 Chronicles 1:13, 14, 35). Nowhere does it appear, as it does in the Book of Mormon, as a female name (Lehi's wife). But in a series of discoveries commencing at the turn of the twentieth century, the word was found as a woman's name on a fifth-century B.C. papyrus from Elephantine, Egypt, and on a number of seals and bullae (seal-impressions) from the Israel of Lehi's own day.[95]

Drawing upon hundreds of arrowheads, seals, and bullae with Hebrew inscriptions that have come to light since the 1960s, three FARMS researchers have found precedents for another 14 Book of Mormon names not present in the Bible. They are Abish, Aha, Ammonihah, Chemish, Hagoth, Himni, Isabel, Jarom, Josh, Luram, Mathoni, Mathonihah, Muloki, and Sam. As they point out, critics offer competing theories of derivation, but they are hardly compelling. Himni suggested to one writer "radical resemblance . . . to the haunting cadences of that blessed name 'Harmony,'" (where Joseph courted Emma).[96] However, the evidence reveals Himni to be "clearly Hebrew, . . . represented by the unvocalized form, *Hmn* on two Israelite seals," one from Megiddo, ca. eighth-century B.C., and the other from a century later.[97] The same critic suggested that Mathoni and Mathonihah were simply lisped versions of the word "mason." Actually, "the Hebrew name *Mtnyhw* appears on a seventh-century B.C. wine decanter, on six seals, and on seven bullae, most of them from the time of Lehi. The hypocoristic [shortened] *Mtn*, which could be vocalized either Mattan (as in the Bible) or Mathoni (as in the Book of Mormon), is found on Ostracon 1682/2 from Khirbet el-Meshash (second half of the seventh-century B.C), seven seals (most from the seventh-century B.C), and eleven bullae (most from the time of Lehi)."[98]

Anachronisms and Improbabilities

B. H. Roberts had found it difficult to respond to charges of anachronistic appearances in the Book of Mormon of horses, steel, silk, and "cimiter." Other candidates for historical bloopers have included the barley mentioned twice in Mosiah (7:22; 9:9) and twice in Alma (11:7; 11:19), and cement (Hel. 3:7).

We have seen already how John Sorenson addresses metallurgical matters and mentions of steel and silk. In the case of the pre-Columbian horse, there is general agreement among scholars that it didn't exist. Nonetheless, researchers at FARMS have ferreted out bits of scattered evidence and dissenting scholars to challenge that consensus. It is clear, for example, that horses were present in this hemisphere in the late glacial age, and at least three archaeologists believe it possible that pockets of the animal survived until the second, third, or fourth millennium B.C.[99] In a little-publicized 1957 discovery, two lots of Yucatan horse remains were "considered to be pre-Columbian on the basis of depth of burial and degree of mineralization."[100] Other finds in the Maya lowlands and southwest Yucatan have turned up horse remains as well.[101] Nevertheless, the prevalent use of horses by a Mesoamerican culture is still, judged in the light of prevailing opinion and evidence, highly unlikely.

Similarly there is no evidence of the other domesticated animals mentioned in the Book of Mormon—swine, cattle, goats. Here William Hamblin cites historical analogies to argue that the level of evidentiary expectation is unrealistic: Norse scholars, he writes, "know that the Norsemen probably introduced the horse, cow, sheep, goats, and pig into North America in the eleventh century. Nonetheless, these animals did not spread throughout the continent and have left no archaeological remains."[102] Perhaps more dramatically, "not a single usable horse bone has been found in the territory of the whole empire of the Huns," probably the most horse-dependent people in history.[103]

Flora of the Book of Mormon presents another challenge to believers. "Barley never grew in the New World before the white man brought it here!" proclaims one vocal critic of Book of Mormon botany.[104] It wasn't until 1983 that *Science* reported the discovery in Arizona of pre-Columbian domesticated barley, and several varieties of wild barley have long been recognized as indigenous to the Americas.[105] And Jared Diamond has recently referred to "little barley" as a staple in the diet of eastern Native Americans in the period 500–200 B.C.[106] Cement is another apparent anachronism that is now commonly known to have been pervasively used throughout the Valley of Mexico and in the Maya regions of southern Mexico, Guatemala, and Honduras.[107]

Summary

After the initial exuberance in the wake of Priest and Stephens, developments in professional archaeology outstripped Mormon efforts to muster the resources of science to Book of Mormon apologetics. At the turn of the century, writes one observer, "advances in knowledge tended to make traditional Mormon beliefs about the pre-Columbian history of all the Americas more and more difficult to sustain." A hundred years later, writes that same author, Mormon scholars "rightly claim a growing sophistication and plausibility for their interpretations."[108] While Book of Mormon historicity may be no less controversial now than it was before, the scholars at FARMS and Brigham Young University have at least raised the level of debate on the subject by professionalizing Mormon apologetics at the same time they have relieved the church's university of the academically problematic burden of Book of Mormon archaeology.

The organization that began as a modest reprint service and informal network for a few scattered LDS scholars working on Book of Mormon subjects has burgeoned into a well-funded organization with substantial resources, dozens of employees (many working on projects involving ancient texts other than the Book of Mormon), a budget of three million dollars, publications that number in the hundreds, and a subscriber list of 20,000. In the 1990s, the organization added staff, Nibley fellowships, and an array of projects. It seems fair to say that FARMS has been a major force in contributing to a realignment of the Book of Mormon's status among evangelical critics, in the international community of scholars, and, perhaps most belatedly, within the LDS church itself.

The Evangelical Response

Only in blithe disregard for the actual particulars of the Book of Mormon, its epic sweep, its narrative complexities, its etymological richness and substantial echoes of Middle Eastern literary structures and patterns were the simplistic and dismissive nineteenth-century counter-theories of origin possible. The ongoing search for cultural parallels between Book of Mormon snippets and everything from horribly written nineteenth-century novels to hermetic texts seems to have exasperated some. Historian Richard Bushman noted in 1984 that

> By any standard the Book of Mormon is a narrative of unusual complexity. . . . The origin of the Indians, the similarities of Masonry to Book of Mormon robber bands, and the apparent Republican tone in certain spots [and, we might add, elements of folk magic, hermeticism, etc.], have been noted as connecting with America in 1830, but the whole Book of Mormon, with its multiplicity of stories and characters, its sketches of an ancient civilization, its involved conception of history, and its unrelenting religious message, has eluded analysis.[109]

Under the burden of Mormon scholarship that is increasingly well credentialed, and in the face of Mormon growth that is alarming to evangelicals,[110] the polemics of nineteenth-century preachers are no longer an adequate response. Until recently, for example, criticisms of barley or pre-Columbian horses in the Book of Mormon would come from writers of anti-Mormon books—not from botanists or archaeologists. The latter have not, for the most part, taken the Book of Mormon seriously enough as a text to analyze its historical credibility. A recent paper by two evangelical scholars suggests that a realignment of the Book of Mormon wars may be coming.

The 1997 address of Carl Mosser and Paul Owen at a regional meeting of the Evangelical Theological Society was remarkable for a number of reasons. First, it accorded high praise to the state of Mormon scholarship. They summarized a number of recent publications to illustrate their assertion that "in recent years the sophistication and erudition of LDS apologetics has risen considerably . . . [and] is clearly seen in their approach to the Book of Mormon." As difficult as it may be to accept the fact, "LDS academicians are producing serious research which desperately needs to be critically examined," they insisted.[111]

In addition, Mosser and Owen are adamant that evangelical responses to Mormon scholarship have been, almost universally, "uninformed, misleading or otherwise inadequate. . . . At the academic level evangelicals are losing the debate."[112] Actually, it hardly resembles a debate, because Mormon scholars, they acknowledge, "have . . . answered most of the usual evangelical criticisms." And, as of 1997, there were "no books from an evangelical perspective that responsibly interact with contemporary LDS scholarly and apologetic writings."[113]

As a consequence, anti-Mormons continue to invoke long-discredited banalities, many of which actually turn to Mormon advantage upon inspection. For example, literature found in any cult section of Christian bookstores still criticizes Alma for writing that Jesus will be "born at Jerusalem, which is the land of our forefathers" (Alma 7:10) a seeming blooper. Actually, of course, such usage is consistent with Middle Eastern practice of naming areas for their principal cities.[114] Or they mock Alma's name itself, an apparent Latin feminine. But in 1960–61, the Israeli scholar Yigael Yadin found a land deed near the western shore of the Dead Sea dating from the early second century. One of the names on the deed was "Alma, son of Yehudah," demonstrating Alma to be "an authentically ancient Semitic masculine personal name."[115]

Whether evangelicals will find the will or the means to engage in scholarly refutation of Nibley, Sorenson, and the scholars of FARMS remains to be seen. For the present, backlists at Christian publishing houses still read much as they did in the 1830s. The major force in anti-Mormon polemics has long been Jerald and Sandra Tanner. But even their recent attempts to embrace statistical methods in attacking the Book of Mormon are more embarrassing than convincing. In the first half of a 164-page exposé, the authors, relying upon a computerized concordance to the LDS scriptures, for the most part simply compare appearances of words, terms, or concepts, in the Bible and the Book of Mormon. When women's names, Passover references, or "discussion of death" appear abundantly in the one but not the other, they claim fraud: "When we searched for the words *castle, castles, prince, prince's, princes, princess, princesses, scepter, scepters, sceptre* and *sceptres,* we found they were used 411 times in the Bible. The Book of Mormon yielded only 7 cases." Exactly why the numbers should be commensurate is not clear, other than alleged Jewish authorship of both. In the second half of their book, rather inconsistently, *duplication* of concepts or wording leads them to insist that the early part of the Book of Mormon plagiarized 41 percent of its material from the Bible.[116] It is no wonder that non-Mormon historian Lawrence Foster has faulted these critics, the most prolific of all anti-Mormon writers, for "twisting" scholarship, resorting to "debaters' ploys," and, in general, demonstrating "lack of balance and perspective."[117] In spite of twentieth-century-sounding titles like *Covering Up the Black Hole in the Book of Mormon,* such works merely evoke the spirit of nineteenth-century diatribes.

The Scholarly Response

"Since the odd contents of the volume lamentably or ludicrously fall before every canon of historical criticism," wrote Walter Prince in 1917, "scholars have not thought it worth while to discuss the notion of [the Book of Mormon's] ancient authorship."[118] Almost a century later, non-

Mormon scholars are little more willing to consider the Book of Mormon as history. Such outside attention as is paid, as evangelicals Mosser and Owen concede, is mostly from professional anti-Mormons and does not rise to the level of scholarship. This is not to say that Book of Mormon scholarship itself does not continue to have more credible detractors, arising largely from within the church. After the evangelicals, those who exhibit the greatest interest in diminishing the status of the Book of Mormon as either ancient document or inspired revelation are those who profess cultural affinity for Mormonism but decry its supernaturalism. Sterling McMurrin, the John Shelby Spong of Mormonism, was a distinguished philosopher embarrassed by the whole angelic entourage of Joseph Smith; he complained that the 1992 *Encyclopedia of Mormonism* "is saturated with references to the Book of Mormon."[119] Indeed, the 200-plus articles in the encyclopedia suggest a centrality of the work that shows no sign of diminishing. McMurrin was understood by some to suggest that this irrepressible scandal of Mormonism might at least be rendered more innocuous by turning it into "a quaint example of rustic, nineteenth-century imaginative magic and myth."[120] That seems to be the point of the impressive array of criticism by a group of scholars claiming some current or prior affiliation to the church, but who dismiss the book's alleged historicity.[121] The best example of this effort, *New Approaches to the Book of Mormon: Explantaions in Critical Methodology* edited by Brent Metcalfe, has been rightly called "the most sophisticated attack on the truth of the Book of Mormon currently available either from standard sectarian or more secularized anti-Mormon sources, or from the fringes of Mormon culture and intellectual life."[122]

As for non-Mormon scholars, they still have little to say on the subject of the Book of Mormon or its people. Owen and Mosser rightly point out that it is up to Mormon scholars to initiate the debate. "The defender of the Latter-day Saint scriptures," they write, "must first offer evidence for historical veracity both of the contents and the production of the works. . . . Objections to the works must then be considered."[123] The question is, at what point does the work of FARMS and kindred research attain a critical mass in volume and quality sufficient to force a serious engagement on the part of academics? Ferguson's work, though flawed and now superseded by more rigorously trained archaeologists, at least aroused significant interest with the public and some scholars outside the mainstream, as we have seen. Robert Wauchope, former president of the Society for American Archaeology, in a 1962 study of offbeat theories about the peopling of America devoted a whole chapter to the Book of Mormon. He mentioned Ferguson's most popular book, *One Fold One Shepherd* (1958), without criticism, and called its author "conscientious and devoted." Still, the chapter is sandwiched between one on Atlantis and another on "Dr. Phuddy Duddy and the Crackpots," making his bottom-line assessment clear.[124]

"Jaredites," "Lamanites," and "Nephites" are actual entries in a reference work subtitled *An Encyclopedia of Visitors, Explorers, and Immigrants*. But the primary title happens to be *Legends and Lore of the Americas Before 1492*.[125] General attitudes may be further reflected in the title of a book that includes a section on Joseph Smith's gold plates: *Fantastic Archaeology: The Wild Side of North American Prehistory* by Stephen Williams. In his long litany of remarkable frauds, he marvels that even today there are "new translations of old hoaxes or new excavations in Middle America for the Mormon cause."[126] Of course, his archaeological cynicism is a response to the Book of Mormon story, not Book of Mormon scholarship of which he never takes note. Robert Wauchope, who appears not to have read the Book of Mormon himself, similarly situates the Book of Mormon alongside Atlantis legends and comparable mythic fare in his *Lost Tribes and Sunken Continents*.[127]

Only a few non-Mormon archaeologists have engaged the actual subject of the Book of Mormon and archaeology. Three of those—Michael Coe, Nigel Davies, and John A. Price—do not consider the Mormon case convincing, to put it mildly. Yale archaeologist Michael Coe does not address the latest or the best scholarship the Mormons have to offer in his blistering attacks. Though he was writing in the early seventies before FARMS existed, even then it was flatly inaccurate to claim, for example, that "Mormon archaeologists over the years have almost unanimously accepted . . . the Kinderhook Plates as a bona fide archaeological discovery."[128] By citing anecdotal stories about the claims of LDS tour guides and claims of archaeological amateurs, he has erected something of a straw man. (Perhaps this is not surprising in a critic who compares church leaders to Soviet totalitarians, and finds little difference "between the old Red Square and Temple Square."[129]) LDS scholars themselves have attacked the same shoddy scholarship that makes Book of Mormon archaeology a playground for hobbyists. John Sorenson laments the premature rush to judgment characteristic of the genre, and what he calls "naive use of sources, logical inconsistencies, cut-and-paste quotations."[130] LDS librarian and art historian Martin H. Raish has also exposed several examples of misleading, unprofessional, and inaccurate attempts to vindicate Book of Mormon historicity.[131]

When appraising Mormon scholarship disconnected from apologetics, even Michael Coe has high praise. He calls the NWAF's program "an unqualified success" that "established one of the longest and best archaeological sequences for any part of the New World." Their archaeologists were "first class." He even approves their study of Stela 5 at Izapa in Chiapas, Mexico, complete with scholarly suggestions of Mesopotamian influence and Old World origin. But when it is read as "a record of the vision or dream of Lehi about the Tree of Life" more particularly, he is scornful. He may be right that "nothing, absolutely nothing, has ever shown up in any New World excavation which would suggest to a dispassionate observer that the Book of Mormon, as claimed by Joseph Smith, is a historical document relating to the history of early migrants to our hemisphere." But his real protest against Book of Mormon archaeology, in the final analysis, is about premises and objectives rather than method and interpretation, as is evident in his concluding comparison: "there is no more chance of finding [the lands of Zarahemla and Bountiful] than of discovering the ruins of the bottomless pit described in the book of Revelations [sic]."[132] (The subsequent discovery in modern day Yemen of altars inscribed with the name Nahom, already referred to, would seem to challenge that optimistic and categorical assessment. Though they are Old World artifacts, they do represent the first confirmation of a Book of Mormon site and place-name lost to the modern age.)

The anthropologist Nigel Davies is another scholar who takes the Book of Mormon semiseriously as an alternative theory of American peopling in his overview of *Voyagers to the New World*.[133] Like Coe, he praises the work of the NWAF for its "valuable contributions to science," but also like Coe, he relies entirely upon one writer—Thomas Ferguson—for his appraisal of scientific claims for the Book of Mormon's relevance to the debate. Assessing only Ferguson's claims that some Hebrew terms are connected to the Mexican Nahuatl language ("word-list games," he scoffs) and that the seventeenth-century Mexican writer Alva Ixtlilxóchitl validates Book of Mormon claims of early Christian elements in Mesoamerica (he is a "Christianized" source, like the author of the *Popul Vuh*), it is easy for him to conclude that Ferguson is "one of the less convincing writers seeking connections between the Old World and the New." [134]

Finally, John A. Price weighs into the debate as an anthropologist examining "the conflicts between [the Book of Mormon] and an anthropological prehistory of the American Indian."[135] His brief paper largely anticipates the objections summarized in the Smithsonian statement. He lists those elements of material culture mentioned in the Book of Mormon—grain, oxen, horses, asses, barges, silk and linen, tools, swords, and metal plates—and sets in opposition a summary of anthropological prehistory: "The aboriginal New World did not have wheat, barley, cows, oxen," etc. Thomas Ferguson, disillusioned after 25 years of inconclusive digging, came to agree that the absence of metals, plant-life and animal-life remains described by the Book of Mormon outweighed even the 300 parallels he had found in the areas he surveyed.[136]

In the face of the obvious lack of corroborative material remains, John Sorenson has cited the example of a Native American culture he finds instructive: "Dr. Julian Steward could only see some 61 items in Paiute archaeological material to represent the 2,500 elements known from live ethnographic descriptions to have been included in [their] cultural inventory."[137] LDS scholars frequently point out as well that the pervasive historical practice of naming unfamiliar species after familiar ones (as with the Greek "river horse" for hippo or the Roman "Lucanian cow" for elephant) effectively throws all criticisms based on the absence of specific flora or fauna into linguistic limbo. And besides, since particular Book of Mormon locations have been posited but not definitively identified, any quest for cultural correlations with specific regions, as Ferguson sought, is itself predicated on highly speculative premises. The lack of geographical certainty is not to be wondered at, writes Hamblin, when only 36 of the 475 Biblical place-names have been identified.[138]

But it isn't just absence of evidence in particular areas that scholars like Price criticize. Cultural institutions such as a seven-day week, gold and silver coinage,[139] and written laws, he believes, are not consistent with anything known of ancient America. Finally, he argues that "there are simply no gaps in the record of archaeological surveys and excavations large enough to admit of the possible existence of Near Eastern style societies anywhere in the New World," and claims of "Near Eastern style wars" fought in upstate New York are, he writes, "simply ridiculous."[140] (It is not clear if Near Eastern style wars fought in Mesoamerica, where most LDS scholars place the final conflict, would be equally ridiculous in his opinion.)

Those few scholars who have spoken more favorably of the Book of Mormon's historical possibilities are not in the mainstream of their disciplines. Even Alfred Kidder and Gordon Ekholm were going against the tide not just for supporting a foundation that considered the Book of Mormon account of Mesoamerican settlement a plausible hypothesis, but for giving any consideration to Old World connections.[141] Cyrus H. Gordon, renowned specialist in Semitic languages and civilizations of the Near East but suspect among colleagues for his diffusionist beliefs[142] (the position that peoples of varied origins arriving via diverse routes settled the Western Hemisphere), called obsession with the Bering Strait model to the exclusion of all others an "intellectual tyranny," and insisted in 1975 that "the climate of opinion is changing thanks to independent spirits."[143] One of those spirits he endorsed was Alexander von Wuthenau, who relied upon pre-Columbian art to establish what appears to be obvious, radical racial differentiation among early American figurines and sculpture. In the context of over a hundred such examples, he wrote that the Book of Mormon "might explain another injection of . . . Semitic elements in the Proto-Mayan era of Mesoamerica."[144]

This formulation actually suggests precisely why the Book of Mormon may never be taken seriously by the larger academic community of anthropologists at least. Even if it could accept angels and seer stones, as we saw with the Smithsonian Institute statement it will reject a priori any text that proffers a theory of transoceanic contact with the Americas long before Columbus (whether Semitic injections or other kinds). The weight brought to bear to crush such unconventional thinking is immense—literally, in the case of 500 tons of rock dumped by the Army Corps of Engineers on the Washington State site of Kenniwick Man in 1998. The 9,300-year-old skeleton appears to be most closely linked not to Native American origins but to groups from southern and eastern Asia known as the Ainu. The corps, apparently acting under a politically motivated directive of the Clinton administration, admitted the earthmoving was meant to ensure "the protection of any additional skeletal or cultural artifacts from further revelation." In a similar case of politics trumping science, a Canadian anthropologist insisted public schools be censored from teaching of possible pre-Columbian contacts since the very idea would be a "dangerous" challenge to "Native identity." These paternalistic precautions seem consistent with safeguarding what one Native American activist and scholar, Vine Deloria, Jr., condemns as "a fictional doctrine that places American Indians outside the realm of planetary human experience."[145]

That the golden plates of Moroni have disappeared makes them only slightly easier to dismiss than the occasional archaeological finds that perplex the academic community, riveted as it is to the doctrine that all pre-Columbian cultures in the Western Hemisphere ultimately are traceable to Siberian origins. Phoenician-era script appearing on a stone found at Grave Creek, West Virginia, in the 1830s has found few defenders since 1894, but Cyrus Gordon refers to the Bat Creek Stone, found in Tennessee, as "the first scientifically authenticated pre-Columbian text in an Old World script or language found in America; and, at that, in a flawless archaeological context." In his opinion, the stone "proves that some Old World people not only could, but actually did, cross the Atlantic to America before the Vikings and Columbus."[146] Still, though some influential archaeologists like David Kelley are unwilling to dismiss all diffusionist arguments out of hand, even he acknowledges that the challenge facing their advocates, like those of the Book of Mormon, is to get a fair hearing. "The problem I see," Kelley says, citing Barry Fell, the distinguished but reviled Harvard diffusionist as an example, "is that the people who can evaluate him accurately are the people who are least likely to be reading him. It needs somebody with . . . a willingness to look at some quite unlikely-seeming material."[147]

So while FARMS scholars continue to focus primarily on evidence that links the Book of Mormon to Near Eastern traditions, critics generally dismiss the diffusionist premise on which the Book of Mormon stands, only occasionally pausing to criticize the lack of evidence supporting the material culture described as well as its incongruity with a New World setting. The double burden of prevailing paradigms in anthropology and the Book of Mormon's insistent claims to supernatural

provenance do not bode well for any change soon in the general scholarly neglect so lamented by C. Wilfred Griggs: "Since nobody could fea-
sibly invent a work the length of the Book of Mormon which represented
ancient Near Eastern society accurately, subjecting the book to the test
of historical integrity would be a rather easy task for any specialist to
undertake."[148] Hugh Nibley parodies the scholarly reluctance of doubters to do so with a parable in which geologists debate the authenticity
of an alleged diamond found by a ploughboy while refusing to simply
examine the diamond.[149] At the same time, he remains highly skeptical
that outside evidence brought to bear by the discipline of archaeology—
the "science of surprises," he calls it—will be of much use in the debate,
at least on the Mormon side. This is not always a welcome opinion in
the Mormon community. In an article the church magazine declined to
publish, he insisted that "as the tub without Diogenes has nothing to do
with philosophy, so archaeology without the prophets has nothing to
do with religion." But what about at least establishing the facticity of an
entire people's existence, like the Nephites or Jaredites? Here he reminded his Mormon audience of an instructive parallel: As a result of
archaeological discoveries, "the Hittites, believed to be a myth by Bible
scholars until 1926, suddenly emerged as one of the greatest civilizations the world has ever seen."[150] (Yet even now, writes another historian, "archaeological evidence cannot be fully reconciled with Hittite
textual data."[151]) The moral, as Nibley wrote the skittish editor, is that
the two-edged sword of science in the service of religion often cuts the
wrong way. Although eventual vindication might be forthcoming, "the
indisputable fact [is] that archaeology has been used and is being used"
more effectively as a tool of the skeptics than the faithful.[152]

When exceptions to the general rule of scholarly neglect do occur, it
is not because Mormon archaeologists—or other scholars—have persuaded colleagues to use the Book of Mormon as a Michelin guide to
pre-Columbian America. In the case of former dean of Harvard Divinity School Krister Stendahl, it is, ironically, something quite different
from the book's historical appeal that he notes:

> It struck me how cavalier we biblical scholars have been in our attitude to
> the biblical "after-history." Every scrap of evidence for elucidating the
> origins of Christianity and its first formative periods receives minute at-
> tention and is treated with great seriousness, however marginal. But . . .
> the laws of creative interpretation by which we analyze material from the
> first and second Christian centuries operate and are significantly eluci-
> dated by works like the Book of Mormon or by other writings of revela-
> tory character.[153]

If Mormon scholars are to be successful in attracting more attention
to their scripture, in other words, it may come as the book is studied as

a sacred text in the context of ancient texts, rather than as an ancient document in the context of Mesoamerican civilization. And certainly the work of LDS scholars in ancient studies has become more conspicuous by its excellence. Mosser and Owen are not the only observers to take note. In 1991, Emanuel Tov, a scholar at Hebrew University, was assigned by the Israeli government to head a project to expedite publication of the Dead Sea Scrolls, at the same time that Weston Fields founded the Dead Sea Scrolls Foundation (DSSF) to raise money for preservation and publication efforts. Soon, an LDS member of the DSSF's advisory board contacted FARMS about possible participation in a project to prepare an electronic library of the Dead Sea Scrolls, and a proposal was prepared in collaboration with Brigham Young University. Initially skeptical, Tov and Fields soon agreed that the FARMS proposal was the most promising of a number they were considering and work began. Over the next few years, the FARMS project would contribute to Provo becoming—"along with Jerusalem itself and the University of Notre Dame—one of the three most active centers for scroll research in the world."[154] As Mosser and Owen note with concern, "at least four Latter-day Saints are on the International Dead Sea Scrolls Editing Team. . . . Latter-day Saint Scrolls research is readily accepted by the larger academic community, and Mormons are increasingly asked to collaborate on, contribute to, or edit books with non-LDS scholars."[155]

At first glance, a project on the Dead Sea Scrolls would appear unrelated to Book of Mormon studies. However, the connection is an implicit part of the lesson Mormons take from the Book of Mormon itself: "For behold, I shall speak unto the Jews and they shall write it; and I shall also speak unto the Nephites and they shall write it; and I shall also speak unto the other tribes of the house of Israel, which I have led away, and they shall write it; and I shall also speak unto all nations of the earth and they shall write it" (2 Nephi 21:12).

In other words, as Daniel Peterson writes,

> Isaiah prophesied of a people who would "be brought down," who would "speak out of the ground," whose "speech shall be low out of the dust," a "whisper out of the dust" (Isaiah 29:4). We generally take this to refer to the coming forth of the Book of Mormon. But the recovery of the Book of Mormon actually unleashed a spectacular flow of ancient documents that have literally begun to be restored to us from "the ground" and "out of the dust." The Dead Sea Scrolls and the Coptic Gnostic library at Nag Hammadi, in Egypt, are probably the most famous of these, but the list is considerably more extensive.[156]

Indeed, the success of the FARMS Dead Sea Scrolls project led FARMS to establish the Center for the Preservation of Ancient Religious Texts, or CPART. Several CPART projects are in various stages of planning or discussion, including electronic libraries of Coptic, Syriac, Arabic, Armenian, and Greek collections.

In this development we can perceive continuity as well as dramatic development. Book of Mormon believers who once touted their volume as "a history of American aborigines" now contextualize it as an ancient document on a par with an array of manuscripts emerging from a span of Middle Eastern venues. Its antiquity and historicity are taken as seriously as ever. But situating its study amidst highly respected document preservation efforts involving international scholars and libraries of the stature of Nag Hammadi and the Dead Sea Scrolls, may elicit unanticipated perspectives on its meaning and significance. At the same time, the inspired value of many of those nonscriptural texts remains a distinct possibility as well. As Truman Madsen has written, "the declaration [by Joseph Smith] that 'there are many things contained [in the Apocrypha] which are true and it is mostly translated correctly' has sometimes been extended by Mormons to apply to other extra-canonical materials. With the Dead Sea Scrolls came the discovery that *many biblical books* have earlier Hebrew and Aramaic texts. . . . They are sympathetic to the view that many extra-canonical writings may reflect inspired source materials."[157]

The LDS Response

When the Talmage committee removed archaeological footnotes from the Pratt edition of the Book of Mormon in 1920, and when B. H. Roberts informed church headquarters the next year that objections to Book of Mormon historicity required further study, the church assumed a position of studied caution with regard to Book of Mormon scholarship that even the enthusiasm of a Thomas Ferguson could not diminish. By 1984, however, pressure again was building to establish a more vigorous Book of Mormon apologetics. The impending publication of a Sterling McMurrin-Brigham Madsen edition of B. H. Roberts's study of the Ethan Smith parallels was apparently perceived by some in the church leadership—and rightly so—as the first salvo in a new wave of attacks upon the Book of Mormon's historicity. That fall, the church responded with two articles in the *Ensign*, in which the limited geography model first appeared in a church-sponsored publication, under the title "Digging into the Book of Mormon: Our Changing Understanding of Ancient America and its Scripture."[158] By this embrace of recent Book of Mormon scholarship, the church preempted many of the objections to the scripture unsuccessfully addressed by Roberts and about to be newly publicized. The church then published the next year, jointly with FARMS, an extended treatment of the geography question authored by John Sorenson (*An Ancient American Setting*).

The professionalism and focus brought to bear on Book of Mormon scholarship by the many scholars of FARMS contributed to a further dramatic shift in 1997. In November of that year, Brigham Young University, with the approval of church leadership, officially invited FARMS to become part of the university. Church president Gordon B. Hinckley, in giving the announcement his blessing, specifically noted the group's professionalism and credibility both inside and outside the LDS community.[159] With this gesture, the LDS church, indirectly albeit officially, gave its stamp of approval to rationalistic, scientific endeavors to strengthen faith in the Book of Mormon through scholarship. But the foundation's recently acquired church affiliation (Brigham Young University is church-owned) may make it harder, not easier, for FARMS to reach a larger non-Mormon audience with a credible voice.

Casting sacred text as secular history, object of faith as object of scholarly investigation, has both advantages and dangers. On the positive side, missionaries immediately broadened the appeal of the book by emphasizing its historical content. As Richard Bushman reminds us, "faith as well as doubt had embraced the Enlightenment by the beginning of the nineteenth century. Christianity claimed to be as reasonable by Enlightenment standards as science or philosophy."[160] So representing a scriptural record as making verifiable claims was clearly playing by the new rules. And indeed, almost from the first, Joseph Smith pointed to contemporary physical evidence to substantiate the credibility of the Book of Mormon. The formations of the Midwestern mound builders that he pointed out to his contemporaries have their modern counterpart in modern editions of the Book of Mormon that include glossy photographs of Mesoamerican ruins and Middle Eastern metal plates.

On the other hand, any effort to subject religious texts to scientific methods or to subsume them within academic disciplines runs some risks as well. First, it remains to be seen what effect an increasing emphasis on historical substantiation of the Book of Mormon will have on the spiritual bases of Mormonism itself. The church has long negotiated a balance between faith and scholarship. Joseph Smith founded a university in the frontier city of Nauvoo at great sacrifice and effort, and today the church subsidizes the largest private university in America. At the same time, more than a few Mormon intellectuals have recurrently felt ostracized and under siege—within their church by cautious leadership and without by sometimes irrational institutional resistance. In the former case, as Mormon gadfly Sterling McMurrin writes, "Mormonism has suffered and continues to experience incursions of anti-intellectualism, but the achievement of knowledge has always been a prominent Mormon ideal; and at least for the past century most Mormons have had a healthy respect for the virtues of reason."[161] Reflecting the latter, one researcher was told it was "easier to get funding to study voodoo snake cults in Latin America than to get money to study the fastest growing religious bodies there." And commenting on the neglect of Mormon studies by his colleagues, sociologist Rodney Stark has lamented "the persistence of considerable prejudice against Mormons and the seeming inability of the mass media to cover adequately much of anything that happens West of Chicago."[162] How continuing developments in Mormon scholarship on their history and their scriptures will affect these forms of resistance is hard to predict.

Second, if a sacred text presents itself as provable, it is by definition disprovable as well. As we have seen, the tendency to treat the work as an empty signifier, to give pride of place to the circumstances rather than the content of the Book of Mormon has long been characteristic of Book of Mormon believers. It is probably safe to say that, by and large, holding the Book of Mormon up to the light of scientific scrutiny has until now been more of a burden than an asset in the continuing effort to convert the public. Nevertheless, writes Sorenson, given the claims made for the Book of Mormon by Mormons from Joseph Smith to the present, comparisons between the LDS scriptural record and the archaeological record are inevitable. "Mormons may play the ostrich or they may excel."[163]

So the church maintains its position of cautious support, recognizing that the discovery of corroborative evidence may be no less problematic than the failure to build a convincing scholarly case. As the First Presidency wrote to Ferguson in denying his initial 1952 request for funding: "The brethren feel that careful exploratory work may very well develop faith-promoting corroborative evidence of the historical value of the Book of Mormon. The Brethren feel that it may be that no discovery will be made which shall establish the historical value of the Book of Mormon. They incline to feel that the faith now required to accept the book is a very considerable factor in the faith of the Restored Gospel, belief in which is the result of faith therein."[164]

SIX

"Devices of the Devil": The Book of Mormon as Cultural Product or Sacred Fiction

When you get at the hard core of the situation, the Book of Mormon as an objective fact, there isn't any middle ground; it becomes as simple a matter as the Mormons and anti-Mormons originally said it was. Either Joseph was all he claimed to be, or during the period at least of the writing of the Book of Mormon he was a "conscious fraud and imposter."

—Dale Morgan to Juanita Brooks

"It's what I call common sense, properly understood," replied Father Brown. "It really is more natural to believe a preternatural story, that deals with things we don't understand, than a natural story that contradicts things we do understand. Tell me that the great Mr. Gladstone, in his last hours, was haunted by the ghost of Parnell, and I will be agnostic about it. But tell me that Mr. Gladstone, when first presented to Queen Victoria, wore his hat in her drawing-room and slapped her on the back and offered her a cigar, and I am not agnostic at all. That is not impossible; it's only incredible."

—G.K. Chesterton

The conundrum of the Book of Mormon is that, on the one hand, as Mormons readily admit, not one single archaeological artifact has been found that conclusively establishes a direct connection between the record and any actual culture or civilization of the Western Hemisphere. On the other hand, as a researcher from FARMS, the organization praised by Carl Mosser and Paul Owen, points out, "there is mounting up a considerable body of analysis demonstrating that at least something of the strangeness of the Book of Mormon is due to the presence in it of other ancient and complex literary forms which Joseph Smith is highly unlikely to have discovered on his own, and showing as well that its contents are rich and subtle beyond the suspicions of even the vast majority of its most devout readers."[1] Or as one determined skeptic admits, it is hard to ignore the "striking coincidences between elements in the Book of Mormon and the ancient world and some notable matters of Book of Mormon style."[2] The naked implausibility of gold plates, seer stones, and warrior-angels finds little by way of scientific corroboration, but attributing to a young farmboy the 90-day dictated and unrevised production of a 500-page narrative that incorporates sophisticated literary structures, remarkable Old World parallels, and some 300 references to chronology and 700 to geography with virtually perfect self-consistency is problematic as well.[3]

A measure of the authorial issue's complexity may be gauged by one group of scholars who have sought escape from the indeterminacy and subjectivism of both archaeological and textual approaches to the Book of Mormon. The element missing in the Book of Mormon debates, they argue, is "an approach that would allow for quantification of the evidence followed by a rigorous and objective statistical analysis as a test of the competing claims." Computational stylistics is based on the premise that all authors exhibit subtle, quantifiable stylistic traits that are equivalent to a literary fingerprint, or wordprint. The method has been used to investigate other instances of disputed authorship, from Plato to Shakespeare to the Federalist Papers. Analyzing blocks of words from 24 of the Book of Mormon's ostensible authors, along with nine nineteenth-century writers including Joseph Smith, three statisticians used three statistical techniques (multivariate analysis of variance, cluster analysis, and discriminant analysis) to establish the probability that the various parts of the Book of Mormon were composed by the range of authors suggested by the narrative itself. They found that all of the sample word blocks exhibit their own "discernible authorship styles (wordprints)," even though those blocks are not clearly demarcated in the text, but are "shuffled and intermixed" throughout the Book of Mormon's editorially complex narrative structure (wherein alleged authorship shifts some 2,000 times). Emphasizing the demonstrated resistance of these methods to even deliberate stylistic imitation, they further conclude that "it does not seem possible that Joseph Smith or any other writer could have fabricated a work with 24 or more discernible authorship styles." The evidence, they write, is "overwhelming" that the Book of Mormon was not written by Joseph Smith or any of his contemporaries or alleged collaborators they tested for (including Sidney Rigdon and Solomon Spaulding).[4] A subsequent, even more sophisticated analysis by a Berkeley group concluded that it is "statistically indefensible to propose Joseph Smith or Oliver Cowdery or Solomon Spaulding as the author of the 30,000 words . . . attributed to Nephi and Alma. . . . The

Book of Mormon measures multiauthored, with authorship consistent with its own internal claims. These results are obtained even though the writings of Nephi and Alma were 'translated' by Joseph Smith."[5]

Trances, Fits, and Fraud

Initial reaction of the general public to the Book of Mormon generally ranged from benign indifference to hostile dismissal. "Horrid Profanities and Unblushing Blasphemies," was how David Reese and local newspapers in New York characterized the record.[6] Others, like Illinois historian Henry Brown, merely yawned: "The frequent communications of 'the prophet' with an angel, the gold plates, the discovery, and afterward the translation of the Book of Mormon in the manner above related; had we not seen in our own days similar impostures practiced with success, . . . [Mormonism] would have excited our special wonder; as it is, nothing excites surprise."[7]

Initially, of course, the easiest route to dismissal was to pass the book off as the fanciful invention of a solitary fraud-meister. Alexander Campbell was absolutely confident in asserting "there never was a book more evidently written by one set of fingers. . . . I cannot doubt for a single moment but that he is the sole author and proprietor of it."[8] The problem was, as all careful readers soon realized, the book was clearly not, in the words of another dismissive editorialist, "a bungling and stupid production . . . [containing] trite, moral maxims."[9] More recent critics like Bernard DeVoto and Edmund Wilson played to popular applause with their witty aspersions ("yeasty fermentation," sniffed the first; "farrago of balderdash," decreed the latter[10]). But even a skeptic like Fawn Brodie was impatient with curt dismissals of the work. As for those who reject it as the ravings of a deluded man, "Its very coherence," she writes, "belies their claims. . . . For it clearly reveals in him what both orthodox Mormon histories and unfriendly testimony denies him: a measure of learning and a fecund imagination."[11]

As Brodie notes, Joseph's friends and his enemies alike insisted that he was an unschooled, barely literate farmboy. In the earliest autograph we have from the prophet (penned two years after the Book of Mormon was published), he described himself as "deprived of the bennifit of an education suffice it to say I was mearly instructid in reading writing and the ground rules of Arithmatic which constuted my whole literary acquirements [sic]."[12]

Smith's close friend and apostle Orson Hyde published this unflattering portrait:

> His only occupation was to plow and cultivate the soil. Because his parents were poor and had to feed a large family, his education was meager.

He was able to read fairly well, but his ability to write was very limited and he had only literary knowledge. His knowledge of letters did not go any further. Most of the subjects which were generally taught in the United States of America were completely unknown to him at the time he was favored with a heavenly message.[13]

His wife, Emma, was perhaps the first to decide that Joseph's talents were not up to such a production. In recalling her own role in the translation process, she insisted that

no man could have dictated the writing of the manuscripts unless he was inspired. For when acting as [Joseph's] scribe, he would dictate to me hour after hour; and when returning after meals, or after interruptions, he would at once begin where he had left off, without either seeing the manuscript or having any portion of it read to him. This was a usual thing for him to do. It would have been improbable that a learned man could do this; and for one so ignorant and unlearned as he was, it was simply impossible.[14]

In fact, this disparity between Joseph's credentials and the obvious complexity and scope of the Book of Mormon were soon adduced as evidence of its divine origin. Sidney Rigdon, one of the first and most influential of early converts, discussed his initial impressions of the prophet and his book with Joseph's scribe Oliver Cowdery:

After a few days Cowdery returned and held a long interview with Rigdon. Rigdon had read a considerable portion of the book. He questioned Cowdery about Smith and found that he was entirely illiterate. Rigdon expressed the utmost amazement that such a man should write a book which seemed to shed a flood of light on all the old scriptures, open all their profoundest mysteries, and give them perfect consistency and complete system. In his fresh enthusiasm he exclaimed that if God ever gave a revelation, surely this must be divine.[15]

Rigdon's son John confirmed the story, saying that when his father learned Joseph had "hardly a common school education," Rigdon replied, "if that is all the education he has got, he never wrote this book."[16]

Of course, the larger public found it easier to simply discount Joseph altogether as translator of an ancient record or as raconteur of ancient American epics—or to blur all distinctions between inspiration and fabrication by recourse to glib psychologizing. A *Tiffany's Monthly* interviewer of Martin Harris concluded that "the whole thing can be accounted for upon purely psychological principles, Joseph Smith, junr., being what is called now-a-days a medium."[17] A generation later, psychologist Woodbridge Riley followed suit, while leaving out the spiritualist bent. He smugly asserted of the Book of Mormon that "the nut is not so hard to crack by literary methods, and the fiction is mixed with enough fact to warrant study." His solution to the riddle was to call it the product of an "automatically-writing hand," Joseph's condition "under the influence of his 'Urim and Thummim'" being "semi-hypnotic."[18] (More recently, historian of religion Lawrence Foster similarly suggests that "the Book of Mormon is probably best understood, at least in part, as a trance-related production."[19]).

Amateur psychologists and doctors have been quick to weigh in as well. Riley had suggested that epilepsy might also have been a factor in Smith's visions. The great German scholar Eduard Meyer picked up on this diagnosis of Joseph as an epileptic in his 1912 history of the church, and combined it with what he believed to be Joseph's impressive power of suggestion to account for the corroborating testimony of the witnesses.[20] Historian Bernard DeVoto endorsed the theory that epileptic fits explained Smith's visionary experiences and productions.[21] (Fawn Brodie rejected the epilepsy theory as too simplistic. In revising her 1945 biography in 1971, she saw "obvious evidences of pathology in Joseph Smith's life." The Book of Mormon, she wrote, reenacted the "numerous conflicts raging within" him, from sibling tensions to identity problems. However, she stopped short of offering "clinical labels" in describing him—not because she was untrained as a psychologist but because of "the difficulties of clinical diagnosis of a man long since dead."[22])

"There is wisdom in the rule laid down by Blass," writes Hugh Nibley, "that whoever presumes to doubt the purported source and authorship of a document cannot possibly escape the obligation of supplying a more plausible account in its stead."[23] Unbelievers, as is apparent, have not been remiss in playing by such a rule. But to be widely plausible, such an alternate theory had to both credit the book's indisputable complexity—its rich mix of history, warfare, theology, allegory, and characters—and to *dis*credit Joseph as author. He had to have received, in other words, the help of a collaborator. Sidney Rigdon, the enthusiastic convert, was the first suspect. He had been an effective Campbellite preacher, and after he defected to Joseph Smith, some of his former co-religionists thought they detected familiar restorationist elements in the rival religion and its new book of scripture. Rigdon's source, they soon alleged, had been one Solomon Spaulding. Though lack of factual evidence has led virtually all scholars to dismiss the theory, it was believed by Alexander Campbell himself and proposed by early writers on Mormonism anxious to present some plausible account of authorship that did not attribute to Joseph Smith either heavenly sponsorship or a rich literary imagination.[24]

Solomon Spaulding

The first to allege publicly the Spaulding connection was Doctor Philastus Hurlbut, who had just been excommunicated from the Mormon church for "unchristianlike" conduct toward some young women.[25] In 1833 he heard that a Reverend Solomon Spaulding had written an unpublished novel with striking similarities to the Book of Mormon, entitled "Manuscript Found." Tracking down former friends and family of Spaulding, Hurlbut collected eight affidavits alleging that Spaulding's work, like Joseph Smith's, referred to a Jewish migration to America, had leading characters named Nephi, Lehi, Laban, and Moroni, and included the locale of Zarahemla. Also similar, they said, was the plotline of two competing factions, one of which eventually perished in internecine warfare.

Hurlbut located Spaulding's widow in Otsego County, New York, where he also managed to find, among Spaulding's effects, the manuscript in question. As it turned out, the manuscript described the adventures not of Jewish seafarers fleeing to America, but Romans blown off course en route to "Brittain." And the main characters were not Nephi and Lehi, but Fabius, Hamboon, Ulipoon, and the like. With the two main contentions of the affidavits discredited (shared names and "leading incidents" between the two works), one would have expected the theory to die a quiet death. It did not. Hurlbut sold his source materials to Eber D. Howe, who rehearsed the hypothesis in his extensive critique of Mormonism that he published in 1834, *Mormonism Unvailed* [sic]. He suggested that the manuscript found in the New York trunk was not the same one described in the affidavits and elaborated the theory by introducing another element—the complicity of Sidney Rigdon. While in Pittsburgh, Spaulding's widow remembered, he delivered his manuscript to a printer named Lambdin. Lambdin, Howe conjectured, delivered the manuscript into the hands of Sidney Rigdon sometime between 1823 and 1824. He and Joseph Smith reworked it and presented it to the world as the Book of Mormon.

So in spite of a radical dissimilarity of style and substance between the two works, the entirely conjectural nature of both the Spaulding-Lambdin and Lambdin-Rigdon handoffs notwithstanding, and ignoring the fact that no evidence could link Sidney Rigdon to Joseph Smith before December of 1830, newspapers in New York picked up the Spaulding-Rigdon theory as a persuasive explanation for the gold bible fraud. By the 1840s, it had become the standard non-Mormon account of the book's origin. Over the next century, the debate would continue. Proponents of the theory would persist in collecting affidavits alleging, at second hand, some connection between the principals. Mormon writers would continue to refute the flimsy case, point by point.

Then, in 1884, the Spaulding manuscript, long thought lost or destroyed, surfaced again and was positively identified as the one first recovered by Hurlbut. Even with the manuscript now available to compare, sporadic attempts to reassert its role as a source would persist until 1945. In that year, Fawn Brodie, writing authoritatively as one of the first Mormon debunkers to be taken seriously as a scholar, gave the Spaulding theory a proper burial.[26] In its place, she revived a more viable candidate.

Ethan Smith

Writing her now famous psychohistory of Joseph Smith, Brodie is often credited with first citing Joseph Smith's knowledge of Ethan Smith's *View of the Hebrews* and alleging it as the likely source of the Book of Mormon. While editor of the church's *Times and Seasons*, Joseph Smith oversaw the publication of an article in 1842 that quoted material from Ethan Smith in support of the Book of Mormon's authenticity. Although Brodie admits there is no evidence for Joseph's knowledge of the Ethan Smith work prior to 1830, she nonetheless insinuates both plagiarism and cover-up when she writes that the prophet, in citing Ethan Smith's material, was "careful to use" as his source a reprint of the relevant passages that appeared in 1833—three years after the Book of Mormon's publication.[27] If it is true, as she argues, that the "striking parallels between the two books hardly leave a case for mere coincidence,"[28] it is also true that a plagiarizing Joseph must be unique among frauds in providing the public with the source of his own plagiarism before anyone else had seen the connection. This peculiarity notwithstanding, several critics continue to support the Ethan Smith book as the most plausible source for Joseph Smith's literary production.[29]

Brodie was not, of course, the first to raise the specter of Ethan Smith's work as source material for the Book of Mormon. B. H. Roberts had addressed the issue more than two decades earlier.[30] First published in 1823, then slightly enlarged upon in an 1825 edition, Ethan Smith's book combines copious excerpts from Isaiah together with descriptions of reported Jewish-Indian parallels (borrowing extensively from Alexander von Humboldt's report of his exploration of Mexico and James Adair's 1775 *History of the American Indians*, which also argues an Indians-Lost Tribes theory). Neither novel nor chronicle, *Views* is an inelegant blend of history, excerpts, exhortation, and theorizing. In Roberts's 1922 study of the parallels, he enumerated 18 similarities between the two works.

Some of the parallels were not unique to Ethan Smith's work. Numbers 2 and 4 of the parallels in Roberts's study, for instance, refer to the American Indian-Lost Tribes of Israel theory. This theory had long and extensive dissemination. (It should be pointed out that in contradistinction to the many preceding versions, the Book of Mormon maintains that its peoples descended from Manasseh and Judah, *not* the ten lost tribes.[31]) And some parallels could be seen as fairly vague, generic conventions. Number 5 compares the discovery of Mormon's buried plates with the discovery of a buried manuscript in Ethan Smith's work.[32] And number 6 compares Nephite seership with Indian divination. Some, on the other hand, are at least more superficially striking. Both works relate the destruction of Jerusalem, mention the Urim and Thummim (although called "interpreters" in the Book of Mormon), and quote copiously from Isaiah in reference to the scattering and gathering of Israel.

Roberts stopped short of concluding an actual influence existed, but he clearly felt the similarities deserved serious consideration. He refrained from publishing his work, although it circulated in small circles from the 1920s, and more generally after it was distributed to the Salt Lake Timpanogos Club in 1946. General publication of his study did not occur until 1985. Far from fleeing the issue, the LDS church addressed it in a 1986 article,[33] and in 1996, through the Brigham Young University's Religious Studies Center, actually subsidized a reprint of Ethan Smith's book itself, so readers could more easily "ascertain whether the claim that it is a source of the Book of Mormon can be substantiated."[34] At present, the Ethan Smith theory is probably the leading contender to challenge the account of the Book of Mormon's origin held by the faithful. To date, over fifty books and articles discuss the pros and cons of the debate.[35]

Whether or not Joseph Smith had access to Ethan Smith's volume, Brodie's mention of the connection and her status as a biographer had powerful consequences beyond the particulars of that specific theory. Bernard DeVoto considered it her "distinction that she has raised writing about Mormonism to the dignity of history for the first time."[36] And insofar as the Book of Mormon inescapably fell under that rubric, her treatment of it set the pattern for subsequent explanations.

Environmental Explanations

This pattern, which has been called an "environmental approach" to the Book of Mormon,[37] has two essential components. Dale Morgan, a friend and collaborator of Fawn Brodie, provides one formulation of the premise. "With my point of view on God, I am incapable of accepting the claims of Joseph Smith and the Mormons, be they however so convincing. If God does not exist, how can Joseph Smith's story have any possible validity? I will look everywhere for explanations except to the ONE explanation that is the position of the Church."[38] Denying, a priori, the possibility of divine origins, the researcher then proceeds to ascertain the sources of the Book of Mormon in its contemporary cultural milieu.

For modern critics who reject both the book's supernatural origins and glib psychologizing (along with romantic notions of authorship as the work of a solitary genius who transcends his historical conditions), textual origins must be sought in the author's cultural environment. David Wright, for example, finds the Book of Mormon and Old World parallels "striking," but he finds equally noteworthy what he considers to be "major textual, ideational, and cultural anachronisms that are found in the Book of Mormon."[39] This position—that the Book of Mormon reflects early nineteenth-century concerns, language, and, ultimately, origins—is actually a throwback to some of the earliest objections raised to the book when Joseph Smith was still alive.

Brodie's and Morgan's approach essentially revisits the first criticism ever published against the work—Alexander Campbell's "Delusions." Campbell there characterized the Book of Mormon as a mishmash of

> every error and almost every truth discussed in New York for the last ten years. He decided all the great controversies:—infant baptism, ordination, the trinity, regeneration, repentance, justification, the fall of man, the atonement, transubstantiation, fasting, penance, church government, religious experience, the call to the ministry, the general resurrection, eternal punishment, who may baptize, and even the question of free masonry, republican government and the rights of man.[40]

Brodie cites the entire passage from Campbell approvingly, insisting that "the book can best be explained, not by Joseph's ignorance nor by his delusions, but by his responsiveness to the provincial opinions of his time." The book, she writes in terms that parallel Campbell's, is "absolutely American, . . . an obscure compound of folklore, moral platitude, mysticism, and millennialism."[41]

Over the next few decades, in an ironic reversal of earlier depictions of Mormonism as profoundly heretical and un-American, scholars began to assert the culturally derivative nature of virtually every Mormon doctrine and practice. Whitney Cross, in his still-important *Burned-Over District*, emphasized the cultural ambience of western New York in Joseph Smith's theological formation.[42] Thomas O'Dea's respected study of the church claimed that "the basic ideas and values of Mormonism were inherited from its cultural background,"[43] and William Mulder characterized Mormonism as "a dynamic reworking of the diverse elements in American culture."[44]

What elements in particular do the environmentalists see reflected in the Book of Mormon? Brodie, following Campbell's lead, believes the antimasonic fervor that broke out over the murder of Mason-exposer William Morgan in 1826 led "directly" to the "crusading spirit" of the Book of Mormon's second half in general, and to the depiction of the

"Gadianton Robbers" in particular.[45] Gadiantons were groups of political subversives and conspirators who appear five times in the Book of Mormon. Their similarity to Masons is limited to the fairly superficial parallel of the secret oaths that characterize membership in both groups. Besides, as Brodie neglects to mention until a few hundred pages later in her study, Joseph's relationship to the Masons, as it developed in the Nauvoo period at least, was that of ardent supporter and borrower, not alarmed critic. Still, the fact that the Book of Mormon designation of Gadiantons as a "secret combination" paralleled contemporary use of that term to refer to Masons has lent weight to claims of borrowing. (Twenty-five years before Brodie, psychologist Walter Franklin Prince had analyzed the Book of Mormon as an elaborate working out of Smith's anti-Mason feelings, with the words "masonry," and "Morgan," obsessively encoded as Book of Mormon characters—MORmoN, MORoNi, MAthONI, to name only a few of his examples—together with "the obsessive prefix ["anti"] clamoring incessantly for deliverance"—as in ANTIpas, mANTI, coriANTumr, etc.)[46]

Brodie also saw the influence of anti-Catholicism in the Book of Mormon. The anti-Catholic crusade, largely connected to the nativist reaction against waves of Irish immigration, would not get under full swing until the 1830s and 1840s with riots in Boston, Charlestown, Baltimore, and eventually the burning of convents and Irish shantytowns. But already in the 1820s, the construction of the Erie Canal led to the influx of enough Irish laborers to stir up resentments in upstate New York, and sporadic attacks on the Catholic church appeared in Rochester and Albany papers.[47] So when the prophet Nephi, as recorded in the Book of Mormon, sees in vision a "great and abominable church," "the whore of all the earth," "whose foundation is the devil," Brodie—and many Mormons—have assumed that such references refer to the Roman Catholic Church in a way that recalls St. John's language in Revelation.[48] Finally, Brodie thinks she detects "Calvinism and Arminianism" in the book, though "they had equal status, depending upon which prophet was espousing the cause, and even universalism received a hearing."[49]

Since Brodie's work, a number of historians have also claimed to hear nineteenth-century echoes in the Nephite record. Marvin Hill, for one, has emphasized early Mormonism as a product of dramatic "social change and social anxiety" of the 1820s and 1830s. As "fugitives from social change and political and social conflict," Mormons erected their kingdom of God into an antipluralistic refuge. The Book of Mormon, he argues, reflects this utopian vision: "The ideal political state depicted in the Book of Mormon was a theocracy, where the chief judge was also the head of the church who promoted social and political unity by preaching the true gospel and by establishing a communistic economic order that eliminated social classes."[50]

The Search for Middle Ground

The universalism Brodie perceived has been explored further by Dan Vogel. Representing a new variety of Book of Mormon critic (who challenges claims of historicity while trying to renegotiate the nature of "inspiration"), he begins by invoking the "well known" historical-critical method, according to which "one must put oneself into the times and into the surroundings in which [the scriptural authors] wrote, and one must see what [concepts] could arise in the souls of those who lived at the time."[51] But in the case of the Book of Mormon, it is hard to see how one can begin a critical investigation by assuming the mindset of a culture whose very existence is doubted by the researcher, and whose conceptual universe is therefore imaginary. What Vogel *can* do is look for evidence that the Book of Mormon addresses nineteenth-century theological issues in terms that are so historically specific as to cast doubt on the possibility of ancient precedent. What he *finds* in the Book of Mormon are a few terms with nineteenth-century counterparts and an otherwise unimpressively generic template. Nephi and Moroni both foresee an age of libertines who will urge all to "eat, drink, and be merry," since the Lord will "uphold such at the last day" and "it shall be well with us" (2 Nephi 28:7; Morm. 8:31). Disbelief in hell and the devil, Nephi says, will accompany these attitudes. More specifically, Alma preaches that Christ will save people from, rather than in, their sins, paralleling a distinction that Universalists were accused of confusing in Joseph Smith's day.

Similarly, in his study of "Nephite sacramental language," Mark Thomas argues that the Book of Mormon "utilizes nineteenth-century literary forms and theological categories" and, as in the case of Universalism, is "anticipating disputations among its nineteenth-century audience" regarding liturgical forms.[52] Specifically, the Book of Mormon enters the "nineteenth-century context of ambiguous statements about the eucharistic covenant" with a "strikingly clear" position that emphasizes remembrance and covenant as a personal contract of works rather than a communal covenant of grace (as in Reformation thought). This Book of Mormon position, he claims, is not a restoration of primitive Christian truths but an echo of one strand of 1830s Protestant thought within a contested set of beliefs. In addition, he argues, when it comes to the question of how often, to whom, and how the Eucharist should be administered, "the Book of Mormon addressed . . . issues which were matters of question and dispute among Christians in the nineteenth century."[53] Elsewhere Thomas writes that the Book of Mormon discussion of atonement in terms of an infinite being dying to remit infinite sins also has parallels in nineteenth-century debates, though it ultimately derives from Anselm of Canterbury in the twelfth century.[54]

Of course, any criticism that builds a case for modern origins upon assertions of modern relevance, as the two examples above, runs the risk of pretending to argue evidence when it really argues premises. Nine-teenth-century Book of Mormon readers were the first to call Book of Mormon characters "universalists," as an 1835 reference work on the vol-ume reveals.[55] Mormon readers expected to find contemporary connec-tions because, first, Nephi charged his audience to consider the words he recorded "and liken them unto [them]selves," and second, as Moroni tes-tified to his future readers, "Jesus Christ hath shown you unto me, and I know your doing" (1 Nephi 19:24; Morm. 8:35). Nineteenth-century par-allels, in other words, are part and parcel of the self-proclaimed prophetic texture of the work and recognizing them is presented as a readerly obli-gation by the keepers of the plates. In the words of Isaiah, quoted by Nephi, "Behold, I have declared the former things from the beginning. . . . And I have even from the beginning declared to thee; before it came to pass I showed them thee" (1 Nephi 20:5; compare Isaiah 48:5).

That is why Vogel's conclusion—that it is unlikely that "ancient American cultures could have debated Universalism in a manner that would have been meaningful to those in nineteenth-century Amer-ica"[56]—is a conclusion predetermined by any naturalistic framework and one that disavows the very nature of the Book of Mormon's pro-phetic pretensions from the start. It is a criticism of fundamentals, not particulars. Ironically, the exact same evidence that Vogel and Thomas adduce to invalidate the book's ancient origin is adduced by believers to confirm its prophetic qualities. We have seen this divide before, of course, most famously in the Isaiah problem. Isaiah's relation of postexilic events is taken, from a naturalistic perspective, as prima facie evidence of his book's dual (or tripartite) authorship.[57] From a believer's point of view, it merely confirms his status as foreteller. For nineteenth-century Mormons, Joseph's living, prophesying presence only confirmed them in their expectations that the Book of Mormon would be oracular. Did he not pronounce an 1832 prophecy that war would "shortly come to pass, beginning at the rebellion of South Carolina, which will eventu-ally terminate in the death and misery of many souls; . . . For behold, the Southern States shall be divided against the Northern States, and the Southern States will call on other nations, even the nation of Great Britain . . ." (D&C 87:1-3). Such accurate prediction does not make him a prophet. But neither does it prove that the 1832 document is actually a post-1861 forgery.

To the Mormon orthodox, then, the Book of Mormon's status would be suspect if it did *not* evince remarkable relevance to the context in which it has been read. The Lord declared that the Book of Mormon would re-solve ambiguous points of doctrine, and from the first, readers found it to do just that, sorting through sectarian confusions far beyond the Univer-salist and liturgical heresies. As the church newspaper declared,

The doubtful points of doctrine, in the Bible, which left one sect to im-
merse for baptism; a second to sprinkle; a third to pour, and a fourth to
do without either, were cleared up by the book of Mormon. That embarrassment under which thousands had labored for years, to learn how the
saints would know where to gather, that all nations might come to Zion,
with songs of everlasting joy, and prepare a house, that the Lord might
suddenly come to his temple, so that the mountain of the Lord's house
might be established in the top of the mountains, and be exalted above
the hills, and the law go forth out of Zion, in the last days, was obviated
by the book of Mormon. That wonderful conjecture, which left a blank as
to the origin, or forefathers of the American Indians, was done away by
the book of Mormon.[58]

Vogel's work is just one example in a rising tide of revisionist essays
on the Book of Mormon, authored largely by Mormon dissidents. The
new direction was signaled in 1990 by a collection Vogel himself edited,
which he hoped would move Mormon religious thinking in a more liberal, progressive direction. "The written word of God does not come to
us direct but through human intermediaries," Vogel reminds us. We need
to attend to "the problem of the human and the divine in scripture,"
and to "challenge . . . simplistic assumptions about the nature of revelation" in order to arrive at a "more refined . . . definition of revelation
and scripture."[59] What these fifteen essays share, along with those in a
subsequent collection entitled *New Approaches to the Book of Mormon* (Brent
Metcalfe, ed., 1993), is this effort to explain the record in terms of a particular social, cultural, or political context. Susan Curtis argues in her
essay, for instance, that "exemplary characters in Smith's Book of Mormon were fundamentally market capitalists" driven by "assumptions
about hard work, regularity, commerce, and accumulation sustained by
a Victorian sensibility."[60]

   In most of these studies, the Book of Mormon itself is considered only
in terms of scattered ideas it contains, but not as a text whose very existence as a whole needs to be reckoned with. The Book of Mormon itself
moved closer to center stage, however, with a new focus on one aspect of
nineteenth-century popular culture in particular—magic. Abner Cole had
first alleged the Mormon magic connection with his 1829 articles; additional allegations came with the first book-length anti-Mormon work already mentioned: Eber D. Howe's 1834 *Mormonism Unvailed: or, a Faithful
Account of That Singular Imposition and Delusion, From Its Rise to the Present
Time. With Sketches of the Character of Its Propagators, and a Full Detail of the
Manner in which the Famous Golden Bible Was Brought Before the World.* Although Howe incorporated Hurlbut's theory that the Book of Mormon
was largely derivative of Spaulding's "Manuscript Found," he also connected Smith's account of miraculous translation with his heavy involvement in treasure-seeking, magic rituals, and divining.

A spate of recent work in the area of American folk-magic traditions has reopened the charge of Joseph Smith's involvement with magic with two consequences: it has established the credibility of early accounts like Howe's that implicate Joseph Smith in a fascinating subculture involving seer stones, guardian spirits, and occult supernaturalism. But it has also diminished the stigma and idiosyncrasy such early characterizations evoked, by emphasizing folk magic's widespread, popular appeal even among the middle classes. As one scholar writes of this period, "truth itself became democratized, and the borders the eighteenth century had painstakingly worked out between science and superstition, naturalism and supernaturalism, were now blurred. Animal magnetism seemed as legitimate as gravity. Dowsing for hidden metals appeared as rational as the workings of electricity."[61] A second writer agrees that it is simply inappropriate to impose our era's "neat distinction between magic and religion," with its "value judgment that magic is superstitious, deluded, and irrational, if not downright evil, while religion is the lofty, abstract expression of our highest ideals."[62]

Raised in a folk culture where magic was commonplace, Joseph Smith's personal circumstances boded a man of special gifts as well. He was born the morning after the winter solstice and had a biblical namesake possessed of a special cup of divination.[63] As a teenager, he found a stone with which, according to his mother, he could see things "invisible to the natural eye."[64] Indian burial mounds—eight were within a dozen miles of his home[65]—afforded ample opportunity to excavate the occasional relic and to speculate about more valuable buried goods, and as we saw, Joseph took his part in the quixotic quest for treasure along with a host of neighbors. Brodie followed Cole in believing Joseph's early experiences with magic in "the mound-haunted landscape of western New York" inspired his tales of visions and gold plates. "Mormonism sprang from the mounds," concludes a historian of American archaeology.[66]

The occult connection received a major boost when two notorious "treasure letters" were made public in 1984, one written by Joseph Smith and one by Martin Harris, replete with references to clever spirits, white salamanders, and charms to defeat their guardianship of treasure. Allegedly written in 1825 and 1830 respectively, they suggested that even the adult Joseph Smith was more profoundly and gullibly immersed in a world of simple-minded superstition than even his earliest detractors alleged. Mark Hoffman admitted forging the letters in 1987. Still, discussions continue to be marred by scholarly ignorance of or disregard for the fraudulent nature of these most sensationalistic pieces of evidence.[67] The appeal of such a cultural context for explaining Joseph's supernatural experiences, however, has only grown more pronounced. As Alan Taylor writes, for instance, treasure-seeking was widespread in

Joseph's time and area, and treasure-seekers "turned increasingly to 'seer stones' or 'peep-stones' as a more ready and reliable alternative to dreams." (Lorenzo Dow, famous Methodist itinerant, endorsed the revelatory function of dreams and claimed he could locate lost and stolen objects by supernatural means—but his methods stopped short of seer stones.[68]) Joseph used just such a stone as a young scryer and later used it in translating the Book of Mormon. So Taylor seems safe in asserting that this same stone "enabled the future Mormon prophet to begin his career as a seer."[69]

When scholars push the occult connection beyond Joseph's seer stone, the case suffers for lack of concrete specifics. Some critics have noted a few references within the Book of Mormon to treasures and riches that become "slippery" (Hel. 13:31-36; Morm. 1:18), but even those occur in the context of condemning rather than condoning "sorceries, and witchcrafts, and magics" (Morm. 1:19). In sum, there is simply little basis for arguing that the worldview of Joseph's era had any influence on the make-up of the Book of Mormon itself. The influential *Early Mormonism and the Magic World View* was the first full-length study to assert the vital role of magic and occult traditions in understanding the scriptures and teachings of the early church, but it suffers from the author's assumption that the Hoffman forgeries were authentic.[70] Even in the decade and more between the original and a second edition, as one reviewer notes, D. Michael Quinn fails to discover "a single primary source written by Latter-day Saints that makes any positive statement about magic."[71] Quinn does not deny that both the Book of Mormon and LDS teachings have consistently condemned magic, but he works hard to build a case that Joseph Smith must have had access to a number of highly esoteric traditions and artifacts that bespeak powerful influence on the Book of Mormon and his theology. In spite of prodigious research, Quinn's case rests on such pillars as his curiously flippant suggestion that if Joseph could read "reformed Egyptian" through the use of his interpreters, surely "he could have also understood sections of the [Aramaic/Hebrew] *Zohar* by the same 'gift and power of God'";[72] on misunderstanding the status of astrology in nineteenth-century almanacs (*not* a medium for the conveyance of significant occult information, zodiac signs notwithstanding); and on tenuous and speculative connections to such curios as a Hyrum Smith family dagger and a silver medallion (neither of which can even be clearly identified as Joseph Smith's). Still, Quinn often succeeds in countering the evidence of genuinely ancient origins (Alma's appearance as an ancient Hebrew name in the Dead Sea Scrolls, for instance) with occult parallels of his own, though readers might well dismiss them as equally unlikely sources and only relatively more contemporary at that. (Alma was a conjuring name in a seventeenth-century magic manuscript, Quinn writes.[73])

In continuing to expand the search from New England folk culture to the entire Western occult tradition, John Brooke has gone further afield than most in his search for occult influences and sources. As one review fairly characterizes his study, *The Refiner's Fire: the Making of Mormon Cosmology, 1644–1844,*

> Brooke attempts to find hermeticism, Freemasonry, and alchemy in the translation process and text of the Book of Mormon. Brooke searches for any and every thought or act of Joseph Smith and other early Mormons that he can see as related—however vaguely—to hermetic, Masonic, alchemical, or other occultic ideas. He first focuses on ideas of priesthood, mysteries, temples, cosmology, and preexistence. . . . Joseph's marriage, sex life, and plural marriages are seen as "replicat[ing] the hermetic concept of conjunctio, the alchemical marriage."[74]

By any measure, Brooke's is a work of impressive scholarship.[75] But the real contribution of his work toward understanding the meaning or genesis of the Book of Mormon is minimal, given his frank admission that "First and foremost, it is not entirely clear how hermeticism might have been conveyed from late-sixteenth-century Europe to the New York countryside in the early nineteenth century. Second, and equally problematic, is the question of how to specify the role of hermeticism in relation to the many obviously Christian elements in Mormon theology."[76] This patent failure to move beyond exotic parallel-hunting becomes at times a curious resistance to those very simple but very mundane explanations that he has just referred to as "obviously Christian." To cite just one example of Brooke's disregard for the principle of Occam's razor, baptism for the dead is explicitly referenced in I Corinthians 15. But Brooke finds it necessary to seek the source for the Mormon practice not in the Bible read by Joseph Smith any day of the week, but rather in "spiritualist doctrine" and in the "radical heritage" of "the German pietist mystics at Ephrata."[77]

Though Brooke may delve further into the past than most in his search for influences, he is certainly not the first non-Mormon scholar to find intriguing connections between the Book of Mormon and ancient sources—or the first to have difficulties turning those connections into a credible theory of cultural influence. Although he seems more intrigued by the writing Joseph later produced purporting to be "the Book of Abraham" than by the Book of Mormon, Harold Bloom is likewise impressed by Joseph's uncanny ability to tie into occult and kabbalistic traditions, with no vehicle of transmission apparent—or even plausible—in the immediate cultural context.[78] (In a similar vein, David Noel Freedman remarked that he had never before encountered an Abraham account in which not only Isaac but the patriarch himself was threatened with sacrifice. Then he recollected that a similar tradition did exist—but in a document not available until the 1890s.[79]) The great scholar of pseudepigrapha James Charlesworth has not concerned himself with Book of Mormon origins, but he also has suggested noteworthy connections between the Book of Mormon and ancient texts. Discussing Book of Mormon Christology in particular, he points to two fairly unusual ideas: "The first is the concept that the Messiah speaks to the lost tribes [3 Nephi 15] and the second is the idea that the advent of the Messiah may be conceived as his return [a strained reading of 2 Nephi 6:14]." Both of these ideas, he maintains, constitute "an interesting link between the Pseudepigrapha and the Book of Mormon." [80]

A look at another parallel may further demonstrate both the appeal and the limitations inherent in those approaches that emphasize parallels. The narrative of Zosimus may originate in the period before the Roman destruction of the Temple, but it may be based on even older traditions. Its basic elements are as follows. A righteous desert dweller named Zosimus is visited by an angel of the Lord, who conducts him on a "journey to the blessed." He wanders for a length of time before a camel conveys him to the banks of a river covered by a "wall of cloud." He is carried over the river by the branches of a tree and set down beneath another, whereupon he feasts upon fruit and water it miraculously provides.

A guide appears whom he mistakes for the Son of God, and who then takes him to a community of righteous elders. These people relate to Zosimus their own story, which is engraved upon soft stone plates. At the time of Jeremiah, their father led them from Jerusalem prior to its destruction. "We also are of you and of your race," they affirm to Zosimus, "except that God has chosen us and set us in this place." Having escaped the scattering of Israel, they inhabit a blessed land, preserved from the knowledge of other peoples by "a wall round this country" and by a "wall of cloud" above.

After relating their history and way of life, the elders bestow their record upon Zosimus, who returns to the desert and deposits the record in a cave. There, he preserves them against the efforts of the Devil to destroy both himself and the plates. Failing to do so, "the Devil wept," fearing lest the "tablets of life . . . get abroad in the world."[81]

The Book of Mormon's parallels with Spaulding's overwrought romance, or even with Ethan Smith's didactic account of Indian-Jewish parallels, are spotty and tenuous compared to the striking correspondences we meet with here. One researcher finds around 15 specific parallels between Zosimus and 1 Nephi alone, from a vision of a tree whose fruit is sweet above all else to keeping records on soft plates to a people fleeing Jerusalem's destruction at the time of Jeremiah.[82] The first version of this narrative to reappear in the modern world was a Russian translation in the 1870s.[83]

Naturalistic explanations for the origin of the Book of Mormon are challenged by that kind of source criticism but not disabled altogether. As we saw with Brooke and Bloom, one may point to the parallel and be content to marvel at the mechanism of cultural transmission. But in what seems to be the unimpeachable absence of any such vehicle, there yet remains one refuge from supernatural explanations.

James Charlesworth, in his study of Book of Mormon messianism, notes examples of what are called *vaticinium ex eventu*, textual details whose apparent anachronicity is heightened by an unusual level of precision. Just as those references in Isaiah to postcaptivity events are construed as evidence of a second, later Isaiah, so does Charlesworth, even in considering the Book of Mormon as an ancient text, find references to Jesus Christ and Mary dead giveaways that those portions of the book were composed after the events narrated:

> How are we to evaluate this new observation? Does it not vitiate the claim that this section of the Book of Mormon, Mosiah, was written before 91 B.C.? Not necessarily so, since Mormons acknowledge that the Book of Mormon could have been edited and expanded on at least two occasions that postdate the life of Jesus of Nazareth. It is claimed that the prophet Mormon abridged some parts of the Book of Mormon in the fourth century A.D. And likewise it is evident that Joseph Smith in the nineteenth century had the opportunity to redact the traditions that he claimed to have received.[84]

This suggestion that Joseph may have had an ancient source that he elaborated or expanded upon has been argued at more length by Blake Ostler. Finding the evidence of the book's antiquity compelling (he cites comparative studies dealing with philology and ancient legal, military, social, and political institutions), he at the same time finds solid evidence of nineteenth-century cultural conditioning (antimasonic rhetoric and the doctrines of baptism and salvation, for instance). To resolve the disparate evidence, he proposes a mode of translation that he calls "creative co-participation," according to which the completed product represents "a modern expansion of an ancient source."[85]

Such a theory addresses a kind of scholarly disconnect between the kind of evidence both Mormon and non-Mormon scholars have brought to bear on the Book of Mormon. To take Alma 36 as an example, we have there an account of a dramatic conversion in which Alma the Younger lapses into unconsciousness to be restored three days later, whereupon he testifies to having been spiritually reborn of God through the mercy of Jesus Christ. In this and similar Book of Mormon episodes, critics are quick to see nineteenth-century influences. Jon Butler, for example, writes that "during Methodist 'love-feasts,' some participants fainted." In one recorded case, a man "'continued so long, that his flesh grew cold.' . . . But the man did not die and, like others, was physically revived and spiritually reborn. 'He began to praise God for what he had done for his soul.'"[86]

But although the content of the Alma conversion story suggests to some the influence of contemporary conditions, the account as narrated in the Book of Mormon exhibits a complex structure of inverted parallelism or chiasmus that has been persuasively connected to ancient Old World forms, as we saw. The same story, in other words, is invoked as telling evidence of both nineteenth-century composition and authentically ancient origins. Ostler sees an example of such divergent readings in King Benjamin's great temple speech (Mos. 2-6), that incorporates elements common to Methodist camp meetings, but at least as convincing are more than a dozen formal elements of Israelite covenant renewal festivals contained in the speech.

By attributing to Joseph Smith real possession of an ancient record as well as powerful cultural influences at work throughout the translation process, Ostler believes he has accommodated both the orthodox reader and those prone to environmental explanations. The plausibility of Ostler's theory would hinge at least in part on the problem of synthesizing seamlessly modern elements into an ancient record. In the case of Alma's narrative, for instance, the chiastic structure of the whole is not separable from the more modern elements of the story. This particular example is not a problem for Ostler, since he does not consider such inverted parallelism a uniquely or convincingly ancient form. Still, it is hard to see the pervasive Christology in the narrative as mere insertions into a preexistent account. As Mark Thomas demonstrates, "the Book of Mormon is christocentric in its understanding of scripture, its theology, and its typology."[87] Such difficulties aside, Ostler's theory is one of the most appealing products of the new détente in the Book of Mormon wars. In his rendering, ancient forms have an ancient source, and apparent anachronisms (like pre-Christian theology) have a plausible explanation. His theory also avoids the charge of conscious fraud since "it would not be necessary for Joseph Smith to be aware of his expansions and interpretations of the Book of Mormon simply because they were a part of his experience."[88]

Thomas Taylor, as we saw, tried to steer a similar course in the nineteenth century, allowing the prophet his metal plates but denying him the status of a Moses. Such compromises didn't work in the nineteenth century, and they seem poorly suited to please most skeptics or Saints today. But the resurrection of such compromises and their increasing reception by many (Ostler's position is "attracting more and more fairly faithful church members" according to Richard Bushman[89]) may reflect the tremendous pressures that have now come to operate at both ends of the debate. These innovative attempts to forge a compromise position are really part of a growing controversy over the status of the Book of Mormon whose roots are in the Latter-day Saint scholarly community itself.

In 1965, Leonard Arrington (called as church historian in 1972) sounded a historic call for the study of Mormon culture and history "in human or naturalistic terms."[90] That same year, a small group of Mormon historians organized around the thesis that "Mormon scholarship seemed to have reached a point that it should be concerned not only with 'proving' the claims of Joseph Smith, but also with recognizing the human side of Church history."[91] In the years since, the study of Mormon history has grown, in one observer's words, from cottage industry into a large-scale enterprise. The Mormon History Association, an example of just one professional group, boasts over 1,100 members. A recent definitive bibliography of Mormon studies corroborates the surge of publications in the field.[92]

The "new Mormon history" that took root in the 1960s is today an umbrella term whose meaning is contentiously disputed. In general, it seems to its advocates to mean Mormon history properly done and to its critics Mormon history that sells out to secularism.[93] The central question it has provoked is: to what degree may secular models of historiography be applied to Mormonism without doing violence to its own account of divine origins and providential involvement?

Louis Midgley may be pointing out the obvious when he writes that "prophetic claims appear questionable, if not absurd, from the perspective of secular modernity, which also provides the ideological grounds for both rival explanations of the faith, and competing secular accounts of the meaning of life."[94] Marvin Hill, on the other side of the dispute, hotly insists that, "To be sure, a dictionary definition of naturalism is that it is a view of the universe which excludes the divine, . . . but the definition is too sweeping." But few would take seriously his suggestion that a professor who asked in his 1940s era graduate class, "Why couldn't Moroni have appeared to Joseph Smith?" either was then or is now typical of an openness on the part of secular academics to either supernaturalism in general or Joseph Smith's divine calling in particular.[95] If Hill were correct, it would hardly be possible for a respected sociologist of religion to write a "heretical" essay in 1999 merely to argue that "normal people can talk to God, while retaining a firm grip on rational thought." In actual fact, as Rodney Stark reminds us in reference to Joseph Smith and other prophets, "even the most unbiased social scientists typically have been unwilling to go further than to grant that the recipients of revelations have made honest *mistakes*."[96]

The stakes in the debate about how to do Mormon history are huge. Historian Martin Marty observed in 1983 that

> Mormon thought is experiencing a crisis comparable to but more pro-found than that which Roman Catholicism recognized around the time of the Second Vatican Council (1962–5). Whatever other changes were oc-curring in the Catholic church, there was a dramatic, sometimes trau-matic shift in ways of regarding the tradition. One of the conventional ways of speaking of this shift comes from the observation of philosopher Bernard Lonergan. He and others argued that Catholicism was moving from a 'classic' view of dogma to a thoroughly 'historical' view of faith. In the classic view Catholic teaching has come intact, as it were, protected from contingency, from a revealing God.[97]

At the present, therefore, while Mormons wait for an increasingly per-suasive Book of Mormon apologetics—or the sheer magnitude of their burgeoning numbers—to attract more serious attention to their scrip-ture, the Book of Mormon wars that rage most furiously are taking place *within* the Mormon scholarly community. For under that controversial rubric of the "new Mormon history," the Book of Mormon has drawn a fresh generation of interpretation and approaches.

One basis for a new middle ground in Book of Mormon studies is a conceptual framework first articulated by the great psychologist Will-iam James. In his monumental *Varieties of Religious Experience*, James erects a distinction between "existential judgments" and "spiritual judg-ments." The first deals with questions like, "Under just what biographic conditions did the sacred writers bring forth their various contributions to the holy volume? And what had they exactly in their several indi-vidual minds, when they delivered their utterances? These are mani-festly questions of historical fact." The second judgments deal with questions of value: "Of what use should such a volume . . . be to us as a guide of life and a revelation?"[98]

James wants to insist that the two can be kept entirely separate, that issues of historicity and accuracy need not impinge on questions of ulti-mate religious value:

> Thus if our theory of revelation-value were to affirm that any book, to pos-sess it, must have been composed automatically and not by the free caprice of the writer, or that it must exhibit no scientific and historic errors and express no local or personal passions, the Bible [or the Book of Mormon?] would probably fare ill at our hands. But if, on the other hand, our theory should allow that a book may well be a revelation in spite of errors and passions and deliberate human composition, if only it be a true record of the inner experiences of great-souled persons wrestling with the crises of their fate, then the verdict would be much more favorable. You see that the

existential facts by themselves are insufficient for determining the value. . . .
With the same conclusions of fact before them, some take one view, and
some another, of the Bible's value as a revelation.[99]

Those scholars who invoke the Jamesian dichotomy are distinct from
earlier "environmentalists" like Brodie in their (at least occasional) insistence that the Book's "scriptural value" would not necessarily be diminished by naturalistic explanations. As James further insisted in this
regard, when he deals with the phenomena of religious experience "as
if they were mere curious facts of individual history, some . . . may think
it a degradation of so sublime a subject, and may even suspect me, until
my purpose gets more fully expressed, of deliberately seeking to discredit the religious side of life. Such a result is of course absolutely alien
to my intention."[100]

Similarly, we find Brigham D. Madsen (who jumped the gun a bit in
declaring there are "overwhelming scientific proofs of [the Book of
Mormon's] fictional character") pleading for an abandonment of Mormon preoccupation with the scripture's historicity, to be replaced by a
focus on its "religious and spiritual values."[101] He quotes approvingly
another Mormon, David P. Wright, who invokes the Jamesian defense
that "some might think that acceptance of the conclusion that Joseph
Smith is the author of the work requires rejecting the work as religiously
relevant and significant. . . . [But] such a rejection does not follow from
this critical judgment. Historical conclusions about a scriptural text, such
as who authored it, are *existential* judgments, . . . and can and should be
separated from judgments about *spiritual* values."[102]

But *can* they, really? A purely "formal" consideration of the Book of
Mormon, to use the language of literary criticism, or a study based on
its "internal persuasiveness," to use Bakhtin's, or a study that brackets
its historical reception and packaging is an approach based on a serious
misperception about the nature of scripture. Such an approach ignores
those ways in which scripture is constituted historically rather than
literarily. That is to say, scripture emerges out of a set of reading practices and from the sacred purposes a text serves for a community. It
does not result from supposed adherence to a set of generic conventions or preconceived rules.[103] The Book of Mormon's status as scripture, we have seen, is inseparable from the role it has come to play as
the very ground of Joseph Smith's authority, a divine sign of the end
times, and as a vehicle for the Mormon conversion experience. Facile
analogies to the Bible too easily ignore the particular features of the Book
of Mormon's historical positioning as scripture. It may sound generous,
as another new Mormon intellectual, Ian Barber, writes, to accommodate Joseph's perceived prophetic fallibility by comparing the Book of
Mormon to the Bible and by redefining scripture "as both record and

metaphor of human striving for the divine, rather than as religious icon or documentary history."[104] But such an attempt at accommodation, based as it is on that writer's experience of the Bible, is oblivious to the utter inappropriateness of such analogizing. Recounting how he discovered to his consternation that both "Mormon scriptures and history were contradictory and unreliable," Barber describes how he salvaged his faith in both upon realizing that in Genesis 1-11, were "scientific, archaeological, and historical problems of the same (or greater) magnitude as those identified for the Book of Mormon."[105]

Joseph Smith may have borrowed the Bible's King James idiom in translating the Book of Mormon. And both texts purport to be inspired testimonies of Christ and his gospel. But a catalogue of their fundamental *dis*similarities—as scripture—would be too long to enter upon here. Questions of origin, reception, canonization, theological function, translation, exegesis, presentation—these and more beside would take us in very different directions. Even if the analogy were otherwise apt, affirming the Bible's status as scripture in spite of historical inaccuracies or transmission errors is not comparable to embracing the Book of Mormon's "spiritual values" in blithe disregard for its being, possibly, fraudulent from conception to execution.

Anthony Hutchinson also tries to promote this same analogy: "It is unclear to me," he earnestly writes, "how the Old Testament's great expression of human fear and hope in God or its message of ethical monotheism and social concern or of human liberation are compromised in the least when we recognize that many of its narratives do not tell accurate history or that its view of the natural world is contrary to the facts." Yet Hutchinson can only profess befuddlement by willfully confusing the question of narrative accuracy with the more fundamental question of prophetic authority and authenticity in order to force an analogy with Moses:

> Likewise I am not clear why currently self-styled orthodox defenders of the "simple truth" of the Book of Mormon seem to believe that the book's message is made irrelevant or less than part of a normative canon of scripture when the book is understood as being written by an inspired prophet of the nineteenth century whose beliefs about anthropology, folk magic, and other matters are not only found in the book but *inform the book's very self-conception and presentation* [my emphasis].[106]

It may be true enough, to make a parallel point, that one may have a dream and then later progressively re-represent it to oneself and the world as an increasingly sublime event of cosmic significance. This is a plausible scenario for any honest fanatic or frenzied poet.[107] But Joseph Smith simply doesn't cooperate in such a reconstruction. Because his self-described excavation of the plates, repeated secreting of them in bean barrels, under hearthstones, and in smocks, his displaying of them to eight corroborating witnesses, and his transcription of them into hieroglyphics and translation of them into English—this continual, extensive, and prolonged engagement with a tangible, visible, grounding artifact is not compatible with a theory that makes him an inspired writer reworking the stuff of his own dreams into a product worthy of the name scripture.

In addition, seeing Joseph Smith's religious contributions as "useless and mischievous," as Brigham Madsen does, or the church's founders as "a corrupt bunch of religious sociopaths" enmeshed in "illicit sex, graft, deceit and duplicity,"[108] as Ian Barber does, and then reconciling those judgments with a positive appraisal of the book's scriptural value is logically inconsistent and historically oblivious. But this, in spite of what many faithful argue, is *not* because a bad man is incapable of producing inspired or inspiring work. Lord Byron may have been an incestuous libertine, and Thomas Chatterton and James Macpherson frauds, yet they all wrote sublime poetry. This is because poetry is defined by its capacity to provoke aesthetic satisfaction, not by its ability to ground some hagiography of the poet. But Joseph Smith could not have produced a fraudulent work that God validates as *His* own designated sign of Joseph's chosenness, as the verifiable emblem of God's renewed presence in human history, or as the most efficacious vehicle ever provided humans for revelatory experience. *Those* roles, as we have seen, are what have defined the Book of Mormon's status as Mormon scripture—not some tortuous "striving for the divine" by a "religious sociopath" who just happened to produce a document pregnant with edifying potential. That is why to consider "the historical validity of the Book of Mormon . . . strangely irrelevant to the experience of finding spirituality through the Latter-day Saint scriptural tradition" is itself a strangely irrational position.[109] All of the Book of Mormon's historically defined functions would be disabled in the presence of fraudulent origins. Joseph's story simply cannot be divorced from the Book of Mormon's scriptural status.

To put it differently, Helaman's miraculous story of the Stripling Warriors, like the Book of Job to many Christians, could be considered fanciful but inspiring mythology to Mormons and the Book of Mormon still be scripture. But the story of the gold plates could not be fanciful mythology and the Book of Mormon still be scripture. And this relationship of Joseph Smith—and his story—to the Book of Mormon simply has no counterpart in the history of the Bible. And any attempt to find middle ground by analogizing the Book of Mormon and the Bible that does not take cognizance of this fundamental and irreducible difference between those two sacred texts may be an exercise in futility.

Mark Thomas, in *Digging in Cumorah: Reclaiming Book of Mormon Narratives*, adopts the same posture in the first full-length treatment of the Book of Mormon as literature divorced from its status as scripture in an attempt to "transcend the history/fiction debate." Thomas adapts Robert Alter's "type-narrative" schema to skillfully describe a number of intricately structured "formulaic plots," "narrative scenes," and other narrative structures that recur throughout the text. From "warning prophet" and "monarchical narrative" forms to the "dying heretic" and "final destruction" forms, he argues that various instances of textual repetition serve to reveal "the sacred in society" (Joseph Smith's, not Mormon's) and to proclaim the universal nature of certain social and historical truths. Not entirely skirting questions of history, Thomas characterizes the Book of Mormon as a "mosaic," or "a kind of jigsaw puzzle," comprised of biblical phrases and contemporary theological problems with which Joseph Smith's mind was saturated.

Thomas's work has the advantage of appealing to religious scholars willing to consider the Book of Mormon without confronting its religious claims.[110] His avowed purpose "to reclaim Book of Mormon narratives" from the debate over its authenticity promises a welcome respite from the Book of Mormon wars: "We have fought for so long over the age of the book that its messages have become accidental casualties. In the end, a book's authority lies less in its origin than in its messages. I believe that the origin of the Book of Mormon is not the most important question that it compels us to ask. The real question is: 'Is the Book of Mormon worth reading?'"[111]

Clearly, Thomas's claim that we should focus on the Book of Mormon's message sounds enticingly reasonable. The question is, what happens to the Book of Mormon message in the process of its historical purgation?[112]

In examining the episode where Jesus endows three Nephite disciples with immortality, for example, Thomas teases out a series of biblical allusions—"figures of deliverance" and "types of the persecuted righteous"—in support of his contention that Joseph's narrative method effected a "complex web of biblical connections united as a whole." But there seems to be something woefully inadequate here in an approach that insists questions of Book of Mormon authenticity can be entirely suspended while we analyze intertextual allusions and "biblical clusters." For though Thomas claims that attention to these "verbal convention(s) increases our ability to listen to the voice of the text," it is precisely the voice of Moroni that is elided in the process. "But behold, I have seen them, and they have ministered unto me" (3 Nephi 28:26), Moroni insists by way of concluding his account of the three Nephites, making a naked claim upon our belief that formal analysis does little to accommodate. In such a light, for Thomas to call his method "a way of talking about what the book actually says" is fairly simplistic question-begging, and rather like saying a swimmer's cry for help is actually a loudly articulated imperative sentence and no more.[113] The plea may be genuine or it may be a ruse, but to analyze its grammatical construction while ignoring its claim to truth is self-indulgence, not transcendence.

Wendell Berry has written of similar deficiencies inherent in "the Bible as literature" approaches generally:

> the interesting question here is not whether young English-speakers should know the Bible—they obviously should—but whether a book that so directly offers itself to our belief or disbelief can be taught "as litera-ture." It clearly cannot be so taught except by ignoring "whatever else [it] may be," which is a very substantial part of it. . . . The fact is that the writers of the Bible did not think that they were writing . . . "literature". . . . It is conceivable that the Bible could be well taught by a teacher who believed that it is true, or by a teacher who believed that it is untrue, or by a teacher who believed that it is partly true. That it could be taught by a teacher uninterested in the question of its truth is not conceivable.[114]

Ultimately, then, Thomas's interpretations may be cogent, and his fathoming of the polyphonic texture of the work does welcome justice to a text too long dismissed as culturally interesting but literarily with-out merit. (Richard Rust's study was the sole predecessor to take the Book of Mormon seriously as literature.[115]) But Thomas's critical fram-ing of the historical question is fatally flawed. When he insists that "in the final analysis, the book's authority cannot depend on its age,"[116] he is either being disingenuous or oblivious to the record's historical con-stitution as scripture. For its authority, as well as Joseph Smith's, was made to depend on precisely that. As we have seen, the historical uses to which the record have been put, as well as the authors' conspicuous self-consciousness about their truth claims, make a purely formal as-sessment of their record precisely the approach it compels us *not* to take.

Similarly appealing as a gesture of compromise, but similarly im-plausible, is the argument of religious historian Lawrence Foster. His compromise position on the Book of Mormon as a "trance-state produc-tion" would mean that "from a Mormon perspective the book could then be described as 'divinely inspired'; from a non-Mormon view-point, it could be seen as an unusually sophisticated product of unconscious and little-known mental processes." Thus, we could shift the focus from "the unrewarding and ultimately irrelevant question of whether any golden plates . . . ever existed or whether the Book of Mormon was a literal history to the far more important and fascinating question of the content and meaning of this most extraordinary religious document."[117]

On the other hand, to consider the "content and meaning" or even the literary merits of the book alone represents progress of a sort. As long ago as 1921, the *Cambridge History of American Literature* made note of the Book of Mormon. Of course, one author of volume 3 thought the book described "the hegira of an adventurous folk moving by successive stages from the East to the Salt Lake Valley."[118] So it is not clear if the silence of the most recent edition of the Cambridge history on the subject of the Book of Mormon represents progress or not.

Given the book's mass distribution and its profound religious impact on millions of people, and especially in light of recent trends in literary criticism, which de-emphasize aesthetic preoccupations in favor of attention to the cultural work that texts perform, neglect of the Book or Mormon in literary studies is surprising. In fact, one non-Mormon observer remarked decades ago that the absence of any "serious or sustained treatment of the Book of Mormon . . . once it has been noticed and reflected upon, begins to look like a conspiracy."[119] In part this may be a result of the fact that, as this same observer notes, "the basic assumptions of Mormon fundamentalists preclude consideration of the Book of Mormon as an 'American' work, in the ordinary sense of the word, and least of all as a product of the nineteenth century."[120]

But it isn't just their assumptions that determine the limits of formal consideration. The forgeries published by James Macpherson a generation earlier were soon recognized by most critics as fraudulent, but doubts about their authenticity did nothing to dampen an almost feverish enthusiasm for the ancient epic attributed to the Celtic bard Ossian. The tragic tales of Carthon and Fingal satisfied the mid-eighteenth-century craving for sentimentalism and melodrama, and those satisfactions had nothing to do with historical provenance. Questions of origin, in other words, were easily divorced in Macpherson's case from the appeal and value of the work as literature. Few people have been able to similarly bracket the more remarkable claims of the Book of Mormon's translator in order to consider the literary or theological or ethical merit of the book itself. It is easy to see why cultural Mormons and accommodationists would see such a step as desirable. As we have seen, historical-minded appraisals of the book have not been persuasive with outsiders. When presented as a literary text or nineteenth-century production, one can at least invite scholars to examine the book on their own terms if not Joseph Smith's, as Mark Thomas does. When one Mormon scholar organized a small conference of non-LDS scholars from "text-oriented disciplines" to examine the book, one Oxford professor of religious history was surprised to find how successfully it bore "the kind of close analysis to which our group of philosophers, political scientists, literary and historical specialists subjected it." He came away, he wrote, with an "enriched appreciation . . . for this complex and inspiring work."[121] But that kind of success can only encourage the "new historians" who continue to search for plausible nineteenth-century sources for the work, in order to naturalize it and thus encourage its study as a respectable endeavor of secular scholars.[122]

Response by the Mormon orthodox to those who would reduce the Book of Mormon to sacred fiction or nineteenth-century potpourri has been, predictably, hostile. In fact, following publication of Dan Vogel's 1990 collection, *The Word of God*, critical reviews by the Foundation for Ancient Research and Mormon Studies and ensuing exchanges between their scholars and Signature Books escalated to an actual threat of lawsuit.[123] Mormon moderates plead for more tolerance, and, indeed, they may be right that Mormon orthodoxy has a wide span capable of embracing great diversity. On the other hand, evangelicals clearly agree that such naturalistic approaches strike at the very heart of Mormonism. Their response to Brent Metcalfe's *New Approaches to the Book of Mormon*, for example, has been gleeful. In fact, Carl Mosser and Paul Owen have complained that their fellow evangelicals offer the book "an enthusiastic endorsement . . . and pronounce the battle over."[124] They are apparently chiding their fellows for a conclusion that is premature— but certainly not illogical. For naturalizing the origins of the Book of Mormon *is* to emasculate its efficacy as Mormon scripture.

"The Book of Mormon is the keystone of our religion," said Joseph Smith, and he chose his words carefully.[125] It was not the edifice on which church teachings and organizations were built. "The Book of Mormon did not become a handbook for doctrine and ecclesiastical practice," in one historian's words.[126] It was not the foundation, but a keystone that, if removed, would precipitate an implosion of the superstructure. That was a reality of the role it played as well as official church doctrine.

But the keystone's integrity, it cannot be overemphasized, depends on the Book of Mormon's being true, not its being inerrant. In a kind of preemptive defense against extravagant expectations, Moroni proclaimed on his title page, "And now, if there are faults they are the mistakes of men; wherefore, condemn not the things of God." Nephi admits that in writing his history, he may well "err, even [as they did] err of old; not that I would excuse myself because of other men, but because of the weakness which is in me, according to the flesh," and later says that what he has written, he has "written in weakness" (1 Nephi 19:6; 2 Nephi 33:4). Joseph himself was reminded in a revelation that what the Lord speaks, he speaks "unto [his] servants in their weakness, after the manner of their language" (D&C 1:24). Joseph's claim that the Book of Mormon was "the most correct of any book on earth"[127] sets a high standard, but his translation is no Qur'an, not an immaculate textual incarnation of God himself.

For criticism of the Book of Mormon to be sufficient to impugn its status as scripture, those criticisms must touch upon questions of origin, not accuracy. Certainly inexplicable anachronisms, wildly implausible scenarios, obvious nineteenth-century imports, and the like would challenge its divine authorship. But it will not do to establish an imperfection and consider the case resolved, as many currently seem wont to do.

As an early LDS publication declared, "Besides, so much depends on an answer to the question, Is the story of its origin true or not: For, on the one hand, if it is not true, then the entire structure of Mormonism is built on a false foundation; and, on the other hand, if it is true, it becomes the strongest physical evidence for the authenticity of Joseph Smith's teachings."[128] Church enemies agreed. Inveterate anti-Mormon Symonds Ryder wrote in 1831 that "if a man once opens his heart to receive the Book of Mormon as a divine record, he is also under the necessity of receiving whatever Joseph Smith, Jr. is pleased to proscribe [sic] by way of commandment."[129]

Some LDS scholars allege that Book of Mormon defender B. H. Roberts was wrong in this regard, that it is simply untrue that if the Book of Mormon "could be proved to be other than it claims to be, . . . then the Church of Jesus Christ of Latter-day Saints . . . must fall."[130] As evidence, one such critic invokes the example of the Reorganized Church of Jesus Christ of Latter Day Saints (RLDS, a small branch—numbering some few hundred thousands by the 1990s—formally organized in 1860 largely of members who rejected the leadership of Brigham Young at the time of the exodus westward). In the 1960s, some members of that group challenged the factualness and literalism of their scripture. As a consequence, their church leaders "soft-pedaled the Book of Mormon in church curricula and publications;"[131] but this critic's expressed hope that the Utah church will follow this "wise practice" seems hopelessly naïve and historically oblivious, both to the scripture's particular roles in Mormon religious life and practice and to the fate of the more progressive offshoot church. For simultaneous with a de-emphasis on the Book of Mormon, there had to necessarily follow a de-emphasis on its translator. And indeed, by the time of that critic's recommendation, the RLDS were already downplaying the founding epiphanies of the Prophet Joseph, calling them "religious experiences" rather than visions or angelic visitations.[132] As for the Book of Mormon itself, the RLDS have gone beyond de-emphasis to virtual repudiation. In one Utah congregation a minister was removed in 1991 for repeatedly "emphasizing the Book of Mormon in his worship meetings" and "mentioning Joseph Smith's name over the pulpit" in spite of warnings to desist.[133] The eventual outcome of such a policy is not surprising. By April of the year 2000, delegates to their world conference voted to rename their church the "Community of Christ," thus severing their last link to a long history rooted in visions, prophecies, glorious angels, and gold plates.

There is no reason to suspect that a comparable move is likely with the Mormons—or that if it were, it would be any less a prelude to Protestant assimilation than has proven to be the case with the RLDS. Whether such assimilation would constitute the fall of the church or an enlightened rebirth may be an open question. But it would not be a church either B. H. Roberts or Joseph Smith would recognize.

SEVEN

"Plain and Precious Truths": The Book of Mormon as New Theology, Part 1—The Encounter with Biblical Christianity

Take away the Book of Mormon and the revelations, and where is our religion? We have none.

—Joseph Smith

The Book of Mormon . . . may not have added enough doctrinal novelty to the Christian tradition to have made Mormonism more than a Protestant sect.

—Rodney Stark

When it became known that I was a Mormon, all crowded around to look at me as though there was some peculiarity about a "Mormon" that was not about any other person. Some wanted to see the Mormon Bible, the golden Bible, etc. I handed them my pocket Bible—a new book, gilt-edged. They took it and looked it all through carefully, then handed it back to me, remarking they could see no difference in it than their own Bible.

—Wandle Mace

We have seen how the Book of Mormon served to alert the world to the prophetic claims of Joseph Smith and the imminence of the last days. And on the night of Moroni's first appearance to Joseph, the angel's first words to Joseph about the Book of Mormon cast it in the role of ancient American record. Seeming almost as an afterthought, the angel "also said that the fulness of the everlasting Gospel was contained in it, as delivered by the Savior to the ancient inhabitants."[1] That claim was later reinforced through several revelations.[2]

It has often been pointed out, however, that those beliefs most commonly associated with Mormonism are nowhere to be found in that text. Those expecting an exposition of a peculiarly Mormon doctrine will be disappointed: the Book of Mormon contains no explicit mention of exaltation (the eventual deification of man), the degrees of glory, tithing, the Word of Wisdom, baptism for the dead, premortal existence,[3] or eternal marriage. In fact, the accounts of early converts to Mormonism confirm that it was the *congruence* of Book of Mormon teachings with the New Testament that dampened their objections to a new scripture and allowed it to affect their conversion for reasons other than doctrinal novelty or innovation.

Brigham Young, for example, related that as a young seeker, he "had searched high and low to find whether there was any such thing as pure religion upon the earth" but concluded "there is not a Bible church upon the earth." Similarly, his brother Joseph "was a man of sad heart," having concluded as well that "there are no Bible Christians upon the face of the earth." Their pessimism lasted until hearing "the everlasting Gospel declared by the servants of God—until [they] heard men testify, by the power of the Holy Ghost, that the Book of Mormon is true."[4] Similarly, first generation member John Murdock was certain that if the Mormon missionaries were true emissaries of God, "the Book of Mormon will contain the same plan of salvation as the Bible."[5] He read the Book of Mormon, and "the spirit of the Lord rested on me, witnessing to me of the truth of the work."[6] And Orson Pratt said that when he heard the message of Mormonism, "As soon as the sound penetrated my ears, I knew that if the Bible was true, their doctrine was true."[7] Eli Gilbert, another early convert, wrote that when presented with a Book of Mormon, he "compared it with . . . the bible, (which book I verily thought I believed,) and found the two books mutually and reciprocally corroborate each other; and if I let go the book of Mormon, the bible might also go down by the same rule."[8] Early Mormon hymnist W. W. Phelps rejoiced to find after studying the Book of Mormon that "its gospel was the same and its ordinances were the same as those I had been taught to observe."[9] And his contemporary Joseph Hovey recorded in his journal that his family was baptized only after they "searched the Bible daily" to ensure that it corroborated Book of Mormon teachings.[10]

Timothy Smith agrees that "the persuasive power of the new scriptures and of the missionaries who proclaimed and expounded them lay in their confident testimony to beliefs that were central to the biblical culture" of their audience. He goes on to enumerate five principal ways in which "the Book of Mormon served to strengthen," rather than chal-

lenge, "the authority of [biblical] scripture in the minds of all who listened seriously to the elders."[11] Other scholars have noted that even the
appearance of the golden bible was calculated to imitate its orthodox
namesake. In the year before and after publication of the Book of Mormon, over half a million copies of the Bible were distributed by the
American Bible Society in two editions. The Book of Mormon, writes
one historian, "was bound in such a way that it looked strikingly similar" to those two imprints.[12]

This congruity, perceived by early converts, was generally not disputed by doubters and critics of the Book of Mormon. Few things could
be clearer than the fact, as we have noted, that it was the miracle the
work embodied, not the doctrine it presented, that gave offense. Even
by their vehement denunciations critics acknowledged this truth. Doctrinally, as far as the public was concerned, the Book of Mormon was "a
feeble and diluted imitation of the Bible revelation and the gospel which
had already been in the possession of the Christian people of this country for over two hundred years."[13] As a New York paper put it rather
more sanguinely, "Setting aside the near approach of the Millennium
and the Book of Mormon, they resemble in faith and discipline the Methodists, and their meetings are marked by the fervid simplicity that characterizes that body of Christians. It is in believing the Book of Mormon
inspired that the chief difference consists; but it must be admitted that
this is an important distinction."[14] It was not believing the Book of
Mormon's teachings, in other words, but believing the story of its origin that set Mormons apart.

Of course, not all unbelievers were so generous. One missionary reported from the field in 1833,

> Some say the book of Mormon is contrary to the bible, because it speaks
> against unconditional election, and reprobation; some because it exhorts
> the saints to continue faithful to the end, lest they fall out by the way and
> perish; some because it teaches immersion for baptism, and discards the
> baptism of infants. The universalist says it reproaches his creed; the athe-
> ist complains that it disorganizes his laws of nature: and thus it is con-
> demned as destructive to every craft under heaven. All parties seem to
> feel a disquietude because of the marvelous and wonderful work that the
> Lord is beginning to accomplish in the earth.[15]

And, as Lucy Mack reported, the Methodists "raged" because it contradicted their creed.[16]

So the Book of Mormon refuted universal salvation, but so did most
Christians. It denied irresistible grace, but so did the Methodists. It de-
nounced infant baptism, but so did the Baptists. It could be said to challenge Methodism, but so did the Presbyterians. Dan Vogel's assertion

that "those in the early nineteenth century who took the time to closely examine the Book of Mormon realized that its theology was far from orthodox" finds little evidence in contemporary accounts, if unorthodox means outside the pale of the Christian establishment as a whole.[17] In the context of mere sectarian quibbling, criticism of the book's *doctrine* was no more or less conspicuous than criticism of any other denomination's version of biblical Christianity, and in the overall picture of anti-Mormonism, it was a nonfactor. W. W. Phelps's assertion, in this regard, is more than self-righteous bluster: "One thing is remarkable, that of all I ever heard said about the work or book, in that day of gross darkness, not one pretended, in truth, to have the least particle of positive proof, that a man or woman joined the church for sinful purposes, or that the book contained one precept of doctrine that was contrary to pure religion."[18]

In fact, the Book of Mormon presents its own relationship to the Bible as one of corroboration, not supplement or replacement. When Nephi himself described in prophetic terms the coming forth of new scripture in the era of restoration, he saw its purpose, in part, as "the convincing of the Gentiles and the remnant of the seed of my brethren, and also the Jews who were scattered upon all the face of the earth, that the records of the prophets and of the twelve apostles of the Lamb are true. And the angel spake unto me, saying: These last records, which thou hast seen among the Gentiles, shall establish the truth of the first, which are of the twelve apostles of the Lamb" (1 Nephi 13:39-40). But as he revealed in his next sentence, to "establish" the truth of the Bible meant to restore its original message and intent. In the process, the Bible's deficiencies, as well as core value, would be emphasized: "and [these records] shall make known the plain and precious things which have been taken away from them."

The process by which those elements were "taken away" to begin with, in a historical process called by Mormons the Great Apostasy, was described as well:

> And the angel of the Lord said unto me: Thou hast beheld that the book [the Bible] proceeded forth from the mouth of a Jew; and when it proceeded forth from the mouth of a Jew it contained the fulness of the gospel of the Lord, of whom the twelve apostles bear record; and they bear record according to the truth which is in the Lamb of God. Wherefore, these things go forth from the Jews in purity unto the Gentiles, according to the truth which is in God. And after they go forth by the hand of the twelve apostles of the Lamb, from the Jews unto the Gentiles, thou seest the formation of that great and abominable church, which is most abominable above all other churches; for behold, they have taken away from the gospel of the Lamb many parts which are plain and most precious;

and also many covenants of the Lord have they taken away. . . . [And] because of the many plain and precious things which have been taken out of the book, which were plain unto the understanding of the children of men, according to the plainness which is in the Lamb of God—because of these things which are taken away out of the gospel of the Lamb, an exceedingly great many do stumble, yea, insomuch that Satan hath great power over them. (1 Nephi 13:24-29)

Describing his own youthful spiritual quest, Joseph had written that "by searching the scriptures I found that mankind did not come unto the Lord but that they had apostatised from the true and liveing [sic] faith and there was no society or denomination that built upon the gospel of Jesus Christ as recorded in the new testament."[19] His experience in the Sacred Grove (site of the First Vision) verified his impression, when God told Joseph that the Christian sects "were all wrong and . . . all their creeds were an abomination in his sight" (JS-H 1:19). Now, the Book of Mormon confirmed the influence of scriptural corruption in the whole process (much as certain Jewish Christian groups in the early Christian church alleged Old Testament corruption had occurred during the process of canonization[20]). Even before he actually saw the plates, Joseph noticed that Moroni was quoting Malachi to him during his first nocturnal visit, "though with a little variation from the way it reads in our Bibles" (JS-H 1:36). The plates merely explained and expanded those "variations."

But what, precisely, was the role of the Book of Mormon to be in the restoration of the "plain and precious things"? Nephi had spoken of "records" to come forth, and indeed, a veritable flood of writings characterized the years of Joseph Smith's ministry. In seeming reference to the Book of Mormon in particular, a revelation that accompanied Joseph's restoration to God's good graces after the Martin Harris fiasco promised the Lord would "bring to light the true points of my doctrine" and "establish my gospel, that there may not be so much contention . . . concerning the points of my doctrine" (D&C 10:62-63).

This paradox of the Book of Mormon as both confirming and impugning the status of the Bible as scripture finds formal expression in a document presented to the church at the time of incorporation and later published as the "Articles and Covenants of the Church of Christ."[21] It begins with a brief history of the then two-year-old church. Passing quickly over the First Vision,[22] the author immediately proceeds to a description of the angel Moroni's visitation to the young prophet and the record he delivered up:

Which Book contained a record of a fallen people, and also the fulness of the Gospel of Jesus Christ to the Gentiles; and also to the Jews, proving

unto them, that the holy Scriptures are true; and also, that God doth inspire men and call them to his holy work, in these last days as well as in
days of old, that he might be the same God forever. Amen. Which Book
was given by inspiration, and is called The Book of Mormon, and is confirmed to others by the ministering of angels, and declared unto the world
by them: Wherefore, having so great witnesses, by them shall the world
be judged, even as many as shall hereafter receive this work.[23]

So, the Book stands as divine witness, "proving . . . that the holy Scriptures are true." But when the editor uses the word "Scriptures," he is
clearly referring to the Bible; the Book of Mormon as "record of a fallen
people" receives no such designation and appears to be subordinate to
that other book in the heavenly hierarchy. At the same time, that ancient
record, and not those holy scriptures, is designated as containing "the
fulness of the Gospel." Furthermore, the 1832 editor then quotes from
Nephi's vision about the loss of "plain and precious things" to emphasize the deficiencies of scripture, and in the process justifies the next
undertaking of Joseph Smith—a new translation of the Bible: "it will be
seen by this that the most plain parts of the New Testament, have been
taken from it by the Mother of Harlots while it was confined in that
Church . . . from the year A.D. 46 to 1400: This is a sufficient reason for
the Lord to give command to have it translated anew: Notwithstanding
King James' translators did very well, all knowing that they had only
the common faculties of men and literature, without the spirit of Revelation."[24] Not all assessments were so understanding, as a subsequent
article revealed: "As to the errors in the Bible, any man possessed of
common understanding, knows, that both the old and new testaments
are filled with errors, obscurities, italics and contradictions, which must
be the work of men. As the church of Christ will soon have the scriptures, in their original purity, it may not be amiss for us to show a few of
the gross errors, or, as they might be termed, contradictions."[25]

Indeed, Joseph Smith's 1842 pronouncement that Latter-day Saints
"believe the Book of Mormon to be the word of God," whereas they
only accord the same credence to the Bible "as far as it is translated
correctly," accords the former *some* kind of preeminence. The error would
be to see, as one scholar has, a definitive "demotion of the Christian
Bible by virtue of his claim that it had been improperly translated."[26]
The matter isn't quite that simple. For one thing, as Philip Barlow has
pointed out, "Nothing . . . captures the evolving but enduring *religious*
quintessence of Mormonism and its relationship to the balance of American religion better than a firm, comparative grasp of the Bible's place
among the Latter-day Saints. This assertion applies even to Mormon
theology and revelation, which . . . is inextricably enmeshed with and
dependent on prior and often unconscious biblical perspectives."[27] One

historian even concludes, based on the relatively few changes Joseph made in his retranslation, that "what the effort demonstrated was not the distance, but the close parallels the early Saints and their first converts saw between the Bible and the Book of Mormon."[28] Apparently, Joseph was not speaking entirely tongue in cheek when he wrote, in response to the question "wherein do you differ from other sects?", that "we believe the Bible."[29] As we saw, early converts used the Bible as the standard against which they measured the Book of Mormon's teachings. Grant Underwood has shown that in early LDS publications the Bible was quoted anywhere from 19 to 40 times as often as the Book of Mormon.[30] Clearly, this is hardly evidence of the Bible's "demotion."

What, then, of the plain and precious things it restores? In exactly what, compared to the Bible, does its "fulness of the Gospel" consist? And a related question is, at just what point does it become clear in the Latter-day Saint mind, and a point of doctrine, that the Book of Mormon is not solely—or even primarily—ancient history, but is sacred scripture? And what, to the Latter-day Saints, might that designation mean? In this latter regard especially, it is important to keep firmly in mind the warning of Miriam Levering, that "'scripture' is a relational term. That is, it refers to kinds of relationships that people enter into with these texts." Speaking of the study of nonbiblical scriptures, she writes that "scholars tended to assume unconsciously that each such text occupied a place in the religious life of its community and tradition similar to that occupied by the Bible in some branches of Protestant life: a freestanding source of religious doctrine, authority, and inspiration, whose meaning could be grasped without too much reference to original or later contexts."[31]

And the noted religious leader Wilfred Cantwell Smith has suggested the shifting nature of that category and the distinctive shape of its Mormon variety. "Scripture as a form and as a concept gradually emerged and developed in the Near East," he writes, "in a process of slow crystallization whose virtually complete stage comes with the Qur'an. . . . When I say that the Qur'an culminates this process, I do not mean to suggest that the process altogether stops at that point. . . . Closer to our own day, Joseph Smith in the United States with his Book of Mormon, for example, illustrates that the notion was still generative as recently as the nineteenth century."[32]

The designation of scripture need not, in other words, suggest for Mormons an authoritative depository of truth that both limits and defines the parameters of religious doctrine and belief; such is the way the word functions for adherents of the *sola scriptura* tradition, but not for Mormons. As we have seen, scripture is a category that is in large measure historically determined. Accordingly, Latter-day Saints have themselves embraced a definition that is expansive, allowing not only for an enlarged canon but for an endless one. W. D. Davies has questioned whether such a concept of progressive or continuous revelation is even compatible with the historic nature and function of "canon": "The word 'canon' implies that there is a list of books, fixed or set in order and authorized, and accepted by a religious community as the norm. . . . For such a community the truth has already been given in the selected scriptures. Revelations received after a canon has been fixed served simply to explicate the same canon."[33]

But for Latter-day Saints, the Book of Mormon went far beyond biblical explication, and it was but the first wave in a flood of canonical dynamism that shows signs of easing but not ending. Following the Book of Mormon's publication in 1830, Joseph immediately began an inspired revision of the Bible, producing the Book of Moses months later. (Joseph was still working intermittently on his revision at the time of his death. By that point, he had altered about 3,700 verses, or 10 percent of the total.[34] Most of Joseph's changes have been incorporated into the official LDS version of the Bible as footnotes or in an appendix.)

Selections from the dozens and dozens of revelations Joseph had received over the previous decade were published as the *Book of Commandments* in 1833. (Its printing disrupted by mob action, a few hundred salvaged copies contained some 65 revelations to the prophet.) Working with Egyptian papyri acquired in 1835, Joseph produced the Book of Abraham, publishing it in installments in 1842. More revelations were added to a new edition of the *Doctrine and Covenants* in 1835 and then again in 1844. (Not all of Joseph's revelations were incorporated into LDS scriptures. At least 40 known revelations given to him have never been included.[35]) In 1851, *Pearl of Great Price* was published, incorporating both the Book of Moses and the Book of Abraham (the volume officially became church scripture in 1880). Additional revelations were again incorporated into a new edition of the *Doctrine and Covenants* in 1876, and a "Manifesto" of Wilford Woodruff from 1908 on; in 1921, Joseph's "Lectures on Faith" were removed. In 1976, two revelations received in 1836 and 1918 (the latter by a subsequent church president, Joseph F. Smith) were added to *Pearl of Great Price*. In 1981, they were transferred to the *Doctrine and Covenants*, along with an "Official Declaration" on the priesthood. Joseph obviously meant it when he wrote to John Wentworth that "we believe all that God has revealed, all that He does not reveal, and we believe that He will yet reveal many great and important things pertaining to the Kingdom of God."[36]

Nevertheless, there is some basis for seeing the Book of Mormon as a guide to doctrine. The second issue of *The Evening and the Morning Star* was already referring to the Book of Mormon as a companion to, rather than either supporter or supplanter of, the New Testament. Elders were reminded that they "must reason from the Bible and the Book of Mormon, with great care and not pervert the meaning of God's sacred word."[37] (Then, as if to repair any damage done to Christian sensibilities by the prior issue's attack on New Testament accuracy, the editor published the first installment of a tribute to "Scripture" written not by Joseph Smith but by the renowned protestant, Bishop Edward Stillingfleet.)

Still, when Joseph Smith outlined the church's "doctrine" and undertook to expound "the facts of [his own] religious principles" in a "Letter to the Elders of the Church" to guide them in their missionary labors in 1835, he quoted at great length from Luke, Acts, Revelation, Matthew, Isaiah, and Hebrews to teach the fundamentals of repentance, baptism, and the gift of the Holy Ghost. The Book of Mormon received not even a mention.[38] (Given the tendency of most writers to cite themselves at every opportunity, Joseph's reluctance—here as elsewhere—to refer to Book of Mormon content is striking.) While W. W. Phelps praises the Book of Mormon in another column for unfolding the "history and doings of the Indians," in a follow-up letter Joseph continued his doctrinal exposition. In recapping the principles of repentance and baptism for the remission of sins, he reminds his audience that he does "positively rely upon the truth and veracity of those principles inculcated in the new testament." Only in passing on to the subject of "the gathering" and after quoting from his new translation of Genesis, from Revelation and Deuteronomy, does he at last cite Nephi and Ether relative to the coming of a New Jerusalem.[39]

On a few occasions, Joseph Smith did refer to the ancient record to buttress his teachings on other gospel themes. In his Lectures on Faith, delivered at the School of the Prophets in Kirtland, Ohio, he alluded to particular Book of Mormon episodes as exemplifying the nature of faith as a "principle of power." But even here, as Timothy Smith notes, he ignores the opportunity to use "many passages that would have sustained" his points, relying instead on favorite Wesleyan New Testament passages.[40]

Joseph's successor Brigham Young was of the same bent. "I never asked for any book when I was preaching to the world," he declared, "but the Old and New Testaments to establish everything I preached, and to prove all that was necessary."[41] Of course, this orientation is in part pragmatic. Among those Christian peoples where most church proselytizing has historically been carried out, it will not do to use as a guide to doctrine a work whose very status is so contested. But some Mormons resist such efforts because they are impatient with even fellow Latter-day Saints who would impose upon the Book of Mormon a doctrinal role it seldom fulfilled initially. Criticizing the very undertaking of a doctrinal commentary on the Book of Mormon, for example, one writes: "If what we needed was an authoritative theological treatise, the

Book of Mormon was an odd way for it to have been made available. Looked at that way, it turns out to have been a failure."[42]

Nevertheless, in the modern era, the Book of Mormon and the Bible have become virtually interchangeable for purposes of doctrine in the Mormon church. The fullest expression of the impulse to simply slip the Book of Mormon into biblical clothing, allowing it to inherit a pre-defined scriptural category rather than carving out a new one, came with the church's 1979–1981 edition of the "Standard Works," the scriptural canon that includes both Bible and Book of Mormon, as well as *Doctrine and Covenants* and *Pearl of Great Price*.[43] In the special edition prepared by Cambridge University Press, the texts of the four works are thoroughly interfused through an elaborate cross-referencing system that effectively assimilates them into one seamless work (even available as one large volume). At the time, it may have appeared a simple exercise in formatting or a pedagogical tool for more efficient scriptural study and teaching. Church apostle Boyd K. Packer, on the other hand, was seeing a larger issue at stake when he referred to the edition as "the most important thing that we [the church] have done in recent generations," and "the crowning achievement in the [long and growth-studded] administration of President Spencer W. Kimball."[44]

As we have seen, Mormons from Joseph Smith's day to the present have cited Ezekiel's vision as a prophecy of the Book of Mormon: "The word of the Lord came again unto me, saying, Moreover, thou son of man, take thee one stick, and write upon it, For Judah, and for the children of Israel his companions: then take another stick, and write upon it, For Joseph, the stick of Ephraim, and for all the house of Israel his companions: And join them one to another into one stick; and they shall become one in thine hand" (Ezekiel 37:15-17).[45] As early as 1833, Joseph planned to publish an edition that would bring the Book of Mormon and his re-working of the New Testament together under one cover,[46] as an apparent sign both of prophetic fulfillment and of authoritative parity of the two scriptures. The 1981 edition finally effected a degree of unity and equality between the two scriptures that seemed, at long last, to fulfill Ezekiel's vision of perfect scriptural harmony and complementarity between the sacred histories of two branches of Israel. In fact, Elder Packer cited that prophecy in pronouncing his judgment on the new scriptural edition, telling a general conference of the church that "The stick or record of Judah—the Old Testament and the New Testament—and the stick or record of Ephraim—the Book of Mormon, which is another testament of Jesus Christ—are now woven together. . . . They are indeed one in our hands. Ezekiel's prophecy now stands fulfilled."[47]

Accordingly, the Book of Mormon seems to have now reached a condition of absolute equality in the Mormon canon, and doctrinally it would seem clearly intended to be every bit as authoritative as its sister scriptures. Of course, in a church that assigns more weight to living oracles than textual ones, the doctrinal role of the canon is in any case limited. In addition to its sheer fluidity, in other words, the Mormon concept of canonicity becomes complicated by the liberal definition of scripture held by its members. In a revelation to Joseph Smith in 1831, the Lord declared that his servants "shall speak when moved upon by the Holy Ghost. And whatsoever they shall speak when moved upon by the Holy Ghost shall be scripture, shall be the will of the Lord, shall be the word of the Lord, and the power of God unto salvation" (D&C 68:3-4).

In was in such a context that Brigham Young in the 1830s made a dramatic statement comparing the claims upon Latter-day Saints of scripture and of modern prophetic utterance:

> Brother Brigham took the stand, and he took the Bible, and laid it down; he took the Book of Mormon, and laid it down; and he took the Book of Doctrine and Covenants, and laid it down before him, and he said: "There is the written word of God to us, concerning the work of God from the beginning of the world, almost, to our day. And now," said he, "when compared to the living oracles those books are nothing to me; those books do not convey the word of God direct to us now, as do the words of a Prophet. . . ."[48]

In 1916, Orson F. Whitney reiterated: "The Latter-day Saints do not do things because they happen to be printed in a book. They do not do things because God told the Jews to do them: nor do they do or leave undone anything because of instructions that Christ gave to the Nephites. Whatever is done by this Church is because God speaking from Heaven in our day has commanded the Church to do it. No book presides over this Church and no books lie at its foundation. You cannot pile up books enough to take the place of God's priesthood inspired by the power of the Holy Ghost."[49] And his words were in turn quoted by another elder at a 1976 general conference of the church.[50]

In the final result, even as Mormon doctrine subordinates its own canon to the principle of living revelation, these distinctions may count for little. Given the very fluidity of the canon we have seen, any opposition between living oracles and printed scripture is always subject to renegotiation. As Mormon canonical history shows, today's inspired utterances may become part of tomorrow's standard works. Ultimately, then, the principle of continuing revelation and living oracles emerges as inseparable from the foremost embodiment of that principle—the Book of Mormon. And the Book of Mormon therefore holds out an alluring promise of continuing divine interaction with the human even as it poses the greatest threat to orthodox notions of canonicity and revelation that Christianity has yet seen.

As W. D. Davies states the dilemma, "Progressive and continuous revelation is certainly an attractive notion, but equally certainly it is not without the grave danger of so altering and enlarging upon the original revelation as to distort, annul, and even falsify it. This is the fundamental question which all the more traditional Christian communions and—indeed, the NT itself—pose to Mormonism."[51] But, as we shall see, it may not be so much the challenge to "the original revelation," as a challenge to the *concept* of revelation, that constitutes the Book of Mormon's real radicalism.

It should be clear by this point that Joseph Smith's claims about the Book of Mormon's foundational role in the Latter-day Saint religion and Rodney Stark's assessment of its theological irrelevance are not as wholly incompatible as they at first seem. The Book of Mormon has had a tremendous role to play in the establishment of the Latter-day Saint church, a role grounded largely in its obtrusiveness as miraculous artifact, portent of the last days, and sign of prophetic power. This role appears to have little or nothing to do with particular doctrines that are explicitly taught in the revealed record. True, we have seen how in the first generation of the church the Book of Mormon was cited frequently to affirm the imminence of Christ's return or the establishment of a New Jerusalem upon the American continent. It was also used to affirm baptism by immersion, the innocence of children, and the conditional nature of salvation.

Most often, however, it was simplicity rather than novelty that converts responded to favorably. To those primitivists, seekers, and restorationists who sought a return to the simple gospel of the New Testament, the Book of Mormon was appealing by virtue of the plain exposition of basic principles that constitute the doctrine of Christ at its core. As quoted before, early Mormon missionary Wandle Mace recorded in his journal that in addition to preaching the Book of Mormon, "We discoursed upon the first principles of the gospel."[52] Indeed, he could have taught those first principles from the New Testament, as Joseph and Brigham suggested, or from the Book of Mormon itself. Nephi, who "delights in plainness," provides this neat summary of the gospel:

> I know that if ye shall follow the Son, with full purpose of heart, acting no
> hypocrisy and no deception before God, but with real intent, repenting of
> your sins, witnessing unto the Father that ye are willing to take upon you
> the name of Christ, by baptism—yea, by following your Lord and your
> Savior down into the water, according to his word, behold, then shall ye
> receive the Holy Ghost; yea, then cometh the baptism of fire and of the
> Holy Ghost; and then can ye speak with the tongue of angels, and shout
> praises unto the Holy One of Israel. . . . And I heard a voice from the

Father, saying: Yea, the words of my Beloved are true and faithful. He
that endureth to the end, the same shall be saved. (2 Nephi 31:13-15)

This basic framework (recast by Joseph Smith as "the first principles
and ordinances of the gospel" in the fourth of the church's Articles of
Faith) is referred to as the "doctrine of Christ" [53] by Nephi, Jacob, and
Mormon and is the only teaching dignified by the word "doctrine" in
the entire Book of Mormon. In fact, as Louis Midgley has pointed out,
"'doctrine' appears in the Book of Mormon twenty-four times, always
with the narrow meaning of the gospel of Jesus Christ; . . . when plural,
the word identifies foolish, vain, and false teachings that deny the gospel—that Jesus is the Christ (see 2 Nephi 28:9, 15; Alma 1:16)."[54]

Doctrinally, then, the Book of Mormon was conservative rather than
radical and fulfilled restorationist hopes by reverting to simple truths
seen by converts as at the heart of biblical religion. Among the early
Disciples of Christ movement especially, these simple formulations were
both familiar and welcome. In the preaching of Walter Scott, for example,
"the great elements of the gospel assumed the following definite, rational, and scriptural order: (1) Faith; (2) Repentance; (3) Baptism; (4) Remission of sins; (5) The Holy Spirit; (6) Eternal life, through a patience
continuance in well doing." Scott himself, and presumably many of his
listeners, found this "arrangement of themes . . . so plain, so manifestly
in harmony with soundest reason, and so clearly correct" that he was
"transported with the discovery." [55]

This public presentation of the Book of Mormon as providing a doctrinal corrective and simple foundation, rather than innovation and
elaboration, had already been emphasized as the translation was nearing completion in June of 1829. Having learned by revelation that a
church was to be established, Joseph Smith, Oliver Cowdery, and David
Whitmer asked for more "instructions relative to building up the Church
of Christ."[56] In apparent reference to the Book of Mormon, the Lord
directed them to "rely upon the things which are written; for in them
are all things written concerning the foundation of my church, my gospel, and my rock" (D&C 18:3-4). In response to this directive, Oliver
Cowdery composed a set of "procedural regulations" for the new church,
relying on the Book of Mormon for over 50 percent of its content.[57]
Cowdery's articles served as the basis for Joseph Smith's expanded and
authoritative document on church administration, the Articles and Covenants. Presented to the members at the first conference of the church in
1830, this "Revelation on Church Organization and Government" defining some of the procedures and regulations of the newly established
church was therefore heavily reliant upon the Book of Mormon itself.
For example, Nephite baptism signaled formal entry into the church,
was practiced by immersion for the remission of sins, and was predi-

cated upon proper priesthood authority. Both Cowdery's and Smith's articles used Book of Mormon language to establish these same principles in the new church. The same was true of the manner of ordaining teachers and priests (and deacons, in Smith's document), and the mode of administering the Lord's supper.[58] The church's actual wording of the baptismal prayer and of the blessing on the bread and wine (later water) come directly from prayers recorded in the Book of Mormon.

Many developments in church organization and doctrine that followed were based more on the principle of continuing revelation than on textual exegesis of either the Bible or the Book of Mormon. The need addressed by Cowdery's preliminary document based on mere gleanings from the Book of Mormon would soon be filled by a proliferation of more contemporary revelation and would come to constitute an additional, entirely distinct, and still-growing book of scripture. And while the Book of Mormon provided a basis for some church procedures and policies, Joseph's experience in translating the Book of Mormon, his growth in revelatory confidence, and the questions provoked in his mind by the ancient record all contributed to the establishment of revelation— not a scriptural canon—as the guiding principle in the new organization about to unfold.

All this is not to say the volume made no doctrinal contributions at all. The scripture does make a number of original claims that go well beyond the mere repackaging of Protestantism. B. H. Roberts, one of the church's greatest students of the Book of Mormon, believed that it contained numerous theological treasures. Among the original contributions of the Book of Mormon, he found

> the definition of truth itself (Jacob 4:13); the doctrine of opposite existences (2 Nephi 2); the doctrine (with cosmological implications) that the universe splits into two categories "things to act and things to be acted upon" (2 Nephi 2:14); a foundation for an unqualified affirmation of man's agency (2 Nephi 2:27, 10:23; Alma 61:21); a doctrine of the fall of Adam as instrumental to a higher good (2 Nephi 2:10-11, 15; Alma 42:16-17); a doctrine of the nature of evil as "among the eternal things"—"as eternal as good; as eternal as law; as eternal as the agency of intelligence" (2 Nephi 2:17; Jacob 5:59; Alma 41:13) and thus a "master stroke" in the solution of the classical problem of theodicy (how can a God of power be responsible for evil and the devil?) (2 Nephi 2:15-25); and a doctrine of the purpose of man's existence (2 Nephi 2:25).

But most significant, he found in Mormonism a distinctive doctrine of Christ and his atonement, "derived almost wholly from the teachings of the Book of Mormon."[59]

Beginning as it does in a familiar Old Testament milieu, with references to Jews and Egyptians, to Zedekiah and Jerusalem's impending destruction, the book loses no time in upsetting expectations in regard to traditional Christology. A mere nine verses into the record, the prophet Lehi sees in vision "One descending out of the midst of heaven," with "twelve others following him," who "came down and went forth upon the face of the earth." And thus we are introduced to one of the most radical and pervasive themes in the Book of Mormon—pre-Christian knowledge of Christ. Unlike the messianic Psalms and Isaiah passages, Book of Mormon prophecies of Christ are unmistakably specific. "Yea, even six hundred years from the time that my father left Jerusalem, a prophet would the Lord God raise up among the Jews," records Nephi, "—even a Messiah, or, in other words, a Savior of the world" (1 Nephi 10:4). Nephi then describes his baptism by "the prophet who should prepare the way before him," his ministry among "multitudes . . . gathered together to hear him," and his eventual death as he is "lifted up upon the cross and slain for the sins for the world." "And according to the words of the prophets, and also the word of the angel of God, his name shall be Jesus Christ, the Son of God," he adds later (1 Nephi 11:27-33; 2 Nephi 25:19). Adding yet more details, King Benjamin indicates that "his mother shall be called Mary," and Alma records that his birth will occur in the land of Jerusalem (Mos. 3:8; Alma 7:12).

As we have seen earlier, it is not just foreknowledge of a coming Christ that the Book of Mormon alleges of the Nephites. From the time Babylonians were depopulating the land of Jerusalem almost till the year in which the Goths sacked Rome, we learn, ancient Americans were baptizing in the name of Christ, praying to the Father in the name of Christ, performing miracles in the name of Christ, and worshiping in the name of Christ (2 Nephi 31:13, 32:9; Alma 14:28; Jacob 4:5).

The Book of Mormon is even subtitled "Another Testament of Christ." Those words were added to every copy of the Book of Mormon printed beginning in 1982, by decision of the church's General Authorities.[60] In the same vein, the church a few years ago redesigned their logo, greatly enlarging the words "Jesus Christ" in their organization's title. The ubiquitous missionary nametags as well as official letterhead now typographically trumpet the shift of focus. Such changes could be interpreted as cosmetic public relations tactics. However, the Book of Mormon supplies ample support for the new emphasis. For sheer number of references to Christ, the Book of Mormon is a scripture without parallel. In one study, for example, an LDS scholar calculates that "a reference to Christ occurs every 1.7 verses, or once every two sentences" throughout that scripture.[61] More frequently per verse than in the New Testament asserts another.[62] The irony of all this is that Mormons find

themselves reviled as non-Christians by many fundamentalist Protes-
tants while holding sacred not two testaments of Christ, but three.

But is it the Christ of the Christian tradition? Given the familiar trappings surrounding Christ in the Book of Mormon—Isaiah's predictions,
recognizable descriptions of his ministry and crucifixion, familiar say-
ings from his Old World Sermon on the Mount—there seems little immediate evidence to suspect he is not.[63] On the other hand, the Mormon
Christ has some important distinctions from the Messiah of other Christians. To start with, Latter-days Saints hold the unique belief that Jehovah was the premortal Christ in his Old Testament garb, the true God of
Israel, of Abraham, Isaac, and Jacob. This position does find clear affirmation in the Book of Mormon. Nephi is the first to equate "the Holy
One of Israel," with "the true Messiah, [Israel's] Redeemer and their
God" (2 Nephi 1:10). Nephi's brother Jacob further clarifies that "the
Lord God, the Holy One of Israel, should manifest himself unto [the
Jews] in the flesh; and after he should manifest himself they should
scourge him and crucify him" (2 Nephi 6:9). Later, King Benjamin teaches
that "the Lord Omnipotent who reigneth, who was, and is from all eternity to all eternity, shall come down from heaven among the children of
men, and shall dwell in a tabernacle of clay," and Abinadi testifies that
the same God who gave the commandments to Moses shall make an
atonement "for the sins and iniquities of his people" (Mos. 3:5; 13:28).

Of course, within a trinitarian framework, such verses suggest nothing outside the ordinary. "Great is the mystery of godliness: God was
manifest in the flesh," writes Paul (1 Tim. 3:16). Critics even hold that
other Book of Mormon passages have distinctly trinitarian echoes, and,
citing scattered editorial changes that later clarify the distinctness of the
godhead's members, conclude that Joseph's Book of Mormon God was
more in line with orthodox Christianity than his later teaching that God,
Christ, and the Holy Ghost are separate and distinct beings.[64] For example, the prophet Abinadi explains to a group of Nephites that "because he [Christ] dwelleth in flesh he shall be called the Son of God, and
having subjected the flesh to the will of the Father, being the Father and
the Son— The Father, because he was conceived by the power of God;
and the Son, because of the flesh; thus becoming the Father and Son—
And they are one God, yea, the very Eternal Father of heaven and of
earth" (Mos. 15:2-4). Later, when Zeezrom asks, "Is the Son of God the
very Eternal Father?", Alma could be seen as either complicating or
clarifying the matter when he answers, "Yea he is the very Eternal Father of heaven and of earth" (Alma 11:38-39). And in 3 Nephi, Jesus
refers to himself and the Father as one on several occasions. Thomas G.
Alexander sees here traces of trinitarian thought that Joseph progressively moved beyond.[65] Finally, Melodie Moench Charles believes there
is "no good way to reconcile Abinadi's words with . . . current Mormon

belief," and Mark Thomas agrees that "the Book of Mormon . . . defends a trinitarian position on the Godhead." [66]

It is true that the Book of Mormon can raise more theological difficulties than it resolves in this regard. To give another example, when the risen Christ appears to the Nephites, he introduces himself as "the God of Israel, and the God of the whole earth" (3 Nephi 11:14). When he also declares that "I am he who gave the law, and I am he who covenanted with my people Israel," the matter seems clear enough. But on the same occasion he promises to "fulfill the covenant which *the Father* hath made unto all the people of the house of Israel" (3 Nephi 15:5, 16:5). So those hard contours that demarcate the members of the godhead as utterly distinct in Joseph Smith's later teachings,[67] extending even to physical, corporeal separateness, are not clearly reflected in the text of the Book of Mormon. For Mormons, the murky intricacies and inconsistencies of these divine interrelationships receive scant attention. If they pose a Gordian knot resolvable for theologians only by borrowings from metaphysics and gnosticism (such as the creedal *"homoousios"*[68]), the LDS First Presidency cuts through it with a simple explanation—"divine investiture:" "The Father placed His name upon the Son; and Jesus Christ spoke and ministered in and through the Father's name; and so far as power, authority, and Godship are concerned His words and acts were and are those of the Father."[69]

This Mormon theology that avoids trinitarianism by imputing to any member of the godhead authority to speak for another may be too convenient for skeptics. But the "modalism" Melodie Moench Charles and Clyde Forsberg[70] impute to the Book of Mormon (the belief that Father, Son, and Holy Ghost are three labels for three functions or modes pertaining to one God) has clear deficiencies of its own, Mormons are quick to point out. It fails utterly to account for a scene like Christ's baptism, or his descent in 3 Nephi, where he appears bodily even as the voice of the Father announces him. It will not do to simply aver that "Book of Mormon authors saw Christ and his Father as one God who manifested himself in different ways."[71] Ultimately, Robert Millet's flippant response to these critics is not so flippant: "the Book of Mormon is about as trinitarian as the New Testament." By which he means, it isn't.[72] Like the New Testament, Mormon's record shows us an incarnate Christ who prays to the Father, a son introduced by the heavenly voice of the Father, and a Christ who refers to his own heavenly Father throughout the course of a mortal ministry. Charles insists that those episodes are theologically less determinative than scriptural, verbal reference to the Father and Son's oneness. [73] Given Christ's plea in his intercessory prayer that his apostles "may be one, even as we are one" (John 17), her logic is less than compelling.

Some distortion of Mormon views on human nature and Christ's role may occur when one neglects the larger theological universe in which the Book of Mormon Christ performs his redemptive work. Many writers, from Fawn Brodie to the present, have emphasized what they take to be Calvinist influences at work in Joseph's mind. Elaborating the connection between the Book of Mormon and nineteenth-century America, for example, Marvin Hill follows Brodie in writing that, "Theologically the Book of Mormon was a mediating text standing between orthodox Calvinists and emerging Arminians" (those who espouse and those who reject predestination), and he points to "passages which are strongly anti-Universalist" as evidence of "the Calvinistic inclinations in the text."[74] Thomas Alexander argues in his influential 1980 essay that Joseph Smith exhibited in the Book of Mormon and in his pre-1835 writings generally a "pessimistic" assessment of human nature and related notions of God,[75] and others have adopted similar views about Joseph's later abandonment of Book of Mormon negativism. For example, Joseph preached a famously radical theology at the funeral sermon of one King Follett toward the end of his ministry, expanding and literalizing the patristic concept of deification (human participation in the divine nature).[76] Contrasting this doctrine with the alleged Nephite view of human nature, one writer asks rhetorically, "Was the Book of Mormon Buried with King Follett?"[77]

These assessments are based in large measure on what seems to be the Book of Mormon's unstinting indictment of human nature as "carnal, sensual, and devilish" (Mos. 16:3; Alma 42:10). Like the Calvinists, Mormon prophets insist that without the redemptive effects of Christ's expiation, "our spirits must have become like unto [the devil,] and we become devils, angels to a devil, to be shut out from the presence of our God" (2 Nephi 9:9). Thus it sounds only fair to claim, as one critic does, that "while human beings are, as some Mormons are fond of repeating, 'gods in embryo' in the sense that they are the spirit offspring of a divine being, the Book of Mormon teaches that humans are also devils in embryo in the sense that, without a savior, they would naturally devolve into diabolical, not divine, beings."[78]

King Benjamin's description of human nature is also less than flattering. In his great sermon, Benjamin preaches that "the natural man is an enemy to God, and has been from the fall of Adam, and will be, forever and ever, unless he yields to the enticings of the Holy Spirit, and putteth off the natural man and becometh a saint through the atonement of Christ the Lord" (Mos. 3:19). And RLDS scholar A. Bruce Lindgren cites Helaman 12:4-7 as proof that the book is "pessimistic about human nature"[79]:

O how foolish, and how vain, and how evil, and devilish, and how quick to do iniquity, and how slow to do good, are the children of men; yea, how quick to hearken unto the words of the evil one, and to set their hearts upon the vain things of the world! Yea, how quick to be lifted up in pride; yea, how quick to boast, and do all manner of that which is iniquity. . . . O how great is the nothingness of the children of men; yea, even they are less than the dust of the earth.

Certainly a view of mankind as fundamentally depraved and incapable of autonomous improvement can legitimately be read in such passages when taken in isolation. But in the Book of Mormon and elsewhere, Joseph revealed a comprehensive vision of human origins and destiny in light of which, as King Benjamin's phrase "putteth off" suggests, fallenness may be a contingent rather than essential feature of the human condition.

The prophet Alma, in an admittedly cryptic passage, refers to children of God "in the first place" who exhibited great faith and good works and were accordingly foreordained and prepared from the foundation of the world, in accordance with a "preparatory redemption," for service in mortal life (Alma 13). Months after the Book of Mormon was published, Joseph revealed further information about this premortal state, when he found Moses to have taught that God "made the world and men before they were in the flesh," and he published a record of Abraham in which the patriarch saw "many of the noble and great ones" among "the intelligences that were organized before the world was."[80]

If mortality is not man's original condition, a view of human nature based on scriptural descriptions of an embodied state is at one remove from the truth of the matter. The Book of Mormon is emphatic in its insistence that the detritus of the fall—sin and death especially—is a dark middle passage, not a point of origin, in humanity's spiritual odyssey. That is why, as regards Adam's transgression, the Book of Mormon weighs in with an unqualified endorsement of the "fortunate fall":

And now, behold, if Adam had not transgressed he would not have fallen, but he would have remained in the garden of Eden. And all things which were created must have remained in the same state in which they were after they were created; . . . And they would have had no children; wherefore they would have remained in a state of innocence, having no joy, for they knew no misery; doing no good, for they knew no sin. But behold, all things have been done in the wisdom of him who knoweth all things. Adam fell that men might be; and men are, that they might have joy. (2 Nephi 2:22-25)

This position of joyful accommodation to a fallen condition, because it is seen as transient rather than innate, was introduced with the record's 1830 publication, and emphatically reaffirmed in Joseph Smith's retranslation of the Bible which he began almost as the Book of Mormon came off the press. From the Book of Moses, we find this addition to the traditional account in Genesis:

> And in that day Adam blessed God, and was filled, and began to prophesy concerning all the families of the earth, saying: Blessed be the name of God, for because of my transgression my eyes are opened, and in this life I shall have joy, and again in the flesh I shall see God. And Eve, his wife, heard all these things and was glad, saying: Were it not for our transgression we never should have had seed, and never should have known good and evil, and the joy of our redemption, and the eternal life which God giveth unto all the obedient.[81]

In fact, the expulsion from the garden was not wrathful punishment of a primal wickedness but merciful forestalling of premature immortality, in accordance with a plan that anticipated a temporary spiritual isolation from God:

> And we see that death comes upon mankind, . . . which is the temporal death; nevertheless there was a space granted unto man in which he might repent; therefore this life became a probationary state; a time to prepare to meet God; a time to prepare for that endless state which has been spoken of by us, which is after the resurrection of the dead. . . . And now behold, if it were possible that our first parents could have gone forth and partaken of the tree of life they would have been forever miserable, having no preparatory state; and thus the plan of redemption would have been frustrated, and the word of God would have been void, taking none effect (Alma 12:24-26).[82]

The fall of man was fortunate, the Book of Mormon explains, not because in some Miltonic sense it called forth a triumphal act of supernal grace, but because its actuality in the world is the sign—and price—of the moral freedom that precedes it. Freedom, in turn, is the precondition for human happiness. As Lehi explains,

> And if ye shall say there is no law, ye shall also say there is no sin. If ye shall say there is no sin, ye shall also say there is no righteousness. And if there be no righteousness there be no happiness. And if there be no righteousness nor happiness there be no punishment nor misery. And if these things are not there is no God. And if there is no God we are not, neither the earth; for there could have been no creation of things, neither to act nor to be acted upon; wherefore, all things must have vanished away. (2 Nephi 2:13)

Thus, the Book of Mormon view of the human condition emphasizes what was validated by the fall—moral freedom—not what was temporarily assumed—sinfulness. In characterizing sin itself as an essential precondition for the very possibility of human happiness, the scripture emphasizes freedom rather than depravity. And in light of the insistent and repeated references to this moral freedom, the Calvinist connection to the Book of Mormon cannot be seriously maintained.

Against this backdrop, then, the Book of Mormon develops a doctrine of the atonement in such a way as to reclaim the principle of justice from a kind of Platonic abstraction or equivalence with God himself and to situate it in the context of human agency. This may well be one of its greatest theological contributions. One Christian doctrine of atonement, with which we may compare the Book of Mormon's teaching, has it that "sin, being an infinite offence against God, required a satisfaction equally infinite. As no finite being . . . could offer satisfaction, it was necessary that an infinite being, i.e. God Himself, should take the place of man and, by His death, make complete satisfaction to Divine Justice."[83] The Book of Mormon (which uses various forms of "atone" 36 times as compared to the New Testament's one reference) similarly connects atonement to justice, explaining that vicarious expiation notwithstanding, "the work of justice could not be destroyed; if so, God would cease to be God" (Alma 42:13).

The theological rub seems to be, why cannot God simply pardon fault? Or as the Book of Mormon's Alma says to his son Corianton, "I perceive there is somewhat more which doth worry your mind, . . . which is concerning the justice of God in the punishment of the sinner" (Alma 42:1). To explain the necessity for atonement in terms of an inflexible principle of eternal justice—as in a conventional soteriology—is to defer the problem; it is not to solve it. We have, in this case, merely elevated one of God's attributes to the status of a universal and then endowed that universal with highly peculiar features. Peculiar, first, because justice manifests itself here as a mathematical rather than moral principle. Since punishment—but not punishment of the guilty—is required, the impersonal demand is in accordance with some abstract calculus that has no earthly counterpart. No terrestrial magistrate would allow an innocent person to die for a guilty one and consider justice to be served. Peculiar, second, because justice here usurps the place of God as a principle before which he himself seems to bow. A wise father given appropriate extenuating circumstances, or by the timely and efficacious exercise of mercy, may remit altogether the punishment of a guilty son. God, apparently, cannot. Explanation of atonement in terms of a Platonic absolute called justice, in other words, begs as many questions as it answers.

Two Book of Mormon disquisitions on the subject, 2 Nephi 2 and Alma 41-42, move beyond such abstracting explanations by situating justice in a larger discussion of moral agency. In the first, Lehi asserts a fundamental dichotomy in the universe between those entities that have agency ("things that act") and those that do not ("things acted upon"). (In a subsequent revelation, Joseph Smith would define the first category as the only true existence: "All truth is independent in that sphere in which God has placed it, to act for itself, as all intelligence also; otherwise there is no existence" [D&C 93:30].) Such agency, to be efficacious, must operate in the presence of alternatives: "Wherefore, man could not act for himself save it should be that he was enticed by the one or the other" (2 Nephi 2:16). But more to the point, genuine moral agency must entail necessary consequences. If choice is to be more than an empty gesture of the will, more than a mere pantomime of decision making, there must be an immutable guarantee that any given choice will eventuate in the natural consequence of that choice. To paraphrase Edmund Husserl, choice must be choice *of something*. Christ, Lehi explains, institutes the terms whereby those consequences are assured and himself stands as the ultimate guarantor of the integrity of such meaningful choice: "Wherefore, the ends of the law [are those] which the Holy One hath given, unto the inflicting of the punishment which is affixed, which punishment that is affixed is in opposition to that of the happiness which is affixed" (2 Nephi 2:10).

It is the certainty of such punishment and reward, defined and differentiated by law and freely chosen by man, that establishes his moral agency: "Wherefore," Lehi concludes, "men are free according to the flesh; and all things are given them which are expedient unto man. And they are free to choose liberty and eternal life, . . . or to chose captivity and death" (2 Nephi 2:27). In this view, justice seems to be another name for the moral order as defined and implemented by "the Holy One."

Alma is even more explicit in defining justice as a moral order that validates human agency. "The plan of restoration," as he calls this principle, "is requisite with the justice of God; for it is requisite that all things should be restored to their proper order" (Alma 41:2). And how is that order defined? "And if their works were good in this life, and the desires of their hearts were good, that they should also, at the last day, be restored unto that which is good. And if their works are evil they shall be restored unto them for evil" (Alma 41:3-4). *Not* simply because that is the "fair" or "just" thing for God to do. For God is also merciful, and if humans can remit a penalty out of compassion or mercy, why cannot God?

Because, as Alma continues, such apparent generosity would undermine the essence of that agency on which moral freedom depends. Consequences are chosen at the time actions are freely committed. To choose to indulge a desire is to choose its fruit—bitter or sweet—assuming, as

Lehi did, that "men are instructed sufficiently" to understand what they are choosing (2 Nephi 2:5). So following the exercise of such agency, "the one [must be] raised to happiness according to his desires of happiness, or good according to his desires of good; and the other to evil according to his desires of evil" (Alma 41:5). It is a truth that harks back to Dante's grim vision of hell in which God is not present as judge or dispenser of punishments, because choices are allowed, inexorably, to bear their own fruit. In Alma's Inferno as well, future states are chosen, not assigned: "For behold," says Alma, "they are their own judges" (Alma 41:7).

The rationale behind such a moral order is not an omnipotent, impersonal, and cruelly inflexible absolute called justice, but rather the protection of a necessary framework for human agency, that in assuring the promise of righteous reward for the righteous must equally guarantee evil (whatever is "contrary to the nature of God" [Alma 41:11]) to those who demonstrate through their actions their choice of evil. Given this framework, Alma emphasizes, Corianton's attribution of punishment to a vindictive God is misplaced: "And now, there was no means to reclaim men from this fallen state, *which man had brought upon himself* because of his own disobedience" (Alma 42:12, emphasis mine).

So, Lehi and Alma agree that human moral autonomy is predicated upon a sacred connection between desire and reward, choice and consequence. And it is law that articulates and clarifies that connection, making sin, righteousness, and happiness possible. As Lehi says, "If ye shall say there is no law, ye shall also say there is no sin. If ye shall say there is no sin, ye shall also say there is no righteousness. And if there be no righteousness there be no happiness" (2 Nephi 2:13). And Alma asks "how could [man] sin if there was no law? How could there be a law save there was a punishment" (Alma 42:17).

Within these parameters that Lehi and Alma have framed, no escape from the consequences of law is possible without destroying the entire moral order of the universe and both the human agency it grounds and the status of the divine guarantor of the whole system ("God would cease to be God"). As long as the penalty is executed, law is safeguarded. As long as man *chooses* to undo the effects of his decisions and then chooses anew (repentance), agency is safeguarded. So Christ offers himself as ransom to the demands of law, as the only being capable of paying a cumulative penalty as "eternal as the life of the soul" (Alma 42:16). The consequence of unrighteous choice unfolds as it must, but the pain it inflicts is vicariously felt. Therefore, "justice exerciseth all his demands, and also mercy claimeth all which is her own; and thus, none but the truly penitent are saved" (Alma 42:24).

As regards its religious teachings, then, the Book of Mormon has been valued by the faithful for teaching the "plain and precious truths" of the gospel while testifying to a historically enlarged role for the embodied Christ and his church. Other than that innovation, the scripture has not been notorious for breaking new ground. In fact, aside from its claim to present an ancient American counterpart to the Book of Acts, there has been little focus—by proponents or detractors—on the Book of Mormon's content. Bruce Lindgren believes that the Mormon belief that man may become as God and the Reorganized Latter Day Saint church's conventional trinitarianism (opposed as he believes them to be to the Book of Mormon's "modalism"), are evidence that Mormons "have tended to use the Book of Mormon primarily as a sign and not as a scripture. We have been concerned about its authorship and historicity. We have been less concerned with understanding the theological content of the Book of Mormon itself." His example may be suspect. But his verdict, as we have seen, is certainly true. The function of the Book of Mormon as a sign of the restoration "tends to make the book opaque as we regard its teachings. We become awed by [or dismissive of] what the book stands for, and our awe [or disdain] distracts us from examining its content."[84]

Nevertheless, one could also make the case that the Book of Mormon's greatest theological value and impact have been underestimated because they have been implicit rather than explicit. The Book of Mormon's real radicalism is in the way it emphatically models, chronicles, and then enacts a version of divine discourse that contests prevailing theologies of revelation. This model, which I call dialogic revelation, may go a long way toward explaining the phenomenal appeal of the book and the church it grounds. Aside from the Book of Mormon's explicitly addressed doctrines, novel or familiar, stands this one principle that thematically frames the work, pervades the work like a leitmotif, preconditions the actual transmission of the work, and is ultimately invoked as the ground on which readers must read and respond to the work.

EIGHT

"Plain and Precious Truths": The Book of Mormon as New Theology, Part 2—Dialogic Revelation

And we also had many revelations, and the spirit of much prophecy. . . .

—Jacob 1:6

There is no such thing as revealed truth. There are truths of revelation; but they are not themselves directly revealed.

—William Temple

". . . the patriotic archbishop of Canterbury found it advisable—"
"Found *what?*" said the Duck;
"Found *it,*" the Mouse replied rather crossly: "of course you know what 'it' means."
"I know what 'it' means well enough, when *I* find a thing," said the Duck: "it is generally a frog, or a worm. The question is, what did the archbishop find?"

—*The Duck and the Mouse* in *Alice's Adventures in Wonderland*

In his important study of *Belief, Language, and Experience*, the ethnographer Rodney Needham makes a powerful case for the impossibility of accurately translating religious vocabularies across cultures. Concepts we translate as "belief" and "faith" meant certain things to the Hebrews, other things to early Christians writing out of a Greco-Roman culture, and something quite different again to the Nuer people of sub-Saharan Africa.[1] Broadly speaking, of course, this is because no concept translates seamlessly across linguistic or cultural boundaries.

In the wake of Saussure and structuralism, we are generally conscious of the role of language in shaping rather than merely reflecting our realities; the French linguist's concept of "negative value" alerts us to the impossibility of ascribing to a word any stable, context-independent meaning. Words will always mean what the surrounding linguistic field conditions and allows them to mean.

But Needham's observation is really a more focused critique of the ways that religious terminology especially is given its particular cast by the underlying cosmology of its users. As he writes, "the translation of the verbal categories which an alien people employ in statements about their cultural universe, especially in the sphere conventionally denoted as that of religion, is a focus of notorious and inescapable difficulty."[2] Or as Evan-Pritchard reported in his famous study of the Nuer, "If I speak of 'spear' or 'cow' everybody will have pretty much the same idea of what I speak of, but this is not so when I speak of 'Spirit,' 'soul,' 'sin,' and so forth."[3] In the comparative study of religions, this incommensurability of vocabularies is a perennial obstacle to accurate understanding.

The metaphysical and cosmological constructs in Mormonism may not be as alien to mainstream American Protestant culture as is the Nuer cultural universe. But the lack of dramatic, visible markers of cultural difference may serve to obscure precisely those differences that do exist. Such may certainly be the case with the principle so central to understanding the Book of Mormon and the religion it founds—the principle of "revelation." As one critic alleges (though in light of Evan-Pritchard's observation, with less injury than was intended), "more than a few well meaning Christians have been totally misled because of the lack of being aware of these [terminological] differences!" A Christian may "think he is in agreement with a Mormon," the same writer warns, when "in reality, they are worlds apart on what is meant by what is said."[4]

Avery Dulles, in his important study of the subject, notes five models in the theology of revelation, three of which have been historically significant. In "revelation as doctrine," "revelation is generally identified with the Bible, viewed as a collection of inspired and inerrant teachings." In "revelation as history," the Bible witnesses to the primary revelation, wherein "God reveals himself . . . in his great deeds." Finally, in "revelation as inner experience," we find a "privileged interior experience of grace or communion with God," such as the mystics have known.[5]

The first two have by and large been normative for Christians and are emphatically resistant to the subjectivist implications of the third. John Baillie, for instance, refers to a "simple identification of revelation with the total content of Holy Scripture" that became a characteristic of both Protestantism and counterreformation. (Certainly not a biblical view of revelation, he adds.)[6] For fundamentalists, this first model—revelation as scriptural content—goes by the name of "propositional" revelation. Clark

Pinnock, for example, defines propositional revelation as "the conceptual truth extractable from Holy Scripture."[7]

But the "revelation as history" definition has held equal sway historically. When Christians in general speak of "special revelation," for instance, they often mean something like "the self-disclosure of God to man through the Bible, and supremely, in Christ."[8] This self-disclosure is emphatically not by way of particularized manifestation. As Baillie writes, "No affirmation runs more broadly throughout recent writing in our subject [of revelation] than . . . that all revelation is given, not in the form of directly communicated knowledge, but through events occurring in the historical experience of mankind, events which are apprehended by faith as the 'mighty acts' of God, and which therefore engender in the mind of man such knowledge of God as it is given him to possess."[9]

In his article on "καλύπτω" ("to cover" or "hide") for *Kittel's Theological Dictionary of the New Testament*, Albrecht Oepke writes in a similar vein. In the Old Testament, "revelation is not the communication of supranatural knowledge, and not the stimulation of numinous feelings. The revelation can indeed give rise to knowledge and is necessarily accompanied by numinous feelings; yet it does not itself consist in these things but is quite essentially the action of Yahweh, an unveiling of His essential hiddenness, His offering of Himself in fellowship." While in the New Testament, "revelation is likewise understood, not in the sense of a communication of supranatural knowledge, but in the sense of a self-disclosure of God." In fact, Baillie writes, "the recovery of this fundamental insight is the first thing we notice as running broadly throughout all the recent discussions."[10] And John Knox agrees that "revelation essentially consists not in the communication of truths about God but in the self-revelation of the divine personality."[11] In other words, both of these models emphatically reject the notion that revelation consists of particular truths or information revealed to individuals outside of the channels of scripture itself or God's historically significant activity.

Dulles's third model of revelation, "revelation as inner experience," holds out the promise of a paradigm in which God communicates particular truths to the individual, but this model is fraught with more qualifiers and limitations than the name suggests. Beginning with the premise that God is transcendent and that he has no "phenomenal existence," the characterization of any revelation as "interior" becomes problematic. As Emmanuel Levinas asks, "How can we make sense of the 'exteriority' of the truths and signs of the Revelation which strike the human faculty known as reason? It is a faculty which, despite its 'interiority,' is equal to whatever the world confronts us with. But how can these truths and signs strike our reason if they are not even of this world?"[12]

So too, given God's immanence, does the distinction between general and special revelation break down, and the boundary between natural and revealed religion.[13] Particularized manifestations or communications are either redundant or illogical in a universe that is itself coextensive with God. Therefore, even within this third model, George Tyrrell writes that there can be no revealed statements or doctrines. Auguste Sabatier insists that "the object of the revelation of God can only be God," and William Ernest Hocking holds that even the mystic, "as he is a mystic pure and simple knows nothing else than God."[14]

More to the point, perhaps, is Baillie's insistence that "according to the Bible, what is revealed to us is not a body of information concerning various things of which we might otherwise be ignorant."[15] Jakob J. Petuchowski quotes other moderns to the same effect, such as Franz Rosenzweig who writes that "all that God ever reveals in revelation is— revelation. Or, to express it differently, He reveals nothing but himself to man." Similarly, Martin Buber writes that "my own belief in revelation . . . does not mean that I believe that finished statements about God were handed down from heaven to earth."[16]

Eventually, the game is up when Dulles says that for the theologians of this third model, "the experience of God . . . may be called grace, and grace, insofar as it brings about a new awareness of the divine, is revelation."[17] In other words, this model seems little more than recognition of the obvious fact that the reality of God and his great acts, however objective and universally valid (as the first two models emphasize), must be intersubjectively experienced to be operative in human life. But when Tyrrell calls this experience "a passive impression," we seem to have in this model a distinction from the others without a clear difference.[18]

William Abraham notes that in spite of the obvious and emphatic historical dilution of the concept of divine speaking (which would entail both intersubjectivity and communicated content), traces of a more literal definition stubbornly persist. The *Catholic Encyclopedia*, for example, defines revelation as "the communication of some truth by God to a rational creature through means which are beyond the ordinary course of nature." And the *Oxford English Dictionary* defines it as "the disclosure or communication of knowledge to man by a divine or supernatural agency." But the movement away from this theory of revelation, or what Abraham calls theology's "vehement reaction against" it, has been pronounced since the nineteenth century.[19]

The equivocal and limiting definitions of "revelation as inner experience" are undoubtedly tied to the many theological dragons that lurk in the domain of experiential religion. But the threat—and historical experience—of heresy, schism, and sectarianism are not the only reasons for preferring historical or textual bases of revelation to subjective ones. Hostility to a model of experiential revelation has been grounded in a variety of other reasons, including fear of irrationalism, the perceived sufficiency of the canon, the concern to preserve the integrity of individual agency, and, perhaps most emphatically, theological resistance to anything tending toward anthropomorphism (the ascription of human form to God).

Baillie traces the emphasis on objectivist definitions of revelation to the late eighteenth and early nineteenth centuries, when Kant, Hegel, Ritschl, and other philosopher-theologians of the post-Enlightenment saw little role for divine communication, wishing instead to see theology develop as the rational elaboration of a religious sensibility.[20] To partisans of natural religion then as with liberal theologians today, any concession to the supernatural or the supersubjective was thought to play into the hands of Christianity's enemies. Not surprisingly (given their view that Christianity quickly apostatized from the primitive gospel), Mormon scholars trace the disparagement of subjective revelation much further back—to the first two Christian centuries, when "the primary targets of these heresy-hunters were the so-called Gnostics, who claimed to receive their doctrine through revelation from heaven rather than by reasoning through the scriptures."[21]

Even William Abraham, while critiquing theological hostility to divine speaking and pleading for greater "openness to divine intervention in the world," acknowledges personal misgivings about the ways fundamentalists "have used the emphasis on propositional revelation to underscore an account of inspiration that is both confused and dangerous."[22]

Most inflammatory to critics are versions of revelation that challenge the notion of a closed and complete canon, and its concomitant understanding of revelation as the canonical word of God. As the Mormons' official newspaper laid out the matter in 1832, "Notwithstanding that nearly all Christendom doubt the propriety of receiving revelations for the government of the church of Christ in this age, and generally adopt the Scriptures of the old and new testament as the only rule of faith and practice, yet we believe, from the Scriptures of truth, that to every church in the past ages, which the Lord recognized to be his, he gave revelations wisely calculated to govern them in the peculiar situation and circumstances under which they were placed, and to enable them by authority to do the peculiar work which they were to perform."[23]

With no gentle irony, the Book of Mormon even anticipates its own initial reception in this regard: "And because my words shall hiss forth— many of the Gentiles shall say: A Bible! A Bible! We have got a Bible, and there cannot be any more Bible" (2 Nephi 29:3). As we saw in Charles Thompson's 1841 defense of the Book of Mormon, five of the six objections he listed as directed at the new revelation were really five variations on the same theme: "the Bible is full and complete."[24]

The poet and sometimes theologian Samuel Taylor Coleridge ("to whom so many looked in the early years of the nineteenth century as the white hope of Christian revival"[25]) gives a different reason for resisting any view of revelation that tends toward more literalist conceptions of God speaking to man. In his opinion, explicit directives from above would compromise individual agency. In support of his view, he cites Romans 8:26 ("Likewise the Spirit also helpeth our infirmities: for we know not what we should pray for as we ought: but the Spirit itself maketh intercession for us with groanings which cannot be uttered"):

> "the Spirit aid[s] our infirmities;" that is, act[s] on the Will by a predisposing influence from without, as it were, though in a spiritual manner, and without suspending or destroying its freedom. . . . Nor is there any danger of Fanaticism or Enthusiasm as the consequence of such a belief, if only the attention be carefully and earnestly drawn to the concluding words of the sentence . . . unutterable or incommunicable. . . . [What is revealed] . . . is something which I cannot, which from the nature of the thing it is impossible that I should, communicate to any human mind.[26]

In other words, such revelation is both so vague as to be linguistically inexpressible and (therefore) so subtle as to have no compelling influence over a person.

So here we have again the retreat into linguistic inadequacy. Only for Coleridge it is not the nature of God alone that is beyond human expressing, but any knowledge revealed by God. Horace Bushnell, one of the most influential American clergymen of that generation, agreed. As one Bushnell scholar paraphrases his view, "little can be said about the content of intuitive moments other than that they involve feelings of some kind, such as a sense of awe, a sense of creatureliness or a conviction of 'oughtness' or some special impression. Nothing really well defined or conceptual in the realm of knowledge can be claimed to be directly communicated. . . . The knowledge of God gotten through this momentary, transient intuition is non-conceptual and void of any definite content so far as describable knowledge is concerned."[27]

Baillie finds in the New Testament ample evidence to end all debate on the subject: "And, according to St. John, Jesus Himself said in answer to Phillip's request to show him the Father, 'He that hath seen me hath seen the Father.' That is the whole essence of the Christian faith, that Jesus Christ has shown us the Father, that in Him there has been revealed to us all we need to know about our ultimate concern. 'All we need to know.'"[28] Here the nature of revelation is not so important as is its sufficiency. We have already had revealed to us "all we need to know," and that need is defined in terms of "ultimate concern"—not our immediate concerns. What we can know from God is general, not personal; it is of eternal, not proximate import.

In theory, at least, one would imagine revelation to encompass a variety of modes and forms. Consistent with God's omnipotence and limitlessness, there should follow an unlimited means of self-disclosure, or revelation. As Baillie writes, "For God is not, like my friend, merely one being among others, but is the source of all being. While therefore my friend's relations with me can only be through the very limited medium of his own psychosomatic organisation, there is nothing through which God cannot reveal Himself to me."[29] Language, in other words, is only one possible means among many God could conceivably employ. Language would seem to be an appropriate medium for a God conceived as a personal God. And, as Walter Eichrodt writes, "An unprejudiced evaluation of the Old Testament" leads to the clear recognition that "the foundation of Old Testament faith . . . is His personhood."[30] Even Baillie admits (grudgingly, says Abraham), that "divine speaking has an important place in the Bible."[31] But there are theological reasons to consider his medium to be anything *but* language. Most importantly, to attribute literal speech acts to Divinity is to defy modern Christianity's persistent hostility to the anthropomorphism that speech implies. That is why, in the western religious tradition, genuine dialogic exchange between God and human beings generally becomes metaphorized into the more nebulous concepts of revelation that we have seen. As Abraham reasons, "when the theist speaks of divine revelation the activity of human revealing serves as the model for conceiving that revelation." But here "we sense immediately a certain awkwardness."[32] This awkwardness, of course, is the possibility that our concept of deity will be tainted with human analogies.

That awkwardness is not without its own theological solutions. As Nicholas Wolterstorff argues,

> The traditional assumption that divine speech is reducible to divine revelation was not just fortuitous error; an interesting reason was sometimes offered. Since God has no vocal cords with which to utter words, and no hands with which to write them down, God cannot literally speak, cannot literally be a participant in a linguistic communication. Accordingly, attributions of speech to God, if not judged bizarrely false, must be taken as metaphorical.[33]

And as Sandra M. Schneider writes, outside of an anthropomorphic model it is "evident" that "divine discourse cannot be taken literally. . . . Language, in other words, is a human phenomenon rooted in our corporeality as well as in our discursive mode of intellection and as such cannot be literally predicated of pure spirit."[34]

Christian rhetoric of prayer often reveals—or at least facilitates—this movement away from a literal understanding of divine discourse. To speak, for example, of an answer to prayer is usually already to speak in a manner inconsistent with models of human communication. When one person "asks" another and is "answered," we can be fairly certain that a request was framed and a rejoinder expressed in a way that was meaningful, decipherable, and that was *understood as a response to the question*. The final condition seems in fact the most essential. Utterance that is meaningful or useful but not responsive to a question is not an answer. Neither is action that is responsive to a request. Handing me a pencil can properly be said to be an "answer" to the query "Do you have a pencil?" only in the same nonliteral sense in which falling rain "answers" the question "will it rain today?"

In the case of prayer, however, the latter example is precisely the model that has characterized a very long conversation on the subject. "But perhaps you ask, How may I know whether my prayers have been answered or not?" writes Joseph Smith's contemporary Edward Bickersteth in his popular *Treatise on Prayer*. "Sometimes the case is so obvious that it cannot be mistaken: Jehoshaphat prays, and he is delivered from his enemies; Hezekiah prays, and he is delivered from sickness. . . . At other times prayers are answered rather in the increase of grace to bear the affliction, than in its removal, as in the case of Paul's thorn in the flesh."[35]

In other words, one may choose to ascribe to prayer the motive force behind an event that follows one's request (healing, escape) or, in the absence of a hoped for eventuality, we posit a consequence that we may not discern (grace, for example). This kind of faithful prayer operates in the context of a presumption that petitionary acts call forth divine activity. But a decision must be made to *interpret* something—or a lack of something—as a response to a question, and that gesture of interpretation is itself the faithful act which constitutes the answer.

"There are," says Edward Gee in his earlier *Treatise on Prayer*, "four ways of God's answering prayers. By giving the things prayed for presently . . . or by suspending the answer for a time, and giving it afterwards . . . or by withholding from you that mercy which you ask, and giving you a much better mercy in the room of it . . . or lastly, by giving you patience to bear the loss or want of it."[36] In petitionary prayer so conceived, then, any answer is once again a product of a preimposed interpretive model. If fulfillment of one's desire is an answer, but deafening silence or continuation of the status quo is likewise read as a response, the process of prayer begins with a cry into the abyss and comes to completion with a faith-backed hermeneutic that, once again, predetermines each and every subsequent development as answer. Such a model entirely exempts God from the responsibility to speak. "Thou art silent," says Manfred to the phantom of his lover Astarte. "And in that silence, I am more than answer'd."[37] Or as Bickersteth writes in a preemptive blow against petitionary failure, "The answer of prayer may be approaching, though we discern not its coming."[38]

Emerson may not be typical of Protestantism when he pointedly calls prayer "the soliloquy of a beholding and jubilant soul," and his formula causes one nineteenth-century preacher to object that "Prayer . . . is *not* 'soliloquy,' but dialogue." But that same preacher goes on to define prayerful "dialogue" in a rather more Emersonian fashion than he intends: "Now, in order to have a real energy of spiritual life, we must have actual intercourse with God himself. . . . And to commune with him, we must have something to say to him. . . . Therefore, God, in order that men may come into real communion with him and so receive real vital energy,—faith, love, peace, joy,—has ordered it so that we may speak to him of our real wants."[39] Strange "intercourse" this, where only man must have something to say, and in consequence of which he receives not an answer but "vital energy" (which may, in any case, be more a product of the act of petition itself than of any response).

Retreating into metaphor, confusing monologue for dialogue, reading heavenly silence or quotidian event as answer—all these strategies cannot belie the fact, as Rodney Stark reminds us in his quest for more terminological rigor, that "a revelation is not an insight or an inspiration. A revelation is a *communication*. . . . A revelation presupposes a divine *being* capable of wishes and intentions."[40]

Obviously, it would be reductive and inaccurate to characterize all prayer in the Christian tradition as a kind of vague projection into the void, operating with such blithe openness to the outcome that it begs the very question of prayer's efficacy. But the kind of prayer that is an asking, rather than an asking for, and that anticipates a personal response, a discernible moment of dialogue or communicated content, would be a distinctive kind of prayer, one that falls outside the models of revelation that we have seen, relegating as they do God's operations to historical events, canonized texts, or the infusion of "vital energy." The response this type of prayer envisions, the experience of "revelation" that follows from a literal conception of divine discourse, is one that William James, for example, characterizes as distinctive, and associates with Catholic saints, George Fox, the Old Testament prophets—and Joseph Smith. Here he quotes W. Sanday: "There is something sharp and sudden about it. He can lay his finger so to speak, on the moment when it came."[41] However, in the case of Joseph Smith and the Book of Mormon, even James's distinction is insufficient. Far beyond a forceful spiritual intimation, one finds in the Book of Mormon that prayer frequently and dramatically evokes an answer that is impossible to mistake as anything other than an individualized, dialogic response to a highly particularized question.

The conception of revelation as a personalized, dialogic exchange pervades the Book of Mormon—as well as the life of the Prophet Joseph—like an insistent leitmotif. It is firmly rooted in a radically anthropomorphic theology. Even though, as critics have long pointed out, Joseph did not fully articulate his belief in a physically finite God until much later in his life, the implications were already inescapable. The model of revelation that we encounter through the Book of Mormon's dozens of examples and illustrations depends upon what Wolterstorff called an emphatic insistence on the literality of divine discourse. The Christian abandonment of this insistence is so pervasive and so pronounced that Abraham finds the very concept of revelation in jeopardy: "To claim that God reveals Himself to man but to reject the [belief that] he reveals Himself by speaking to man is to so whittle away the analogy on which the concept of divine revelation is built that it must be seriously asked whether the concept of divine revelation has enough content to license its continued use. Revelation in the fully personal sense characteristic of personal agents has been abandoned."[42]

In the face of this assessment, it is clear that the Book of Mormon presents Christianity with a radical challenge, one that may reinvigorate even as it threatens to unacceptably reshape the theology of revelation.

The Book of Mormon and Dialogic Revelation

Speaking of Augustine's belief that God spoke through the mouth of a child, Nicholas Wolterstorff has written: "What would Judaism, Christianity, and Islam look like if no one spoke of God commanding, no one, of God promising, no one, of God telling?"[43] Like the three major religions Wolterstorff mentions, Mormonism comes with its unique scriptural canon. One of the functions of a sacred text is to ground or establish a coherent cosmology. By so doing, it establishes the possible parameters of religious experience, at the same time that it provides for the meaningful interpretation of that religious experience.[44] Since the extent, shape, and meaning of "revelation" in Mormon thought, like "spirit" or "god" in Nuer religion, are best understood in the context of that religion's worldview, the Book of Mormon may provide the best basis for such an understanding. When in the Book of Mormon God commands, promises, tells, speaks, exhorts, chastises, and directs in myriad circumstances and settings, such revelation may indeed be understood in ways particular to Mormonism.

Nowhere is the concentration of heavenly utterances more intense than in 1 Nephi. (Considering he labels his own account the record of "sacred" things as opposed to political history [1 Nephi 9; 19:6], this is not surprising.) In the first 50 pages alone, we read of eight visions, various angelic visitations, several occasions on which Nephi is "visited" by the Lord, "constrained by the Spirit," "led by the Spirit," "commanded" by the Lord, and so forth. But more to the point, Nephi and his father describe several occasions that cannot be interpreted as mere dreams, spiritual promptings, or heaven-sent impressions. In response to his pleadings on behalf of his wicked brothers, Nephi records, "the Lord spake unto me, saying . . ." Subsequently, he records that "the Lord spake unto" his father, telling him to obtain wives for the journey to the promised land. Later, the "voice of the Lord came unto my father" and "chastened" him for his murmuring, then "the voice of the Lord came and did speak many words" to the rebellious Laman. Preparatory to building a ship for their journey, "the voice of the Lord came unto" Nephi, the "Lord spake" unto him about the ship, "showed" him how to construct it, and "told him" where to find ore. When the time comes to depart, "the voice of the Lord came unto my father, that we should arise and go down into the ship" (1 Nephi 2:19; 7:1; 16:25; 16:39; 17:7-10; 18:5).

In fact, we hear Nephi recount how "the voice of the Lord came" to him, to his father, to Laman and Lemuel so often that it becomes a refrain almost as pervasive as the numbingly common "and it came to pass." The precise expression occurs more than two dozen times. Variations of it, including the voice of the spirit or of angels, dozens more. No shadowy spiritual intimations these, no merely intuited guidance or inspiration, but direct divine discourse that frequently rises to the level of genuine dialogic exchange. For example, upon returning to Jerusalem to obtain the plates of brass, Nephi encounters the record-keeper Laban in a drunken stupor. At that point, he is "constrained by the Spirit" to slay Laban. As he recounts, "I said in my heart: Never at any time have I shed the blood of man. And I shrunk and would that I might not slay him." The dialogue develops when "the Spirit said unto me again: Behold the Lord hath delivered him into thy hands." Nephi continues to hesitate, so the Spirit persists, articulating an entire rationale behind the original directive: "And it came to pass that the Spirit said unto me again: Slay him, for the Lord hath delivered him into thy hands; Behold the Lord slayeth the wicked to bring forth his righteous purposes. It is better that one man should perish than that a nation should dwindle and perish in unbelief" (1 Nephi 4:10-13).

A similar example of conversational revelation occurs at the time of the conversion of Enos, Nephi's nephew. Hungering for "eternal life and the joy of the saints," he spends a night and a day in prayer, after which "there came a voice unto me, saying: Enos, thy sins are forgiven thee, and thou shalt be blessed." Marveling at the miracle of forgiveness, Enos asks, "Lord, how is it done? And he said unto me: Because of thy faith in Christ, whom thou hast never before heard nor seen. And many years pass away before he shall manifest himself in the flesh; wherefore, go to, thy faith hath made thee whole." But he does not go to. "When I had heard these words," he writes, thus revealing the exchange's linguistic rather than impressionistic nature, he turns his thoughts to his brethren the Nephites, praying fervently on their behalf. Soon, "the voice of the Lord came into my mind again," promising them conditional blessings. Once more, after he "had heard these words," he struggles in spirit for his enemies the Lamanites. And once more, the Lord speaks his assurances to him. Yet a final time, Enos prays for the preservation of the records of which he is now guardian. The exchange ends when the Lord not only speaks to but covenants with Enos to do according to his desire. "And I, Enos, knew it would be according to the covenant which he had made; wherefore my soul did rest" (Enos 1:3-17).

The Book of Ether recounts how neglect of prayerful communication by a Jaredite leader resulted in what must surely be the longest dressing-down in sacred history: "For the space of three hours did the Lord talk with the brother of Jared, and chastened him because he remembered not to call upon the name of the Lord" (Ether 2:14). Thereafter, communication is reestablished, and in an especially notable exchange, the Lord prods this same prophet to move from general pleading to specific petition. Hearing the brother of Jared's complaint that the sea-going barges of his people have no interior light, the Lord replies provocatively, "What will ye that I should do that ye may have light in your vessels?" (Ether 2:23). Returning with a specific proposal, the brother of Jared asks the Lord to touch and illuminate 16 molten stones. Having made the guided journey from chastised listener to petitioner and now to interlocutor, the brother of Jared is rewarded with the most spectacular epiphany recorded in the Book of Mormon, seeing first the finger of the Lord, then beholding the premortal Christ in his full glory: "ye are brought back into my presence," the Lord says, "therefore I show myself unto you" (Ether 3:13).

At first glance, some of these experiences may suggest the pattern of Old Testament prophets, and, as we saw, William James for one likened Joseph Smith himself to such ancient patriarchs. Indeed, it is true that "The Lord spake" to Moses dozens of times, engaged in a protracted negotiation with Abraham over the fate of Sodom, and obviously revealed his mind and will to a canon of major and minor prophets. So to some extent, one could consider that Joseph's personal ministry, as well as the Book of Mormon record, reenacts an Old Testament paradigm. But on closer inspection, the Book of Mormon model of revelation diverges in at least one crucial way. In the Bible, outside of prophets acting in the role of national leadership, personal revelation is almost unheard of.[45] Prophets and prophecy are not just linguistically but textually synonymous. Or to state the matter as principle: "Prophecy was preeminently the privilege of the prophets."[46] And the concern of these prophets is with the fate of kings, nations, and tribes, with the workings and purposes of God in history, with the spiritual destinies of covenant peoples and fledgling churches. Even more grandly, as the great

Abraham Heschel writes, "Prophecy . . . may be described as *exegesis of existence from a divine perspective.*"[47]

The Book of Mormon here becomes a study in contrast. Through chiastic form, thematic structure, numerous textual examples, and a final concluding instance of readerly invitation, the scripture hammers home the insistent message that revelation is the province of everyman. As a consequence, in the world of the Book of Mormon, concepts like revelation, prayer, inspiration, mystery find powerful and substantive redefinition. That may well be the Book of Mormon's most significant and revolutionary—as well as controversial—contribution to religious thinking. The particularity and specificity, the vividness, the concreteness, and the accessibility of revelatory experience—those realities both underlie and overshadow the narrated history and doctrine that constitute the record. The "knowability" of all truth, the openness of mystery, the reality of personal revelation find vivid illustration within the record and invite reenactment outside it.

Nephi, as chronicler of the record that bears his name, postpones until chapter 10 (chapter 3 in the 1830 edition) an account of his own "proceedings and reign and ministry," having spent the previous sections emphasizing those of his father, Lehi. But this is more than a gesture of filial respect. Because now when Nephi records his own spiritual epiphany, it is within a context that gives the principle of revelation its first radically new contours in the Book of Mormon. Following a number of briefly narrated revelations and dreams, Lehi had received an expansive vision of the tree of life, which he related to his family. After hearing his father's account, Nephi writes that he "was desirous also that I might see, and hear, and know of these things, by the power of the Holy Ghost, which is the gift of God unto all those who diligently seek him" (1 Nephi 10:17).

Believing that "the Lord was able to make [those things] known unto [him]," after much pondering in his heart, Nephi is "caught away in the Spirit of the Lord," to a place where he immediately engages that Spirit in conversation. When Nephi expresses his desire "to behold the things which [his] father saw," the Spirit responds, "Believest thou that thy father saw the tree of which he hath spoken?" At this critical juncture, two points are highly important. First, Lehi, not Nephi, is still functioning as the unquestioned prophetic figure in the story. Nephi has even gone out of his way to acknowledge the spiritual preeminence of his father, by pointedly asking him for guidance even in the midst of his father's recent murmurings. (Afflicted by hunger and the loss of weapons while in the Old World wilderness, Lehi "did murmur against the Lord." Nephi takes the initiative to fashion new arms and asks his father, "Whither shall I go to obtain food?" after which Lehi humbles himself and successfully inquires of the Lord [1 Nephi 16].) In the divine economy of the Old Testament, Nephi's inquiry of the Spirit would thus seem to be faithless at worst and redundant at best. The Spirit's inquiry, worded as it is, might even have been construed as implicit criticism. Even so, Nephi answers unhesitatingly, "Yea, thou knowest I believe all the words of my father."

Second, as John Welch has pointed out, this query occurs at the moment of the book's most extreme narrative tension, as the culmination of an expansive chiastic structure that organizes all of 1 Nephi.[48] Framed by symmetrical prophetic modes, quest elements, characters, and motifs, Nephi's interview is the fulcrum on which the entire, complexly organized account of 1 Nephi balances. The reply of the angel to Nephi's answer is therefore fraught with special significance. And that answer comes as heavenly exultation: "Hosanna to the Lord, the most high God; for he is God over all the earth, yea, even above all. And blessed art thou, Nephi, because thou believest in the Son of the most high God; wherefore, thou shalt behold the things which thou hast desired" (1 Nephi 11:1-6).

Nephi is commended, not reproved, for seeking access to the mysteries of heaven for personal, rather than public, edification. To forestall any misperception that his prerogative is related to some special spiritual status (or his eventual inheritance of the prophetic role), his brothers are explicitly associated with such a misguided perspective and harshly condemned as a result. Confused by Lehi's account of his vision, Laman and Lemuel complain to Nephi that "we cannot understand the words which our father hath spoken" (1 Nephi 15:7). The exchange that follows anticipates and frames, together with the closing chapters of Moroni, the entire thousand-year history of righteousness and apostasy that constitutes the body of the Book of Mormon record. The warning these verses carry will be grimly fulfilled by the end of the book and will be tragically echoed by the last guardian of the records, while looking hopefully to a different audience.

> And I said unto them: Have ye inquired of the Lord?
> And they said unto me: We have not; for the Lord maketh no such thing known unto us. ["Because we are not prophets," in other words.]
> Behold, I said unto them: How is it that ye do not keep the commandments of the Lord? How is it that ye will perish, because of the hardness of your hearts?
> Do ye not remember the things which the Lord hath said? —If ye will not harden your hearts, and ask me in faith, believing that ye shall receive, with diligence in keeping my commandments, surely these things shall be made known unto you. (1 Nephi 15:8-11)

The brothers do not heed the message, and they and their posterity are spiritually blighted as a result. Nephi's belief in revelatory experience outside official channels and his brothers' disbelief in the same principle seem clearly calculated to establish the pivotal importance of the principle that divides them.

The opening verse of the Book of Mormon actually portends just such a theme, when Nephi introduces himself as "having . . . had a great knowledge of the goodness and mysteries of God." New Testament uses of the word mystery (Μυστήριον) are quite unlike this epistemology. Occurring some 24 times in the New Testament, the word almost always refers to something hidden from the world, revealed through a historical process connected to the providence of God. Romans 16:25-26 is typical: "Now to him that is of power to stablish you according to my gospel, and the preaching of Jesus Christ, according to the revelation of the mystery, which was kept secret since the world began, But now is made manifest, and by the scriptures of the prophets, according to the commandment of the everlasting God, made known to all nations for the obedience of faith."[49] As Baillie writes, "In the Bible the word is always used in its proper and exalted sense." Not only is revelation always "the revelation of a mystery which was kept secret for long ages but is now disclosed," but the mystery thus disclosed is nothing less than God's own will and purpose.[50]

For Nephi, as for others in the Book of Mormon, the cognates of mystery (that appear in numbers comparable to New Testament occurrences) appear always in the context of a valuable truth revealed through the spirit to the seeking individual. They are *supposed* to be studied and apprehended by the individual. As Mosiah teaches, "were it not for these things, which have been kept and preserved by the hand of God, *that we might read and understand of his mysteries,* . . . we should have been like unto our brethren, the Lamanites, who know nothing concerning these things, or even do not believe them when they are taught them" (Mos. 1:5). Later, he exhorts them to "open your ears that ye may hear, . . . and your minds that the mysteries of God may be unfolded to your view" (Mos. 2:9). Similarly, Alma promises that "he that repenteth and exerciseth faith, . . . unto such it is given to know the mysteries of God" (Alma 26:22).

Because the Book of Mormon is compiled largely by Nephite prophets, we get few portraits of religious life at the level of common individuals. But in addition to Nephi, we do have instances wherein other individuals—acting outside any prophetic role—are privy to revelations and the mysteries of God. Mosiah fears for his sons' lives when they plan to preach in hostile territory. He "inquired of the Lord if he should let his sons go up among the Lamanites to preach the word. And the Lord said unto Mosiah: Let them go up" (Mos. 28:6-7). Similarly, the missionary Ammon watches helplessly as thousands of his converts, now pacifist, suffer death rather than retaliate or defend themselves. He proposes a migration to the Nephite lands, but they are reluctant. "And Ammon said: I will go and inquire of the Lord, and if he say unto us, go down unto our brethren, will ye go?" They give their consent. "And it came to pass that Ammon went and inquired of the Lord, and he said unto him: Get this people out of this land . . ." (Alma 27:7, 11-12). Centuries earlier in the Book of Mormon, a similar migration had been prompted by direct communication from God: "And it came to pass that Jared spake again unto his brother, saying: Go and inquire of the Lord whether he will drive us out of the land. . . . And it came to pass that the Lord did hear the brother of Jared, . . . and said unto him: Go to and gather together thy flocks . . . and thy families . . ." (Ether 1:38-41).

Who, then, has rightful access to revelations, epiphanies, visions, and utterances? To the extent that the spirit of prophecy and the spirit of revelation are the same (the Book of Mormon uses the expressions in tandem and almost interchangeably), the Book of Mormon powerfully refutes the claim that prophecy is "preeminently the privilege of the prophets." Joseph learned the lesson fully. ""No man can receive the Holy Ghost without receiving revelations. The Holy Ghost is a revelator" he would teach in the years after the translation.[51] Consignment of revelatory prerogatives to prophets, priests, or popes alone, the implication seems to be, is but an invitation to priestcraft.

If the Book of Mormon was a template for early church organization because it pronounced doctrine on such matters as baptism and sacramental prayers, how much more its significance as a model for the how, who, and what of revelation. In laying out the doctrine of personal revelation, the Doctrine and Covenants merely elaborates what was implicit throughout the Book of Mormon. "Yea, behold, I will tell you in your mind and in your heart, by the Holy Ghost, which shall come upon you and which shall dwell in your heart. Now, behold, this is the spirit of revelation; behold, this is the spirit by which Moses brought the children of Israel through the Red Sea on dry ground" (D&C 8:2-3). For Mormons, as for Catholics, Christ's words to Peter specified the conditions of the church's very foundation. But whereas Catholics interpret the rock as Peter himself, Mormons assert that the rock on which the church was—and is—built is the rock of personal revelation, the process whereby truth is "revealed" not by "flesh and blood . . . but my Father which is in heaven" (Matthew 16:17-18). The Book of Mormon reasserts this principle while clarifying its democratic, rather than hierarchical, application.

(It is essential to point out that for present-day Mormons, personal revelation *is* circumscribed by principles of ecclesiastical stewardship or jurisdiction. In early church history, Hiram Page claimed revelations through a seer stone and was instructed in a precedent-setting reproof that only the president of the church is entitled to receive revelation for the church as a whole. "For, behold, these things have not been appointed unto him, neither shall anything be appointed unto any of this church contrary to the church covenants. For all things must be done in order," he was told [D&C 28:12-13]. And sixth church president Joseph F. Smith officially declared that members' "visions, dreams, tongues, prophecy, impressions, or any extraordinary gift or inspiration" must be in "harmony with the accepted revelations of the church [and] the decisions of its constituted authorities," and pertain only to "themselves, their families, and . . . those over whom they are appointed and ordained to preside."[52])

What then of the substance of revelation? The Book of Mormon may indeed grapple with the exegesis of existence or matters of ultimate concern, but that doesn't seem to be the point of most of the revelatory process we witness here. Questions that prompt divine replies are in turn quotidian, pragmatic, and at times almost banal in their mundane specificity. While still in the wilderness on their way to the promised land, Nephi and his brothers lose their weapons and their people suffer hunger and discouragement. Nephi fashions a new bow and asks his father where to hunt. "And it came to pass that he did inquire of the Lord. . . ." The answer comes (this time by means of the Liahona) directing him to a successful hunt (1 Nephi 16:24-31).

Much later in the record, on two occasions, military plans are informed by divine revelation. Alma is asked by Zoram, a chief captain, to inquire "whither the Lord would that they should go into the wilderness in search of their brethren, who had been taken captive by the Lamanites." So "Alma inquired of the Lord concerning the matter. And Alma returned and said unto them: Behold, the Lamanites will cross the river Sidon in the south wilderness. . . . There shall ye meet them . . . and there the Lord will deliver unto thee they brethren" (Alma 16:5-6). A few years and campaigns later, Captain Moroni "sent certain men unto him, desiring him that he should inquire of the Lord whither the armies of the Nephites should go to defend themselves against the Lamanites" (Alma 43:23). Once again, the Lord reveals the enemy's plans.

Queries can also be of a strictly doctrinal nature. Alma is curious about the space of time between physical death and resurrection. He "inquire[s] diligently of the Lord to know," and receives by angelic intermediary a detailed account that he then imparts to his son Corianton (Alma 40:9). The prophet Jacob, Nephi's successor, prays for guidance in his ministry and records that "as I inquired of the Lord, thus came the word unto me, saying: Jacob, get thou up into the temple on the morrow, and declare the word which I shall give thee . . ." (Jacob 2:11). He then transmits a discourse on humility and chastity. And Moroni, troubled by reports of infant baptism, but apparently unsure of its merits, appeals to the Lord for guidance. "And the word of the Lord came unto me by the power of the Holy Ghost, saying: Listen to the words of Christ. . . . Little children are whole, for they are not capable of committing sin; . . . wherefore . . . I know that it is solemn mockery before God, that ye should baptize little children" (Moro. 8:7-9).

When Moroni inquires of the Lord in another context, it seems only slightly more than pious curiosity that prompts him. Pondering the fate of three Nephite disciples, he "inquired of the Lord, and he hath made it manifest unto me that there must needs be a change wrought upon their bodies, or else it needs be that they must taste of death" (3 Nephi 28:37). Thus is their immortality confirmed to Moroni.

In at least one instance, prayer about a difficult political problem elicits an answer. Unsuccessful in his effort to transfer jurisdiction over zealous apostates to the king, Alma takes his dilemma to the Lord in prayer. "And it came to pass that after he had poured out his whole soul to God, the voice of the Lord came to him, saying" that ecclesiastical dilemmas require ecclesiastical solutions (Mos. 26:14).

We may contrast these examples with Shlomo Biderman's assertion that "Christianity is centered on revelation, which contains within it a message ('good news') meant for the believer. Given this message, what is important is the *content* of revelation."[53] In the Book of Mormon, what is important is not one ultimate Truth it embodies, but rather the ever-present reality of revelation it depicts, a kind of egalitarian access to truths that range from the sublime to the mundane, from principles of salvation to the location of game.

The redemptive role of Jesus Christ is the central tenet of which the Book of Mormon testifies. But conditioned as that knowledge is on spiritual channels, the Book of Mormon gives at least as much attention to the mode as to the object of revelation. When Amaleki concludes the record known as the Small Plates of Nephi, his closing words, spoken as both summation of past experience and admonition to posterity, is an exhortation to "believe in prophesying, and in revelations," and other spiritual gifts (Omni 1:25).

Alma, a few years later, will testify to his sons of his own experience with revealed knowledge: "Behold, I have fasted and prayed many days that I might know these things of myself. And now I do know of myself that these things are true." And again, "I would not that ye should think that I know these things of myself, but it is the Spirit of God which is in me which maketh these things known unto me" (Alma 5:46; 38:6). Helaman will continue the theme, writing "Behold now, I do not say that these things shall be, of myself, because it is not of myself that I know these things; but behold, I know that these things are true because the Lord God has made them known unto me" (Hel. 7:29).

In spite of the recurrent testimonies of the Nephite prophets who affirm the principle of personal revelation, the majority of Nephite history, like the Old Testament counterpart, is one of spiritual blindness and apostasy. But in this case, the reader is invited to locate a different culprit than the idolatry of Baal. Moroni, final prophet and editor of the record, proclaims his intention of writing a moral history of particular relevance to futurity ("Behold, I speak unto you as if ye were present, and yet ye are not. But behold, Jesus Christ hath shown you unto me, and I know your doing" [Morm. 8:35]). Writing with particular poignancy in the aftermath of his entire people's destruction, Moroni predicts that the same truth lost on Laman and Lemuel may well be lost on generations yet to come, and he repeats the same condemnation. "And again I speak unto you who deny the revelations of God, and say that they are done away, that there are no revelations, nor prophecies, nor gifts. . . . Behold I say unto you, he that denieth these things knoweth not the gospel of Christ . . ." (Morm. 9:7-8). And yet, in concluding his record, Moroni turns from lament to hopefulness. In his apostrophe to futurity (the most oft-invoked verse in the Book of Mormon), Moroni renews Nephi's testimony, presumably with the intention of shaping a more successful history than the one he has just witnessed: "I would exhort you that ye would ask God, the Eternal Father, in the name of Christ, if these things [contained in the Book of Mormon] are not true; and if ye shall ask with a sincere heart, with real intent, having faith in Christ, he will manifest the truth of it unto you, by the power of the Holy Ghost" (Moro: 10:4-5).

Judging from the near perfect symmetry of Nephi's testimony-rebuke directed at his brothers earlier in the days preceding first settlement and Mormon's rebuke-testimony at the twilight of his people's history, and given the unrelenting affirmations of numerous writers throughout the record, the moral of this sprawling epic seems to be the indispensability of personal revelation as a key to spiritual survival—of the individual as well as the nation. This is clearly at least one of the morals the early Mormons drew from it. As a church editorial warned,

> The Bible contains revelations given at different times to different people, under different circumstances, as will be seen by editorial articles in this paper. The old world was destroyed for rejecting the revelations of God, given to them through Noah. The Israelites were destroyed in the wilderness for despising the revelations given to them through Moses; and Christ said that the world, in the days of the apostles, should be condemned for not receiving the word of God through them: thus we see that the judgments of God in the past ages have come upon the people, not so much for neglecting the revelations given to their forefathers, as for rejecting those given immediately to themselves.[54]

But Moroni, as prophet but also editor and spokesman to future generations, has done more than derive a moral from a millennium of record-keeping. He serves to link the principle of personal revelation witnessed within the text to its enactment in regard to the text. His expression of the principle thus echoes this theme, but also transposes the text from a record that provides a unified treatment of the principle as enacted by the various prophets—from Nephi onward, we do not hear sermons *about* revelation, we observe the transformation of their lives and the catalyst behind their ministries as tangible products *of* such revelation—into something else.

Moroni's editorial position outside the text allows him to objectify it as the proving ground for contemporary readers to have their own experience of spiritual validation. In other words, our knowing that the particulars of Moroni's history are true (like Laman and Lemuel understanding the allegory of Lehi's vision) is clearly not the point of his challenge. Knowing they are knowable is. In effect, Moroni has transformed the Book of Mormon's status from signified to signifier; its ability to emphatically call into play the validating power of the spirit becomes more important than the particulars of its history or its doctrine.

In the context of the theologies of Christian revelation we have surveyed, Joseph Smith's golden bible was radically distinctive. The Book of Mormon patterned a variety of revelation that emphatically affirmed revelation's dialogic nature, a paradigm mostly at odds with historical conceptions of revelation though not without some parallels and antecedents in nineteenth-century American frontier religion. In addition, the Book of Mormon was itself a locus of special revelatory activity that swirled around the prophet. Finally, the Book of Mormon served to initiate susceptible readers into a new paradigm of personal revelation, appealing in a highly successful way to a spirit of religious individualism. The invitation extended by Moroni was echoed and generalized by Joseph Smith and the Mormon missionaries, and was combined with an appeal to uniquely American sensibilities: "To the Honorable Men of the World," began one of his open letters,

> we, in a spirit of candor and meekness, [and] bound by every tie that makes man the friend of man . . . say unto you, Search the Scriptures search the revelations which we publish, and ask your heavenly Father, in the name of his Son Jesus Christ, to manifest the truth unto you, and if you do it with an eye single to his glory, nothing doubting, he will answer you by the power of his Holy Spirit: You will then know for yourselves and not for another: You will not then be dependent on man for the knowledge of God; . . . Then again we say, Search the Scriptures; search the prophets, and learn what portion of them belongs to you, and the people of the nineteenth century. . . . You stand then in these last days, as all have

stood before you, agents unto yourselves, to be judged according to your
works. Every man lives for himself. . . .[55]

It could be pointed out that certain forms of personal, unmediated
knowledge of God and his truths have persisted in spite of the evolution in Christian concepts of revelation—an evolution that confines heavenly communication to divine enactment or historically delimited
inspiration, rather than continuing utterance. In most general terms, we
could treat mysticism as that tradition historically most resistant to such
developments. Indeed, in his investigation of the nature of Mormon religious experience, Thomas Alexander has found comparisons to mysticism useful. Not to what he calls "the negative mysticism," the *via
negativa* of the medievals who reveled in the ineffability of it all, but to
"Primitive Christian or affirmative mysticism," emphasizing "the open
revelation of God to man."[56] In Joseph Smith's own day, his region so
abounded in prophets and mystics that a contemporary wrote an account entitled *Humbugs of New York*,[57] and Sir Walter Scott's heroine
Jennie Dean provides a glimpse of an Old World religious tradition similarly rich in revelatory epiphanies. In the "auld and wrastling times,"
she says,

> folk were gifted wi' a far look into eternity, to make up for the oppres-
> sions whilk they suffered here below in time. She freely allowed that many
> devout ministers and professors in times past had enjoyed downright
> revelation, like the blessed Peden, and Lundie, and Cameron, and
> Renwick, and John Caird the tinker, wha entered into the secrets, and
> Elizabeth Melvill, Lady Culross, wha prayed in her bed, . . . and Lady
> Robertland, whilk got sic rare outgates of grace, and many other in times
> past; and of a specialty, Mr John Scrimgeour, minister of Kinghorn. . . .
> She contended that those ministers who had not seen such vouchsafed
> and especial mercies, were to seek their rule in the records of the ancient
> times. . . .[58]

Indeed, Joseph Smith's role seems aptly captured by Scott's description of another figure in his litany of seers, one "John Scrimgeour, that
blew open the gates of heaven as an it had been wi' a sax-pund cannon-
ball."[59]

Recent studies of Mormonism's beginnings have emphasized the
movement's commonalities with contemporary religious contexts, its
growth out of democratizing tendencies that permeated the religious
sphere. Harriet Martineau, writing in the church's first decade, captured
the essence of this spirit of American democracy when she wrote, "It is
common to say 'Wait; these are early days. The experiment will yet fail.'
The experiment of the particular constitution of the United States may

fail; but the great principle, which, whether successful or not, it strives to embody, the capacity of mankind for self-government—is established forever."[60]

Ronald Walker has written that "as we come to understand the New England folk culture more fully, we may find that it was not an inappropriate precursor to the Restoration. It is already apparent that this culture tended to be anti-traditional church in orientation. It strongly embraced the idea of personal revelation and the ministry of spirits."[61] Historian Timothy Smith has likewise emphasized that this "'witness of the Spirit,' as the Methodists called it, [was] a coveted goal in all evangelical witness."[62] Dan Vogel writes that "seekers" and other religionists of the day were looking for just that paradigm held out by Mormonism: "Direct revelations from God—the desire of Seekers—especially in restoring the true church and true doctrine of Christ, was the promise of Mormonism. The Book of Mormon—echoing the gospel according to the Seekers—criticizes rational religion for denying the operations of spirit while at the same time criticizing revivalism for not embracing a radical enough concept of spiritual gifts."[63]

Gordon Wood finds in the age evidence that growing spiritual individualism often meant greater personal access to the mysteries of heaven. Although, he writes, in America "church membership had long been a matter of an individual's conversion experience," still, in this period the emphasis was growing more emphatic: "Countless numbers of people were involved in a simultaneous search for individual autonomy," and "people were given personal responsibility for their salvation as never before."[64] As he elaborates: "The disintegration of older structures of authority released torrents of popular religiosity into public life. Visions, dreams, prophesyings, and new emotion-soaked religious seekings acquired a validity they had not earlier possessed. The evangelical pietism of ordinary people, sanctioned by the democratic revolution of these years, had come to affect the character of American culture in ways it had not at the time of the Revolution."[65]

This search for a more democratic religion increasingly took the particular form of "insisting on direct, individual encounters with divinity," as one historian puts it. "Seekers longed for the reassurance of regular spiritual encounters in dreams, visions, inner voices, and uncanny coincidences." Many of these primitivists eventually became Methodists or Freewill Baptists.[66] Another writer notes the appeal of such "experiential religion" to at least two other contemporary movements: "Thus there was a confessed likeness between the spiritualists and the primitive Quakers, who 'also believed in manifestations through outward voices and appearances, through dreams, and through inward spiritual impressions.'"[67]

Finally, A. S. Hayden has pointed out that one such parallel between
Mormonism and other primitivists could be a cause of concern. The Disciples of Christ, he notes, were particularly susceptible to Mormon preaching based on their similar claims about prayer: "The misfortune governing
the case was that many people, victims of excitement and credulity, and
taught in nearly all pulpits to pray for faith, now found themselves met
on their own grounds. . . . Finding an emotion or impulse answerable to
an expected response from heaven, [they] dared not dispute the answer
to their own prayers, and were hurried into the [Mormon] vortex."[68] It
may be only a slight exaggeration, then, to describe the setting for early
Mormonism in the words of the spiritual, in which everyone wanted to
"see bright angels stand/ and waiting to see me."[69]

Situating Mormonism in the context of related religious movements
and developments of the nineteenth century has become an increasingly
popular historical enterprise. When considering the setting of Mormon
origins, however, it is important to remember that the quest for cultural
consistencies can undermine the very project of historical inquiry that
attempts to assess the particularity of a given phenomenon. As religious
historian John Gager has warned,

> If early Mormonism or early Christianity are merely warmed-over ver-
> sions of mid-nineteenth or mid-third century culture, then we are at a
> loss to explain why these particular movements, and not their many con-
> temporary competitors, not only survived but also flourished in such a
> remarkable fashion. In other words, the more we are able to demonstrate
> fundamental similarities between these movements and their surround-
> ing cultures and the more we must dismiss their own self-understanding
> in relation to their cultural environment, the more we find ourselves un-
> able to explain their success.[70]

In response to this warning, it may be useful to consider that, like many
religions of its day and before, Mormonism relied upon "the voluntary
acceptance of revealed truth and thus on personal mystical confirmation."[71] On the other hand, unlike other religions of its day, Mormonism
had a book of scripture that provided an unprecedented model for such
confirmatory experience. And one should not be too quick to assume that
Mormon emphasis on personal revelation alone made it indistinguish-
able in that regard from contemporary movements that emphasized spiritual manifestations. For example, it may be true, as Adolph Koch has
suggested, that "the Great Awakening, the first movement to unite the
American colonies from Maine to Georgia in a common experience, opened
the doors of salvation to all classes on the same terms."[72] But some versions of the democratic impulse in American religion could work more to
impugn elitism than to promote spiritual populism, to reduce religious

experience to a common denominator rather than empower individuals with new spiritual authority. As the *Theophilanthropist* of 1810 ranted, "The teachers of religion of all denominations assume an arrogant, dictatorial style, in order to convince their followers that they are in possession of the secrets of Heaven." But, as another issue asks, "What can a Doctor of Divinity . . . know of his maker, which is not known to the illiterate ploughman?" Of course, such spiritual egalitarianism does not necessarily make of everyone a prophet. In this instance, the writer suggests, the spiritual equality that is invoked is an equality of limitations: "The ploughman knows that there is a God, that he is just and good. What more is necessary?"[73]

The prominent preacher Alexander Campbell, who accused Joseph Smith of plagiarizing most of his restoration principles, parted company sharply on the principle of revelation. Realizing the unmistakable centrality of dialogic revelation in the Book of Mormon, he saw it not as typical of the age or of primitive Christianity but as ludicrous and downright unscriptural:

> I would ask [Book of Mormon witnesses Oliver Cowdery, David Whitmer, and Martin Harris] how they knew that it was God's voice which they heard—but they would tell me to ask God in faith. *That is, I must believe it first, and then ask God if it be true!* . . . If there was anything plausible about Smith, I would say to those who believe him to be a prophet, hear the question which Moses put into the mouth of the Jews, and his answer to it—"And if thou say in thine heart, *How shall we know the word which the Lord hath not spoken?*"—Does he answer, *"Ask the Lord and he will tell you?"* . . . Nay, indeed [emphases his].[74]

Similarly, Gilbert Wardlaw, an Edinburgh minister, admonished his American audience in 1830 in words uncannily pertinent to the Mormon example: "I am aware that prayer for the outpouring of the Holy Spirit has been, and may be recommended in terms which Scripture sobriety does not justify. Some have spoken of this divine gift as if they expected something actually miraculous, something altogether new to the church in the present day, conferred independently of the word, and in a manner almost perceptible to the senses."[75]

When it comes to models of personal revelation, the stakes are enormous. When religious ideas like these operate at the popular level, Rodney Stark reminds us, with their potential for social and theological disruption, "religious organizations take pains to filter, interpret and otherwise direct such activities."[76] A hundred years before the aggressive editing of the Cambuslang accounts, Boston preacher John Cotton was advising his church "not to be afraid of the word *Revelation*," even as he warned them "not to look for any *revelation* out of the Word."[77]

This effort to restrain revelatory anarchy is clear in the editor's introduction to Wardlaw's treatise. Believing the minister's message was especially apropos of the "Revivals of Religion" sweeping America, he betrays obvious alarm at a society in which prophets and revelators were popping up everywhere.[78] Wardlaw asks "whether we have not misunderstood, and interpreted too largely, the ample assurances which God has given with regard to the answering of prayer." True, he admits, both biblical testaments affirm that, "among the various operations of the Spirit of God . . . were those which communicated *miraculous* powers of different kinds." But it is to the "more common, and still more precious influences in the souls of all whom he renews" that we should look for our own answers.[79]

Wardlaw here echoes John Wesley, who distinguished between what he called "the 'extraordinary' gifts of the Spirit—languages and their interpretation, healing and other miracles—and the 'ordinary' one of hallowing, or sanctifying grace . . . available to all Christians." But who was susceptible to such outpourings, and to what degree and in what form, was clearly a subject of profound renegotiation during the religious ferment of the early nineteenth century. Caught in the center of these shifting theological winds, the Book of Mormon was alternately repellant and welcome, and both responsive to and a catalyst behind changing spiritual sensibilities. Historian Timothy Smith, for example, believes that after 1830, and reflecting the "constant appeal by Mormon apologists to the presence of the Holy Spirit in their community," attempts like Wesley's to confine and limit the operations of the Spirit diminished among evangelicals.[80]

A modern evangelical, in articulating just where Mormonism pushes the envelope of orthodoxy too far, finds danger precisely where Campbell and Wardlaw did more than a century and a half earlier: "Without some external checks and balances, it is simply too easy to misinterpret God's answer when we try to apply a test like that of Moroni 10:4-5 and ask him to reveal through his Spirit the truth or falsity of the Book of Mormon."[81] Similarly, scholar of early Christianity W. D. Davies wonders if Mormonism's error is in taking "conventional modes of revelation found in the OT . . . so literally . . . as to give a facticity to what was intended as symbolic." After all, he writes, "the revelation to Moses as recorded in the Old Testament can hardly be taken literally as an event in which the Divine handed over or dictated to Moses Ten Commandments."[82]

But of course, this tenacious embrace of revelatory literalism is neither an arbitrary biblical fundamentalism *nor* a Book of Mormon innovation. It is in fact rooted in Joseph Smith's own, first hand experience with revelation, a dialogic encounter with deity that gave indelible redefinition to the promise of James the Apostle by simply taking it at face value, thereby setting both Joseph and the church he would found on a collision course with orthodoxy. In his personal history, Joseph's concluding sentence about the glorious theophany in which he participated as a fourteen-year-old boy was an unadorned affirmation striking for its matter-of-fact simplicity: "I had found the testimony of James to be true—that a man who lacked wisdom might ask of God, and obtain, and not be upbraided" (JS-H 1:26, citing James 1:5). Subsequent Mormons would find in that theophany the basis for a radical conception of God's corporeality, one that abruptly and decisively shattered the Trinity of traditional Christendom.[83] For millions, the event has become, in retrospect, the first scene in the unveiling of the great and final era in human history. Church president Gordon B. Hinckley has called that event "the first, the Great Vision, the visit of the Father and the Son to the boy Joseph Smith, the opening of the heavens in this the Dispensation of the Fulness of Times, the great bringing together of all of the work of God in all the past dispensations throughout the history of the world. The curtain was parted with that First Vision," he added. [84] But Joseph's own summative comment was that when man puts a question to God in guileless faith and humility, God may choose to answer with articulate, discernible, unmistakably human words. "I asked the Personages who stood above me in the light, which of all the sects was right . . . and which I should join. I was answered that I must join none of them" (JS-H 1:18-19).

Whether or not Mormonism's model was the first to appeal to radically individualistic cravings for spiritual experience by means of a literalized understanding of divine discourse, the Book of Mormon *was* apparently the most effective vehicle of the age for eliciting, condoning, and affirming such personal encounter with divine powers. Martin Marty has remarked that "historians cannot prove that the Book of Mormon was translated from golden plates and have not proven that it was simply a fiction of Joseph Smith. Instead they seek to understand its revelatory appeal, the claims it makes, and why it discloses modes of being and of believing that millions of Saints would not otherwise entertain."[85] But attempts to understand that "revelatory appeal" and its new "modes of believing" have never really focused on how the Book of Mormon describes and models a version of dialogic revelation that pushes the boundaries of revelatory theology. And this, in spite of the fact that, from Samuel Smith to the present, Mormon missionaries have exploited that revelatory appeal deliberately and successfully.

None of this is to say that Latter-day Saints, as a rule today, hold dialogic revelation on the order of Enos's or Nephi's experience as normative in religious life. The description of revelation given in the Doctrine and Covenants 9:8-9 is important: "But, behold, I say unto you, that you must study it out in your mind; then you must ask me if it be right, and if it is right I will cause that your bosom shall burn within you; therefore, you shall feel that it is right. But if it be not right you shall have no such feelings, but you shall have a stupor of thought that shall cause you to forget the thing which is wrong." Though given to Oliver Cowdery by way of instructing him in the proper method of translation, the scripture has been widely appropriated as relevant to personal prayer generally. Thus, confirmatory impression rather than more dramatic varieties of revelation becomes normative for most Latter-day Saints. But now, as then, the Book of Mormon serves as the instrument for a personal, sacred confirmation of spiritual realities sufficient to constitute a conversion experience.

The Reader and Revelation

It was primarily in terms of its authenticity and evidence of larger truths, not its inherent value, internal persuasiveness, or theological merits, that Joseph Smith and early missionaries presented the Book of Mormon to the world. And this role was inextricably tied to its role as a catalyst for the experience of dialogic revelation. And it was in these same terms that the brunt of popular opposition to the book was framed. In general, then, the status of the Book of Mormon as a historical narrative or body of theology recedes in the face of the events that surround its appearance and its affirmation for the contemporary reader. The lack of *conspicuously* distinctive doctrine on the one hand and the myth of supernatural origins on the other mean that the book's primary claim to the reader's attention will be as a pointer to meaning, rather than an embodiment of meaning. And the way this sign becomes operative in the experience of the convert is through the exercise of the kind of revelation it both enacts and invites. This fact is made clear in the rhetoric of conversion as expressed by virtually every convert to Mormonism. The typical conversion account would seldom include a statement such as, "I studied the Book of Mormon and found the doctrinal exposition of the atonement as recorded in Alma 42 especially compelling." The near-universal formula would read more like Mormon luminary Parley P. Pratt's: "As I read, the spirit of the Lord was upon me, and I knew and comprehended that the book was true."[86] Writing in 1977, Grant Underwood noted that there had been no study of Mormonism's meaning and attraction for early converts that relied on "quantitative study of first-person accounts." When he examined 45 conversion accounts, he found the first common feature to appear was the effectiveness of church literature, and "by far and away the most effective literary missionary for the message of Mormonism was the Book of Mormon."[87] Joseph Hovey's account was typical: "I, Joseph, for the first time bowed myself before God in secret and implored his mercy and asked him if what I had read out of the Book of Mormon was true and if the man, Joseph Smith, was the one who translated these marvelous records. I, Joseph, asked God for a testimony by the Holy Spirit and truly got what I asked for and more abundantly."[88]

The experience of early convert Luman Shurtliff is even more striking. He doubted the claims of the Mormon missionaries and so sought out David Whitmer, one of the original witnesses to the gold plates. Whitmer rehearsed the miraculous manifestation by the angel, but Shurtliff still was unconvinced. He started for home, purchasing a Book of Mormon on his way. Consumed by doubt and still skeptical about a book he apparently had not yet examined, he that day "began to call on the Lord in earnest." He soon heard a "sweet melodious voice about me say, 'Joseph Smith, Jr. is a prophet . . . and the Book of Mormon which you hold under your arm is true.'"[89]

Now it may seem that Shurtliff's request for divine endorsement of the Book of Mormon (presumably) even before reading it would suggest the book could hardly have provided him with a model for such a strategy.[90] But Mormon missionaries, then as now, presented the Book of Mormon in such a way as to foreground its status as candidate for divine manifestation. We have a vivid description, for example, of how Samuel Smith, brother of the prophet himself, introduced the volume, in this case to one Phinehas Young:

> "There's a book, sir, I wish you to read."
> Phinehas hesitated. "Pray, sir, what book have you?"
> "The Book of Mormon, or as it is called by some, the Golden Bible."
> "Ah, so then it purports to be a revelation?"
> "Yes, a revelation from God."
> The young man showed Phinehas the last two pages of the book.
> "Here is the testimony of three witnesses, which said they had seen the
>   plates from which the book had been translated, that an angel had
>   shown these plates to them and that a voice had declared it to be true."
> Then he read the testimony of eight others. . . .
> The young man continued: "If you will read this book with a prayerful
>   heart and ask God to give you a witness, you will know the truth of
>   the work."[91]

Richard Bushman also notes that for the prophet's brother, it was the Book of Mormon's role as vehicle for revelation, not its internal persuasiveness, that was the key to its effectiveness:

> The experience of reading the book transcended the specific contents. Samuel Smith, who carried books to some of the towns around Palmyra shortly after publication, made no arguments on its behalf. When he gave a copy to the wife of John P. Greene, a Methodist preacher in Bloomington,

Samuel explained "the most profitable manner of reading the book . . . which was to ask of God, when she read it, for a testimony of the truth of what she had read, and she would receive the Spirit of God, which would enable her to discern the things of God." Mr. and Mrs. Greene followed his directions and soon joined the church. . . . From all reports the converts seem to have acted on their spiritual feelings more than sympathy with specific ideas.[92]

Joseph's mother, Lucy Mack, advocated the same strategy. While the book was in production, a group of men came to her home to make inquiries:

"Mrs. Smith, we hear that you have a gold bible; we have come to see if you will be so kind as to show it to us?" "No, gentlemen," said I, "we have no gold bible, but we have a translation of some gold plates, which have been brought forth for the purpose of making known to the world the plainness of the Gospel, and also to give a history of the people which formerly inhabited this continent." I then proceeded to relate the substance of what is contained in the Book of Mormon, dwelling particularly upon the principles of religion therein contained. I endeavored to show them the similarity between these principles, and the simplicity of the Gospel taught by Jesus Christ in the New Testament.

She then asked, "Will you, Deacon Beckwith, take one of the books, when they are printed, and read it, asking God to give you an evidence that you may know whether it is true?"[93]

In more recent times, a study of the Book of Mormon's role in Latter-day Saint conversions found a similar pattern. A sampling of almost 400 converts revealed that the "most impressive" factor in their reading of the Book of Mormon was neither "its teachings," nor "its stories," but "feelings received in reading."[94]

It is easy to mistake the Mormon emphasis on personal, confirmatory revelation as a practice of simple sign-seeking. That, however, did not appear to be the perception of contemporary critics of Mormonism. Quite the contrary. As Richard Bushman has pointed out, the display of miracles was, in the age of enlightened Christianity, "the evidence separating true faith from imposture." But Mormonism was perceived to fall short on this point. Bushman has noted the complaint in the *Painsville Telegraph* that "when Jesus sent his disciples to preach, he gave them power against all unclean spirits, to cast them out, to heal all manner of diseases, and to raise the dead." But "these newly commissioned disciples have totally failed thus far in their attempts to heal, and as far as can be ascertained, their prophecies have also failed." When Mormon leader Sidney Rigdon protested that "the new revelation was not to be confirmed by miracles," Bushman continues, "the man wanted to know

'How then are we to obtain faith?'"[95] The shape of the Mormon conversion experience, then, was one that relied upon a divine manifestation, but one that was vouchsafed in a private, rather than public, manner.

As further evidence of rationalism's role in frontier religion, Bushman cites Alexander Campbell's eight-day debate with atheist Robert Owen. "Campbell attempted to prove that hard evidence—well-attested miracles—supported Christian belief. His mode of defense illustrated how faith as well as doubt had embraced the Enlightenment by the beginning of the nineteenth century."[96] Still, in spite of some efforts to consider the miraculous as just one more form of evidence, it seems clear that popular opinion, then as now, generally saw rationalism and charismatic experiences as mutually opposed. One 1809 book about art jibed, "Those who talk rationally on other subjects, no sooner touch on this, than they go off in a literary delirium; fancy themselves, like Longinus, 'the great sublime they draw,' and rave like methodists, of inward lights, and enthusiastic emotions."[97]

Personal revelation in the Book of Mormon's model had the advantage of following upon, rather than substituting for, thoughtful consideration of the book. Religious experience that validated its truthfulness was not seen by early—or modern—converts as hostile to rationalism. So Orson Hyde, later to be a leading Mormon intellectual, was not unusual in writing that he "read the 'Mormon' bible carefully through" and spent "three months of careful and prayerful investigation, reflection, and meditation." As Steven Harper demonstrates, "one finds the word 'reasonable' and its relatives used frequently by writers trying to describe what it was in Mormon theology that caused conversion in them."[98]

The fact remains, however, that the primary mode of both proselytizing and conversion was through an emphasis on a logical sequence of steps in which the Book of Mormon elicits an initiation into spiritual dialogue with heaven, so that Joseph Smith's larger work can be vindicated. Knowing *that* the Book of Mormon is true, therefore, in the logic of Mormon conversion, makes it possible—even necessary—to accept Smith's spiritual authority. One is then bound to conclude that the church he founded, with its prophetic office, ordinances, doctrines, and teachings, is necessarily "true." The book functions primarily, then, as an object for the exercise of faith and the vehicle through which personal revelation confirms a truth larger than the book itself.

Certainly it could be argued that the Bible also functions as authoritative discourse in this same way, and that conversion to Christianity is similarly dependent upon a revelatory experience that endows the Bible, as a whole, with a demand to our assent. Indeed, millions of believers have "found Christ" not through biblical exegesis but merely by reading the New Testament and being "moved upon." The difference is this: the Bible is not construed primarily as a sign of either a prophetic or doctrinal authority that resides outside of the text—the Book of Mormon is. No one reads the Bible, in other words—at least *primarily*—in order to be able to have an experience that affirms or denies Moses' stature as a prophet.

Because neither the canon of the Old Testament nor the "received text" of the New (as that term makes clear) has been transmitted, preserved, or authorized by ostensibly supernatural mechanisms, and because the theological claims of both *are* conspicuously different from a non-Jewish or a non-Christian set of beliefs, their theological function is not to serve as evidence of an authority external to themselves but to establish and embody truth within themselves.

The meaning of the Book of Mormon, by contrast, may be said to reside in the experience of dialogic revelation it elicits. As the poet John Greenleaf Whittier wrote, the Book of Mormon spoke "a language of hope and promise to weak, weary hearts, tossed and troubled, who have wandered from sect to sect, seeking in vain for the primal manifestations of the divine power."[99] For millions of believers, the Book of Mormon has been the vehicle through which they could find their own sacred grove and reenact on a personal scale the epiphany that ushered in a new dispensation.

NINE

"A Standard Unto My People":
The Book of Mormon as Cultural Touchstone

> It is now more than four years since this church was organized in these
> last days, and though the conferences have always shown by their min-
> utes, that they took no other name than the name of Christ, the church
> has, particularly abroad, been called *"Mormonite."* . . . Others may call
> *themselves* by their own, or by other names, and have the privilege of
> wearing them without our changing them or attempting so to do; but we
> do not accept the above title, nor shall we wear it as our name, though it
> may be lavished out upon us double to what it has heretofore been.
>
> —Editor, *Evening and Morning Star*, May 1834

In 1834, church leaders had good reason to confidently predict that
the designation "Mormonites," or "Mormons" as they were already
being called by some, would be as transient a label as it was unwel-
come.[1] The Book of Mormon had been out since 1830 and did not find
wide readership. Indeed, after its publication, one study has found, "the
sale and distribution of the Book of Mormon did not receive major emphasis."[2] Other scriptural projects had followed, beginning with the Book
of Commandments in 1833. Joseph's work on the new translation of the
New Testament was mostly complete, and the Book of Abraham translation would follow the next year, as would the first edition of the Doctrine and Covenants; the golden bible no longer seemed set to occupy
the dominant role in Mormon belief or practice that "Mormonite" suggested. Indeed, except for its abiding centrality in the conversion experience of proselytes, the Book of Mormon has been virtually invisible
throughout most of the church's history. Joseph acknowledged the trend
of general disregard only two years after the book's publication through

a damning revelation on the subject: "And your minds in times past have been darkened because of unbelief, and because you have treated lightly the things which you have received—Which vanity and unbelief have brought the whole church under condemnation. And this condemnation resteth upon the children of Zion, even all. And they shall remain under this condemnation until they repent and remember the new covenant, even the Book of Mormon" (D&C 84:54-57).

Historically, there seems little doubt the censure was deserved. Doctrinally, as we have seen, the Book of Mormon exerted little influence. At the level of general church use, two studies that review church speeches and publications in the nineteenth and early twentieth centuries reveal the unmistakable fact that "a very low percentage of early LDS speeches and writings overtly encouraged the study or distribution of the book."[3] As recently as the pre-World War II years, even Brigham Young University and LDS Institutes (religious instruction targeted at college-age Mormons worldwide) did not feature the Book of Mormon prominently or regularly. Brigham Young University would not require that students study the Book of Mormon until 1961, and only in 1972 did churchwide study of that scripture become institutionalized in the Sunday school curriculum. In the latter half of the century (until 1986), church authorities cited the Book of Mormon a paltry 12 percent of the time when drawing upon scriptural support for their general conference addresses.[4] Even at the level of church hymnody, where one might expect the Book of Mormon to claim space proportional to its scriptural status, it is conspicuous by its virtual absence. Five of the selections in the church's first official hymnal touched on Book of Mormon themes or language, even though half of the ninety hymns were authored by Latter-day Saints. In the latest (1985) church hymnal, the number is proportionally even fewer—six out of some four hundred.[5]

This situation began to change dramatically with the inaugural sermon of president Ezra Taft Benson to the church in April of 1986. On that occasion he warned that the 1832 condemnation was still in force, sounding a theme that would become the hallmark of his ministry. In a subsequent address he spoke with even greater emphasis about the scripture, urging members to make its study "a lifelong pursuit," and reaffirming its role as "keystone of the church." He had long championed a greater role for the Mormon scripture, emphasizing its relevance to a contemporary audience. "The Nephites never had the book; neither did the Lamanites of ancient times," he reminded members. "Each of the major writers of the Book of Mormon testified that he wrote for future generations."

By 1988, it was clear that Benson had launched the church into a new era in which the Book of Mormon received unprecedented attention and respect. In that year he issued a stirring summons for a "massive flooding of the earth with the Book of Mormon," reaffirmed its role as "the instrument that God designed . . . to gather out [His] elect,"[6] and emphatically designated it as of more immediate spiritual relevance and value than the other scriptures. Noting the current churchwide curriculum that apportioned one year of study to every volume of scripture in a four-year sequence, he said: "This four-year pattern, however, must not be followed by church members in their personal and family study. We need to read daily from the pages of the book that will get a man 'nearer to God by abiding by its precepts, than by any other book.'"[7]

Even in 1972 it was an exaggeration to say, as Sydney Ahlstrom did: "A few isolated individuals can still read [the Book of Mormon] as a religious testimony, . . . but not even loyal Mormons can be nourished by it as they were a century ago."[8] Today, it is simply dead wrong. The Book of Mormon is now the focus of vigorous scholarly research by Mormon academics that is unprecedented in scope, professionalism, and church support. The Foundation for Ancient Research and Mormon Studies (FARMS) has a subscribing audience of many thousands for its publications on the Book of Mormon. An army of over 60,000 missionaries continues to use the Book of Mormon as the centerpiece of a proselytizing effort that was bringing in over a quarter of a million converts a year by the new century.[9] In LDS worship services and Sunday schools, the Book of Mormon is now absolutely central rather than peripheral. Hundreds of thousands of young Mormons daily attend early morning seminary, a four-year program of gospel study, throughout their high school years. Every participant spends one full year immersed in the keystone of their religion, the Book of Mormon. And perhaps most tellingly, Benson's prophetic promises keyed specifically to Book of Mormon attentiveness mean that in countless LDS homes throughout the world, devout families meet together every day for a devotional in which they read together from the Book of Mormon. Ironically, then, though Latter-day Saints tend to be extremely Bible-literate, rising generations of children are more likely to associate scripture reading with the stories of Nephi and Alma than of Matthew and Mark, and to bask imaginatively in the courage of Captain Moroni than of Samson or Daniel.

The Book of Mormon and Cultural Identity

In spite of the Book of Mormon's shifting fortunes among skeptics, scholars, and even saints, the scripture has remained a constant in anchoring Mormon identity and distinctiveness. The gathering remarked as a curiosity by Dickens, the polygamy pilloried by preachers and politicians, the pioneer trek still commemorated in Utah with more fanfare than a Fourth of July in Philadelphia, these and other aspects of the Mormon religion have come and gone. But from the start, the record bearing Mormon's name has served to identify and unify the Mormon people. Even those members who feel more cultural than doctrinal affinity to the church, even those Mormons who are oblivious to the sacred record's origins and teachings, cannot escape its power to name them and to shape the language of their religious culture.

Today legions of Mormon children around the world can be heard singing a rousing anthem about being part of "the army of Helaman," and many a fine young Mormon man has been referred to as a "stripling warrior" (and may well bear the name Alma, Moroni, or Nephi). One can buy Book of Mormon action figures, watch animated videos of the adventures of Nephi retrieving the brass plates, or read novels about "Tennis Shoes Among the Nephites." Especially orthodox members are sometimes called "Iron Rod" Mormons, while a more free-thinking approach to their religion garners the epithet "Liahona Mormon." Parents with wayward children console each other that even the prophet Lehi had his Laman and Lemuel, and every youth in the church can recite the stirring words of Nephi: "I will go and do the things which the Lord hath commanded, for I know that the Lord giveth no commandments unto the children of men, save he shall prepare a way for them that they may accomplish the thing which he commandeth them" (1 Nephi 3:7).

The Book of Mormon, in other words, is an essential ingredient in that thoroughly unique subculture of Christianity called Mormonism. In addition to shoring up faith in their modern prophets and in the principle of revelation, the Book of Mormon provides the Latter-day Saints with archetypal heroes and villains, a store of folk wisdom, and myriad instances of scriptural shorthand for diverse cultural plots, life scenarios, character types and attitudes. The 16 molten stones that the brother of Jared brought to the Lord to be touched by his finger have become a miniparable about personal initiative and a faith that can pierce the veil. The slaying of Laban stands as a shocking demonstration that God's commands may supersede even conventional morality, while it also serves as the single most potent lesson to Mormons about the incalculable significance of scripture. They find in the tragicomic institution of the Rameumptom—the ramp where cultists stood to proclaim their own blessedness—a memorable warning against the universal proclivity for self-righteousness and pride and often refer to modern day Korihors, by which they mean sophists or intellectualizers.

Of course, at one level, the Book of Mormon has long served as a source for a unique Mormon cultural vocabulary, unique cultural perspectives, and unique cultural productions. From the days of Kirtland and Nauvoo, Mormons have borrowed from the scripture to refer to American Indians as Lamanites and to nonmembers as Gentiles. Hymns sung in the Utah Territory—like "O Stop and Tell Me, Red Man," and

"Great Spirit Listen to the Red Man's Wail"—took their cue from the Book of Mormon's emphasis on the Lamanites as children of the covenant, as did the church's longstanding Indian Student Placement Program that provided school-year adoptions of Navajo and other Native American children into Latter-day Saint homes.[10] Around the turn of the century, a play with a popular run in the Salt Lake Valley was "Corianton," based on the wayward son of Book of Mormon prophet Alma. Written originally by B. H. Roberts, then adapted by Orestes Bean for the stage, it even had a run on Broadway.[11] Over the years, Latter-day Saints have produced a considerable corpus of dramas, musicals, novels, short stories, and poetry, as well as sculpture and paintings—all based on Book of Mormon themes.[12] Still, there is something new in the modern infiltration of the Book of Mormon into Latter-day Saint culture. Quaint borrowings from an exotic text, made in all the privacy and secret understanding that a besieged and insular culture affords, have been transformed into something far different.

Perhaps it began when B. H. Roberts planned and wrote an elaborate centennial commemoration of Joseph Smith's first view of the golden plates at Hill Cumorah in upstate New York. His evocation of Book of Mormon history that culminated in a final battle at Cumorah was described by one journalist as "like some graphic panorama of the past," like a "Norse saga."[13] Soon thereafter, the church acquired the hill and environs, and before long the spectacle described by Roberts was being reenacted annually on a grand scale. The first performance of "America's Witness for Christ" took place in 1937, and within ten years annual attendance would surpass 100,000.[14] (In the 1997 season, Donny Osmond tried out for one of the 640 parts—Samuel the Lamanite.[15]) America's equivalent of Germany's Oberammergau passion play, the Hill Cumorah Pageant is the country's largest and oldest outdoor drama, featuring volcanoes, earthquakes, hundreds of armored warriors, priests, court dancers, kings, and peasants, a seven level stage, ten light towers, digitally recorded music, water curtains, and a spectacular descent of Christ from heaven.

Each day in Salt Lake City's opulent Joseph Smith Building, thousands view a 70 mm film with state-of-the-art production values presenting an exquisitely detailed epic set in Book of Mormon lands and times.[16] The Brigham Young University alumni magazine regularly advertises an array of guided tours to "Book of Mormon Lands," complete with archaeological experts and local guides. A coffee table book with large glossy format, replete with photographs of Mesoamerican artifacts, assists the reader in "visualizing Book of Mormon life."[17] Sci-fi writer Orson Scott Card has based a five-volume series on the Book of Mormon, deflecting charges of plagiarism and irreverence with the assertion that "you can't plagiarize history."[18] In sum, even as revisionists and New Historians within the church push to downplay or soft-pedal the scripture's claims to historicity, a mix of vast resources, high-tech savvy, public respectability, and scholarly confidence have worked to make the book more, not less, historically compelling and vivid.

It appears that the Book of Mormon is poised to become increasingly central to Mormon worship, identity, and culture. Even as their renewed emphasis on being called the Church of Jesus Christ affirms their ties to Christian origins and a larger Christian community, the obtrusive presence of Joseph Smith and his gold bible will remain an irreducible sign of difference. For Mormons, that paradoxical tension is best captured in one of the most distinctive emblems of Mormonism, the spires of their temples visible on skylines from Salt Lake City to Washington and from Tokyo to Samoa, often crowned by the gold-plated angel, trumpet to mouth and precious book tucked snugly under angelic arm. The angel may be Moroni himself, sealer and guardian of the records, and link between a Nephite past and a modern era of restoration—but the scriptural reference that inspired the version that first crowned the temple in Nauvoo is pure Bible. "And I saw another angel fly in the midst of heaven," wrote John the Revelator, "having the everlasting gospel to preach unto them that dwell on the earth, and to every nation, and kindred, and tongue, and people" (Rev. 14:6).

Just what angel John saw or whose gospel the Book of Mormon proclaims will continue to be debated for generations to come, as will a host of other questions the Book of Mormon imposes on its vast public, willingly or no. Does the brazen integration of things human and divine that it embodies represent a collapse of sacred distance tantamount to heresy or a challenge to Hellenic dualisms that heralds a new and welcome orthodoxy? "Haunting Christian theology and Western philosophy throughout the centuries," notes Nicholas Wolterstorff, "has been the picture of time as bounded, with the created order on this side of the boundary and God on the other. Or sometimes the metaphor has been that of time as extending up to a horizon, with all creaturely reality on this side of the horizon and God on the other. All such metaphors, and the ways of thinking they represent, must be discarded. Temporality embraces us along with God."[19] The Book of Mormon, with its literal reconceiving of dialogic revelation and its enshrouding tale of divine appearances, angelic visitants, and sacred, material oracles and relics, may be the most dramatic example to date of what Wolterstorff sees as a growing twentieth-century process of "the dehellenization of Christian theology."[20]

The Book of Mormon's controversial origins notwithstanding, serious consideration of the scripture by scholars and hardened skeptics alike is increasingly consistent with its status as what an early twentieth-century historian was already calling "the most famous and widely discussed book ever first published in America."[21] Lutheran pastor Robert N. Hullinger begins his study of the Book of Mormon with an expression of realpolitik refreshingly new to Protestant engagement with the record: "Even if one holds that Smith was the worst scoundrel of his day, one still must account for the content of the Book of Mormon."[22] (Like many others of this new middle ground, he interprets the prophet as a sincere but self-appointed "defender of God" in an age of skepticism, who forged the Book of Mormon out of biblical, masonic, and Ethan Smith borrowings.)

Recognizing the ultimate insufficiency of cultural influences to account for the Book of Mormon taken as a whole, an intrigued observer like Harold Bloom, perhaps the most famous contemporary (non-Mormon) admirer of Joseph Smith, refers to the prophet as an "authentic religious genius."[23] Many Mormons would be happy for the compliment. Such a tribute, however, as foremost historian of Mormonism Richard Bushman realizes, is still just another kind of intellectual failure to come to terms with the golden bible. "Genius, by common admission, carries human achievement beyond the limits of simple historical explanation, just as revelation does. To say that the Book of Mormon could only be written by a genius is logically not much different from saying God revealed it. In both cases, we admit that historical analysis fails us."[24]

Of course, Joseph left indications that even the best efforts to solve the Book of Mormon conundrum may always elude us all, forgetful as we are of its dynamic nature. But if the time ever does arrive when Saints, scholars, or skeptics achieve a firm handle on its origins and message, the picture may grow rather more complicated with no warning at all. As Orson Pratt reminded an assembly in the Salt Lake Tabernacle in 1856, "You recollect that when the Book of Mormon was translated from the plates, about two-thirds were sealed up, and Joseph was commanded not to break the seal; that part of the record was hid up. The plates which were sealed contained an account of those great things shewn unto the brother of Jared; and we are told that all those things are preserved to come forth in the due time of the Lord."[25]

"When the people of the Lord are prepared, and found worthy," wrote Joseph's scribe Oliver Cowdery, "then it will be unfolded unto them."[26]

Notes

INTRODUCTION

1. The editor, John Wentworth, had asked for a "sketch of the rise, progress, persecution and faith of the Latter-day Saints" to be used in a New Hampshire history written by Wentworth's friend George Barstow. Never used by Barstow, the letter did appear in the March 1, 1842 issue of the Nauvoo newspaper, *Times and Seasons*, and has been widely disseminated as one of the most succinct accounts of Mormonism by the church's founding prophet. It also contains the closest thing Mormons have to a creed: the "Thirteen Articles of Faith."

2. Paul Tucker, *Claude Monet: Life and Art* (New Haven: Yale University Press, 1995), 103.

3. Miriam Levering, "Scripture and Its Reception: A Buddhist Case," in *Rethinking Scripture: Essays from a Comparative Perspective*, ed. Miriam Levering (Albany: SUNY Press, 1989), 59.

4. Shlomo Biderman, *Scripture and Knowledge: An Essay on Religious Epistemology* (New York: Brill, 1995), 50.

5. Jan Shipps, "The Mormons: Looking Forward and Outward," in *Where the Spirit Leads: American Denominations Today*, ed. Martin E. Marty (Richmond, Va.: John Knox, 1980), 29–30.

6. Forty of those translations are abridgments. David Whittaker, "An American Scripture: A Printing History of the Book of Mormon," paper presented at Society for the History of Authorship, Reading, and Publishing (5 July 2000), Mainz, Germany, 1.

7. See John Brooke, *The Refiner's Fire: the Making of Mormon Cosmology, 1644–1844* (Cambridge: Cambridge University Press, 1994), 149–83.

8. The original theory was laid out by Fawn Brodie in *No Man Knows My History: The Life of Joseph Smith* (New York: Knopf, 1945; 2nd ed., Vintage, 1995). D. Michael Quinn published *Early Mormonism and the Magic World View* in 1987 (Salt Lake City: Signature Books; 2nd ed., 1999).

9. A revised version of the 25 April 1997 address was subsequently published by Carl Mosser and Paul Owen, "Mormon Apologetic, Scholarship and Evangelical Neglect: Losing the Battle and Not Knowing It?" *Trinity Journal* (1998): 179–205.

10. Jacob Neusner, "Religious Studies: The Next Vocation," *Council on the Study of Religion Bulletin* 8.5 (December 1977): 118.

11. Harold Bloom, *The American Religion: The Emergence of the Post-Christian Nation* (New York: Simon & Schuster, 1992), 98–117; *Omens of Millennium: The Gnosis of Angels, Dreams, and Resurrection* (New York: Riverhead, 1996), 79.

12. Ernst Wilhelm Benz, "Der Mensch als Imago Dei," *Eranos Jahrbuch* 1971, published in *Urbild und Abbild: Der Mensch und die Mythische Welt* (Leyden: E. J. Brill, 1974); Heikki Raisanen, "Joseph Smith und die Bibel: Die Leistung des mormonischen Propheten in neuer Beleuchtung," *Theologische Literaturzeitung* (February 1984): 83–92.

13. Seth Daniel Kunin, "The Death/Rebirth Mytheme in the Book of Mormon," in *Mormon Identities in Transition,* ed. Douglas Davies(London: Cassell, 1996), 192–203; Viola Sachs, ed., *L'Imaginaire-Melville: A French Point of View* (Saint-Denis: Presses Universitaires de Vincennes, 1992), 21–22.

14. Nathan Hatch, *The Democratization of American Christianity* (New Haven: Yale University Press, 1989), 115. The Shipps citation is from *Mormonism: The Story of a New Religious Tradition* (Urbana: University of Illinois Press, 1985), 32–33. Hatch's reference to the book as "an extraordinary work of popular imagination" is a quote of Gordon S. Wood's judgment, in "Evangelical America and Early Mormonism," *New York History* 61 (October 1980): 381.

15. Jan Shipps, "The Prophet Puzzle: Suggestions Leading Toward a More Comprehensive Interpretation of Joseph Smith," *Journal of Mormon History* 1 (1974): 11.

16. Foremost in the first category would be the writings of LDS luminary Hugh Nibley. His full-length treatments include *Lehi in the Desert, The World of the Jaredites,* and *There Were Jaredites* in *The Collected Works of Hugh Nibley,* vol. 5, ed. John W. Welch et al. (Salt Lake City and Provo, Utah: Deseret Book and Foundation for Ancient Research and Mormon Studies [FARMS], 1988); *An Approach to the Book of Mormon* (*Collected Works,* vol. 6, 1988); *Since Cumorah* (*Collected Works,* vol. 7, 1988); and *The Prophetic Book of Mormon* (*Collected Works,* vol. 8, 1989). An approach based more on geography and anthropology is that of Brigham Young University's John L. Sorenson. His most important contribution is *An Ancient American Setting for the Book of Mormon* (Salt Lake City and Provo, Utah: Deseret Book and FARMS, 1996). See also his *Images of Ancient America: Visualizing Book of Mormon Life* (Provo, Utah: Research Press, 1998). Titles on the Book of Mormon or Mormonism found in Christian bookstores, such as John Ankerberg and John Weldon's *Facts on the Mormon Church* (Harvest House, 1991), usually appear in series with titles like the "Zondervan Guides to Cults and Religious Movements."

ONE

1. The standard account of Joseph's first vision is recounted in "Joseph Smith-History" (JS-H), *Pearl of Great Price* (Salt Lake City: Church of Jesus Christ of Latter-day Saints, 1981).

2. Between 1832 and 1842, Joseph would write or dictate several accounts of this vision. In the first, he mentions only one personage. See Dean C. Jessee, ed., *The Papers of Joseph Smith*, vol. 1, *Autobiographical and Historical Writings* (Salt Lake City: Deseret Book, 1989), for those versions as well as some contemporary secondhand accounts.

3. Richard L. Bushman's account of early Mormonism is the best to date. See his *Joseph Smith and the Beginnings of Mormonism* (Urbana and Chicago: University of Illinois Press, 1984), 55, 57.

4. Joseph Smith, Jr., *History of the Church of Jesus Christ of Latter-day Saints*, 7 vols., ed. James Mulholland, Robert B. Thompson, William W. Phelps, Willard Richards, George A. Smith, and later B. H. Roberts (Salt Lake City: Deseret News Press, 1902–12; 2nd rev. ed., Salt Lake City: Deseret Book, 1951), 1:6. Bushman observes that the confusion of the prophet's mother, Lucy Mack Smith, over the details of Joseph's first vision seems to confirm that he shared few particulars of his experience even with close family. As Bushman notes, "even twelve years after the event the First Vision's personal significance for him still overshadowed its place in the divine plan" (Bushman, *Joseph Smith*, 56).

5. Disapproval by "one of the Methodist preachers"—probably George Lane—is the only specific instance he provides of the "severe persecution at the hands of all classes of men, both religious and irreligious" referred to in his personal history (JS-H 1:21-27).

6. Two years before the publication of Joseph's official version in 1842, his friend Orson Pratt had published an account related to him by the prophet. See *An Interesting Account of Several Remarkable Visions and of the Late Discovery of Ancient American Records* (Edinburgh: Ballyntyne and Hughes, 1840). For a study of the different accounts of the First Vision, see Milton V. Backman Jr., *Joseph Smith's First Vision* (Salt Lake City: Bookcraft, 1980).

7. See James B. Allen, "The Significance of Joseph Smith's 'First Vision' in Mormon Thought," *Dialogue* 1 (autumn 1966): 29–45; Marvin Hill, "On the First Vision and Its Import in the Shaping of Early Mormonism," *Dialogue* 12 (spring 1979): 90–99; James B. Allen, "The Emergence of a Fundamental: The Expanding Role of Joseph Smith's First Vision in Mormon Thought," *Journal of Mormon History* 7 (1980): 43–61.

8. *Doctrine and Covenants* (D&C) 20:5. In 1833, a compilation of revelations received by Joseph Smith was published as the *Book of Commandments*. In 1835, the volume was expanded and republished as the *Doctrine and Covenants*. This volume, along with the Bible, the Book of Mormon, and the *Pearl of Great Price*, is one of the "standard works" considered scripture by Latter-day Saints.

9. The hundred million milestone was reached on April 22, 2000. *Deseret News 2001–2002 Church Almanac* (Salt Lake City: Deseret News, 2000), 568.

10. According to sociologist Rodney Stark, some now living may see it grow from its 11 million in the year 2000 to the neighborhood of 267 million by the year 2080. See his "The Rise of a New World Faith," *Review of Religious Research* 26.1 (September 1984): 19, 22–23. Though criticized as extravagant by some sociologists, Stark argues more recently that his estimate may have been too conservative. As of 1999, "membership is substantially higher than my most optimistic projection." "Extracting Social Scientific Models from Mormon History," *Journal of Mormon History* 25.1 (spring 1999): 176.

11. "When did the dumbing of America begin? . . . Some rude skeptics might want to locate the origins of 'creeping nincompoopism' . . . in the 1830s, when Joseph Smith took from dictation a number of miserably written narratives and injunctions conveyed to him by the angel Moroni and then persuaded a number of hicks to begin a new religion." Paul Fussell, *BAD: The Dumbing of America* (New York: Summit, 1991), 197.

12. Harold Bloom, *The American Religion: The Emergence of the Post-Christian Nation* (New York: Simon & Schuster, 1992), 80.

13. For a discussion of those passages cited by Moroni, see Kent P. Jackson, "Moroni's Message to Joseph Smith," *Ensign* 20.8 (August 1990): 13–16.

14. Here and throughout this book Bible citations are from the King James Version. It was the version Joseph Smith read and referred to, and would later revise in a project known as the "Inspired Translation." The King James is also the translation used in the official version of the LDS scriptures.

15. Though not included in Joseph's catalogue of scriptures he heard that night, Wilford Woodruff referred to Moroni's mention of the Daniel prophecy in a sermon of July 20, 1883 in *Journal of Discourses*, 26 vols., reported by G. D. Watt et al. (Liverpool: F. D. and S. W. Richards et al., 1851–1886; reprint, Salt Lake City: n.p., 1974), 24:241. Cited in David J. Whittaker, "The Book of Daniel in Early Mormon Thought," in John M. Lundquist and Stephen D. Ricks, eds., *By Study and Also by Faith: Essays in Honor of Hugh W. Nibley*, 2 vols. (Salt Lake City and Provo: Deseret Book and Foundation for Ancient Research and Mormon Studies [FARMS], 1990), 1:159.

16. *The Evening and the Morning Star* 1.10 (March 1833): 79. The first 14 numbers of this paper were published in Independence, Missouri (June 1832–July 1833). After mobs forced the Mormons out of Independence, publication resumed in Kirtland, Ohio, in December 1833 under the old title. The first 14 issues were also reprinted there, under the title *Evening and Morning Star*.

17. Andrew F. Ehat and Lyndon W. Cook, eds., *The Words of Joseph Smith: The Contemporary Accounts of the Nauvoo Discourses of the Prophet Joseph* (Orem, Utah: Grandin, 1994), 367. Cited in Whittaker, "The Book of Daniel," 159.

18. Jessee, *Papers*, 1:8.

19. Scot Facer Proctor and Maurine Jensen Proctor, eds., *The Revised and Enhanced History of Joseph Smith by his Mother* (Salt Lake City: Bookcraft, 1996), 123. Lucy's version of events, however, associates this failure and reprimand with Smith's *second* visit to the hill, one year later.

20. *Messenger and Advocate* 2.1 (October 1835): 198.

21. In Smith's account, the four-year period was established at the time of his first visit to the hill. His mother, however, recorded that he was told he could try to retrieve the plates again in one year's time, and was grievously disappointed when he failed on the second attempt as well. JS-H 1:53; Proctor, *History of Joseph Smith*, 122–23.

22. Proctor, *History of Joseph Smith*, 111–12.

23. Proctor, *History of Joseph Smith*, 111, 119.

24. "William Smith Notes," in Dan Vogel, ed., *Early Mormon Documents*, 3 vols. (Salt Lake City: Signature Books, 1996–), 1:486–87.

25. Proctor, *History of Joseph Smith*, 124.

26. Willard Chase, a Methodist preacher who glossed over his own role as a treasure-seeker in his later accounts of events, became a vociferous enemy to Joseph Smith. See his affidavit in Vogel, *Early Mormon Documents*, 2:65.

27. See in this regard D. Michael Quinn, *Early Mormonism and the Magic World View* (Salt Lake City: Signature Books, 1987; 2nd ed., 1999).

28. For a study of the perseverance of magical practices—including money-digging—throughout the American Enlightenment, see Herbert Leventhal, *In the Shadow of the Enlightenment: Occultism and Renaissance Science in Eighteenth-Century America* (New York: New York University Press, 1976), especially pages 107–19.

29. This is probably the same Winchell ("Winchell or Wingate") whom a nineteenth-century writer named "one source, if not the main source from which came this monster—Mormonism." That Winchell was a Vermont counterfeiter who was part of a group that claimed to be restoring Christianity using the Bible and divining rods. Apparently, Winchell was hosted at one time by Oliver Cowdery's father, William. Since the young Cowdery later became Joseph Smith's scribe, the grounds were there for a very tenuous and convoluted connection between Winchell and Mormonism. Barnes Frisbie, *The History of Middletown, Vermont* (Rutland, Vt.: Turtle, 1867), 64. The story is recounted and assessed in Richard Lloyd Anderson, "The Mature Joseph Smith and Treasure Searching," *BYU Studies* 24.4 (fall 1984): 489–546.

30. The fullest treatment of this seer stone is Richard Van Wagoner and Steve Walker, "Joseph Smith and the Gift of Seeing," *Dialogue* (summer 1982): 48–68.

31. See the affidavits of several neighbors, many of whom were co-participants in money-digging, originally published in E.D. Howe, *Mormonism Unveiled* (Painesville, Ohio: E. D. Howe, 1834), and reprinted in Vogel, *Early Mormon Documents*, 2:59–63. William Stafford, who lost the sheep, passed off his involvement as "gratif[ication of] my curiosity" (61).

32. In response to the question, "was not Jo Smith a money digger?" he replied in series of question and answers, "Yes, but it was never a very profitable job to him, as [he] only got fourteen dollars a month for it," *Elders' Journal of the Church of Jesus Christ of Latter-day Saints* 1.3 (July 1838): 43.

33. Martin Harris interview with Joel Tiffany, "Mormonism—No. II," *Tiffany's Monthly* (August 1859): 163–70, in Vogel, *Early Mormon Documents*, 2:309.

34. The comment was recorded at Joseph's 1826 trial for disorderly conduct and imposture by W. D. Purple. Donna Hill, *Joseph Smith, the First Mormon* (1977; reprint, Salt Lake City: Signature Books, 1999), 66. See Bushman, *Joseph Smith,* 74–76, for an overview of the available sources for the trial.

35. "Peter Ingersoll Statement, 1833," in Vogel, *Early Mormon Documents,* 2:43. Hale recorded that "Smith stated to me, that he had given up what he called 'glass-looking,' and that he expected to work hard for a living."

36. Proctor, *History of Joseph Smith,* 140, 151. Many years later, Harris said that he didn't hear of the plates until October of 1827, from his brother Preserved. See Harris interview with Tiffany, in Vogel, *Early Mormon Documents,* 2:307–08.

37. Willard Chase, not an entirely reliable witness, claimed that Joseph Jr. had a close working relationship with Lawrence, consulted with him about the plates, and even asked him to recommend him to the young Emma Hale. See "Willard Chase Statement, 1833" in Vogel, *Early Mormon Documents,* 2:68–69. Joseph Knight, a friend of Joseph Smith, also claimed Lawrence had been to the hill, and so threatened to intrude himself into Smith's dealings with the angel Moroni that Smith had to warn him away. See Dean Jessee, "Joseph Knight's Recollection of Early Mormon History," *BYU Studies* 17.1 (autumn 1976): 33; Bushman, *Joseph Smith,* 216n1.

38. *Wayne Sentinel,* 26 June 1829, found in Francis W. Kirkham, *A New Witness for Christ in America,* 2 vols. (Independence, Mo.: Zion's Printing and Publishing, 1951), 2:28.

39. *The Saints Herald* 28 (1881): 167. Cited in Hill, *Joseph Smith,* 71. Hill points out that in 1810, De Witt Clinton recorded that copper kettles and other artifacts had been unearthed near Canandaigua (71–72).

40. Harris interview with Tiffany, in Vogel, *Early Mormon Documents,* 2:308.

41. Joseph Knight Jr., "Incidents of History from 1827 to 1844," compiled by T. Thomas Bullock from loose sheets in Joseph Knight's possession, August 16, 1862. In Larry C. Porter, "The Colesville Branch and the Coming Forth of the Book of Mormon," *BYU Studies* 10.3 (spring 1970): 369.

42. Jessee, "Joseph Knight's Recollection," 33.

43. Lucy places the event "soon after" Joseph's January return to Palmyra, at which time the angel promised delivery of the plates in "the following September" (Proctor, *History of Joseph Smith,* 135). She is frequently confused about dates, but there is no evidence to suggest the visit could not have occurred in early 1827 as she suggests, rather than late in that same year as Bushman and Hill assume (Bushman, *Joseph Smith,* 78; Hill, *Joseph Smith,* 69).

44. Proctor, *History of Joseph Smith,* 135.

45. "I have been laboring in this cause for eight years," he wrote in a letter published in *Messenger and Advocate* 1.12 (September 1835): 179.

46. "Joseph Knight's Recollection" is the fullest account of that evening's event (Jessee, 32–33). Lucy Mack revealed that Joseph borrowed his transportation without permission—early the next morning, Knight assumed "some rogue had stolen" both horse and carriage (Proctor, *History of Joseph Smith,* 139).

47. Important in this regard is one of the reasons Ezra Booth gave for leaving the church only months after joining: Joseph's "habitual proneness to jest-

ing and joking." Letter to Reverend I. Eddy, *Ohio Star*, 24 (October 1831). Thus one reasonable interpretation of the William Stafford incident involving the sheep would see him as a resentful dupe of Smith's practical joking, like the priests of Baal being egged on to more frenzied worship by an earnest sounding Elijah.

48. Jessee, "Joseph Knight's Recollection," 33.

49. Proctor, *History of Joseph Smith*, 139.

50. William Smith interview with J. W. Peterson and W. S. Pender, 1890, in Vogel, *Early Mormon Documents*, 1:508. Both William and Lucy reported that Joseph often kept the interpreters on his person. William concluded from this that they were actually detachable from the breastplate.

51. Reuben Miller, 1859 account of Oliver Cowdery's 1848 Council Bluffs testimony, in Vogel, *Early Mormon Documents*, 2:495. Miller's journal entry, made at the time, omits the tactile testimony.

52. Several affidavits and interviews are collected in Vogel, *Early Mormon Documents*, 2:352–58.

53. While most scholars follow the Septuagint's translation of "lights and perfections" for the Hebrew terms Urim and Thummim, the idea is not universally accepted. John Tvedtnes, for example, sees in them an Egyptian origin: "*iri*, 'do, act, achieve, perform' and the negative particle, *tm*, 'don't.' We can thus read, very simply, 'DOs and DON'Ts'." John A. Tvedtnes, "Egyptian Etymologies for Biblical Religious Paraphernalia," in Sarah I. Groll, ed., *Egyptological Studies*, Scripta Hierosolymitana, vol. 28 (Jerusalem: Magnes Press of the Hebrew University, 1982), 219.

54. Adam Clarke, *The Holy Bible Containing the Old and New Testaments with a Commentary and Critical Notes*, 3 vols. (Nashville: Abingdon, n.d. [reprint]), 1:448.

55. James E. Lancaster, "The Translation of the Book of Mormon," in Dan Vogel, ed., *The Word of God: Essays on Mormon Scripture* (Salt Lake City: Signature Books, 1990), 112.

56. Cornelius van Dam, *The Urim and Thummim: A Means of Revelation in Ancient Israel* (Winona Lake, Ind.: Eisenbrauns, 1997), 229–30.

57. "The book of Mormon, as a revelation from God, possesses some advantage over the old scripture: it has not been tinctured by the wisdom of man, with here and there an Italic word to supply deficiencies. It was translated by the gift and power of God, by an unlearned man, through the aid of a pair of Interpreters, or spectacles—(known, perhaps, in ancient days as Teraphim, or Urim and Thummim)." *The Evening and the Morning Star* 1.8 (January 1833): 58. Once Joseph began to employ the term, he apparently used it to refer to both the interpreters and the seer stone. Accordingly, I will use the latter terms whenever possible, and the former when it is impossible to determine which of those two instruments Joseph meant.

58. The closest parallel at the time would have been a reference in the Apocrypha (still included in many editions of the King James Bible in Joseph Smith's era). There, we read, a tribute to Simon, son of Mattathias, and his sons was inscribed on "tables of brass" and placed within the precincts of the temple (1 Macc. 14; see also 8:22). Of course, numerous ex-

amples of ancient writings on metal plates have emerged since 1827. See, in this regard, the overview by H. Curtis Wright, "Ancient Burials of Metal Documents in Stone Boxes," in Lundquist and Ricks, *By Study and Also by Faith*, 2:273–334.

59. Proctor, *History of Joseph Smith*, 139.

60. Jessee, "Joseph Knight's Recollection," 33.

61. Harris interview with Tiffany, in Vogel, *Early Mormon Documents*, 2:307.

62. Lyndon W. Cook, ed., *David Whitmer Interviews: A Restoration Witness* (Orem, Utah: Grandin 1991), 60.

63. According to Joseph Knight, Joseph threatened, through his father, to "thrash the stumps with him" if Lawrence showed up at the hill at the time the plates were to be delivered. Jessee, "Joseph Knight's Recollection," 33.

64. Martha Campbell letter to Joseph Smith, December 19, 1843, in Vogel, *Early Mormon Documents*, 2:307n29.

65. Sally Parker letter to John Kempton, August 26, 1838, in Vogel, *Early Mormon Documents*, 1:219.

66. William Smith interview with J. W. Peterson and W. S. Pender, 1890, in Vogel, *Early Mormon Documents*, 1:508.

67. Reminiscence of H. S. Salisbury, 1954, in Vogel, *Early Mormon Documents*, 1:524–25.

68. Emma's description is given in Vogel, *Early Mormon Documents*, 1:525n5.

69. Hill, *Joseph Smith*, 69.

70. Harris interview with Tiffany, in Vogel, *Early Mormon Documents*, 2:308–10.

71. Lucy Mack implies that it was Joseph's idea to relocate (Proctor, *History of Joseph Smith*, 153). Harris, however, is emphatic in explaining that, hearing of mob threats to tar and feather Joseph, he saw it was "unsafe for him to remain, so I determined that he must go to his father-in-law's." Harris interview with Tiffany, in Vogel, *Early Mormon Documents*, 2:310.

72. "It was agreed upon that Martin Harris should follow him as soon as Joseph should have sufficient time to transcribe some of the Egyptian characters." Proctor, *History of Joseph Smith*, 154.

73. Jessee, "Joseph Knight's Recollection," 34. Bushman reads in Lucy Mack Smith's account as well the suggestion that Joseph wanted "a translation of all the basic characters, [so] he could carry on by himself." Bushman, *Joseph Smith*, 86.

74. Jessee, *Papers*, 1:9.

75. Smith, *History*, 1:19.

76. Clark described the visit in a letter full of factual errors and inconsistencies. John A. Clark to Dear Brethren, August 24, 1840, *The Episcopal Recorder* 18 (5 September 1840): 94, in Vogel, *Early Mormon Documents*, 2:261–69.

77. Hill, *Joseph Smith*, 75.

78. Anthon letter in Milton V. Backman Jr., *Eyewitness Accounts of the Restoration* (Salt Lake City: Deseret, 1986), 219.

79. Smith, *History*, 1:20.

80. Charles Anthon to E. D. Howe, 17 February 1834, in Backman, *Eyewitness*, 215–19.

81. Charles Anthon to Rev. T. W. Coit, 3 April 1841, in Backman, *Eyewitness*, 215–19.

82. See Stanley B. Kimball, "The Anthon Transcript: People, Primary Sources, and Problems," *BYU Studies* 10.3 (spring 1970): 335–36.

83. This vow, cited by Anthon in his 1841 letter, is highly improbable in this context. Publication of the book, and the need for Martin to guarantee its financing through a mortgage on his farm, were still two years away.

84. Smith, *History*, 1:20.

85. Emma Smith Bidamon interview with Edmund C. Briggs, 1856, in Vogel, *Early Mormon Documents*, 1:530.

86. *St. Louis Republican*, July 26, 1884, in Cook, *David Whitmer Interviews*, 139–40.

87. Reuben Miller Journal, October 21, 1848, in Vogel, *Early Mormon Documents*, 2:494.

88. John H. Gilbert letter to James T. Cobb, 10 February 1879, in Vogel, *Early Mormon Documents*, 2:522–23.

89. Backman, *Eyewitness*, 173; Stan Larson, "A Study of Some Textual Variations in the Book of Mormon. . . " (master's thesis, Brigham Young University, 1974); Royal Skousen, "How Joseph Smith Translated the Book of Mormon: Evidence from the Original Manuscript," in Noel B. Reynolds, ed., *Book of Mormon Authorship Revisited: The Evidence for Ancient Origins* (Provo, Utah: FARMS, 1997), 61–93.

90. B. H. Roberts has seen no particular problem in believing that Joseph would rely upon a printed text, as long as it was in substantial agreement with the text before him. See discussion and references in Stan Larson, "The Historicity of the Matthean Sermon on the Mount," in Brent Lee Metcalfe, ed., *New Approaches to the Book of Mormon: Explorations in Critical Methodology* (Salt Lake City: Signature Books, 1993), 116.

91. Royal Skousen, "Textual Variants in the Isaiah Quotations," in Donald W. Parry and John W. Welch, eds., *Isaiah in the Book of Mormon* (Provo, Utah: FARMS, 1998), 377–78.

92. William Smith wrote that the large figure-eight shaped bow attached to a breastplate was held "before the eyes much like a pair of spectacles," but that Joseph took to placing it in a hat to relieve the strain on his eyes. The problem is, William was not at Harmony during the only time that they were, apparently, used. Oliver Cowdery and others, in describing Joseph's employment of the Urim and Thummim, are actually referring to his use of the seer stone, which appears to have been the only instrument he used after the summer of 1828. William Smith interview with J. W. Peterson and W. S. Pender, 1890, in Vogel, *Early Mormon Documents*, 1:508–09.

93. Jerald and Sandra Tanner, *Covering Up the Black Hole in the Book of Mormon* (Salt Lake City: Utah Lighthouse Ministry, 1990), 160.

94. "Last Testimony of Sister Emma," *Saints' Herald* 26 (1 October 1879), in Vogel, *Early Mormon Documents*, 1:541.

95. Edward Stevenson, "Incidents in the Life of Martin Harris," *Latter-day Saints Millennial Star* 44 (February 6, 1882): 87.

96. *Latter-day Saints Millennial Star* 44 (February 6, 1882): 86–87.

97. A number of articles address this issue—which may have considerable theological significance—of how mechanical and how tightly controlled

the process was. Some (secondhand) accounts go even further than Harris in arguing for rigid control, such as Truman Coe's claim that Joseph said he saw the translation "in plain English, on a screen placed before him." (Truman Coe to Editor, *Ohio Observer*, August 11, 1836, in Vogel, *Early Mormon Documents*, 1:46.) Book of Mormon textual scholar Royal Skousen refers to theories of "loose," "tight," and "iron-clad" control in "How Joseph Smith Translated the Book of Mormon: Evidence from the Original Manuscript," *Journal of Book of Mormon Studies* 7.1 (1998): 23–31. He concludes that "Joseph Smith could actually see (whether in the interpreters or in his mind's eye) the translated English text—word for word and letter for letter" (31). And recently, LDS scholars have used wordprint analysis of the Book of Mormon to argue that "the demonstrated presence of distinguishable authorship wordprints in the Book of Mormon argues for a formal translation in which information was transferred but the imprint of the original language remained." Thus, "the process was both direct and literal." Wayne A. Larsen, Alvin C. Rencher, and Tim Layton, "Who Wrote the Book of Mormon? An Analysis of Wordprints," *BYU Studies* 20.3 (spring 1980): 244. On the other hand, given the fact that Joseph did not scruple to make minor changes to the text over the next few years, he clearly understood his role to be that of an imperfect medium in a process that was far from mechanical.

98. Smith, *History*, 1:220.

99. Proctor, *History of Joseph Smith*, 157.

100. Dean C. Jessee, comp. and ed., *The Personal Writings of Joseph Smith* (Salt Lake City: Deseret Book, 1984), 210.

101. Proctor, *History of Joseph Smith*, 165–66.

102. It is unclear what Harris himself believed. Donna Hill writes that Harris agreed Lucy was part of such a conspiracy (*Joseph Smith*, 82), but there is evidence he rejected the idea of his wife's guilt or complicity in such a design. A first edition of the Book of Mormon once owned by B. H. Roberts (1857–1933) contains an enigmatic note in this regard. In the margin above the preface, where Joseph rehearses the Lord's warning that evil-minded people—presumably Lucy among others—stole the manuscript with intent to alter it and discredit him, an apparent contemporary has penned: "Martin says that preface is all incorrect and should not be regarded or read." Next to which is the notation, "I do not know who wrote the above [signed] BHR." (Book of Mormon in private collection of George W. Givens.)

103. Bushman believes Joseph lost the Urim and Thummim at the time Harris went off with the manuscript, based on Joseph's remark that they "had been taken from me in consequence of my having wearied the Lord" on Harris's behalf (Smith, *History*, 1:21). But Lucy Mack recorded that *after* Joseph's return to Harmony, an angel required him to deliver up the Urim and Thummim because "he had sinned in delivering the manuscript into the hands of a wicked man." (Proctor, *History of Joseph Smith*, 173–74.) There is no reason to think her dating wrong, since she writes that the punishment was "in consequence of," but not at the time of, Smith's impolitic and excessive intervention on behalf of Harris.

104. Proctor, *History of Joseph Smith*, 174.

105. Emma Smith Bidamon to Emma Pilgrim, March 27, 1870, in Vogel, *Early Mormon Documents*, 1:532.

106. David Whitmer to *Kansas City Journal*, in Cook, *David Whitmer Interviews*, 72.

107. Apparently, Joseph did not give the entirety of their work to that date over to Harris. Section 10 of the *Doctrine and Covenants* distinguishes between the 116-page portion Joseph gave to Harris ("words which . . . have gone out of your hands"–v. 10) and a further portion, presumably miniscule, he kept ("that which you have translated, which you have retained"–v. 41).

108. Smith, *History*, 1:28.

109. Joseph Knight and Emma both remembered her brother Reuben Hale assisting during the winter of 1828–29 as well. Jessee, "Joseph Knight's Recollection," 35; "Last Testimony of Sister Emma," in Vogel, *Early Mormon Documents*, 1:541.

110. Jessee, "Joseph Knight's Recollection," 35–36.

111. Smith, *History*, 1:32–33.

112. "Last Testimony of Sister Emma," in Vogel, *Early Mormon Documents*, 1:542.

113. The date in current editions, summer of 1828, is in error. In verse 41, Joseph is commanded to "translate the engravings which are on the [small] plates of Nephi, down even till you come to the reign of king Benjamin, or until you come to that which you have translated, which you have retained." But in summer 1828, Joseph had virtually *no* translated portion in his possession, and handwriting analysis of the manuscript reveals that the Nephi sections were *not* translated, per these instructions, until over a year later. See a fuller discussion of the evidence for erroneous dating in Bushman, *Joseph Smith*, 223.

114. It is possible that part of Mosiah had been translated and lost as part of the 116 pages. Both original manuscript notations and the text of Mosiah chapter 1 suggest it may originally have been chapter 3.

115. Smith, *History*, 1:39.

116. *Book of Commandments* (Independence, Mo.: 1833), 4:5.

117. Except for the "few pages" translated before Cowdery arrived, the entire section from Mosiah through Moroni—pages 153–588 in the 1830 edition—was probably translated before the move to Fayette. First Nephi to the Words of Mormon would have come last. See John W. Welch and Tim Rathbone, "The Translation of the Book of Mormon: Basic Historical Information," (Provo, Utah: FARMS, 1986). The rate for the entire translation would have been eight printed pages a day, according to Welch's estimate. John Welch, "How Long Did It Take Joseph Smith to Translate the Book of Mormon?" *Ensign* 18.1 (January 1988): 47.

118. Smith, *History*, 1:44.

119. David Whitmer wrote that "the translation at my father's occupied about one month, that is from June 1st to July 1st, 1829." *Kansas City Journal*, June 5, 1881, in Cook, *David Whitmer Interviews*, 62.

120. Quoted in Philip Barlow, *Mormons and the Bible* (New York: Oxford, 1991), 19.

121. Joseph Smith mentioned this verse, as well as 2 Nephi 11:3, which predicts that "by the words of three" God "will establish [his] word."

122. Smith, *History*, 1:54–55.
123. Proctor, *History of Joseph Smith*, 199.
124. Reuben Miller, "Last Days of Oliver Cowdery," *Deseret News* 9 (April 13, 1859), in Vogel, *Early Mormon Documents*, 2:495.
125. In fall of 1837, opposition to Joseph Smith grew as he claimed the right to advise and counsel in areas beyond what some members saw as spiritual matters. The collapse of the Kirtland Anti-Banking Society in early 1838 was invoked by his critics as confirmation that he had overreached—and therefore forfeited—his authority. Many members left the church as a consequence. See Ronald K. Esplin, "The Emergence of Brigham Young and the Twelve to Mormon leadership, 1830–1841," (Ph.D. diss., Brigham Young University, 1981).
126. Keith W. Perkins, "David Whitmer," in Daniel Ludlow, ed., *Encyclopedia of Mormonism*, 4 vols. (New York: Macmillan, 1992), 4:1566.
127. Vogel, *Early Mormon Documents*, 2:255.
128. Leigh Eric Schmidt, *Holy Fairs: Scottish Communions and American Revivals in the Early Modern Period* (Princeton: Princeton University Press, 1989), 148.
129. "Evangelists and Their Hearers: Popular Interpretation of Revivalist Preaching in Eighteenth-Century Scotland," *Journal of British Studies* 28.2 (April 1989): 139.
130. Statement of Reuben P. Harmon, in Vogel, *Early Mormon Documents*, 2:255. He cites secondhand testimony of three or four others to similar effect.

TWO

1. John Sorenson, *An Ancient American Setting for the Book of Mormon* (Salt Lake City: Deseret Book and Foundation for Ancient Research and Mormon Studies [FARMS], 1996), 138.
2. C. S. Lewis, *Perelandra* (New York: Scribner, 1996), 142.
3. Stephen E. Robinson, "The 'Expanded' Book of Mormon?" in Monte S. Nyman and Charles D. Tate Jr., eds., *The Book of Mormon: Second Nephi, The Doctrinal Structure* (Provo, Utah: Brigham Young University, Religious Studies Center, 1989), 396. The paraphrase of Robinson is by Melodie Moench Charles, who critiques the historical plausibility of "Book of Mormon Christology" in her article of that name, in Brent Lee Metcalfe, ed., *New Approaches to the Book of Mormon: Explorations in Critical Methodology* (Salt Lake City: Signature Books, 1993), 95.
4. Howard N. Wallace, in Frank Moore Cross Jr., ed., *The Eden Narratives* (Atlanta: Scholars, 1985), 18–21; Umberto Cassuto, *A Commentary on the Book of Genesis. Part I: From Adam to Noah*, trans. Israel Abrahams (Jerusalem: Magnes, 1961), 72–74; Robert Gordis, "The Knowledge of Good and Evil in the Old Testament and the Qumran Scrolls," *Journal of Biblical Literature* 76 (1857): 127n16. These examples, and several others, are in Bruce M. Pritchett Jr., "Lehi's Theology of the Fall in Its Preexilic/Exilic Context," *Journal of Book of Mormon Studies* 3.2 (fall 1994): 49–81. In addition to several Old Testament passages discussed in his article, his appendix includes 36 others that commentators have connected with the fall.

5. The sources are given in John A. Tvedtnes, "Jeremiah's Prophecies of Jesus Christ," in *The Most Correct Book* (Salt Lake City: Cornerstone, 1999): 101–02.
6. John Tvedtnes, "The Messiah, The Book of Mormon, and the Dead Sea Scrolls," in *The Most Correct Book*, 343. Tvedtnes cites examples from scrolls 11Q13, 4Q246, and 4Q521 (328–43).
7. Margaret Barker, *The Great Angel: A Study of Israel's Second God* (Louisville: John Knox, 1992), 2. See also her *The Older Testament: The Survival of Themes from the Ancient Royal Cult in Sectarian Judaism and Early Christianity* (London: SPCK, 1987).
8. Moses 6:59–66, *Pearl of Great Price*.
9. For example, a writer to the *Salt Lake Tribune* called it "a feeble and diluted imitation of the Bible revelation and the gospel which had already been in the possession of the Christian people of this country for over two hundred years." Reprinted in B. H. Roberts, *Defense of the Faith and the Saints*, 2 vols. (Salt Lake City: Deseret News, 1907–12), 1:348. More famously, Mark Twain called it "a tedious plagiarism of the New Testament." *Roughing It*, 2 vols. (Hartford, Conn.: American Publishing, 1899), 1:132.
10. *Rochester Daily Advertiser*, April 2, 1830, in Francis W. Kirkham, *A New Witness for Christ in America*, 2 vols. (Independence, Mo.: Zion's Printing, 1951), 1:267.
11. For a discussion of the epic features of the Book of Mormon, see Richard Rust, *Feasting on the Word: The Literary Testimony of the Book of Mormon* (Salt Lake City: Deseret Book and FARMS, 1997), 47–64.
12. Sorenson, *Ancient American Setting*, 50.
13. In a preface to the first printing of the Book of Mormon, Joseph Smith referred to those 116 pages as "The Book of Lehi" and said they came from Mormon's abridgment of "The plates of Lehi." Apparently, then, the plates of Lehi are another name for the first section of the large plates of Nephi. (In similar manner, Jacob will refer to his writings on Nephi's small plates as "the plates of Jacob"–Jacob 3:14).
14. John W. Welch, "Authorship of the Book of Isaiah," in Donald W. Parry and John W. Welch, eds., *Isaiah in the Book of Mormon* (Provo, Utah: FARMS, 1998), 431.
15. Sorenson discusses six such elements in "The 'Brass Plates' and Biblical Scholarship," *Dialogue* 10.4 (autumn 1977): 31–39. But his challenge to biblical scholars that "this congruence should invite serious attention to the Book of Mormon for what it may reveal to them about Old Testament sources" has met with no response.
16. As Eugene England points out, "the Book of Mormon . . . is mainly patterned by a single mind, that of Mormon, and the resulting unity is remarkably similar to the patterns only now being explicated in the Bible by such critics as [Northrop] Frye." See England's "A Second Witness for the *Logos*: The Book of Mormon and Contemporary Literary Criticism," in John M. Lundquist and Stephen D. Ricks, eds., *By Study and Also by Faith: Essays in Honor of Hugh W. Nibley*, 2 vols. (Salt Lake City and Provo: Deseret Book and FARMS, 1990), 2:91–125.
17. Mormon is here quoting the words of Nephi, son of Helaman (Helaman 7:7). The other instances of the term in his abridgment are Alma 36:28, Alma 37:44–45, and 3 Nephi 20:29.

18. Cowdery apparently first designated the New York mount as Hill Cumorah in the *Messenger and Advocate* (July 1835): 158–59. For further discussion, see William Hamblin, "Basic Methodological Problems with the Anti-Mormon Approach to the Geography and Archaeology of the Book of Mormon," (Provo, Utah: FARMS, 1993), 10; and John Sorenson, *The Geography of Book of Mormon Events: A Source Book* (Provo, Utah: FARMS, 1992), 372.

19. Harris sold his farm in April of 1831 to pay the bill. See Richard Bushman, *Joseph Smith and the Beginnings of Mormonism* (Urbana and Chicago: University of Illinois Press, 1984), 108.

20. David Whitmer said of the occasion, "2 rooms were filled with members—about 20 from Colesville, 15 from Manchester Church and about 20 from around about Father Whitmers. About 50 members & the 6 Elders were present." From Journal of Edward Stevenson, 2 January 1887. Cited in Larry C. Porter, "'The Field is White Already to Harvest': Earliest Missionary Labors and the Book of Mormon," in Larry C. Porter and Susan Easton Black, eds., *The Prophet Joseph: Essays on the Life and Mission of Joseph Smith* (Salt Lake City: Deseret Book, 1988), 74.

21. David Whitmer interview with a reporter of the *Kansas City Journal*, June 5, 1881. This and several of the examples to follow of prepublication proselytizing are collected in Porter, "The Field is White," 73–89.

22. Joseph Smith Jr., *History of the Church of Jesus Christ of Latter-day Saints*, 7 vols., ed. James Mulholland, Robert B. Thompson, William W. Phelps, Willard Richards, George A. Smith, and later B. H. Roberts (Salt Lake City: Deseret News Press, 1902–12; 2nd rev. ed., Salt Lake City: Deseret Book, 1951), 1:51.

23. Smith, *History*, 1:75. Fearing for the safety of the manuscript, Joseph had Cowdery make out a second "printer's manuscript," which was delivered a few pages at a time for typesetting. Occasionally, when the printers outpaced the copyist, original pages were used as well.

24. David Whitmer, *An Address to All Believers in Christ*, (Richmond, Mo.: David Whitmer, 1887), 32; "History of Thos. Baldwin Marsh," *Deseret News*, 24 March 1858; Solomon Chamberlain, "A Short Sketch of the Life of Solomon Chamberlain." All three sources are quoted in Porter, "The Field is White," 79–81. See also Larry C. Porter, "Solomon Chamberlain—Early Missionary," *BYU Studies* 12.3 (spring 1972): 314–18.

25. Letter of Joseph Smith, Jr., to Oliver Cowdery, Harmony, Pennsylvania, October 22, 1829, Joseph Smith Collection, Archives of the Church of Jesus Christ of Latter-day Saints, Salt Lake City. Quoted in Porter, "The Field is White," 32.

26. *Wayne Sentinel*, June 26, 1829, reprinted in Kirkham, *New Witness*, 2:28.

27. *Palmyra Freeman*, August 29, 1829, quoted in Donna Hill, *Joseph Smith, the First Mormon* (1977; reprint, Salt Lake City: Signature Books, 1999), 95.

28. Lucy Mack said the group threatened Grandin "with evil consequences" if he proceeded with the printing. Joseph came back from New York and "went immediately with Martin Harris [who had guaranteed payment] and succeeded in removing his fears." Scot Facer Proctor and Maurine

Jensen Proctor, eds., *The Revised and Enhanced History of Joseph Smith by his Mother* (Salt Lake City: Bookcraft, 1996), 221.

29. William Alexander Linn, *The Story of the Mormons* (New York: Macmillan, 1902), 48, quoted in Porter, "The Field is White," 85.
30. Dean Jessee, "Joseph Knight's Recollection of Early Mormon History," *BYU Studies* 17.1 (autumn 1976): 36–37.
31. Proctor, *History of Joseph Smith*, 152.
32. Pomeroy Tucker, *Origin, Rise, and Progress of Mormonism* (New York: Appleton, 1867), 60. Quoted by Porter, "The Field is White," 85.
33. Benjamin Winchester, "Introduction to the Subject of the Book of Mormon," *Gospel Reflector* 1.5 (March 1, 1841): 99.
34. Smith, *History*, 1:84.

THREE

1. At least early as 1831, Joseph Smith employed the term "saints" in a revelation referring to the righteous of the "last days" (*Doctrine and Covenants* [D&C] 61:17). The church was incorporated as "The Church of Christ" in 1830, was being called "The Church of the Latter-Day Saints" by April of 1834 (*The Evening and the Morning Star* 2.19 [April 1834]: 150, 152), and adopted its present name in 1838 (see D&C 115:4).
2. Dean C. Jessee, comp. and ed., *The Personal Writings of Joseph Smith* (Salt Lake City: Deseret Book, 1984), 218–19.
3. David J. Whittaker has written a thorough account of "how saturated early Mormon thought was with Daniel typology." See his "The Book of Daniel in Early Mormon Thought," in John M. Lundquist and Stephen D. Ricks, eds., *By Study and Also by Faith: Essays in Honor of Hugh W. Nibley*, 2 vols. (Salt Lake City and Provo: Deseret Book and FARMS, 1990), 1: 155–201.
4. *Messenger and Advocate* 2.14 (November 1835): 221.
5. *Messenger and Advocate* 2.15 (December 1835): 227.
6. George M. Marsden, *Religion and American Culture* (New York: Harcourt Brace Jovanovich, 1990), 80.
7. Monte S. Nyman and Lisa Bolin Hawkins, "Book of Mormon: Overview," in Daniel Ludlow, ed., *Encyclopedia of Mormonism*, 4 vols. (New York: Macmillan, 1992), 1:139.
8. These terms were popularized by French linguist Ferdinand de Saussure. The distinction is between that aspect of a linguistic sign that points to a meaning (a sound-image or symbol) and that part that constitutes its meaning (the concept or idea). *Course in General Linguistics* (New York: McGraw-Hill, 1966), 66–7.
9. "Joseph Smith-History" (JS-H), *Pearl of Great Price* (Salt Lake City: Church of Jesus Christ of Latter-day Saints, 1981), 1:40.
10. "In the Name of the Prophet—Smith!," *Household Words* 8 (19 July 1851): 340. For a discussion of the role of gathering in the Mormon persecutions, see Terryl Givens, *Viper on the Hearth: Mormons, Myths, and the Construction of Heresy* (New York: Oxford University Press, 1997), 52–54.
11. *The Evening and the Morning Star* 1.1 (June 1832): 6.

12. Joseph Smith, Jr., *History of the Church of Jesus Christ of Latter-day Saints*, 7 vols., ed. James Mulholland, Robert B. Thompson, William W. Phelps, Willard Richards, George A. Smith, and later B. H. Roberts (Salt Lake City: Deseret News Press, 1902–12; 2nd rev. ed., Salt Lake City: Deseret Book, 1951), 1:359.

13. See Terryl Givens, "'An Age of Humbugs': The Contemporary Scene," in *Viper on the Hearth*, 60–75.

14. Jan Shipps, "Another Side of Early Mormonism," in Jan Shipps and John W. Welch, eds., *The Journals of William McLellin 1831–1836* (Provo, Utah: BYU Studies and Brigham Young University; Urbana: University of Illinois Press, 1994), 5–6.

15. J. H. Beadle, *Life in Utah; or, the Mysteries and Crimes of Mormonism* (Philadelphia: National Publishing Company, 1870), preface.

16. Laurence Moore, *Religious Outsiders and the Making of Americans* (New York: Oxford University Press, 1986), 38.

17. Shipps, "Another Side," 7.

18. The other two signs were "the covenants given to the Latter-day Saints, also the translation of the Bible." Joseph considered a new translation of the Bible to be "a branch of [his] calling" (Smith, *History of the Church* 1:238). He began it in March 1831. "To the Elders of the Church," *Messenger and Advocate* 2.3 (December 1835): 229.

19. Parley P. Pratt detailed the journey in his *Autobiography* (Salt Lake City: Deseret Book, 1975), 47–52.

20. Charles Thompson, *Evidences in Proof of the Book of Mormon* (Batavia, N.Y.: D. D. Waite, 1841), 3.

21. *Times and Seasons* 3.5 (1 January 1842). From this date on, there occur increasing references to "the Book of Mormon [coming] forth as an 'ensign to the nations.'" See *Times and Seasons* 3.6, 3.21, 4.3, etc.

22. Benjamin Winchester, "The Object of a Continuation of Revelation," *Gospel Reflector* 1.5 (March 1, 1841): 98.

23. Marvin S. Hill, "The Shaping of the Mormon Mind in New England and New York," *BYU Studies* 9.3 (spring 1969): 352. The best study that situates Mormonism within the context of millenarian expectations is Grant Underwood's *The Millenarian World of Early Mormonism* (Urbana: University of Illinois Press, 1999).

24. Hyrum L. Andrus, "The Second American Revolution: Era of Preparation," *BYU Studies* 1.2 (autumn 1959): 78.

25. A. S. Hayden, *Early History of the Disciples in the Western Reserve, Ohio* (Cincinnati: Chase and Hall, 1876), 183.

26. Alexander Campbell, *The Christian System*, 10, cited in Andrus, "Second American Revolution," 80.

27. In Grant Underwood's study of Book of Mormon usage in pre-1846 Mormon publications, he finds 59 references to "the restoration of Israel." The next highest incidence is for "Prophecy relating to Gentiles," with 37 occurrences. See his chapter "The Book of Mormon and the Millenarian Mind" in *Millenarian World*.

28. Now canonized as the tenth "Article of Faith," the complete thirteen were first made public in Joseph Smith's letter to John Wentworth, cited earlier in this chapter.

29. Smith, *History of the Church*, 2:450.

30. Smith, *History of the Church*, 1:391.

31. Smith, *History of the Church*, 1:437.

32. *The Evening and the Morning Star* 2.16 (January 1834): 122.

33. Smith, *History of the Church*, 2:129. "We learn from the Book of Mormon the very identical continent and spot of land upon which the New Jerusalem is to stand," confirmed Joseph Smith elsewhere. (2:261–62).

34. Alexander Campbell, *Delusions: An Analysis of the Book of Mormon* (Boston: Benjamin H. Greene, 1832), 12.

35. Underwood, *Millenarian World*, 63.

36. Stephen E. Berk, *Calvinism versus Democracy: Timothy Dwight and the Origins of American Evangelical Orthodoxy* (Hamden, Conn.: Archon, 1974), 21. (See his entire chapter, "The New American Jerusalem," 18–32). See also Ernest Lee Tuveson, *Redeemer Nation* (Chicago: University of Chicago Press, 1966), in which he credits Timothy Dwight with "the first comprehensive statement of America's millennial destiny." Dwight's phrase is from his *Valedictory Address to the Young Gentlemen, Who Commenced Bachelors of Arts at Yale College*, July 25, 1776 (New Haven, 1776), 6–7.

37. Underwood, *Millenarian World*, 96.

38. Shipps, "Another Side," 6. See also her "Difference and Otherness: Mormonism and the American Religious Mainstream" in *Minority Faiths and the American Protestant Mainstream* (Urbana: University of Illinois, 1998) in which she writes that "Mormon preachers pointed to the coming forth of the Book of Mormon as a sure sign of the nearness of the end of time" (83).

39. Hayden, *Early History*, 121.

40. *Millennial Harbinger* I (January 4, 1830): 1. The passage is Campbell's translation of Revelation 14:6–7. Cited in Andrus, "Second American Revolution," 81.

41. Clara E. H. Lloyd, ed., "Journal of Levi W. Hancock" (n.p., n.d.), 23. Cited in Richard Anderson, "Impact of the First Preaching in Ohio," *BYU Studies* 11.4 (summer 1971): 483.

42. "John Murdock Autobiography," 12, quoted in Anderson, "First Preaching," 482.

43. Journal of Lyman Wight, quoted in Anderson, "First Preaching," 484.

44. Donna Hill, *Joseph Smith: The First Mormon* (1977; reprint, Salt Lake City: Signature Books, 1999), 122.

45. From the *Brookville Enquirer*, reprinted in *Messenger and Advocate* 1.5 (February 1835): 77.

46. Gordon Shepherd and Gary Shepherd, *A Kingdom Transformed: Themes in the Development of Mormonism* (Salt Lake City: University of Utah Press, 1984), 196. The passage is included in a fuller discussion of "Mormonism, Millenarianism, and Modernity," in Underwood, *Millenarian World*, 139–42.

47. Gordon Wood, "Evangelical America and Early Mormonism," *New York History* 61 (October 1980): 381.

48. Herbert A. Wiseby Jr., *Pioneer Prophet: Jemima Wilkinson, the Publick Universal Friend* (Ithaca: Cornell University Press, 1964), 12.

49. Hill, *Joseph Smith*, 53.

50. Bushman's tally does not include visionary experience embedded in longer narratives. "The Visionary World of Joseph Smith," *BYU Studies* 37.1 (1997/

98): 183–204. For several examples of revelations and visions in the Puritan era, see Michael G. Ditmore's "A Prophetess in Her Own Country: An Exegesis of Anne Hutchinson's 'Immediate Revelation,'" *William and Mary Quarterly* 57.2 (April 2000): 352n5, 354. In assessing the intensely private experience of Joseph Smith against the context of so much prior visionary experience, Leigh Eric Schmidt's observation about the abundance of "extraordinary revelations" in the seventeenth, eighteenth, and nineteenth centuries is pertinent: "From Shotts to Cambuslang to Booth Bay to Gaspar River, ecstatic religious experience was part of the communion occasion" associated with "festival events." *Holy Fairs: Scottish Communions and American Revivals in the Early Modern Period* (Princeton: Princeton University Press, 1989), 145.

51. The essential difference between a mystic and prophet, as William James has argued, is that "no authority emanates from [mystical states] which should make it a duty for those who stand outside of them to accept their revelations uncritically." *Varieties of Religious Experience* (Cambridge, Mass.: Harvard University Press, 1985), 422. And as Thomas Weiskel writes, "there is the odd literalism of the visionary tradition, a persistent atavism." *The Romantic Sublime: Studies in the Structure and Psychology of Transcendence* (Baltimore: Johns Hopkins, 1976), 6. For both those reasons, Joseph Smith is more accurately aligned with visionaries than mystics. Jan Shipps very early treated Joseph and the Book of Mormon as a mystic and mystical text, respectively, but has since retreated from the position she argued in "Mormons in Politics" (Ph.D. diss., University of Colorado, 1965), 31–32. As should be evident, my focus here in not on those distinctions (however important), but on certain of the shared problems of linguistic representation as they occur across the whole spectrum of visionary experience. For discussion of Joseph Smith's particular status in the spectrum, see Hugh Nibley (who argues for the emphatic differentiation of prophet from mystic) in "Prophets and Mystics," in *The World and the Prophets, The Collected Works of Hugh Nibley,* 15 vols. (Salt Lake City: Deseret Book and FARMS, 1986), 3:98–107. Also see, for further discussion and relevant sources, Louis Midgley, "The Challenge of Historical Consciousness: Mormon History and the Encounter with Secular Modernity" in Lundquist and Ricks, *By Study and Also by Faith,* 2: 532n.

52. See Carlo Ginzburg's *The Cheese and the Worms* (Baltimore: Johns Hopkins, 1980), for a masterful study of Menocchio's radical cosmology, trial, and execution for heresy.

53. Wiseby, *Pioneer Prophet*, 153.

54. Fawn Brodie, *No Man Knows My History: The Life of Joseph Smith*, 2nd ed. (New York: Vintage, 1995), vii.

55. Following a decree of the city council, the town marshal destroyed the press. As one legal scholar has argued, the action was not "entirely illegal" (libelous presses had been legally destroyed in other cities), but neither was it calculated to allay friction. See Dallin H. Oaks, "The Suppression of the *Nauvoo Expositor*," *Utah Law Review* 9 (winter 1965): 862–903.

56. Hans L. Martensen, *Jacob Boehme: Studies in his Life and Teaching*, rev. ed., trans. T. Rhys Evans, ed. Stephen Hobhouse (New York: Harper & Brothers, 1949), xi, xii.

57. Martensen, *Jacob Boehme*, xxii, 29.
58. Augustine, *Confessions* XII, trans. R. S. Pine-Coffin (New York: Penguin, 1961), 281–309. The parables of Jesus obviously set a precedent for nonliteral reading of sacred discourse, and Paul suggested an early form of typological interpretation when he said of the Jews, "But their minds were blinded: for until this day remaineth the same vail untaken away in the reading of the old testament; which vail is done away in Christ" (2 Corinthians 3:14).
59. Augustine, *Confessions*, XII, 290.
60. Augustine, *Confessions*, XII.
61. Samuel T. Coleridge, "Notebooks," *Samuel Taylor Coleridge*, ed. H. J. Jackson (Oxford: Oxford University Press, 1985), 555.
62. James, *Varieties*, 362.
63. Evelyn Underhill, *Mysticism* (New York: Doubleday, 1990), 335, 337.
64. Underhill, *Mysticism*, 347–48.
65. Ralph Waldo Emerson, "Swedenborg; or, the Mystic," *Complete Writings of Ralph Waldo Emerson* (New York: Wise, 1929), 363.
66. Emerson, "Swedenborg," 365.
67. For an argument that he did have significant—albeit termporary—influence on the development of an anthropocentric heaven, see Colleen McDannell and Bernhard Lang, *Heaven: A History* (New Haven: Yale University Press, 1988), 181–227.
68. Sheldon Cheney, *Men Who Have Walked with God* (New York: Knopf, 1945), 313.
69. McDannell and Lang, *Heaven*, 322.
70. Emerson, "Swedenborg," 370.
71. Emanuel Swedenborg, *Heaven and its Wonders, and Hell. From Things Heard and Seen* (New York: Dutton, 1920), 2–3.
72. Swedenborg's "doctrine of correspondence," by which he attempts to explain the relationship of the material to spiritual worlds, is often misunderstood in this regard as some kind of neodualism.
73. Emanuel Swedenborg, *The Universal Human and Soul-Body Interaction*, ed. and trans. George F. Dole (New York: Paulist Press, 1984), xiii–xiv.
74. Swedenborg, *Heaven*, 3.
75. Emerson, "Swedenborg," 368–69.
76. Statement of the Roman Congregation for the Doctrine of the Faith, 1979, quoted in McDannell and Lang, *Heaven*, 322–23. They cite Renée Haynes as saying, more simply, "The more detailed pictures of life after death are, the less acceptable they seem to be" (322).
77. James, *Varieties*, 393.
78. Emerson, "Swedenborg," 369.
79. Edmund Burke, *Philosophical Enquiry into the Origin of our Ideas of the Sublime and Beautiful* (New York: Oxford University Press, 1998), 58.
80. *Messenger and Advocate* 1.5 (February 1835): 79; Dean C. Jessee, ed., *The Papers of Joseph Smith* vol. 1, *Autobiographical and Historical Writings* (Salt Lake City: Deseret Book, 1989), 431. For a further discussion of hostility to this particularlizing aspect of early Mormonism, see Givens, *Viper on the Hearth*, 88–92.

81. Schmidt, *Holy Fairs*, 44, 146; Ned Landsman, "Evangelists and Their Hear-ers: Popular Interpretation of Revivalist Preaching in Eighteenth-Century Scotland," *Journal of British Studies* 28.2 (April 1989): 143.

82. Douglas Wilson, "Prospects for the Study of the Book of Mormon as a Work of American Literature," *Dialogue* 3 (spring 1968): 37, 39. "A mythic approach to the Book of Mormon," he explains, "would be concerned with the character and significance of its dramatic configuration and struc-ture, not with its historical validity."

83. One may take as typical in regard to this trend the title of a paper pre-sented at the 1998 Conference of the Modern History Association, "The Case for a Nonliteral 19th Century Mormonism." Stalwart defender B. H. Roberts allegedly proposed a reading of the Book of Mormon in which "the plates were not objective but subjective with Joseph Smith." How-ever, that dubious allegation exits only as a single secondhand report. See Wesley P. Lloyd, Personal Journal (7 August 1933), cited in B. H. Roberts, *Studies in the Book of Mormon*, ed. Brigham D. Madsen, (Salt Lake City: Signature Books, 1992), 23.

84. Mikhail Bakhtin, "Discourse in the Novel," *The Dialogic Imagination: Four Essays*, ed. Michael Holquist (Austin: University of Texas Press, 1981), 42.

85. *Times and Seasons* 4.13 (May 15, 1843): 194. B. H. Roberts believed there was evidence suggesting W. W. Phelps, and not Joseph, was the author of this article, which he felt was "based on inaccurate premises and was offensively pedantic." Truman G. Madsen, *Defender of the Faith: The B. H Roberts Story* (Salt Lake City: Bookcraft, 1980), 291–92.

86. Joseph Fielding Smith, ed., *Teachings of the Prophet Joseph Smith* (Salt Lake City: Deseret Book, 1973), 350.

87. Bakhtin, "Discourse," 42.

88. Bakhtin, "Discourse," 47.

89. Bruce R. McConkie, *Mormon Doctrine* (Salt Lake City: Deseret book, 1989), 99.

90. Pope A. Duncan, "Crawford Howell Toy: Heresy at Louisville," in George H. Shriver, *American Religious Heretics: Formal and Informal Trials* (Nash-ville: Abingdon, 1966), 68.

91. As noted above, Joseph apparently used a seer stone for much or even most of the translation, although he seems to have used the term "Urim and Thummim" to refer to either means of translation.

92. Hendrik C. Spykerboer, "Urim and Thummim," *The Oxford Companion to the Bible*, ed. Bruce M. Metzger and Michael D. Coogan (New York: Ox-ford University Press, 1993), 786. The terms are mentioned in Exod. 28:30; Lev.8:8; Deut. 33:8; Ezra 2:63; Neh. 7:65; and in the Apocrypha.

93. Steven Harper, "Infallible Proofs, Both Human and Divine: The Persua-siveness of Mormonism for Early Converts," *Religion and American Cul-ture* 10.1 (winter 2000): 104.

94. W. W. Phelps, "Letter No. 6," *Messenger and Advocate* 1.7 (April 1835): 97.

95. *Elders' Journal of the Church of Latter-day Saints*, 1:2 (November 1837): 28 and 1:3 (July 1838): 43.

96. Klaus J. Hansen, *Mormonism and the American Experience* (Chicago: Uni-versity of Chicago Press, 1981), 40.

97. Wandle Mace autobiography in Milton V. Backman Jr. and Keith W. Perkins, eds., *Writings of Early Latter-day Saints and Their Contemporaries, A Database Collection*, 2nd ed., rev. (Provo, Utah: Brigham Young University, Religious Studies Center, 1996), 23.

98. John W. Welch, "Acts of the Apostle William E. McLellin," in Shipps and Welch, *Journals*, 19.

99. Shipps and Welch, *Journals*, 148, 37.

100. Smith, *History of the Church*, 2:52.

101. Andrew F. Ehat and Lyndon W. Cook, eds., *The Words of Joseph Smith: The Contemporary Accounts of the Nauvoo Discourses of the Prophet Joseph* (Orem, Utah: Grandin, 1994).

102. Ehat and Cook, *Words*, 35.

103. Daniel Tyler, "Incidents of Experience," *Juvenile Instructor* (1883): 23. Cited in Steven C. Harper, "The Restoration of Mormonism in Erie County, Pennsylvania," *Mormon Historical Studies* 1.1 (spring 2000): 10.

104. Amos N. Merrill and Alton D. Merrill, "Changing Thought on the Book of Mormon," *Improvement Era* 45 (September 1945): 568.

105. Ann Taves, *Fits, Trances, and Visions: Experiencing Religion and Explaining Experience from Wesley to James* (Princeton: Princeton University Press, 1999), 18. Somewhat astonishingly, Taves neglects to include in her impressive study any mention of the most influential American visionary between Wesley and James—Joseph Smith.

106. Thompson, *Evidences*, 149–67.

107. "The Mormons," *Religious Herald* 59:1 (9 April 1840).

108. Thomas O'Dea, *The Mormons* (Chicago: University of Chicago Press, 1957), 26.

109. "The Book of Mormon brings men to Christ through two basic means. First, it tells in a plain manner of Christ [not the nature of the Godhead] and His gospel. It testifies of His divinity and of the necessity for a Redeemer and the need of our putting trust in Him. . . . Second, the Book of Mormon exposes the enemies of Christ." Ezra Taft Benson, "The Book of Mormon Is the Word of God," Regional Representatives Seminar, Salt Lake City, April 4, 1986.

110. Shlomo Biderman, *Scripture and Knowledge: An Essay on Religious Epistemology* (New York: Brill, 1995), 12–13.

111. The most comprehensive study of the Book of Mormon witnesses is by Richard Lloyd Anderson, *Investigating the Book of Mormon Witnesses* (Salt Lake City: Deseret Book, 1981). As he demonstrates, "each witness . . . reiterated his printed testimony" throughout his life (3). In spite of later disaffection with Joseph or the church on the part of some, no reliable evidence has surfaced to indicate that any of the eleven witnesses ever revoked his testimony.

112. William E. McLellin to James T. Cobb, 14 August 1880, in Larry C. Porter, "William E. McLellan's Testimony of the Book of Mormon," *BYU Studies* 10.4 (summer 1970): 486.

113. *Nauvoo Expositor* June 7, 1844. The publishers were William Law, Wilson Law, Charles Ivins, Francis M. Higbee, Chauncey L. Higbee, Robert D. Foster, and Charles A. Foster.

FOUR

1. Jeffery L. Sheler, *Is the Bible True?* (New York: HarperCollins, 1999), 111.
2. Wilfred Cantwell Smith, "The Study of Religion and the Study of the Bible," in Miriam Levering, ed., *Rethinking Scripture: Essays from a Comparative Perspective* (Albany: SUNY Press, 1989), 26.
3. For a Mormon view that echoes Wilfred Cantwell Smith's, see Leonard J.Arrington. Citing the influence of George Santayana's *Reason in Religion* (1905), the long-time church historian told an interviewer that "sacred history" is "separate and distinct" from the kind of history professional historians do. In Malise Ruthven, *The Divine Supermarket: Shopping for God in America* (New York: William Morrow, 1989), 120. See also Arrington's "Why I am a Believer," *Sunstone* 10 (1985): 36–38.
4. Trude Dothan, interview (January 23, 1994), in Sheler, *Is the Bible True?*, 120.
5. Dean C. Jessee, ed., *The Papers of Joseph Smith*, vol. 1, *Autobiographical and Historical Writings* (Salt Lake City: Deseret Book, 1989), 431.
6. Jessee, *Papers*, 1:432–33.
7. Scot Facer Proctor and Maurine Jensen Proctor, eds., *The Revised and Enhanced History of Joseph Smith by his Mother* (Salt Lake City: Bookcraft, 1996), 111–12.
8. Wandle Mace autobiography in Milton V. Backman Jr. and Keith W. Perkins, eds., *Writings of Early Latter-day Saints and Their Contemporaries, A Database Collection*, 2nd ed., rev. (Provo, Utah: Brigham Young University, Religious Studies Center, 1996), 45.
9. *Wayne Sentinel*, March 26, 1830.
10. Joseph Smith said of this title page, "I wish to mention here that the title-page of the Book of Mormon is a literal translation, taken from the very last leaf, on the left hand side of the collection or book of plates, which contained the record which has been translated, the language of the whole running the same as all Hebrew writing in general; and that said title page is not by any means a modern composition, either of mine or of any other man who has lived or does live in this generation." Joseph Smith, Jr., *History of the Church of Jesus Christ of Latter-day Saints*, 7 vols., ed. James Mulholland, Robert B. Thompson, William W. Phelps, Willard Richards, George A. Smith, and later B. H. Roberts (Salt Lake City: Deseret News Press, 1902–12; 2nd rev. ed., Salt Lake City: Deseret Book, 1951), 1:71.
11. Francis W. Kirkham, *A New Witness for Christ in America*, 2 vols. (Independence, Mo.: Zion's Printing, 1951), 2:29. Joseph Smith deposited this title page with the clerk of the Northern District of New York (and obtained a copyright) on June 11, 15 days before it was printed in the news article. Richard Bushman, *Joseph Smith and the Beginnings of Mormonism* (Urbana and Chicago: University of Illinois Press, 1984), 107.
12. Some accounts made vague allusions to religious content: *Rochester Advertiser and Telegraph* (August 31, 1829) reported that the Book of Mormon was said to have "language and doctrine . . . far superior to those of the book of life." And after publication, the *Painesville Telegraph* (November

16, 1830) referred to the book as "purporting to contain new revelations from Heaven." Reprinted in Kirkham, *New Witness*, 2:32, 33.

13. Daniel Gookin, *Historical Collections of the Indians in New England* (1674), 144–47. Quoted in Richard W. Cogley, "John Eliot and the Origins of the American Indians," *Early American Literature* 21.3 (winter 1986/87): 210.

14. Stuart J. Fiedel, *Prehistory of the Americas*, 2d ed. (New York: Cambridge University Press, 1992), 3. As Stan Larson remarks, Fiedel goes "beyond the available evidence when he concluded that 'one avid reader of mound-builder fantasies was Joseph Smith, whose Book of Mormon . . . seems to reflect his familiarity with this literature.'" Stan Larson, *Quest for the Gold Plates: Thomas Stuart Ferguson's Archaeological Search for the Book of Mormon* (Salt Lake City: Freethinker Press/Smith Research Associates, 1996), 168.

15. J. M. Peck, *A Gazeteer of Illinois* (Jacksonville, Ill.: Goudy, 1834), 53–54.

16. Ethan Smith, *View of the Hebrews: 1825 2nd Edition*, ed. Charles D. Tate Jr. (Provo, Utah: Brigham Young University, Religious Studies Center, 1996), xxix.

17. See Roger G. Kennedy, *Hidden Cities: The Discovery and Loss of Ancient North American Civilization* (New York: Free Press, 1994), esp. 225–28; Lee E. Huddleston, *Origins of the American Indians: European Concepts 1492–1729*, Latin American Monographs 11 (Austin: University of Texas Press, 1967); Dan Vogel, *Indian Origins and the Book of Mormon* (Salt Lake City: Signature Books, 1986).

18. John Lloyd Stephens, *Incidents of Travel in Central America, Chiapas, and Yucatan* (Washington: Smithsonian Institute Press, 1993), 36. First published 1841.

19. The remark represents one consensus between the debaters in a fictitious dialogue on the Book of Mormon, published in the *Times and Seasons* 2.18 (July 15, 1841): 473.

20. *Palmyra Reflector*, July 7, 1830, reprinted in Kirkham, *New Witness*, 52–54.

21. Joseph Smith to N. E. Seaton (January 4, 1833) in *Times and Seasons* 5.21 (November 15, 1844): 707.

22. *Messenger and Advocate* 1.5 (February 1835): 80.

23. *The Evening and the Morning Star* 1.1 (June 1832): 6.

24. Underwood's study examines pre-1846 periodicals and publications, and classifies 32 of the Book of Mormon citations he finds as "Archaeological Evidences." The next largest single topic is "Gathering of Israel," with 28 citations. (For "Gathering" in general he finds 59.) See his "Book of Mormon Usage in Early LDS Theology," *Dialogue* 17:3 (autumn 1984), 41.

25. Thomas Stuart Ferguson, letter to the LDS First Presidency, January 27, 1955, cited in Larson, *Quest*, 50.

26. Hugh Nibley, "New Approaches to Book of Mormon Study: Part I, Some Standard Tests," *The Improvement Era* 56 (November 1953): 831. Cited in Larson, *Quest*, 211.

27. *The Evening and the Morning Star* 1.5 (October 1832): 37.

28. John Sorenson, "The Book of Mormon as a Mesoamerican Record," in Noel B. Reynolds, ed., *Book of Mormon Authorship Revisited: The Evidence for Ancient Origins* (Provo, Utah: Foundation for Ancient Research and Mormon Studies [FARMS], 1997), 489.

29. *Times and Seasons* 2:22 (September 15, 1841); 3:5 (January 1, 1842); 3:15 (June 1, 1842); 3:18 (July 15, 1842); and 3:19 (August 1, 1842).

30. Excerpted in *Times and Seasons* 3.5 (January 1, 1842): 641. From Charles B. Thompson, *Evidences in Proof of the Book of Mormon Being a Divinely Inspired Record* (Batavia, N.Y.: D.D. Waite, 1841).

31. *The Evening and the Morning Star* 1.9 (February 1833): 71.

32. Matthias F. Cowley, *Wilford Woodruff, History of his Life and Labors* (Salt Lake City: Bookcraft, 1975), 40–41. Kenneth W. Godfrey collates ten different versions of the episode in "The Zelph Story," *BYU Studies* 29.2 (spring 1989): 31–56. The versions are essentially the same in their major details.

33. Dean C. Jessee, comp. and ed., *The Personal Writings of Joseph Smith* (Salt Lake City: Deseret Book, 1984), 324.

34. Smith, *History of the Church*, 3:35. "Nephitish," reads the original manuscript, suggesting he possibly intended to indicate similarity rather than identity.

35. On the back of one is written, "Got it from Br. Robert Dickinson. He got it from Patriarch Wm. McBride at Richfield in the Sevier and also from Andrew M. Hamilton of same place. And they got it from Joseph Smith the Prophet." H. Donl Peterson, "Moroni, the Last of the Nephite Prophets," in Paul R. Cheesman, Monte S. Nyman, and Charles D. Tate Jr., eds., *Fourth Nephi Through Moroni: From Zion to Destruction*, Book of Mormon Symposium Series (Provo, Utah: Brigham Young University, Religious Studies Center, 1988–1995), 244–47.

36. Joseph's statement was recorded by Frederick G. Williams and published in Franklin D. Richards and James A. Little, *A Compendium of the Doctrines of the Gospel* (Salt Lake City: Deseret News, 1882). *After* he had written his major studies of the Book of Mormon, largely predicated on a geography suggested by the prophet's purported revelation, B. H. Roberts examined the Williams document and found the phrase "revelation to Joseph the Seer" had been added by publishers. John A. Widtsoe also doubted the accuracy of Williams's statement, and even Williams later contradicted his own account. See Frederick G. Williams III, "Did Lehi Land in Chile? An Assessment of the Frederick G. Williams Statement," (Provo, Utah: FARMS, 1988).

37. Benjamin Winchester, "The Claims of the Book of Mormon Established," *Gospel Reflector* 1.5 (March 1, 1841): 105.

38. Karl Ackerman, introduction in Stephens, *Incidents*, 6.

39. Stephens, *Incidents*, 35.

40. Ackerman, introduction in Stephens, *Incidents*, 4.

41. Stephens, *Incidents*, 38–40.

42. Joseph Smith, letter to John M. Bernhisel, November 16, 1841, in Jessee, *Personal Writings*, 502.

43. "American Antiquities," *Times and Seasons* 3.18 (July 15, 1842). As of March 15, 1842, Joseph Smith had assumed editorial responsibility for the paper, with John Taylor acting as managing editor.

44. Stephens, *Incidents*, 36, 8.

45. Orson Pratt, "Divine Authenticity of the Book of Mormon," (Liverpool, 1850), reprinted in *Orson Pratt's Works* (Salt Lake City: Modern Microfilm, n.d.), 1.

46. Orson Pratt, *An Interesting Account of Several Remarkable Visions* (Edinburgh: Ballantyne and Hughes, 1840), 4. Oliver Cowdery's account was published in the *Messenger and Advocate* 2.1 (October 1835): 196–97.

47. *Chicago Times*, August 7, 1875, in Lyndon W. Cook, ed., *David Whitmer Interviews: A Restoration Witness* (Orem, Utah: Grandin, 1991), 7.

48. The claim appeared in *Times and Seasons* 3:22 (September 15, 1842). Smith was still responsible editorially at this point.

49. *Times and Seasons* 3.23 (October 1, 1842). Archaeologists now date Palenque after A.D. 600 and Quiriguá from A.D. 478 to 805. Since the Nephites were exterminated around A.D. 385, these ruins could be held to spring from the surviving Lamanite peoples, but not, strictly speaking, the Nephites themselves. See Larson, *Quest*, 22–24.

50. *Times and Seasons* 4.22 (October 1, 1843): 346–47.

51. *Times and Seasons* 4.13 (May 15, 1843): 201. Little progress in the collection occurred during Joseph's lifetime.

52. George Givens, *In Old Nauvoo: Everyday Life in the City of Joseph* (Salt Lake City: Deseret Book, 1990), 260.

53. *Times and Seasons* 4.11 (April 15, 1843): 185.

54. An entry in the *History of the Church*, dated May 1, 1843, has Joseph writing, "I have translated a portion of them, find they contain the history of the person with whom they were found." But the original source of that statement is actually the journal of William Clayton, edited and put in the first person at the time Joseph Smith's "History" was being composed. See the thorough treatment by Stanley B. Kimball, "Kinderhook Plates Brought to Joseph Smith Appear to be a Nineteenth-Century Hoax," *Ensign* 11.8 (August 1981): 66–74.

55. Orson Pratt, *Divine Authority—or the question, was Joseph Smith Sent of God?* (Liverpool, 1848). Reprinted in *Orson Pratt's Works*, 13.

56. *Millennial Star* 28 (June 16, 1866): 370. The "Chili" location was claimed by Orson's brother Parley P. Pratt, both in *Proclamation! to the People of the Coasts and Islands of the Pacific* (pamphlet, 1851) and in *Key to the Science of Theology* (Liverpool: F. D. Richards, 1855), 23.

57. *Book of Mormon* (Chicago: Henry Etten, n.d.), 572n, 582n, 606n, 589n, 606n, 589.

58. Sterling M. McMurrin, "Brigham H. Roberts: A Biographical Essay," in B. H. Roberts, *Studies of the Book of Mormon*, 2nd ed., ed. Brigham D. Madsen (Salt Lake City: Signature Books, 1992), xiii. See E. E. Ericksen, *The Psychological and Ethical Aspects of Mormon Group Life* (1922: reprint, Salt Lake City: University of Utah Press, 1975).

59. *Commentary on the Book of Mormon*, 7 vols., ed. Philip C. Reynolds (Salt Lake City: Deseret Book, 1955–61). Though almost always cited in tandem, Reynolds and Sjodahl were not collaborators and actually differed on a number of issues. Philip Reynolds elided many of those differences in the commentary he edited. See Bruce Van Orden, "George Reynolds and Janne M. Sjodahl on Book of Mormon Geography," *The Thetean* (April 1982): 60–79.

60. Madsen, introduction to Roberts, *Studies of the Book of Mormon*, 3.

61. B. H. Roberts, *New Witnesses for God*, 3 vols. (Salt Lake City: Deseret News, 1895–1911) 2:356–70, 415–16.

62. Roberts, *New Witnesses*, 3:559.
63. McMurrin, "Brigham H. Roberts," xvi.
64. The very use of this expression, "Book of Mormon archaeology," is fraught with peril. Ross T. Christensen, an associate professor of archaeology at Brigham Young University, believed "Book of Mormon archaeology is a specialized branch of general archaeology which searches out any information which throws light upon the Book of Mormon, be it direct, indirect, or diffused light." "A History of Book of Mormon Archaeology," in *Book of Mormon Institute* 5 December 1959 (Provo, Utah: BYU Education and Extension Services, 1959), 9. By contrast, Dee Green insists that the first myth we need to dispel in that area is the myth "that Book of Mormon archaeology exists." Dee Green, "Book of Mormon Archaeology: The Myths and the Alternatives," *Dialogue* 4 (summer 1969): 77.
65. An overview of the expedition is found in Ernest L. Wilkinson and W. Cleon Skousen, *Brigham Young University: A School of Destiny* (Provo, Utah: Brigham Young University Press, 1976), 151–62. Another appraisal, much harsher than theirs (and Cluff's), is that the venture "ended in embarrassment for all involved, [and] affected the school's academic advancement over the next three decades." Gary James Bergera and Ronald Priddis, *Brigham Young University: A House of Faith* (Salt Lake City: Signature Books, 1985), 10. Journals from several expedition members and several photographs are housed in Special Collections, Harold B. Lee Library, Brigham Young University, Provo, Utah.
66. Stephen Williams, *Fantastic Archaeology: The Wild Side of North American Prehistory* (Philadelphia: University of Pennsylvania Press, 1991), 181.
67. Even as cynical a writer as Stephen Williams called Talmage's investigation "instructive" compared to less rigorous examinations in the area where archaeology and religion intersect. Williams, *Fantastic Archaeology*, 181.
68. Though James E. Talmage was head of the committee, footnotes were the responsibility of Janne M. Sjodahl, who had recently worked out his own Book of Mormon geography. See Talmage letter to First Presidency, May 27, 1920, in the James E. Talmage Journals, Special Collections, Harold B. Lee Library, Brigham Young University, Provo, Utah.
69. W. E. Riter to James E. Talmage, August 22, 1921, in Roberts, *Studies of the Book of Mormon*, 35.
70. B. H. Roberts to Heber J. Grant et al., December 29, 1921, in Roberts, *Studies of the Book of Mormon*, 46.
71. Roberts, *New Witnesses*, 2:iii–viii.
72. Roberts, "Book of Mormon Difficulties," in *Studies of the Book of Mormon*, 115.
73. James E. Talmage, Journals, January 1922, cited in McMurrin, "Brigham H. Roberts," in *Studies of the Book of Mormon*, 22.
74. Arguing for his ultimate conviction are the following articles: Truman G. Madsen, "B. H. Roberts and the Book of Mormon," *BYU Studies* 19.4 (summer 1979): 427–45; and Truman G. Madsen and John W. Welch, "Did B. H. Roberts Lose Faith in the Book of Mormon?" (Provo, Utah: FARMS, 1985). For the view that he abandoned his faith in the book's historicity, see Brigham D. Madsen, "B. H. Roberts' 'Studies of the Book of Mormon,'"

Dialogue 26 (fall 1993): 77–86; and "Reflections on LDS Disbelief in the Book of Mormon as History" *Dialogue* 30.3 (fall 1997): 87–97; also see Sterling McMurrin's biographical essay on Roberts in Roberts, *Studies of the Book of Mormon*, xiii–xxxi.

75. Letter to Heber J. Grant, Council, and Quroum of Twelve Apostles, March 15, 1922, in Roberts, *Studies of the Book of Mormon*, 57–58.

76. Rey L. Pratt, in *Conference Reports of the General Conference of the Church of Jesus Christ of Latter-day Saints* (April 1923): 39.

77. John A. Widtsoe, in *Conference Reports of the General Conference of the Church of Jesus Christ of Latter-day Saints* (October 1927): 26.

78. Levi Edgar Young, in *Conference Reports of the General Conference of the Church of Jesus Christ of Latter-day Saints* (October 1928): 106.

79. Elder Antoine R. Ivins, in *Conference Reports of the General Conference of the Church of Jesus Christ of Latter-day Saints* (April 1939): 129.

80. Paul Henning, a German convert born in 1872, was apparently the first Latter-day Saint "to become a professional archaeologist and Mesoamerican scholar." He participated in the Cluff expedition and later encouraged Book of Mormon related studies, but never published his many papers on the subject. See Robert F. Fullmer, "Paul Henning: The First Mormon Archaeologist," *Journal of Book of Mormon Studies* 9.1 (2000): 64–65.

81. Thomas Stuart Ferguson, letter to Ralph E. Henderson, June 28, 1950, in Larson, *Quest*, 16. For the helicopter episode, see Larson, *Quest*, 57.

82. Alfred V. Kidder and Ferguson, "Plan for Archaeological Work in an Important Zone in Middle America," in Larson, *Quest*, 43.

83. Ferguson complained about the rejection ("no explanation given") to Wells Jakeman: "a million dollars for a field house but not a cent for Book of Mormon archaeology." Letter to Wells Jakeman, January 16, 1952, in Thomas Stuart Ferguson Collection, 4.13, Special Collections, Harold B. Lee Library, Brigham Young University, Provo, Utah.

84. W. F. Albright letter to Thomas Stuart Ferguson, July 21, 1952; Thomas Stuart Ferguson letter to John A. Widtsoe, July 23, 1952. Both in Thomas Stuart Ferguson Papers, 1.17, Special Collections, Harold B. Lee Library, Brigham Young University, Provo, Utah.

85. Alfred V. Kidder letter to don Ignacio Marquina, Director of the Mexican National Institute of Anthropology and History, July 21, 1952, in Thomas Stuart Ferguson Papers, 6.7, Special Collections, Harold B. Lee Library, Brigham Young University, Provo, Utah. At other times, the foundation could be more coy about Book of Mormon connections, as when an NWAF report refers to "certain ecclesiastical documentary sources." J. Alden Mason, "Resumé of the Work of the New World Archaeological Foundation in Chiapas, Mexico," 2, unpublished typescript, [c. 1959] Thomas Stuart Ferguson Papers, 8.19, Special Collections, Harold B. Lee Library, Brigham Young University, Provo, Utah.

86. J. Alden Mason, "Foreward," *Research in Chiapas, Mexico. Papers of the New World Archaeological Foundation*, nos. 1–4 (Orinda, Calif.: New World Archaeological Foundation, 1959), iii.

87. See Mason, "Resumé." Michael Coe writes that the Mesoamerican endeavor represented "the largest and most ambitious archaeological project

ever funded by a religious institution (including the Vatican)." Coe, "Mormons and Archaeology: An Outside View," in *Dialogue* 8 (winter 1973): 45. In 1961, the NWAF became officially attached to Brigham Young University.

88. John L. Sorenson and Martin H. Raish, *Pre-Columbian Contact with the Americas Across the Oceans: An Annotated Bibliography*, 2 vols. (Provo, Utah: Research Press, 1990), 1:151. David Perlman, "Where Did We Come From," *San Francisco Chronicle*, December 22, 1958, 36, reported him as referring to "clearly recognizable Egyptian hieroglyphs." Other scholars feel the glyphs are too few for a positive identification.

89. Thomas Stuart Ferguson, *One Fold and One Shepherd* (San Francisco: Book of California, 1958).

90. The popular Lowell Thomas even agreed to narrate the proposed film. See assorted correspondence on the projects in the Thomas Stuart Ferguson Papers, 4.7 and 4.8, Special Collections, Harold B. Lee Library, Brigham Young University, Provo, Utah.

91. Form letter issued by the Smithsonian Institute, 1979. Reprinted in Bob Witte, *Where Does It Say That?* (Grant Rapids, Mich.: Gospel Truths, nd), 9–5. A slightly shorter version of their statement dated 1965 is reproduced in Jerald and Sandra Tanner, *Archaeology and the Book of Mormon* (Salt Lake City: Modern Microfilm, 1969), 2.

FIVE

1. *Times and Seasons* 3.22 (September 15, 1842): 3:922.

2. Austin Farrer, "Grete Clerk," in Jocelyn Gibb, comp., *Light on C. S. Lewis* (New York: Harcourt & Brace, 1965), 26. Cited by Elder Neal A. Maxwell, "Discipleship and Scholarship," *BYU Studies* 32.3 (summer 1992): 5; Dallin H. Oaks, "The Historicity of the Book of Mormon" (Provo, Utah: Deseret Book and Foundation for Ancient Research and Mormon Studies [FARMS], 1993), 2.

3. Oral interview, quoted in John W. Welch, "Hugh Nibley and the Book of Mormon," *Ensign* 15.4 (April 1985): 50.

4. Hugh W. Nibley, *Lehi in the Desert*, in *The Collected Works of Hugh Nibley*, 15 vols. (Provo, Utah: Deseret Book and FARMS, 1986–), 5:4.

5. Hugh W. Nibley, "Teachings of the Book of Mormon"—Semester 1: Transcripts of [29] Lectures Presented to an Honors Book of Mormon Class at Brigham Young University, 1988—1990. Introduction and 1 Nephi 1–Mosiah 5 (Provo, Utah: FARMS, 1993).

6. Nibley, *Lehi in the Desert*, xiii.

7. Nibley, *Lehi in the Desert*, 14.

8. Hugh Nibley, *Since Cumorah*, 2nd ed., in *Collected Works of Hugh Nibley*, 7:169. Edward Ashment has criticized Nibley's discussion of the historical "Pa-ankh" and "Herihor" as erroneous in light of recent scholarship. But except for quibbling about Nibley's transliteration of the initial 'H' as 'Kh,' Ashment does not dispute they are authentic Egyptian names. See his "A Record in the Language of My Father": Evidence of Ancient Egyp-

tian and Hebrew in the Book of Mormon," in Brent Metcalfe, ed., *New Approaches to the Book of Mormon: Explorations in Critical Methodology* (Salt Lake City: Signature Books, 1993), 343–45.

9. William F. Albright to Grant S. Heward (July 25, 1966). Cited in John A. Tvedtnes, John Gee, and Matthew Roper, "Book of Mormon Names Attested in Ancient Hebrew Inscriptions," *Journal of Book of Mormon Studies* 9.1 (2000): 45.

10. Nibley, *Lehi in the Desert*, 49.

11. W. E. Jennings-Bramley, "The Bedouin of the Sinaitic Peninsula," *Palestinian Exploration Fund Quarterly* (1908): 257. In Nibley, *Lehi in the Desert*, 75.

12. Nibley, *Lehi in the Desert*, 79. S. Kent Brown points out that the Old South Arabic meaning of "NHM" is "chipped masonry." It is possible," he suggests, "on the basis of a number of stone artifacts that have survived and on the basis of the meaning of the root NHM in Old South Arabian, that the people of the Nihm tribe were stone artisans. According to . . . David Johnson, who has excavated at Marib in Yemen (which is in the neighborhood of the Nihm tribal area), the tribe anciently inhabited an area which included an important quarry." Letter to author, February 3, 2001.

13. Ross T. Christensen, "The Place Called Nahom," *Ensign* 8.8 (August 1978): 73; S. Kent Brown, "'The Place That Was Called Nahom': New Light From Ancient Yemen," *Journal of Book of Mormon Studies* 8.1 (1999): 66–68.

14. Nibley, *Lehi in the Desert*, 85–90. His sources for this discussion include Ignac Goldziher, *Abhandlungen zur arabischen Philologie* (Leiden, 1896), 1:58–71; Gustav Richter, "Zur Entstehungsgeschichte der altarabischen Qaside," *Zeitschrift des Deutsch-Palästina Vereins* 92 (1938): 557–58; Ibn Qutayba, *Introduction au livre de la poesie et des poetes* (Paris: l'Association Guillaume Budé, 1947), 13–25.

15. Though Nibley mentions several precedents in *Lehi in the Desert*, 100, the ampler references I cite here are in his later work, *Since Cumorah*, 56–57, 220.

16. Nibley, *Since Cumorah*, 245, 242, 247. Nibley first cast the coronation (Benjamin) speech as an ancient rite in a yearly festival in 1957. See Nibley, *An Approach to the Book of Mormon*, 3rd ed., in *Collected Works of Hugh Nibley*, 6:295–310.

17. Though he is working with a relatively late account, Nibley argues that the Jews in exile would presumably be maintaining as faithfully as possible their ancient coronation customs. The account is found in Benzion Halper, *Postbiblical Hebrew Literature* (Philadelphia: Jewish Publication Society of America, 1946), 1:37–38. Nibley's discussion of the text and its Book of Mormon parallels is in "Assembly and Atonement" in John W. Welch and Stephen D. Ricks, eds., *King Benjamin's Speech: That Ye May Learn Wisdom* (Provo, Utah: FARMS, 1998), 119–45.

18. Nibley, *Approach*, 255–56.

19. John A. Tvedtnes, "King Benjamin and the Feast of Tabernacles," in John M. Lundquist and Stephen D. Ricks, eds., *By Study and Also by Faith, Essays in Honor of Hugh Nibley*, 2 vols. (Salt Lake City: Deseret Book and FARMS, 1990), 2:197–237.

20. Terrence L. Szink and John W. Welch, "King Benjamin's Speech in the Context of Ancient Israelite Festivals," in Welch and Ricks, *King Benjamin's Speech*, 200.

21. Stephen D. Ricks, "Kingship, Coronation, and Covenant in Mosiah 1-6" in Welch and Ricks, *King Benjamin's Speech*, 233, 265.

22. Nibley, *Lehi in the Desert*, xiii.

23. The first five of these have contributed to Nibley's Festschrift, *By Study and Also by Faith*. Evangelicals Carl Mosser and Paul Owen mention those names, as well as the now legendary MacRae remark, in "Mormon Apologetic, Scholarship and Evangelical Neglect: Losing the Battle and Not Knowing It?" *Trinity Journal* (1998): 184.

24. In order to illustrate the caliber of training behind current LDS work in ancient scripture and Book of Mormon apologetics, Mosser and Owen cite the following: Stephen E. Robinson, Ph.D. in Biblical Studies (under W. D. Davies and James Charlesworth), Duke; S. Kent Brown, Ph.D. working on the Nag Hammadi texts, Brown; Wilfred Griggs, Ph.D. in Ancient History (Egyptian Christianity), Berkeley; Kent P. Jackson, Ph.D. in Near Eastern Studies (working under David Noel Freedman and Frank Moore Cross on the Ammonite language), Michigan; Stephen D. Ricks, Ph.D. in Near Eastern Religions (under Jacob Milgrom), Berkeley and Graduate Theological Union; John Gee, Ph.D. in Egyptology, Yale; Daniel Peterson, Ph.D. in Near Eastern Languages and Cultures, UCLA; Donald W. Parry, Ph.D. in Hebrew, University of Jerusalem and University of Utah; Abraham Gileadi, Ph.D. in Hebrew (with R. K. Harrison directing), BYU. The only FARMS employees who have written scholarly material on the Book of Mormon are John Gee, Daniel Peterson, Matthew Roper, and John Tvedtnes.

25. Kent Appleberry, "Foundation Coordinates Book of Mormon Scholarship," *Seventh East Press*, June 28, 1982.

26. John Jebb, *Sacred Literature* (London: T. Cadell and W. Davies, 1820), 57. Jebb was building upon the work of Robert Lowth, with whom "the modern study of parallelism begins" (he first gave lectures on the subject in 1753). Nils Wilhelm Lund, *Chiasmus in the New Testament* (Chapel Hill: University of North Carolina Press, 1942), 36. J. A. Bengel published *Gnomon novi testamenti* (Tübingen: Henr. Philippi Schrammii) in 1742.

27. Welch describes the discovery in an interview by James P. Bell, "Taking the Stand," *This People* (February–March 1987), 49–63.

28. Interview with John Welch in *Church News Ogden Standard-Examiner*, 1 December 1984, 12; Bell, "Taking the Stand," 63.

29. John Sorenson, *An Ancient American Setting for the Book of Mormon* (Salt Lake City and Provo, Utah: Deseret Book and FARMS, 1996), 31–32, 342. First published in 1985; *Images of Ancient America: Visualizing Book of Mormon Life* (Provo, Utah: Research Press, 1998), 2. In the latter book, Sorenson makes clear that his examples often come from pre- and post-Nephite times, but may still serve to present "generic pictures of their culture" (4). Striking in a similar way, by its title alone, is Sorenson's book, *Nephite Culture and Society* (Salt Lake City: New Sage Books, 1997).

30. Mark Thomas, "Scholarship and the Future of the Book of Mormon," *Sunstone* 5.3 (May–June 1980): 26.

31. Janne M. Sjodahl, *An Introduction to the Study of the Book of Mormon* (Salt Lake City: Deseret News Press, 1927), 28; William E. Berrett, Milton R. Hunter, et al., *A Guide to the Study of the Book of Mormon* (Salt Lake City: Department of Education of the Church of Jesus Christ of Latter-day Saints, 1938), 48. The limited geography model centered in Mesoamerica was originally put forth by a Reorganized Church of Jesus Christ of Latter Day Saints researcher, Louis E. Hill, in two books: *Geography of Mexico and Central America from 2234 b.c. to 421 a.d.* (Independence, Mo.: n.p., 1917) and *Historical Data from Ancient Records and Ruins of Mexico and Central America* (Independence, Mo.: n.p., 1919). It was widely introduced to Latter-day Saints by Jesse A. and Jesse N. Washburn beginning in the 1930s.

32. For an overview of Book of Mormon geographical models, together with statements on the subject by LDS leaders, see John L. Sorenson, *The Geography of Book of Mormon Events: A Source Book* (Provo, Utah: FARMS, 1992).

33. John L. Sorenson, "Digging into the Book of Mormon: Our Changing Understanding of Ancient America and Its Scripture," *Ensign* 14.9 and 14.10 (September and October, 1984): 26–37, 12–23; Sorenson, *Ancient American Setting.*

34. In another article, Sorenson points out that the Book of Mormon contains "over seven hundred statements . . . that involve geographical matters." See "The Book of Mormon as a Mesoamerican Record," in Noel B. Reynolds, ed., *Book of Mormon Authorship Revisited: The Evidence for Ancient Origins* (Provo, Utah: FARMS, 1997), 392. In recognizing and attempting to correlate the prodigious number of references with actual Mesoamerican geography, he far outstrips his predecessors in complexity of argument. Richard F. Hauck published a book that built upon but modified several particulars of Sorenson's geography: *Deciphering the Geography of the Book of Mormon* (Salt Lake City: Deseret, 1988). It was not as well received critically. See the reviews by John Clark and William Hamblin in *FARMS Review of Books on the Book of Mormon* 1 (1989): 20–77.

35. John L. Sorenson, *Mormon's Map* (Provo, Utah: FARMS, 2000), 78.

36. Brigham D. Madsen, "Reflections on LDS Disbelief in the Book of Mormon as History" *Dialogue* 30.3 (fall 1997): 87–97.

37. Sorenson, *Ancient American Setting*, 16.

38. Roberts did consider, but never could embrace, a model in which Book of Mormon peoples occupied limited or already inhabited lands: "Moreover, there is also the possibility that other peoples may have inhabited parts of the great continents of America, contemporaneously with the peoples spoken of by the Book of Mormon, though candor compels me to say that nothing to that effect appears in the Book of Mormon." He goes on to admit it may be true that "the Book of Mormon peoples were restricted to much narrower limits in their habitat on the American continents, than have generally been allowed." Letter to William E. Riter, February 6, 1922, in B. H. Roberts, *Studies of the Book of Mormon*, 2nd ed., ed. Brigham D. Madsen (Salt Lake City: Signature Books, 1992), 49–50.

39. John L. Sorenson, "When Lehi's Party Arrived in the Land, Did They Find Others There?" in *Nephite Culture*, 65–104.

40. Sorenson, *Ancient American Setting*, 46–47, 31.

41. Hugh Nibley is here translating from W. Krickeberg's *Altmexikanische Kulturen* (Berlin: Safari-Verlag, 1966), 566. In Nibley, "The Book of Mormon and the Ruins: The Main Issues," (Provo, Utah: FARMS, 1993).

42. The 1995 updated version by John Sorenson is entitled "A New Evaluation of the Smithsonian Institution 'Statement Regarding the Book of Mormon,'" (Provo, Utah: FARMS, 1995).

43. Juan Comas, *Cuadernos Americanos* 152 (May–June 1967): 117–25 and *Antropología de los Pueblos Ibero-Americanos* (Barcelona: Editorial Labor, 1974), 35–42, 52ff; Earnest Hooton is quoted to this effect in Harold Gladwin, *Men Out of Asia* (New York: McGraw-Hill, 1947), 63–65; Joseph B. Birdsell, "The problem of the early peopling of America as viewed from Asia," in W. S. Laughlin, ed., *Papers on the Physical Anthropology of the American Indian* (New York: Viking Fund, 1951), 14; also Andrzej Wierçinski, "Inter- and Intrapopulational Racial Differentiation of Tlatilco, Cerro de las Mesas, Teotihuacan, Monte Alban and Yucatan Maya," *Actas, Documentos y Memorias de la 36a. Congresso Internacional de Americanistas, Lima, 1970*, 1:1, 231–48. In Sorenson, "New Evaluation," 6–7.

44. Quoted material is from E. James Dixon, *Quest for the Origins of the First Americans* (Albuquerque: University of New Mexico Press, 1983), 130–32.

45. Alison T. Stenger, "Japanese-influenced Ceramics in Precontact Washington State: a View of the Wares and Their Possible Origin," in Terry Stocker, ed., *The New World Figurine Project* (Provo, Utah: Research Press, 1991), 1:111–22; Otto J. Sadovszky, "The New Genetic Relationship and the Paleolinguistics of the Central California Indian Ceremonial Houses, "*Tenth LACUS Forum, Quebec City, 1983* (Columbia, S.C.: Linguistic Association of Canada and the United States, 1984), 516–30.

46. John L. Sorenson and Martin H. Raish, *Pre-Columbian Contact with the Americas Across the Oceans: An Annotated Bibliography*, 2 vols. (Provo, Utah: Research Press, 1990), 1:x.

47. Gisela M. A. Richter, "Silk in Greece," *American Journal of Archaeology* 33 (1929): 27–33; Alfred M. Tozzer, ed., Landa's Relación de las Cosas de Yucatan, *Harvard University Peabody Museum of American Archaeology and Ethnology, Papers* 18 (1941): 201; I. W. Johnson, "Basketry and Textiles," in Archaeology of Northern Mesoamerica, Part I, *Handbook of Middle American Indians* (Austin: University of Texas Press, 1971), 10:312. In Sorenson, "New Evaluation," 14–15.

48. Robert J. Forbes, *Metallurgy in Antiquity: A Notebook for Archaeologists and Technologists* (Leiden: E. J. Brill, 1950), 402. In Sorenson, "New Evaluation," 17.

49. Forbes, *Metallurgy*, 402. Sorenson cites several papers that document the discovery of iron artifacts and minerals throughout Mesoamerica. The mention of "brass," not invented until Roman times, is also not a clear-cut anachronism. In King James English, "brass" referred to all forms of copper alloys, including what would come to be called bronze in the eighteenth century. See "Iron Ore Occurrences in Oman," *Insights* (May 2000): 7.

50. David H. Kelley, "Proto-Tifinagh and Proto-Ogham in the Americas," *Review of Archaeology* (spring 1990): 1–9; William R. McGlone et al., *An-*

cient American Inscriptions: Plow Marks or History? (Long Hill, Mass.: Early Sites Research Society, 1993).

51. Sorenson, "New Evaluation," i (1998 addendum).

52. Donald W. Parry, Jeanette W. Miller, and Sandra A. Thorne, *A Comprehensive Annotated Book of Mormon Bibliography* (Provo, Utah: Research Press, 1996).

53. John A. Tvedtnes, "Hebraisms in the Book of Mormon: A Preliminary Survey," *BYU Studies* 11.1 (autumn 1970): 50. A more recent study is his "Hebrew Background of the Book of Mormon," in John L. Sorenson and Melvin J. Thorne, eds., *Rediscovering the Book of Mormon* (Salt Lake City: Deseret Book and FARMS, 1991). See also Sidney B. Sperry, *Our Book of Mormon* (Salt Lake City: Bookcraft, 1950), chapter 3.

54. John Tvedtnes, *The Most Correct Book* (Salt Lake City: Cornerstone Publishing, 1999), 80. For further discussion of the phenomenon, with bibliography, see also John A. Tvedtnes and Stephen D. Ricks, "Jewish and Other Semitic Texts Written in Egyptian Characters," *Journal of Book of Mormon Studies* 5.2 (fall 1996): 156–63.

55. John Gee, "La Trahison des Clercs: On the Language and Translation of the Book of Mormon," review of *New Approaches to the Book of Mormon*, ed. Brent Metcalfe, in *FARMS Review of Books* 6.1 (1994): 98–99.

56. This copy, once owned by David Whitmer who verified its authenticity, is now in the possession of the Reorganized Church of Jesus Christ of Latter Day Saints. A second transcript, discovered in 1980, matched more nearly Anthon's description of what Harris showed him and was authenticated by handwriting experts, only to be revealed as a forgery of Mark Hofmann in 1987.

57. Charles A. Shook, *Cumorah Revisited, or, The Book of Mormon and the Claims of the Mormons Re-examined from the Viewpoint of American Archaeology and Ethnology* (Cincinnati: Standard, 1910), 538.

58. Richard Lloyd Anderson, review of Walter R. Martin's *Maze of Mormonism*, *BYU Studies* 6.1 (autumn 1964): 58.

59. Nibley, *Since Cumorah*, 149–50.

60. William J. Hamblin, "Reformed Egyptian," (Provo, Utah: FARMS, 1995).

61. John Welch's published work on chiasmus began with his article on "Chiasmus in the Book of Mormon," *BYU Studies* 10.1 (autumn 1969): 69–84. More recently, he edited *Chiasmus in Antiquity* (1981; reprint, Provo, Utah: Research Press, 1999), which addresses chiasmus in the Book of Mormon and in a range of ancient literatures.

62. Mark Twain, *Roughing It*, 2 vols. (Hartford, Conn.: American Publishing, 1899), 1:132.

63. I. Woodbridge Riley, *The Founder of Mormonism: A Psychological Study of Joseph Smith, Jr.* (New York: Dodd, Meade, 1903), 118.

64. Ed Decker, *Decker's Complete Handbook on Mormonism* (Eugene, Ore.: Harvest House, 1995), 112–13.

65. Tvedtnes, "Hebraisms in the Book of Mormon," 50.

66. Although no published record exits, John Tvedtnes reports that one of his professors and past president of the Hebrew Language Academy, Haim Rabin, "occasionally used the Book of Mormon to illustrate principles of

the Hebrew language, both in class and in public lectures." Personal correspondence, November 3, 2000.

67. Royal Skousen, "How Joseph Smith Translated the Book of Mormon: Evidence from the Original Manuscript," in Reynolds, *Book of Mormon Authorship Revisited*, 88–89. In subsequent editions, the construction in Helaman was modified to make it grammatical (Hel. 12:13–21).

68. See Edward H. Ashment, "'A Record in the Language of My Father': Evidence of Ancient Egyptian and Hebrew in the Book of Mormon," in Metcalfe, *New Approaches*, 361–63, 385. Ashment confuses pronouns with nouns in the first case and simply misunderstands the grammatical issues relevant to the second, as is readily seen in his examples.

69. Abner Cole, "Gold Bible, No. 5," *Palmyra Reflector* 28 February 1831, in Dan Vogel, ed., *Early Mormon Documents*, 3 vols. (Salt Lake City: Signature, 1996–), 2:247.

70. Sydney E. Ahlstrom, *A Religious History of the American People*, 2 vols., (Garden City, N.J.: Image Books, 1975), 1:608. Philip L. Barlow, *Mormons and the Bible: The Place of the Latter-day Saints in American Religion* (New York: Oxford University Press, 1991), 27–28.

71. Riley, *Founder of Mormonism*, 112.

72. "Book of Isaiah," in F. L. Cross and E. A. Livingstone, eds., *Oxford Dictionary of the Christian Church* (Oxford: Oxford University Press, 1997), 850.

73. John Russell, *The Mormoness, or, The Trials of Mary Maverick* (Alton, Ill.: Courier Steam Press, 1853), 38.

74. Royal Skousen doubts Joseph would have even known that italics signified translator interpolations, since no explanation is ever given in the King James Bible. See his "Textual Variants in the Isaiah Quotations in the Book of Mormon," in Donald W. Parry and John W. Welch, eds., *Isaiah in the Book of Mormon* (Provo, Utah: FARMS, 1995), 381. However, Joseph and fellow Mormons apparently knew they signified something suspicious or corrupt, as witness a church editorial claiming that "the old and new testaments are filled with errors, obscurities, italics and contradictions, which must be the work of men." *The Evening and the Morning Star* 2.13 (June 1833): 106.

75. Stan Larson, "The Historicity of the Matthean Sermon on the Mount," in Metcalfe, *New Approaches*, 130. His essay appeared earlier in *Trinity Journal* 7 (spring 1986): 23–45.

76. John A. Tvedtnes, "The Isaiah Variants in the Book of Mormon," (Provo, Utah: FARMS, 1981), 128.

77. Royal Skousen credits a student, Andrew Steward, with discovering the Coverdale exception. "Textual Variants," 377.

78. John Welch, review of *New Approaches to the Book of Mormon*, ed. Brent Metcalfe, in *FARMS Review of Books on the Book of Mormon* 6.1 (1994): 152.

79. The destructions occurred in the "thirty and fourth year, in the first month," his appearance "in the ending of the thirty and fourth year" (3 Nephi 8:5, 10:18).

80. Krister Stendahl, "The Sermon on the Mount and Third Nephi" in Truman G. Madsen, ed., *Reflections on Mormonism: Judaeo-Christian Parallels* (Provo, Utah: Brigham Young University, 1978), 152.

81. Stendahl, "Sermon on the Mount," 143.
82. Larson, "Historicity," 117. Larson originally proposed 12 such problem areas but revised his argument in response to John Welch's criticism. See John W. Welch, *The Sermon at the Temple and the Sermon on the Mount* (Provo, Utah: FARMS, 1990), chapter 8.
83. "What Larson fails to describe here is the basic unity of all these critical editions, that their practice derives from a single school of textual criticism whose foundation was established by the German scholar Johann Jakob Griesbach in the late eighteenth century." Royal Skousen, review of *New Approaches to the Book of Mormon*, ed. Brent Metcalfe, in *FARMS Review of Books on the Book of Mormon* 6.1 (1994): 122.
84. John W. Welch, "The Sermon at the Temple and the Greek New Testament Manuscripts," in *Illuminating the Sermon at the Temple and the Sermon on the Mount* (Provo, Utah: FARMS, 1999), 202.
85. "The absence of the phrase . . . is evidenced by the following manuscripts: *p*64, *p*67, Sinaiticus (original hand), Vaticanus, some minuscules, the Latin Vulgate (Jerome mentions that it was not found in the oldest manuscripts known to him), the Ethiopic texts, the Gospel of the Nazarenes, Justin, Tertullian, Origen, and others." Welch, *Illuminating the Sermon*, 200. As Larson points out, the omission had also been suggested in Adam Clarke's 1810 commentary, as well as other sources, and might have been known to Joseph through those avenues. Larson, "Historicity," 128.
86. Welch, *Illuminating*, 199–200.
87. Welch, *Illuminating*, 23–24.
88. Specifically mentioned in the record are the elderly Lehi and his wife Sariah and the widow of Ishmael, Laman, Lemuel, Sam, Nephi, and Zoram who are married to the five daughters of Ishmael, two sons of Ishmael and "their families," young Jacob and Joseph, unnamed children of Nephi, as well as "sisters" of Nephi.
89. Martin Thomas Lamb, *The Golden Bible; or the Book of Mormon, Is It from God?* (New York: Ward and Drummond, 1887).
90. John C. Kunich, "Multiply Exceedingly: Book of Mormon Population Sizes," in Metcalfe, *New Approaches*, 250.
91. John A. Tvedtnes, review of Kunich, "Multiply Exceedingly" in *FARMS Review of Books on the Book of Mormon* 6.1 (1994): 26.
92. Kunich, "Multiply Exceedingly," 250. He is taking the 600,000 figure from John Sorenson.
93. James E. Smith, "Nephi's Descendants? Historical Demography and the Book of Mormon," review of Kunich, "Multiply Exceedingly," in *FARMS Review of Books on the Book of Mormon* 6.1 (1994): 231–67; Tvedtnes, review of Kunich, "Multiply Exceedingly," 8–50. See also the lengthy defense of Book of Mormon population figures in James E. Smith, "How Many Nephites? The Book of Mormon at the Bar of Demography," in Reynolds, *Book of Mormon Authorship Revisited*, 255–94. On the annexation issue, see John L. Sorenson, "When Lehi's Party Arrived in the Land, Did They Find Others There?," in *Nephite Culture and Society* (Salt Lake City: New Sage Books, 1997), 65–104.

94. A summary of particularly dramatic results from a 1997 California study is given in Richard N. Ostling and Joan K. Ostling, *Mormon America* (New York: HarperCollins, 1999), 176. George K. Jarvis cites other studies confirming that "Mormons were found to have low incidence and mortality rates for a wide range of diseases, not only those diseases believed to be related to tobacco and alcohol use. "Mormon Mortality Rates in Canada," *Social Biology* 24.1 (spring 1977): 295.

95. Its appearance on three seals and two bullae is documented in Jeffrey R. Chadwick, "Sariah in the Elephantine Papyri," *Journal of Book of Mormon Studies* 2.2 (1993): 196–200.

96. Walter Franklin Prince, "Psychological Tests for the Authorship of the Book of Mormon," *American Journal of Psychology* 28 (1917): 386–87.

97. John A. Tvedtnes, John Gee, and Matthew Roper, "Book of Mormon Names Attested in Ancient Hebrew Inscriptions," *Journal of Book of Mormon Studies* 9.1 (2000): 47.

98. Tvedtnes et al., "Book of Mormon Names," 50–51.

99. Paul S. Martin, "The Discovery of American," *Science* 179 (1973): 974n 3; Robert A. Martin, in S. David Webb, ed., *Pleistocene Mammals of Florida* (Gainesville: University of Florida, 1974), 132, 144; Paul S. Martin and H. E. Wright Jr., eds., *Pleistocene Extinctions*, Proceedings of the VII Congress, International Association for Quartenary Research (New Haven: Yale University Press, 1967), 183, 186. The above are referenced in John L. Sorenson, "Once More: The Horse," in John W. Welch, ed., *Reexploring the Book of Mormon* (Provo, Utah: FARMS, 1992), 98–100.

100. Clayton E. Ray, "Pre-Columbian Horses from Yucatan," *Journal of Mammalogy* 38 (1957): 278; Harry E. D. Pollock and Clayton E. Ray, "Notes on Vertebrate Animal Remains from Mayapan," *Current Reports* 41 (August 1957): 638 (Carnegie Institution, Washington, D.C., Dept. of Archaeology). In Sorenson, "Once More," 99–100.

101. Henry Chapman Mercer, *The Hill-Caves of Yucatan: A Search for Evidence of Man's Antiquity in the Caverns of Central America* (Philadelphia: Lippincott, 1896), 172; Institute of Maya Studies, Miami Museum of Science, *Newsletter* 7: 11 (November 1978): 2. In Sorenson, "Once More," 99–100.

102. Gwyn Jones, *The Norse Atlantic Saga* (New York: Oxford, 1986), 119, 129–30, cited in William J. Hamblin, "Basic Methodological Problems with the Anti-Mormon Approach to the Geography and Archaeology of the Book of Mormon," (Provo, Utah: FARMS, 1993), 28.

103. Denis Sinor, "The Hun Period," in Denis Sinor, ed., *The Cambridge History of Inner Asia* (Cambridge: Cambridge University Press, 1990), 203, cited in Hamblin, "Basic Problems," 28.

104. Latayne Colvett Scott, *The Mormon Mirage* (Grand Rapids: Zondervan, 1980), 82. Quoted in Daniel C. Peterson, "Is the Book of Mormon True? Notes on the Debate," in Reynolds, *Book of Mormon Authorship Revisited*, 149.

105. John L. Sorenson and Robert F. Smith, "Barley in Ancient America," in Welch, *Reexploring*, 130–32.

106. Jared Diamond, *Guns, Germs, and Steel: The Fate of Human Societies* (New York: Norton, 1997), 150.

107. See a number of examples and references in Matthew G. Wells and John W. Welch, "Concrete Evidence for the Book of Mormon," in Welch, *Reexploring*, 212–13.

108. Ronald H. Fritz, "Jesus Christ in America," *Legend and Lore of the Americas Before 1492: An Encyclopedia of Visitors, Explorers, and Immigrants* (Santa Barbara: ABC-CLIO, 1993), 184–85.

109. Richard Bushman, *Joseph Smith and Beginnings of Mormonism* (Urbana and Chicago: University of Illinois Press, 1984), 119–20.

110. The famous prediction of sociologist Rodney Stark that Mormon growth could reach 265 million by 2080 is quoted in a variety of evangelical publications (*Review of Religions Research* 26.1 [Sept. 1984]: 18–27.) For example, Mosser and Owen, in their call for more effective evangelical rebuttals to Mormon apologetics, invoke Stark's assessment: "The fact is that the growth of Mormonism is outpacing even the highest predictions of professional sociologists of religion, and is on its way, within eighty years, to become the first world-religion since Islam in the seventh century." "Mormon Apologetic," 204.

111. Mosser and Owen, "Mormon Apologetic," 181, 185, 189. James White is an evangelical who does not share Owen's and Mosser's respect for the work at FARMS. An author of anti-Mormon works, White provides some anecdotal evidence to support his claim that FARMS scholarship is at times smug, ad hominem, and misapplied. See his "The Impossible Task of Mormon Apologetics," *Christian Research Journal* 19.1 (summer 1996), 28–35. Of this article, Mosser and Owen say it is "nothing more than straw man argumentation" (202). The only other example of an attempt to refute Mormon scholarship they can identify is *Behind the Mask of Mormonism: From Its Early Schemes to its Modern Deceptions* by John Ankerberg and John Weldon (Eugene, Ore.: Harvest House, 1992). They dismiss it as "ugly, unchristian, and misleading" (203).

112. Mosser and Owen, "Mormon Apologetic," 204.

113. As this book went to press, Carl Mosser and Paul Owen together with Francis J. Beckwith produced a collection of essays designed at least in part to address this deficit. See *The New Mormon Challenge* (New York: Zondervan/Harper Collins, 2002).

114. The Amarna letters (ca. 1400 B.C.), for example, refer to "a town of the land of Jerusalem, Bit-Lahmi." Peterson, "Is the Book of Mormon True?" 156.

115. Peterson, "Is the Book of Mormon True?" 145–46. Terence L. Szink provides evidence of an even earlier provenance, third millennium B.C., in "Further Evidence of a Semitic Alma," *Journal of Book of Mormon Studies* 8.1. Of course, Hebrew script at that time did not include vowels, so "Alma" is a reconstruction from 'lm'. It is, however, the reconstruction favored by Yigael Yadin himself, as well as Paul Hoskisson, "Alma as a Hebrew Name," *Journal of Book of Mormon Studies* 7.1 (1998): 72–73.

116. Jerald and Sandra Tanner, *Covering Up the Black Hole in the Book of Mormon* (Salt Lake City: Utah Lighthouse Ministry, 1990).

117. Lawrence Foster, "Apostate Believers: Jerald and Sandra Tanner's Encounter with Mormon History," in Roger D. Launius and Linda Thatcher, eds., *Differing Visions: Dissenters in Mormon History* (Urbana: University of Illi-

nois Press, 1994), 350; and "Career Apostates: Reflections on the Work of Jerald and Sandra Tanner," *Dialogue* 17 (summer 1984): 35–60.

118. Prince, "Psychological Tests," 373. Prince's article tellingly follows one entitled "Visual, Cutaneous, and Kinaesthetic Ghosts."

119. Sterling McMurrin, "Toward Intellectual Anarchy," *Dialogue* 26.2 (summer 1993): 209–13.

120. Louis Midgley, "The Current Battle over the Book of Mormon: 'Is Modernity Itself Somehow Canonical?'" review of Anthony A. Hutchinson, "The Word of God Is Enough: The Book of Mormon as Nineteenth-Century Scripture," *FARMS Review of Books* 6.1 (1994): 1.

121. The term "cultural Mormons," coined perhaps by Louis Midgley and now used pervasively, refers to this kind of Latter-day Saint. Their intense, quasi-ethnic identification with the Church is often reinforced by pioneer ancestry (the blue bloods of Mormonism), but they reject church orthodoxy and especially the religion's supernaturalism. Midgely borrowed the term from post-WWI Protestantism, but as Mormonism gains increasing credibility among sociologists as an ethnic community, comparison with secular Jews seems more apt.

122. Midgley, "Current Battle," 4.

123. Paul L. Owen and Carl A. Mosser, review of Craig L. Blomberg and Stephen E. Robinson, *How Wide the Divide? A Mormon and an Evangelical in Conversation*, in *FARMS Review of Books* 11.2 (1999): 25. In the case of the Blomberg and Robinson book, the reviewers wonder why the LDS author, Robinson, "prefers not to make use of the works of Nibley, FARMS, and so forth" in rebutting challenges to the Book of Mormon's historicity (25). The omission is curious, given the LDS-lamented fact that the work of those apologists so seldom attains a readership outside of Mormon circles and a few evangelicals.

124. Robert Wauchope, *Myth and Method in the Study of American Indians* (Chicago: University of Chicago Press, 1962), 66.

125. Fritz, *Legend and Lore of the Americas Before 1492*. In spite of the title, the entries are fairly balanced in their discussions of Book of Mormon civilizations as potentially historical.

126. Stephen Williams, *Fantastic Archaeology: The Wild Side of North American Prehistory* (Philadelphia: University of Pennsylvania Press, 1991), 185.

127. Robert Wauchope, *Lost Tribes and Sunken Continents: Myth and Method in the Study of American Indians* (Chicago: University of Chicago Press, 1974).

128. Michael Coe, "Mormons and Archaeology: An Outside View," in *Dialogue* 8 (winter 1973): 40–41. As just one example of Coe's inaccuracy, one could point to a 1966 letter in which Thomas Stuart Ferguson, then the most active and enthusiastic "Book of Mormon archaeologist," wrote to an inquirer on the subject that "the [Kinderhook] plates were not genuine. They were manufactured . . . in order to deceive Joseph Smith." Letter to Jay Stone, December 2, 1966, in Thomas Stuart Ferguson Papers, 4.7, Special Collections, Harold B. Lee Library, Brigham Young University, Provo, Utah.

129. Michael Coe quoted in Hampton Sides, "This is Not the Place," *Doubletake* 16 (spring 1999): 54.

130. John L. Sorenson, "Instant Expertise on Book of Mormon Archaeology," *BYU Studies* 16.3 (spring 1976): 429.

131. Martin H. Raish, "All that Glitters: Uncovering Fool's Gold in Book of Mormon Archaeology," *Sunstone* 6 (January 1981): 10–15.

132. Coe, "Outside View," 44–48.

133. Nigel Davies, *Voyagers to the New World* (New York: Morrow, 1979). Other advocates of diffusionism he evaluates range from the "cultist" Von Däniken to the more "serious" Thor Heyerdahl, as well as Harvard's Barry Fell, who fares more poorly at his hands than Joseph Smith.

134. Davies, *Voyagers*, 142–43. Of course, Davies' own position is clear when he quotes John H. Rowe on his first page as writing that "diffusionism is the wave of the past."

135. John A. Price, "The Book of Mormon vs. Anthropological Prehistory," *Indian Historian* 7.3 (summer 1974): 35–40.

136. Disillusioned also by developments that threw doubt on Joseph Smith's *Pearl of Great Price* writings (the Book of Abraham especially), Ferguson completely renounced his faith in the Book of Mormon. See, among others, his letter of December 3, 1979 to James Still in which he asserts that he had "lost faith in Joseph Smith as one having a pipeline to deity." In Stan Larson, *Quest for the Gold Plates: Thomas Stuart Ferguson's Archaeological Search for the Book of Mormon* (Salt Lake City: Freethinker Press/Smith Research Associates, 1996), 155. See also, "Response of Thomas S. Ferguson to the Norman & Sorenson Papers," Written Symposium on Book of Mormon Geography, Brigham Young University, 1975, reprinted in Jerald and Sandra Tanner, eds., *Ferguson's Manuscript Unveiled* (Salt Lake City: Utah Lighthouse Ministry, 1988), 11–39.

137. John Sorenson, "What Archaeology Can and Cannot Do for the Book of Mormon," 3. Typescript in Special Collections, Harold B. Lee Library, Brigham Young University, Provo, Utah.

138. William J. Hamblin, "Basic Problems with the Anti-Mormon Approach to the Geography and Archaeology of the Book of Mormon," (Provo, Utah: FARMS, 1993), 4. The figures come from Yohanan Aharoni, *The Land of the Bible: a Historical Geography*, trans. A. F. Rainey (Philadelphia: Westminster, 1979), 128–29.

139. Actually, an editorial heading, not the text, uses the term coins in Alma 11. "The editors fell into an easy anachronism, but the book didn't," says Sorenson. "What Archaeology Can and Cannot Do," 6.

140. Price, "Book of Mormon," 38–39. For an LDS position, see Stephen D. Ricks and William J. Hamblin, *Warfare in the Book of Mormon* (Salt Lake City: Deseret Book and FARMS, 1990).

141. Melvin Fowler, a Reorganized Church of Jesus Christ of Latter Day Saints archaeologist, noted in a letter to Thomas Ferguson that "Kidder, Ekholm and others have become almost heretical to American archaeology in suggesting that the possibility of Old World connections needs to be investigated." Letter dated May 25, 1952. In Thomas Stuart Ferguson Papers, 1.17, Special Collections, Harold B. Lee Library, Brigham Young University, Provo, Utah.

142. "[It is] clear that men crossed the Atlantic to our shores at least by the mid second millennium B.C.," he writes in his preface to Alexander von Wuthenau, *Unexpected Faces in Ancient America, 1500 BC–1500 AD: The Testimony of pre-Columbian Artists* (New York: Crown, 1975), xii. "To put it mildly, some of Cyrus Gordon's notions on ancient America are most questionable," comments Nigel Davies in *Voyagers*, 181.

143. Von Wuthenau, *Unexpected Faces*, xii.

144. Von Wuthenau, *Unexpected Faces*, 51.

145. Marc K. Stengel, "The Diffusionists Have Landed," *Atlantic Monthly* (January 2000): 46. Stengel's is an overview of the diffusionist controversy, arguing that it is time to "start paying attention" to a diverse group of scholars (and scholarship) that have been misrepresented as "crackpot theorists," because of institutional intransigence and political agendas. Not all his diffusionist evidence is equally meritorious. See the critique by James Wiseman, "Camelot in Kentucky," *Archaeology* 54.1 (January–February 2001): 10–14.

146. Stengel refers to the Grave Creek Stone as authentic ("Diffusionists Have Landed," 37), but Wiseman writes that only Barry Fell has recently championed it ("Camelot in Kentucky," 13). For the Bat Creek Stone, see Cyrus Gordon, "A Hebrew Inscription Authenticated," in Lundquist and Ricks, *By Study and Also by Faith*, 1:71.

147. Stengel, "The Diffusionists," 42.

148. C. Wilfred Griggs, "The Book of Mormon as an Ancient Book," in Reynolds, *Book of Mormon Authorship Revisited*, 77.

149. Nibley, *Lehi in the Desert*, 121.

150. Hugh Nibley, "Archaeology and Our Religion," in *Old Testament and Related Studies* in *Collected Works of Hugh Nibley*, 1:32.

151. Hamblin, "Basic Methodological Problems," 3.

152. Letter to "Mr. [Loren] W[heelwright]," September 16, 1965, in Special Collections, Harold B. Lee Library, Brigham Young University, Provo, Utah.

153. Stendahl, "Sermon on the Mount," 99.

154. The statement, attributed to Weston Fields, is cited by Daniel C. Peterson, "Ancient Documents and Latter-day Saints Scholarship," (Provo, Utah: FARMS, 1999), 3. The essay was first presented as a Brigham Young University Devotional Address, August 2, 1999.

155. Mosser and Owen, "Mormon Apologetic," 189. The scholars are Donald W. Parry, Andrew Skinner, Dana M. Pike, and David Rolph Seely. Mosser and Owen cite several examples of these collaborative publications.

156. Peterson, "Ancient Documents," 2.

157. Truman G. Madsen to W. D. Davies, June 20, 1985, in Davies, "Reflections on the Mormon 'Canon,'" *Harvard Theological Review* 79 (January 1986), 46n. The Smith quote is from *Doctrine and Covenants* 91:1.

158. Sorenson, "Digging into the Book of Mormon." 14.9:26–37 and 14.10: 2–23.

159. "Scholarly foundation to become part of BYU," *Deseret News*, November 4, 1997.

160. Bushman, *Joseph Smith*, 6.

161. Sterling M. McMurrin, "Brigham H. Roberts: A Biographical Essay," in Roberts, *Studies of the Book of Mormon*, xv.

162. David Whittaker to the author, October 20, 2000; Rodney Stark, "The Rise of a New World Faith," *Review of Religious Research* 26:1 (September 1984): 22. An additional example: a letter from the National Endowment for the Humanities denies funding of a Mormon studies project because "it will probably find a limited audience, in part because of the very legacy of prejudice the study outlines" (NEH to the author, June 30, 1993).

163. Sorenson, "What Archaeology Can and Cannot Do," 4.

164. Letter to Thomas Stuart Ferguson, January 18, 1952, in Thomas Stuart Ferguson Papers, 1.17, Special Collections, Harold B. Lee Library, Brigham Young University, Provo, Utah.

SIX

1. Daniel C. Peterson, "Editor's Introduction: By What Measure Shall We Mete?" in *FARMS Review of Books* 2 (1990): xxiii.

2. David P. Wright, "'In Plain Terms that We May Understand': Joseph Smith's Transformation of Hebrews in Alma 12–13," in Brent Metcalfe, ed., *New Approaches to the Book of Mormon: Explorations in Critical Methodology* (Salt Lake City: Signature Books, 1993), 165n.

3. For the number and discussion of geographical references, see John Sorenson, "The Book of Mormon as a Mesoamerican Record," in Noel B. Reynolds, ed., *Book of Mormon Authorship Revisited: The Evidence for Ancient Origins* (Provo, Utah: Foundation for Ancient Research and Mormon Studies [FARMS], 1997), 392. For discussion of two alleged dating errors and one of place, see the references in Stan Larson, *Quest for the Gold Plates: Thomas Stuart Ferguson's Archaeological Search for the Book of Mormon* (Salt Lake City: Freethinker Press/Smith Research Associates, 1996), 32.

4. Wayne A. Larsen, Alvin C. Rencher, and Tim Layton, "Who Wrote the Book of Mormon? An Analysis of Wordprints," *BYU Studies* 20.3 (spring 1980): 225, 244–45. Royal Skousen, leading authority on the text of the Book of Mormon, believes that a new, more accurate critical text is necessary before such studies can claim real validity. "Towards a Critical Edition of the Book of Mormon," *BYU Studies* 30.1 (winter 1990): 42. Since 1988, Skousen has been working on producing a definitive critical text. (FARMS published a preliminary critical text of the Book of Mormon in 1984–87.) The final product, as envisioned, will be published by FARMS in five volumes: (1) a facsimile transcript of the existing portions of the original manuscript; (2) a facsimile transcript of the printer's manuscript; (3) a history of the text; (4) the changes the text has undergone; and (5) the critical text itself (a re-creation of the original English text as far as it can be determined). "FARMS Update," *Insights* (January 1992): 2.

5. John L. Hilton, "On Verifying Wordprint Studies: Book of Mormon Authorship," in Reynolds, *Book of Mormon Authorship Revisited*, 225–53.

6. David Reese, *Humbugs of New York* (New York: J. S. Taylor, 1838), 264.

7. Henry Brown, *The History of Illinois from Its First Discovery and Settlement to the Present Time* (New York: Winchester, 1844), 394.

8. Alexander Campbell, "Delusions: An Analysis of the Book of Mormon," *Millennial Harbinger* II (February 7, 1831): 85–96. Partially reprinted in Francis W. Kirkham, *A New Witness for Christ in America*, 2 vols. (Independence, Mo.: Zion's Printing, 1951), 2:104–09. A useful overview of Book of Mormon critics, with a lively rebuttal, is the nine-part series by Hugh Nibley, "'Mixed Voices': A Study on Book of Mormon Criticism" first published in the *Improvement Era* (May–June 1959) and reprinted in *The Collected Works of Hugh Nibley*, 15 vols. (Salt Lake City: Deseret Book and FARMS, 1986–), 8:148–206.

9. *Religious Herald* 59.1 (April 9, 1840).

10. Bernard deVoto, "The Centennial of Mormonism," *American Mercury* 19 (1930): 5; Edmund Wilson, *The Dead Sea Scrolls 1947–1969* (Glasgow: William Collins & Sons, 1985), 275.

11. Fawn Brodie, *No Man Knows My History: The Life of Joseph Smith*, 2nd ed. (New York: Vintage, 1995), 68–69.

12. Joseph Smith, "1832 History" in Dean C. Jessee, ed., *The Papers of Joseph Smith* vol. 1, *Autobiographical and Historical Writings* (Salt Lake City: Deseret Book, 1989), 5. Richard Bushman cautions against taking his lack of formal schooling too far, pointing out that since Joseph's father had been a schoolteacher in Sharon, Vermont, young Joseph was not without qualified instruction in the home. *Joseph Smith and the Beginnings of Mormonism* (Urbana and Chicago: University of Illinois Press, 1984), 31.

13. Orson Hyde, "A Cry from the Wilderness" ("Ein Ruf aus der Wüste," trans. Marvin Folsom) Frankfurt, 1842, in Jessee, *Papers of Joseph Smith*, 1:405.

14. "Last Testimony of Sister Emma," *Saints' Herald* 26 (1 October 1879), in Dan Vogel, ed., *Early Mormon Documents*, 3 vols. (Salt Lake City: Signature Books, 1996–), 1:542.

15. A. W. Cowles, "The Mormons," *Moore's Rural New Yorker* (23 January 1869), 61, in Richard Anderson, "The Impact of the First Preaching in Ohio," *BYU Studies* 11.4 (summer 1971): 479.

16. John W. Rigdon, "Lecture on the Early History of the Mormon Church," in Anderson, "Impact of First Preaching," 479.

17. Martin Harris interview with Joel Tiffany, "Mormonism—No. II," *Tiffany's Monthly* (August 1859), in Vogel, *Early Mormon Documents*, 2:301.

18. I. Woodbridge Riley, *The Founder of Mormonism* (New York: Dodd, Mead, 1903), 79, 84–86.

19. Lawrence Foster, *Religion and Sexuality* (Urbana: University of Illinois Press, 1981), 296.

20. Eduard Meyer, *Ursprung und Geschichte der Mormonen*, available in English as *The Origin and History of the Mormons, with Reflections on the Beginnings of Islam and Christianity*, transl. by Heinz F. Rahde and Eugene Seaich (Salt Lake City: University of Utah, 1961).

21. DeVoto, "The Centennial of Mormonism," 5.

22. Brodie, *No Man Knows*, 413–19.

23. Hugh Nibley, *The Prophetic Book of Mormon*, in *Collected Works*, 8:113.

24. Two now-dated accounts that invoke the theory are George Arbaugh, *Revelation in Mormonism* (Chicago: University of Chicago Press, 1932) and

William Alexander Linn, *The Story of the Mormons* (New York: Macmillan, 1902).

25. For a thorough treatment of the Spaulding hypothesis and its fortunes, see Lester Bush, "The Spalding [*sic*] Theory Then and Now," *Dialogue* 10.4 (autumn 1977): 40–69.

26. She summarizes the theory's crippling flaws in introducing a lengthy appendix on the subject. Among them are the obvious Hurlbut authorship of the affidavits, the stylistic consistency of Joseph's entire corpus and its inconsistency with Rigdon's, the illogic and impracticality of their collaboration given their respective circumstances, and the unlikelihood of Rigdon's acquiescence to the role of silent partner, receiving no credit even while suffering discipline and eventual disaffection from both Joseph and the Mormon church. Brodie, *No Man Knows*, 442.

27. The material in question involved an ancient Hebrew phylactery discovered in Pittsfield, Massachusetts, and the legend recounted by "an old Indian" that "his fathers in this country had not long since, been in the possession of a book, which they had for a long time, carried with them, but having lost the knowledge of reading it, they buried it with an Indian chief." The article cited Ethan Smith's *View of the Hebrews* (1825, 2nd ed.) as the original source, and Josiah Priest's *American Antiquities*" (1835, 5th ed.) as the reprint source. *Times and Seasons* 3.15 (June 1, 1842).

28. Brodie, *No Man Knows*, 47.

29. Robert Hullinger, for instance, argues that "Joseph Smith's probable dependence upon *View of the Hebrews* has all the strengths that others looked for in the Spaulding manuscript theories but none of their weaknesses." Robert N. Hullinger, "The Lost Tribes of Israel and the Book of Mormon," *Lutheran Quarterly* 22.3 (August 1970): 319–29. He cites as supporters of his view Larry W. Jonas, *Mormon Claims Examined* (Grand Rapids, Mich.: Baker, 1961); Wesley M. Jones, *A Critical Study of Book of Mormon Sources* (Detroit: Harlo Press, 1964); and famous anti-Mormon critics Jerald and Sandra Tanner, *Mormonism—Shadow or Reality* (Salt Lake City: Modern Microfilm, 1964).

30. Before Roberts, I. Woodbrige Riley mentioned that Ethan Smith's work "by 1825 had circulated to westernmost New York" (*Founder of Mormonism*, 125). It was for Brodie, however, to give general currency to the theory of borrowing.

31. Lehi, we are told, "was a descendant of Manasseh, who was the son of Joseph who was sold into Egypt by the hands of his brethren" (Alma 10:3). The numerous Mulekites, by contrast, with whom the Nephites unite several hundred years into their history, claimed descent from Mulek, a son (not mentioned in the Bible) of King Zedekiah: "And now will you dispute that Jerusalem was destroyed? Will ye say that the sons of Zedekiah were not slain, all except it were Mulek? Yea, and do ye not behold that the seed of Zedekiah are with us . . . ?" (Hel. 8:21).

32. The discovery of a lost manuscript that founds a literary work is almost a cliché in world literature. That it is *buried* in the Ethan Smith work seems less than striking, given the antiquity of the "author."

33. John W. Welch, "B. H. Roberts: Seeker after Truth," *Ensign* 16.3 (March 1986): 56–62.

34. Ethan Smith, *View of the Hebrews: 1825 2nd Edition*, ed. Charles D. Tate, Jr. (Provo, Utah: Brigham Young University, Religious Studies Center, 1996), vii. The church also published a reprint of the Spaulding manuscript. *Manuscript Found: The Complete Original "Spaulding Manuscript,"* ed. Kent P. Jackson (Provo, Utah: Brigham Young University, Religious Studies Center, 1996).

35. Charles D. Tate, Jr., provides a bibliography in his introduction to the Ethan Smith reprint. Smith, *View*, xix–xxii.

36. Quoted by Leonard J. Arrington and Davis Bitton in *Mormons and Their Historians* (Salt Lake City: University of Utah Press, 1988), 115.

37. David Paulsen presented an excellent and thorough review of "The Search for Cultural Origins of Mormon Doctrines," in his paper delivered at a Mormon Studies Symposium at the University of Durham, U.K., April 24, 1999. See also Gary F. Novak, "Naturalistic Assumptions and the Book of Mormon," *BYU Studies* 30.3 (summer 1990): 23–40.

38. John Phillip Walker, ed., *Dale Morgan on Early Mormonism: Correspondence and a New History* (Salt Lake City: Signature Books, 1986), 87.

39. Wright, "In Plain Terms," in Metcalfe, *New Approaches,* 165n.

40. Campbell, "Delusions," 85.

41. Brodie, *No Man Knows*, 69, 67.

42. Whitney R. Cross, *The Burned-Over District: The Social and Intellectual History of Enthusiastic Religion in Western New York, 1800–1850* (New York: Cornell University Press, 1950).

43. Thomas O'Dea, *The Mormons* (Chicago: University of Chicago Press, 1958), 21, 31, 54, 57. The characterization is David Paulsen's ("Search for Cultural Origins," 9).

44. William Mulder, "The Mormons in American History," *Utah Historical Quarterly* 27.1 (January 1959): 60.

45. Brodie, *No Man Knows*, 63–66.

46. Walter Franklin Prince, "Psychological Tests for the Book of Mormon," *American Journal of Psychology* 28.3 (July 1917): 373–89. In a later note, Prince reiterated the possibility that, though probably a conscious production, the work could have been written "in a secondary or dreamy state." "Authorship of the Book of Mormon," *American Journal of Psychology* 30.4 (October 1919): 428.

47. Brodie, *No Man Knows*, 59.

48. Stephen E. Robinson, in "Nephi's 'Great and Abominable Church,'" argues that the identification is "untenable, primarily because Roman Catholicism as we know it did not yet exist when the crimes described by Nephi were committed." Technically, of course, he is correct. But to propose, instead, "Hellenized Christianity" as the culprit, will not likely appease those who see themselves as the lineal descendents of Hellenized Christianity. *Journal of Book of Mormon Studies* 7.1 (September 1, 1998): 38–39.

49. Brodie, *No Man Knows*, 70.

50. Marvin S. Hill, "Quest for Refuge: An Hypothesis as to the Social Origins and Nature of the Mormon Political Kingdom," in *Journal of Mormon His-*

tory 2 (1975): 4–5, 14. Hill cites Mosiah 29:42, where Alma assumes duties of both chief judge and high priest, and 2 Nephi 3:12, which prophecies the role of the Book of Mormon in resolving religious controversies.

51. Quoting Jean Alphonse Turrentius, in Dan Vogel, *The Word of God: Essays on Mormon Scripture* (Salt Lake City: Signature Books, 1990), 22.

52. Mark D. Thomas, "A Rhetorical Approach to the Book of Mormon: Rediscovering Nephite Sacramental Language," in Metcalfe, *New Approaches*, 54, 55.

53. Thomas, "Rhetorical Approach," in Metcalfe, *New Approaches*, 73–74.

54. Mark D. Thomas, "The Meaning of Revival Language in the Book of Mormon," *Sunstone* 8 (May–June 1983): 19–25.

55. The term appears in *References to the Book of Mormon* (Kirtland, Ohio: Church of Jesus Christ of Latter-day Saints, 1835). Vogel himself cites this precedent.

56. Dan Vogel, "Anti-Universalist Rhetoric in the Book of Mormon," in Metcalfe, *New Approaches*, 47.

57. Stylistic and conceptual differences are cited as well. But the predominant reason for the exploding of one Isaiah into multiples was, as Gerald Bray writes, "the rationalistic rejection of predictive prophecy" that accompanied the growth of the historical-critical method. *Biblical Interpretation, Past and Present* (Leicester, England: Apollos, 1996), 311.

58. *The Evening and the Morning Star* 1.8 (January 1833): 57.

59. Vogel, *Word of God*, viii–ix.

60. Susan Curtis, "Early Nineteenth-Century America and the Book of Mormon," in Vogel, *Word of God*, 67.

61. Gordon S. Wood, "Evangelical America and Early Mormonism," *New York History* 61 (October 1980): 369.

62. Alan Taylor, "Rediscovering the Context of Joseph Smith's Treasure Seeking," *Dialogue* 19.4 (winter 1986): 19.

63. Of the silver cup hidden in his brother's sack of grain, the biblican Joseph's steward was instructed to say, "Is not this it in which my lord drinketh, and whereby indeed he divineth?" Gen. 44:5.

64. Scot Facer Proctor and Maurine Jensen Proctor, eds., *The Revised and Enhanced History of Joseph Smith by his Mother* (Salt Lake City: Bookcraft, 1996), 124.

65. Brodie, *No Man Knows*, 19.

66. The cited phrase and quotation are both from Roger G. Kennedy, *Hidden Cities: The Discovery and Loss of Ancient North American Civilization* (New York: Free Press, 1994), 230.

67. Sometimes a smoking gun is too convenient to ignore—even if it fires blanks. Alan Taylor, for example, leads off his essay on Smith's treasure-seeking with those two remarkable letters. Their authenticity was impugned before his piece made it to press, but rather than pull or rewrite he instead inserts this unabashed explanation: even if "forged, the documents skillfully summarize treasure seeking's nuances and links to early Mormonism as amply documented in other sources." "Rediscovering the Context," 19n1. More egregious is the carelessness in Jon Butler's discussion of Mormonism. He takes note in his 1992 book of the Hoffman forg-

eries, but nonetheless refers to the "toads or salamanders Smith describes as guarding the golden plates" as evidence of his connection to an ancient occult tradition. Jon Butler, *Awash in a Sea of Faith* (Cambridge: Harvard University Press, 1992), 243. Without the "Salamander Letter," there is no credible evidence to suggest Smith ever referred to amphibious sentries. The secondhand report by the hostile Willard Chase (Vogel, *Early Mormon Documents*, 2:67), is dubious to say the least.

68. Butler, *Awash in a Sea of Faith*, 241.

69. Alan Taylor, "The Early Republic's Supernatural Economy: Treasure Seeking in the American Northeast, 1780–1830," *American Quarterly* 38.1 (spring 1986): 10. In this essay also he relies on material forged by Mark Hoffman, but on many other sources as well.

70. D. Michael Quinn, *Early Mormonism and the Magic World View* (Salt Lake City: Signature Books, 1987; 2nd ed., 1999). Quinn distanced himself from the forgeries as the book went to press, but indications are that the letters provided a major impetus to his thesis. See Rhett S. James, "Writing History Must Not Be an Act of Magic," *FARMS Review of Books* 12.2 (2000): 407–09.

71. William J. Hamblin, "That Old Black Magic," *FARMS Review of Books* 12.2 (2000): 226. Quinn was quite respected as a historian earlier in his career, but his work draws harsh criticism for his vitriolic response to his critics (some LDS apologists are, he suggests in his revised work, "sociopaths" [x]) and for an undeniable tendency to misrepresent his sources. For some egregious examples in this last regard, see Hamblin, 278–79, 299, 322–23.

72. Quinn, *Early Mormonism*, 302.

73. Quinn, *Early Mormonism*, 197–98.

74. John Brooke, *The Refiner's Fire: the Making of Mormon Cosmology, 1644–1844* (Cambridge: Cambridge University Press, 1994). William J. Hamblin, Daniel C. Peterson, and George L. Mitton, "Mormon in the Fiery Furnace, Or, Loftes Tryk Goes to Cambridge," review of John L. Brooke, *The Refiner's Fire*, in *FARMS Review of Books on the Book of Mormon* 6.2 (1994): 8.

75. One reviewer writes, "Brooke's approach is refreshingly old-fashioned: he simply stayed in the library until he had read everything that pertained to Smith's spiritual and religious ideas and their antecedents." Paul E. Johnson, "The Alchemist," *New Republic* 212.24 (1995): 46.

76. Brooke, *Refiner's Fire*, xiv.

77. Brooke, *Refiner's Fire*, 28, 243.

78. Harold Bloom, *The American Religion: The Emergence of the Post-Christian Nation* (New York: Simon & Schuster, 1992), 98–117.

79. "The Ebla Tablets and the Abraham Tradition," in Truman G. Madsen, ed., *Reflections on Mormonism: Judaeo-Christian Parallels* (Provo, Utah: Brigham Young University, Religious Studies Center, 1978), 67. For some LDS treatments of the complex analogues between Joseph Smith's ancient writings, LDS temple practice, and ancient religious ideas and practices, see Donald W. Parry, ed., *Temples of the Ancient World: Ritual and Symbolism* (Salt Lake City: Deseret Book and FARMS, 1994); Truman G. Madsen, ed., *The Temple in Antiquity: Ancient Records and Modern Perspectives* (Provo, Utah: Brigham Young University, Religious Studies Center,

1984); Hugh W. Nibley, *The Message of the Joseph Smith Papyri: An Egyptian Endowment* (Salt Lake City: Deseret Book, 1975).

80. James H. Charlesworth, "Messianism in the Pseudepigrapha and the Book of Mormon," in Madsen, *Reflections on Mormonism,*129.

81. "The Narrative of Zosimus Concerning the Life of the Blessed," *The Ante-Nicene Fathers. Translations of the Writings of the Fathers Down to A.D. 325* (Buffalo: Christian Literature, 1885–96), 9:220–24.

82. John W. Welch, "The Narrative of Zosimus (History of the Rechabites) and the Book of Mormon," in Reynolds, *Book of Mormon Authorship Revisited*, 323–74.

83. Welch, "Zosimus," in Reynolds, *Book of Mormon Authorship Revisited*, 313.

84. Charlesworth, "Messianism," in Madsen, *Reflections*, 125.

85. Blake T. Ostler, "The Book of Mormon as a Modern Expansion of an Ancient Source," *Dialogue* 20.1 (spring 1987): 109.

86. Butler, *Awash in a Sea of Faith*, 240.

87. Mark Thomas, *Digging in Cumorah: Reclaiming Book of Mormon Narratives* (Salt Lake City: Signature Books, 1999), 11.

88. Ostler, "Modern Expansion," 111.

89. Richard Bushman to the author, December 4, 2000.

90. Leonard J. Arrington, "Scholarly Studies of Mormonism in the Twentieth Century," *Dialogue* 1 (1966): 28. Arrington delivered an earlier version of the essay at the Western History Association, October 16, 1965.

91. James B. Allen and Leonard J. Arrington, "Mormon Origins in New York: An Introductory Analysis," *BYU Studies* 9.3 (spring 1969): 241.

92. James B. Allen, Ronald W. Walker, and David J. Whittaker, *Studies in Mormon History, 1830–1997: An Indexed Bibliography* (Urbana: University of Illinois Press, 2000). They do not organize by chronology, but their work includes citations for over 2,600 books, 10,400 articles, and 1,800 theses and dissertations.

93. For Robert Flanders, the new history represents a "significantly different understanding of the Latter-day Saint past" because of its "shift of interest and emphasis from polemics, from attacking or defending assumptions of faith." "Additionally," he claims, "it has provided a new location where 'marginal' Latter-day Saints, who hold some faith assumptions but reject others, or who are attached to Mormon societies or social networks but not to the religion per se, can share in the dialogue." "Some Reflections on the New Mormon History," *Dialogue* 9 (spring 1974): 34, 40. Thomas G. Alexander describes the movement as employing "techniques derived from historical, humanistic, social-scientific, and religious perspectives." It pays "more attention to the relationship between Mormon and general U.S. historiography" and insists "upon an understanding of development, rather than just doctrinal exegesis." "Toward the New Mormon History: An Examination of the Literature on the Latter-day Saints in the Far West," in Michael P. Malone, ed., *Historians and the American West* (Lincoln: University of Nebraska Press, 1983), 344, 352, 357. Both sources are cited by Gary F. Novak in "Naturalistic Assumptions and the Book of Mormon," *BYU Studies* 30.3 (summer 1990): 19. More negative

assessments would include Novak's complaint that "much of the New Mormon History is written in such a way as to exclude or bracket what scripture understands as the mighty acts of God. These mighty acts are precisely what are essential for the collective memory of the Saints—what Yerushalmi calls 'God's acts of intervention in history.' But perhaps the most prominent modernist feature of the New History, and certainly one of the features it emphasizes, is its appeal to naturalistic assumptions." Novak, "Naturalistic Assumptions," 35.

94. Louis Midgley, "The Challenge of Historical Consciousness: Mormon History and the Encounter with Secular Modernity," in John M. Lundquist and Stephen D. Ricks, eds., *By Study and Also by Faith: Essays in Honor of Hugh Nibley*, 2 vols. (Provo and Salt Lake City: Deseret Book and FARMS, 1990), 2:505.

95. Marvin S. Hill, "Afterword," *BYU Studies* 30.4 (fall 1990): 119.

96. Rodney Stark, "A Theory of Revelations," *Journal for the Scientific Study of Religion* 38.2 (1999): 305, 288.

97. Martin E. Marty, "Two Integrities: An Address to the Crisis in Mormon Historiography," *Journal of Mormon History* 10 (1983): 3.

98. William James, *The Varieties of Religious Experience* (Cambridge, Mass.: Harvard University Press, 1985), 13–14..

99. James, *Varieties*, 24.

100. James, *Varieties*, 14.

101. Brigham D. Madsen, "Reflections on LDS Disbelief in the Book of Mormon as History," *Dialogue* 30.3 (fall 1997): 96.

102. David P. Wright, "'In Plain Terms That We May Understand': Joseph Smith's Transformation of Hebrews in Alma 12–13," in Metcalfe, *New Approaches*. Cited in Madsen, "Reflections," 94. Wright was excommunicated from the Mormon church some time after his article was published. Since Mormon at times can refer to something more akin to cultural affiliation than doctrinal orthodoxy and formal standing, I use the label in the most general sense. (Theological dissenters like Sterling McMurrin have often been adamant in claiming the label of Mormon in spite of their disbelief in Mormon supernaturalism.)

103. As Jonathan Culler writes, "genres are not special varieties of language but sets of expectations." *Structuralist Poetics: Structuralism, Linguistics, and the Study of Literature* (Ithaca, N.Y.: Cornell University Press, 1975), 129. Peter Rabinowitz has also demonstrated the usefulness of an approach in which "genres can be seen not only in the traditional way, as patterns or models that writers follow in constructing texts, but also from the other direction, as different bundles of rules that readers apply in constructing texts." "The Turn of the Glass Key: Popular Fiction as Reading Strategy," *Critical Inquiry* 11 (March 1985): 420. These reading practices are not whimsical or idiosyncratic, but are sanctioned by what another critic calls "interpretive communities." A peculiar individual may find the Sears catalogue "inspirational." That doesn't make it scripture, at least not in any meaningful sense. See Stanley Fish, "Interpreting the Variorum," *Critical Inquiry* 2 (spring 1976): 465–85.

104. Ian G. Barber, "Beyond the Literalist Constraint: Personal Reflections on Mormon Scripture and Religious Interpretation," *Sunstone* 20.3 (October 1997): 21.

105. Barber, "Beyond the Literalist," 21.

106. Anthony A. Hutchinson, "The Word of God is Enough: The Book of Mormon as Nineteenth-Century Scripture," in Vogel, *Word of God*, 5.

107. Marvin S. Hill, following Fawn Brodie's thesis, has suggested this explanation of Joseph Smith's career. See his "Secular or Sectarian History? A Critique of *No Man Knows My History*," *Church History* 43 (March 1974): 78–96; and "Brodie Revisited: A Reappraisal," *Dialogue* 7 (winter 1972): 72–85.

108. Madsen, "Reflections," 95; Barber, "Beyond the Literalist," 21.

109. Barber, "Beyond the Literalist," 22.

110. Robert Price of the Jesus Seminar and editor of *Journal of Higher Criticism*, for instance, applauds Thomas's *Digging in Cumorah* for "inaugurating a new era in Book of Mormon studies," on the book's jacket blurb.

111. Thomas, *Digging in Cumorah*, 1–2.

112. Thomas's bracketing of historical questions is not entirely sincere—since his book is replete with reference to nineteenth-century cultural factors that constitute the tiles of Joseph's "mosaic." He is quite clearly an "environmentalist."

113. Thomas, *Digging in Cumorah*, 23, 15, 3.

114. Wendell Berry, "The Loss of the University," in *Home Economics* (San Francisco: North Point Press, 1987), 91–92.

115. Richard Rust, in his *Feasting on the Word*, provides an eloquent survey of the variety of literary forms and dimensions of the Book of Mormon. As its subtitle indicates ("The Literary Testimony of the Book of Mormon"), Rust's study, unlike Thomas's, presumes the book's sacred origin and status. (Provo and Salt Lake City: Deseret Book and FARMS, 1997).

116. Thomas, "Rhetorical Approach," in Metcalfe, *New Approaches*, 53.

117. Lawrence Foster, *Religion and Sexuality*, 294, 296–97. As one reviewer notes, "Foster does not indicate what consequences, if any, his reinterpretation may have upon the community of faith or even if that community can survive such a shift." Novak, "Naturalistic Assumptions," 40.

118. Lyman P. Powell, *Cambridge History of American Literature* (New York: Putnam, 1921), 3:522. Writing in 1969, one Mormon scholar found the benign neglect of a standard reference like Robert E. Spiller's *Literary History of the United States* preferable to the Cambridge travesty. Robert E. Nichols, Jr., "Beowulf and Nephi: A Literary View of the Book of Mormon," *Dialogue* 4 (fall 1969), 41.

119. Douglas Wilson, "Prospects for the Study of the Book of Mormon as a Work of American Literature," *Dialogue* 3 (spring 1968): 29. Ironically, Wilson laments that the few studies to appear have been in "exclusively Mormon periodicals." *Dialogue* is, of course, a Mormon periodical.

120. Wilson, "Prospects," 32.

121. Daniel W. Howe, letter to G. M. Curtis III, in Noel B. Reynolds, "The Coming Forth of the Book of Mormon in the Twentieth Century," *Dialogue* 38.2 (1999): 39.

122. One example of such motivation laid bare is provided by Marvin S. Hill. Attacked by an orthodox critic for his naturalistic approach to the Book of Mormon, he remarked defensively, "It seems of no worth to him that I tried to create a more favorable view of the Church among professional historians." "Afterword," 119.

123. Signature Books is the main vehicle for publications that challenge the borders of Mormon orthodoxy. Called "Korihor's Press" and anti-Mormon by reviewer Stephen Robinson in response to the Vogel volume, the publisher responded with threat of legal action. (Korihor was a famous anti-Christ in the Book of Mormon.) The journals *Sunstone* and *Dialogue* provide comparable forums for intellectual inquiry that from time to time takes the form of dissent or outright hostility (or of waging "a campaign against Mormon orthodoxy" in the words of a FARMS reviewer).

124. Carl Mosser and Paul Owen, "Mormon Apologetic, Scholarship and Evangelical Neglect: Losing the Battle and Not Knowing It?," *Trinity Journal* (1998): 203.

125. Joseph Smith Jr., *History of the Church of Jesus Christ of Latter-day Saints*, 7 vols., ed. James Mulholland, Robert B. Thompson, William W. Phelps, Willard Richards, George A. Smith, and later B. H. Roberts (Salt Lake City: Deseret News Press, 1902–12; 2nd rev. ed., Salt Lake City: Deseret Book, 1951), 4:461.

126. Bushman, *Joseph Smith*, 142.

127. Smith, *History of the Church*, 4:461.

128. Church Radio, Publicity, and Missionary Literature Committee, *A Short History of the Church of Jesus Christ of Latter-day Saints* (Salt Lake City: Church of Jesus Christ of Latter-day Saints, 1938), 20.

129. Symonds Ryder, Letter to *Ohio Star*, December 29, 1831.

130. B. H. Roberts, *New Witnesses for God*, 3 vols. (Salt Lake City: Deseret News, 1895–1911), 2: preface. See also his letter to church leaders, in which he states "it is inconceivable that the Book of Mormon should be untrue in its origin or character and the Church of Jesus Christ of Latter-day Saints be a true Church." Letter to Heber J. Grant, Council, and Quorum of Twelve Apostles, in Roberts, *Studies of the Book of Mormon* (Salt Lake City: Signature Books, 1992), 56.

131. William D. Russell, review, *Utah Historical Quarterly* 55 (fall 1987): 376. Cited in Madsen, "Reflections," 96.

132. Their web site, for example, mentions neither the First Vision nor the Book of Mormon.

133. Diane Butler Christensen, "Disillusioned RLDS Faithful Form New Flock," *Utah County Journal*, September 15, 1991.

SEVEN

1. "Joseph Smith-History" (JS-H), *Pearl of Great Price* (Salt Lake City: Church of Jesus Christ of Latter-day Saints, 1981), 1:34.

2. The Lord referred to the Book of Mormon as having "the fulness of the gospel" in *Doctrine and Covenants* (D&C) 20:9; 27:5; 42:12, etc.

3. Mormons often cite Alma 13 as substantiating the doctrine of premortal existence. It must be pointed out, however, that the references are cryptic—certainly no more compelling than the biblical references Latter-day Saints cite in Jeremiah 1:5, Job 38, or John 9.

4. *Journal of Discourses*, 26 vols., reported by G. D. Watt et al. (Liverpool: F. D. and S. W. Richards, et al., 1851–1886; reprint, Salt Lake City: n.p., 1974), 10:311, 8:129.

5. "John Murdock Autobiography," 12. Quoted in Richard Anderson, "Impact of the First Preaching in Ohio," *BYU Studies* 11.4 (summer 1971): 482.

6. "Murdock Autobiography," 15.

7. Deseret News IX, 153–55, cited in Hyrum L. Andrus, "The Second American Revolution: Era of Preparation," *BYU Studies* 1.2 (autumn 1959): 85.

8. *Messenger and Advocate* 1.1 (October 1824): 10.

9. Susan Easton Black, *Stories from the Early Saints Converted by the Book of Mormon* (Salt Lake City: Bookcraft, 1992), 44, 62.

10. Journal of Joseph Grafton Hovey, Special Collections, Harold B. Lee Library, Brigham Young University, Provo, Utah. In Grant Underwood, "The Meaning and Attraction of Mormonism Reexamined," *Thetean* (March 1977): 3.

11. Timothy Smith, "The Book of Mormon in a Biblical Culture," *Journal of Mormon History* 7 (1980): 8, 10–11. The five ways are 1) affirmation of Old and New Testament prophecies and teachings; 2) ecumenical vision of a common humanity as declared by the stories of creation, Noah, and Abraham; 3) call to ethical righteousness; 4) prominent role of the workings of the Holy Spirit among God's people; 5) belief in literal fulfillment of latter-day prophecies.

12. See Paul Gutjahr, "The Golden Bible in the Bible's Golden Age: *The Book of Mormon* and Antebellum Print Culture," *ATQ* 12 (December 1998): 276, 278.

13. Letter of "M" to the Salt Lake Tribune, 6 December 1903, in B. H. Roberts, *Defense of the Faith and the Saints*, 2 vols. (Salt Lake City: Deseret News, 1907–1912), 1:348.

14. Quoted in *Times and Seasons* 2.7 (February 1, 1841): 305–06.

15. Letter of Sylvester Smith, May 16, 1833, in *The Evening and the Morning Star* 2.14 (July 1833): 108.

16. Scot Facer Proctor and Maurine Jensen Proctor, eds., *The Revised and Enhanced History of Joseph Smith by his Mother* (Salt Lake City: Bookcraft, 1996), 212. As recently as May 2000, delegates to the United Methodist Church's General Conference approved a new policy statement declaring Mormonism outside the "tradition of Christian faith." "Methodists Will Baptize Ex-Mormons," *Los Angeles Times* (May 13, 2000): B3.

17. Dan Vogel argues that what the Book of Mormon teaches about the nature of God is radically heterodox. "The Earliest Mormon Concept of God," in Gary James Bergera, ed., *Line Upon Line: Essays on Mormon Doctrine* (Salt Lake City: Signature Books, 1989).

18. *Messenger and Advocate* 1.7 (April 1835): 96.

19. Dean C. Jessee, ed., *The Papers of Joseph Smith* vol. 1, *Autobiographical and Historical Writings* (Salt Lake City: Deseret Book, 1989), 5.

20. W. D. Davies notes this parallel with "certain Jewish Christian sects [who] claimed that ideas in the primitive Jewish tradition concerning the Temple, sacrifice, and the cult had been changed when the Bible was assembled." He cites Hans Joachim Schoeps, *Theologie und Geschichte des Judenchristentums* (Tübingen: Mohr-Siebeck, 1949), 148–87, in "Reflections on the Mormon 'Canon,'" *Harvard Theological Review* 79 (January 1986): 61.

21. The "Articles and Covenants" were published in *The Evening and the Morning Star* 1.1 (June 1832): 1–2, and later in sections 20 (which was drafted by Oliver Cowdery) and 22 of the D&C.

22. The article actually makes a veiled allusion to Smith's first vision ("after that it truly was manifested unto this first Elder, that he had received a remission of his sins"), but it is too cryptic and fleeting to draw attention to that experience as in any way miraculous.

23. *The Evening and the Morning Star* 1.1 (June 1832): 1.

24. *The Evening and the Morning Star* 1.1 (June 1832): 3

25. *The Evening and the Morning Star* 2.14 (July 1833): 106.

26. John G. Gager, "Early Mormonism and Early Christianity: Some Parallels and their Consequences for the Study of New Religions," *Journal of Mormon Studies* 9 (1982): 59.

27. Philip Barlow, *Mormons and the Bible* (New York: Oxford, 1991), xi.

28. Smith, "Book of Mormon in a Biblical Culture," 21.

29. *Elders' Journal of the Church of Jesus Christ of Latter-day Saints* 1.3 (July 1838): 43.

30. Grant Underwood, "Book of Mormon Usage in Early LDS Theology," *Dialogue* 17 (autumn 1984): 53.

31. Miriam Levering, ed., *Rethinking Scripture: Essays from a Comparative Perspective* (Albany: SUNY Press, 1989), 3.

32. Wilfred Cantwell Smith, "Scripture as Form and Concept," in Levering, *Rethinking Scripture*, 32.

33. Davies, "Reflections on the Mormon 'Canon,'" 63.

34. Robert J. Matthews, *A Plainer Translation, Joseph Smith's Translation of the Bible, A History and Commentary* (Provo, Utah: Brigham Young University Press, 1975), 424–25.

35. John W. Welch and David Whittaker, "Mormonism's Open Canon: Some Historical Reflections on Its Religious Limits and Potentials" (Provo, Utah: FARMS, 1986), 10.

36. "Articles of Faith," *Pearl of Great Price*.

37. *The Evening and the Morning Star* 1.2 (July 1832): 14.

38. *Messenger and Advocate* 1.12 (September 1835): 179–82.

39. *Messenger and Advocate* 2.2 (November 1835): 209.

40. Joseph Smith, Jr., *Lectures on Faith*, ed. Nels B. Lundwall (Salt Lake City: Bookcraft, n.d.), 11; Smith, "Book of Mormon in a Biblical Culture," 20. Though scholarship has long raised authorship questions about the lectures, the opinion of Leland H. Gentry appears still accurate: "even if it could be shown that the Prophet did not write or deliver the lectures personally, it cannot be denied that he had much to do with their final published form." "What of the Lectures on Faith," *BYU Studies* 19.1 (fall 1978): 17.

41. *Journal of Discourses* 8:129–30.
42. Louis Midgley, "Prophetic Messages or Dogmatic Theology? Comment-
    ing on the Book of Mormon," review essay on Joseph Fielding McConkie
    and Robert L. Millet, *Doctrinal Commentary on the Book of Mormon*, vols. 1
    and 2, in *FARMS Review of Books on the Book of Mormon* 1 (1989): 100.
    Midgley is here expanding upon the position of B. H. Roberts who in-
    sisted that "the Book of Mormon is not a formal treatise on the subject of
    theology." *Mormon Doctrine of Deity* (1903; reprint, Bountiful, Utah: Hori-
    zon, 1975), 213.
43. The new edition of the Bible had been published two years earlier, in
    1979. Standard Works became, around 1900, the term that designates the
    official corpus of Latter-day Saint scripture.
44. Boyd K. Packer, "Scriptures," *Ensign* 2.11 (November 1982): 53.
45. An intriguing reference to Ezekiel 37 was made by John Eliot in the sev-
    enteenth century. The Roxbury, Massachusetts, clergyman and "Apostle
    to the Indians" was an enthusiastic proponent of the view that American
    Indians were descendents of the House of Israel who were soon to be
    gathered back into the covenant. A contemporary named Samuel Sewall
    noted that shortly before Eliot's death, he had written "a small paraphrase
    . . . upon Ezekiel 37." But Sewall didn't say whether Eliot, like Smith, saw
    in that scripture biblical confirmation of the Indian-Israelite connection.
    See Richard W. Cogley, "John Eliot and the Origins of the American Indi-
    ans," *Early American Literature* 21.3 (winter 1986/87): 222
46. "At no very distant period, we shall print the book of Mormon and the
    [New] Testament, and bind them in one volume," reported *The Evening
    and the Morning Star* 2.14 (July 1833): 109.
47. Packer, "Scriptures," 53.
48. Wilford Woodruff, *Conference Reports of the General Conference of the Church
    of Jesus Christ of Latter-day Saints* (October 1897): 22–23.
49. *Conference Reports of the General Conference of the Church of Jesus Christ of
    Latter-day Saints* (October 1916), 55.
50. Loren C. Dunn, "A Living Prophet," *Ensign* 6.5 (May 1976): 65–66.
51. Davies, "Reflections on the Mormon 'Canon,'" 64. For a response to the
    warning posed by Davies, see Welch and Whittaker, "Mormonism's Open
    Canon."
52. Wandle Mace autobiography in Milton V. Backman Jr. and Keith W.
    Perkins, eds., *Writings of Early Latter-day Saints and Their Contemporaries,
    A Database Collection*, 2nd ed., rev. (Provo, Utah: Brigham Young Univer-
    sity, Religious Studies Center, 1996), 23.
53. This expression is also used by Paul in reference to a slightly expanded
    list of principles (Hebrews 6:1) and by John (2 John 1:9) in the King James
    Version. Noel B. Reynolds has written two essays that discuss the permu-
    tations of this core doctrine throughout the Book of Mormon. See "The
    True Points of My Doctrine," *Journal of Book of Mormon Studies* 5.2 (fall
    1996): 26–56; and "The Gospel of Jesus Christ as Taught by the Nephite
    Prophets," *BYU Studies* 31.3 (summer 1991): 31–50.
54. Midgley, "Prophetic Messages," 100.

55. A. S. Hayden, *History of the Disciples in the Western Reserve, Ohio* (Cincinatti: Chase & Hall, 1876), 71.

56. Joseph Smith, Jr., *History of the Church of Jesus Christ of Latter-day Saints*, 7 vols., eds. James Mulholland, Robert B. Thompson, William W. Phelps, Willard Richards, George A. Smith, and later B. H. Roberts (Salt Lake City: Deseret News Press, 1902–12; 2nd rev. ed., Salt Lake City: Deseret Book, 1951), 1:62.

57. The expression is from Scott H. Faulring. See his excellent study of the subject, "The Book of Mormon: A Blueprint for Organizing the Church," *Journal of Book of Mormon Studies* 7.1 (1998): 60–71.

58. Faulring, "Blueprint," 65–69.

59. B. H. Roberts, *The Seventy's Course in Theology*, 5 vols. (Salt Lake City: Deseret News, 1911), 4:113–14.

60. Announced by Boyd K. Packer in the October 1982 General Conference in his address, "Scriptures."

61. Susan Easton Black, *Finding Christ Through the Book of Mormon* (Salt Lake City: Deseret Book, 1987), 10–34.

62. Robert Matthews, "What the Book of Mormon Tells Us About Jesus Christ," in Paul R. Cheesman, S. Kent Brown, Charles D. Tate Jr., eds., *The Book of Mormon: The Keystone Scripture* (Provo, Utah: Brigham Young University, Religious Studies Center, 1988), 33.

63. Dan Vogel finds an instance of "one outsider [who] commented on the Book of Mormon's unorthodox view of God." But that person was himself a "binitarian" associated with the "Christian Connection"—not exactly a representative of normative Christianity. Dan Vogel, "The Earliest Mormon Concept of God," in Gary James Bergera, ed., *Line Upon Line: Essays on Mormon Doctrine* (Salt Lake City: Signature Books, 1989), 20–21.

64. In the 1837 edition, the words "Son of" were inserted before "God" in four verses: 1 Nephi 11:19; 11:21; 11:32; and 13:40. This change is clearly less than revisionist when one considers that in 1 Nephi and elsewhere, "Son of God" was already present as a common Book of Mormon formulation.

65. Thomas G. Alexander, "The Reconstruction of Mormon Doctrine: From Joseph Smith to Progressive Theology," *Sunstone* 5 (July–August 1980): 24–33, and *Mormonism in Transition: A History of the Latter-day Saints, 1890–1930* (Urbana: University of Illinois Press, 1986), chap. 14. An excellent critique of Alexander's position is David L. Paulsen, "The Doctrine of Divine Embodiment: Restoration, Judeo-Christian, and Philosophical Perspectives," *BYU Studies* 35.4 (1996): 7–94. See also Robert L. Millet, "Jesus Christ, Fatherhood and Sonship of," in Daniel Ludlow, ed., *Encyclopedia of Mormonism*, 4 vols. (New York: Macmillan, 1992), 2:739–40.

66. Melodie Moench Charles, "Book of Mormon Christology," in Brent Metcalfe, ed., *New Approaches to the Book of Mormon: Explorations in Critical Methodology* (Salt Lake City: Signature Books, 1993), 81; Mark Thomas, "A Rhetorical Approach to the Book of Mormon: Rediscovering Nephite Sacramental Language," in Metcalfe, *New Approaches*, 58.

67. A few days before his own death, Smith affirmed that he had "always declared God to be a distinct personage, Jesus Christ a separate and dis-

tinct personage from God the Father, and the Holy Ghost a distinct personage or spirit, and these three constitute three distinct personages and three Gods." Andrew F. Ehat and Lyndon W. Cook, eds., *The Words of Joseph Smith* (Provo, Utah: Brigham Young University, Religious Studies Center, Brigham Young University, 1980), 378. Joseph's clearest pronouncement on the subject would come in his 1843 revelation that declared, "The Father has a body of flesh and bones as tangible as man's; the Son also; but the Holy Ghost has not a body of flesh and bones, but is a personage of Spirit" (D&C 130:22).

68. The Greek term, meaning "of the same substance as," was used in the Nicene creed to express the interrelations of the members of the godhead. It had made an earlier appearance in Gnostic thought.

69. First Presidency and the Council of the Twelve Apostles of the Church of Jesus Christ of Latter-day Saints. "The Father and the Son: A Doctrinal Exposition by the First Presidency and the Twelve." In James E. Talmage, *A Study of the Articles of Faith*, (Salt Lake City: Deseret Book, 1973), 471. The statement has its roots in the 1890s although it was first publicly released in 1912 .

70. Clyde Forsberg argues in a master's thesis that the Book of Mormon christology has elements of Arianism, Trinitarianism, Sabellianism, and inverted Sabellianism, but is largely Sabellian (or modalistic). "The Roots of Early Mormonism: An Exegetical Inquiry," M.A. thesis, University of Calgary, 1990, cited in Charles, "Christology," in Metcalfe, *New Approaches*, 98. To this litany, a Mormon apostle and former president of Brigham Young University replies, "Is this said with a straight face?" Jeffrey R. Holland, "A Standard unto My People," Church Educational Symposium, Brigham Young University, August 9, 1994. A. Bruce Lindgren also argues strongly that the Book of Mormon's doctrine of deity is "modalistic Monarchianism" in "Sign or Scripture: Approaches to the Book of Mormon," *Dialogue* 19.1 (September 1986): 73.

71. Charles, "Christology," in Metcalfe, *New Approaches*, 99.

72. Robert L. Millet, "Joseph Smith and Modern Mormonism: Orthodoxy, Neoorthodoxy, Tension, and Tradition" *BYU Studies* 29.3 (summer 1989): 53. As Millet cites Bernhard Lohse: "one does not find in [the New Testament] an actual doctrine of the Trinity;" it was "well into the fourth century before the doctrine of the Trinity was dogmatically clarified" (53). See Lohse's *A Short History of Christian Doctrine* (Philadelphia: Fortress, 1966), 37, 38. See also R. L. Richard's assertion that "among Apostolic Fathers, there had been nothing even remotely approaching such a mentality or perspective." R. L. Richard, "Trinity, Holy," *New Catholic Encyclopedia* (New York: McGraw-Hill, 1967), 14:299.

73. Charles, "Christology," in Metcalfe, *New Approaches*, 100.

74. Marvin S. Hill, *Quest for Refuge: The Mormon Flight from American Pluralism* (Salt Lake City: Signature Books, 1989), 21.

75. Alexander, "The Reconstruction of Mormon Doctrine," 24–33.

76. Famous expressions of this principle include St. Athanasius's dictum that "the Word became flesh . . . that we, partaking of His Spirit, might be deified," and the teaching of Irenaeus that "as God shared our life in the

Incarnation, so we are destined to share the Divine life and 'become what he is.'" See "Deification," in F. L. Cross and E. A. Livingstone, eds., *Oxford Dictionary of the Christian Church* (Oxford: Oxford University Press, 1997), 465.

77. J. Frederic Voros Jr., "Was the Book of Mormon Buried with King Follett?," *Sunstone* 11:2 (March 1987): 15–18.

78. Voros, "Was the Book of Mormon Buried," 16. At the same time, it is important to note another passage that suggests a view of man almost Rousseauean in its optimism. In arguing for elected judges, King Benjamin reasons that "it is not common that the voice of the people desireth anything contrary to that which is right; but it is common for the lesser part of the people to desire that which is not right; therefore this shall ye observe and make it your law—to do your business by the voice of the people" (Mosiah 29:26).

79. Lindgren, "Sign or Scripture," 73. See also his "Sin and Redemption in the Book of Mormon," *Restoration Studies II* (Independence, Mo.: Herald House, 1983), 201–06.

80. Moses 6:51; Abraham 3:22, *Pearl of Great Price.*

81. Moses 5:10–11, *Pearl of Great Price.*

82. See also Alma 42:5: "For behold, if Adam had put forth his hand immediately and partaken of the tree of life, he would have lived forever, according to the word of God, having no space for repentance; . . . and the great plan of salvation would have been frustrated."

83. "Atonement," in Cross and Livingstone, *Oxford Dictionary of the Christian Church*, 123.

84. Lindgren, "Sign or Scripture," 73.

EIGHT

1. Rodney Needham, *Belief, Language, and Experience* (Chicago: University of Chicago Press, 1972).

2. Needham, *Belief, Language, and Experience*, 15.

3. Evan-Pritchard, *Nuer Religion* (Oxford: Oxford University Press, 1956), vi, cited in Needham, *Belief, Language, and Experience*, 19.

4. Bob Witte, *Where Does it Say That?* (Grant Rapids, Mich.: Gospel Truths, n.d.), 13–1.

5. Avery Dulles, S. J., *Models of Revelation* (New York: Doubleday, 1983), 27–28. Two less historically significant models are "revelation as dialectical presence," as developed by a group of post-World War I theologians, that emphasizes the utter transcendence of God and the word of God that "simultaneously reveals and conceals the divine presence," and "revelation as new awareness," that more recent theologians have postulated as "an expansion of consciousness or shift of perspective when people join in the movements of secular history."

6. John Baillie, *The Idea of Revelation* (New York: Columbia University Press, 1956), 29.

7. Clark H. Pinnock, *A Defense of Biblical Infallibility* (Philadelphia: Presbyterian and Reformed Publishing, 1967), 4n15, in William J. Abraham, *Divine Revelation and the Limits of Historical Criticism* (New York: Oxford University Press, 1982), 22.

8. John Lawson, *Comprehensive Handbook of Christian Doctrine* (Englewood Cliffs, N.J.: Prentice-Hall, 1967), 24.

9. Baillie, *Idea of Revelation*, 62.

10. Albrecht Oepke quoted in Baillie, *Idea of Revelation*, 28–29.

11. John Knox, *Our Knowledge of God* (New York: Scribner's, 1939), 175–77.

12. In Nicholas Wolterstorff, *Divine Discourse: Philosophical Reflections on the Claim that God Speaks* (Cambridge: Cambridge University Press, 1995), 8–9.

13. Dulles, *Models of Revelation*, 70–71.

14. George Tyrrell, *Through Scylla and Charybdis* (London: Longmans, Green, 1907), 326–27; A. Sabatier, *Outlines of a Philosophy of Religion Based on Psychology and History* (London: Hodder & Stoughton, 1897), 35; W. E. Hocking, *The Meaning of God in Human Experience* (New Haven: Yale University Press, 1963), 448. All cited in Dulles, *Models of Revelation*, 72–73.

15. Baillie, *Idea of Revelation*, 28.

16. Nahum N. Glatzer, *Franz Rosenzweig: His Life and Thought* (Philadelphia: Jewish Publication Society, 1953), 285; Martin Buber, *Eclipse of God* (New York: Harper, 1952), 173f. Both cited in Jakob J. Petuchowski, *Studies in Modern Theology and Prayer*, ed. Elizabeth R. Petuchowski and Aaron M Petuchowski (Philadelphia: Jewish Publication Society, 1998), 101.

17. Dulles, *Models of Revelation*, 70.

18. Dulles, *Models of Revelation*, 73. Dulles himself as much as agrees, claiming weakly that since the two prior models are grounded in historically circumscribed events, this model, "in its acceptance of continuing revelation . . . contrasts with the two preceding models."

19. Abraham, *Divine Revelation*, 8–9.

20. Baillie, *Idea of Revelation*, 3–15; William Abraham agrees that in this era, "interest centered less on the nature of revelation than on its necessity" (*Divine Revelation*, 8). Compare this development with Kaufmann Kohler's account of revelation in Judaism, where "this supernatural element disappears gradually and passes over into sober, self-conscious thought, in which the writer no longer thinks of God as the Ego speaking through him." *Jewish Theology* (New York: Macmillan, 1918), 39, cited in Petuchowski, *Studies in Modern Theology*, 102.

21. C. Wilfred Griggs, "Rediscovering Ancient Christianity," *BYU Studies* 38.4 (1999): 73–90. Griggs notes that one of the earliest Christian controversies, the Valentinian Crisis, was precipitated when that popular Alexandrian "claimed to have received his doctrine through revelatory experience" (74).

22. Abraham, *Divine Revelation*, 189, 10.

23. *The Evening and the Morning Star* 1.2 (July 1832): 13.

24. Charles B. Thompson, *Evidences in Proof of the Book of Mormon Being a Divinely Inspired Record* (Batavia, N.Y.: D.D. Waite, 1841), 149–67.

25. A. N. Wilson, *God's Funeral* (New York: Norton, 1999), 19.

26. Samuel Taylor Coleridge, *Aids to Reflection*, ed. John Beer, in *The Collected Works of Samuel Taylor Coleridge*, 14 vols. (Princeton: Princeton University Press, 1969–), 9:78–79.

27. Eddie Lo, *Horace Bushnell's Religious Epistemology in Relation to His Major Christian Doctrines: A Historical, Philosophical, and Theological Consideration* (Ph.D. diss., Claremont, 1977), 155.

28. Baillie, *Idea of Revelation*, 148.

29. Baillie, *Idea of Revelation*, 26.

30. Walter Eichrodt, *Theology of the Old Testament*, trans. J. A. Baker (London: SCM Press, 1961), 209, 211, cited in Edmond LaB. Cherbonnier, "In Defense of Anthropomorphism," in Truman G. Madsen, ed., *Reflections on Mormonism: Judeo-Christian Parallels* (Provo, Utah: Brigham Young University, Religious Studies Center, 1978), 161.

31. Abraham, *Divine Revelation*, 21.

32. Abraham, *Divine Revelation*, 11.

33. Wolterstorff, *Divine Discourse*, 10.

34. Sandra M. Schneider, *The Revelatory Text* (San Francisco: Harper, 1991), 27–29, cited in Wolterstorff, *Divine Discourse*, 10. He does cite a contrary view of Karl Barth that "we have no reason not to take the concept of God's word primarily in its literal sense" (*Church Dogmatics* I/I, 132). Some contemporaries of Joseph Smith saw the body-speech problem in similar terms but from the other side of orthodoxy. In addition to criticizing Mormons, Hiram Mattison cites the heretical view of William Kinkade (1783–1832) that "Ears, hands, and eyes, are part of an intelligent ruler, and if God has none of these he cannot hear, handle, nor see us." *A Scriptural Defence of the Doctrine of the Trinity, or a Check to Modern Arianism as Taught by Campbellites, Hicksites, etc.* (New York: 1846), 44.

35. Rev. Edward Bickersteth, *A Treatise on Prayer; Designed to Assist the Devout in the Discharge of that Duty* (New York: American Tract Society, n.d.), 186–87. The book had at least 20 printings during its author's life (1786–1850).

36. Edward Gee, *A Treatise on Prayer* (London: 1653), cited in Bickersteth, *Treatise on Prayer*, 187.

37. Lord Byron, *Manfred*, in *The Complete Poetical Works of Lord Byron* (Boston and New York: Houghton Mifflin, 1905), 490.

38. Bickersteth, *Treatise on Prayer*, 183.

39. James Freeman Clarke, *The Christian Doctrine of Prayer* (1854; reprint, Boston: American Unitarian Association, 1890), 166, xi.

40. Rodney Stark, "A Theory of Revelations," *Journal for the Scientific Study of Religion* 38.2 (1999): 289.

41. William James, *The Varieties of Religious Experience* (Cambridge, Mass.: Harvard University Press, 1985), 373.

42. Abraham, *Divine Revelation*, 24.

43. Wolterstorff, *Divine Discourse*, 8.

44. As Alan Grossman has written, "Men conserve Scripture, first, as the final map of all reality and, then, as the possibility of any mapping of reality which time and the accidents of historicity—the general rage against meaning—threaten to snatch from the hand." Alan Grossman, "Summa

Lyrica: A Primer of the Commonplaces in Speculative Poetics," in *The Sighted Singer: Two Works on Poetry for Readers and Writers*, with Mark Halliday (Baltimore: Johns Hopkins Press, 1992), 245. Ian Barbour, more simply, describes the function of religious language as providing models that "are used in the interpretation of experience." *Myths, Models, and Paradigms: A Comparative Study in Science and Religion* (New York: Harper & Row, 1971), 57.

45. Rebekah is one notable exception. Bewildered by the twins struggling in her womb, "she went to enquire of the Lord. And the Lord said unto her . . . " (Gen 25:23).

46. "Prophecy," in F. L. Cross and E. A. Livingstone, eds., *Oxford Dictionary of the Christian Church* (Oxford: Oxford University Press, 1997), 1336.

47. Abraham Heschel, *The Prophets* (New York: Harper & Row, 1962), xviii.

48. Welch details the chiastic elements in "Chiasmus in the Book of Mormon," in *Chiasmus in Antiquity* (1981; reprint, Provo, Utah: Research Press, 1999), 199–200.

49. Though the term usually refers to the gospel in general, or its new inclusivity, it can also refer to particular truths of that gospel, as it does for Paul: "Behold, I shew you a mystery; We shall not all sleep, but we shall all be changed. . . " (1 Cor. 15:51).

50. Baillie, *Idea of Revelation*, 28.

51. Joseph Smith Jr., *History of the Church of Jesus Christ of Latter-day Saints*, 7 vols., eds. James Mulholland, Robert B. Thompson, William W. Phelps, Willard Richards, George A. Smith and later B. H. Roberts (Salt Lake City: Deseret News Press, 1902–12; 2nd rev. ed., Salt Lake City: Deseret Book, 1951), 6:58.

52. James R. Clark, ed., *Messages of the First Presidency* (Salt Lake City: Bookcraft, 1965), 4:285.

53. Shlomo Biderman, *Scripture and Knowledge: An Essay on Religious Epistemology* (New York: Brill, 1995), 11.

54. *The Evening and the Morning Star* 1.2 (July 1832): 13.

55. *The Evening and the Morning Star* 1.3 (August 1832): 22.

56. Thomas G. Alexander, "Wilford Woodruff and the Changing Nature of Mormon Religious Experience," *Church History* (March 1976): 61.

57. David Reese, *Humbugs of New York* (New York: J. S. Taylor, 1838).

58. Walter Scott, *The Heart of Midlothian* (New York: Penguin, 1994), 471–72.

59. Scott, *Heart of Midlothian*, 472.

60. Harriet Martineau, *Society in America* (London: Saunders & Otley, 1837), 1:2–3.

61. Ronald W. Walker, "The Persisting Idea of American Treasure Hunting," *BYU Studies* 24.4 (fall 1984): 430.

62. Timothy Smith, "The Book of Mormon in a Biblical Culture," *Journal of Mormon History* 7 (1980): 6.

63. Dan Vogel, *Religious Seekers and the Advent of Mormonism* (Salt Lake City: Signature Books, 1988), 90. Vogel has been criticized for reifying the generic "seekers"—"spiritual nomads of [any age]" into a sect or movement of Joseph Smith's day. Grant Underwood, review of Vogel's *Religious Seekers*, *BYU Studies* 30.1 (winter 1990): 120.

64. Gordon S. Wood, "Evangelical America and Early Mormonism," *New York History* 61 (October 1980): 364, 367, 361. Wood's is a thorough treatment of the pervasive demand, voiced by the Baptist Elias Smith in 1809, to be "wholly free to examine for ourselves, what is truth" (374).

65. Wood, "Evangelical America," 368.

66. Alan Taylor, "Rediscovering the Context of Joseph Smith's Treasure Seeking," *Dialogue* 19.4 (winter 1986): 22.

67. I. Woodbridge Riley, *The Founder of Mormonism: A Psychological Study of Joseph Smith, Jr.* (New York: Dodd, Meade, 1903), 238.

68. A. S. Hayden, *Early History of the Disciples in the Western Reserve, Ohio* (Cincinatti: Chase & Hall, 1876), 197, 209–18. Cited in Hyrum L. Andrus, "The Second American Revolution: Era of Preparation," *BYU Studies* 1.2 (autumn 1959): 82.

69. Wood, "Evangelical America," 371.

70. John G. Gager, "Early Mormonism and Early Christianity: Some Parallels and Their Consequences for the Study of New Religions," *Journal of Mormon History* 9 (1982): 58.

71. Alexander, "Wilford Woodruff," 61.

72. G. Adolph Koch, *Religion of the American Enlightenment* (New York: Crowell, 1968), 286.

73. *Theophilanthropist*, 278, 338 in Koch, *Religion*, 181, 183.

74. Alexander Campbell, "Delusions: An Analysis of the Book of Mormon," *Millennial Harbinger* II (7 February 1831): 85–96. Reprinted in part in Francis W. Kirkham, *A New Witness for Christ in America*, 2 vols. (Independence, Mo.: Zion's Printing and Publishing, 1951), 2:101–109.

75. Gilbert Wardlaw, *The Testimony of Scripture to the Obligations and Efficacy of Prayer* (Boston: Peirce & Williams, 1830), 97.

76. Stark, "Theory of Revelations," 292.

77. John Cotton, *A Treatise of the Covenant of Grace* (1636), cited in Michael G. Ditmore, "A Prophetess in Her Own Country: An Exegesis of Anne Hutchinson's 'Immediate Revelation,'" *William and Mary Quarterly* 57.2 (April 2000): 353.

78. Wardlaw, *Testimony of Scripture*, v–vi.

79. Wardlaw, *Testimony of Scripture*, 8, 59.

80. John Wesley, "Scripturalizing Christianity," *Works* 5:37–38, cited in Smith, "Book of Mormon in a Biblical Culture," 16.

81. Craig L. Blomberg and Stephen E. Robinson, *How Wide the Divide: A Mormon and an Evangelical in Conversation* (Downers Grove, Ill: InterVarsity Press, 1997), 40.

82. W. D. Davies, ""Reflections on the Mormon 'Canon,'" *Harvard Theological Review* 79 (January 1986): 64n.

83. The First Vision "undergirds the doctrine of an anthropomorphic God and theomorphic man, [and] of the relationships of the persons of the Godhead." Milton V. Backman, "The First Vision," *Encyclopedia of Mormonism* (New York: Macmillan, 1992), 2:516.

84. Gordon B. Hinckley, Salt Lake Bonneville Stake Conference Address (November 23, 1997), quoted in *LDS Church News, Deseret News*, March 7, 1998.

85. Martin Marty, "Two Integrities: An Address to the Crisis in Mormon Historiography" in George D. Smith, ed., *Faithful History: Essays on Writing
Mormon History* (Salt Lake City: Signature Books, 1992), 186–87.

86. Susan Easton Black, *Stories from the Early Saints Converted by the Book of
Mormon* (Salt Lake City: Bookcraft, 1992), 64.

87. Grant Underwood, "The Meaning and Attraction of Mormonism Reexamined," *Thetean* (March 1977): 2–3.

88. Journal of Joseph Grafton Hovey, Special Collections, Harold B. Lee Library, Brigham Young University, Provo, Utah, quoted in Underwood,
"Meaning and Attraction," 3.

89. Black, *Stories from the Early Saints*, 71–72.

90. Shurtliff's experience has an echo in the contemporary story, printed by
the official LDS magazine, of a Yugoslavian woman who gained fervent
conviction of the Book of Mormon's truthfulness though her copy was
printed in a language she could not read: she had "looked through the
book and studied the pictures and . . . prayed about the truthfulness of
the book as I had told her Moroni had admonished readers to do." Arlin
P. Neser, "A Witness from the Holy Ghost," *Ensign* 4.7 (July 1984): 24.

91. Black, *Stories from the Early Saints*, 85.

92. Richard Bushman, *Joseph Smith and the Beginnings of Mormonism* (Urbana:
University of Illinois Press, 1984), 141.

93. *Biographical Sketches of Joseph Smith the Prophet, and his Progenitors for Many
Generations* (Liverpool, 1853; reprint, Arno Press, 1969), 146–47.

94. M. Richard Maxfield, "The Book of Mormon and the Conversion Process
to the Church of Jesus Christ of Latter-day Saints: A Study of Recent Converts" (Ph.D. diss., Brigham Young University, 1977), 70.

95. The Painsville articles are collected in Kirkham, *A New Witness for Christ*
and are quoted by Bushman, *Joseph Smith*, 123.

96. Bushman, *Joseph Smith*, 6.

97. Martin Shee, in *Elements of Art* (1809), quoted by Samuel H. Monk, *The
Sublime* (Ann Arbor: University of Michigan Press, 1960), 3.

98. Steven C. Harper, "Infallible Proofs, Both Human and Divine: The Persuasiveness of Mormonism for Early Converts," *Religion and American Culture*
10.1 (winter 2000): 101. His work, like Bushman's, is a powerful corrective
to the nineteenth-century propaganda that had Mormonism drawing its
converts "from the ranks of the superstitious and the gullible."

99. J. F. C. Harrison, *The Second Coming: Popular Millenarianism, 1780–1850* (New
Brunswick, N.J.: 1979), 191. Cited in Wood, "Evangelical America," 380.

NINE

1. The church editor would have been well-advised to learn from the history of "Yankee" and comparable terms of intended reproach. For it was
not long at all before the disdainful designation was wholeheartedly embraced by the rank and file of the church. So much so, in fact, that by the
1980s, the LDS first presidency and other leaders were asking members
not to refer to themselves as Mormons. See *Member-Missionary Class—*

Instructor's Guide (Salt Lake City: The Church of Jesus Christ of Latter-day Saints, 1982), 2. As recently as 2001, the church initiated another series of press releases and a letter to members in which they "discourage referring to the church as 'The Mormon Church.'" Letter of First Presidency, February 23, 2001.

2. Amos N. Merrill and Alton D. Merrill, "Changing Thought on the Book of Mormon," *Improvement Era* 45 (September 1945): 568.

3. Noel B. Reynolds, "The Coming Forth of the Book of Mormon in the Twentieth Century," *BYU Studies* 38.2 (1999): 8. The two studies are Grant Underwood, "Book of Mormon Usage in Early LDS Theology," *Dialogue* 17:3 (autumn 1984), 35–74; and Alton D. Merrill, "An Analysis of the Papers and Speeches of Those Who Have Written or Spoken about the Book of Mormon, Published during the Years of 1830 to 1855 and 1915 to 1940, to Ascertain the Shift of Emphasis" (Master's thesis, Brigham Young University, 1940).

4. Reynolds, "Coming Forth," 7, 28, 32, 10.

5. See Karen Lynn Davidson's survey of the subject in "The Book of Mormon in Latter-day Saint Hymnody," *Journal of Book of Mormon Studies* 9.1 (2000): 14–27.

6. "Flooding the Earth with the Book of Mormon," *Ensign* 18.11 (November 1988): 4–5. Benson is here quoting Moses 7:62 (from *Pearl of Great Price*).

7. "Flooding," 4. Benson here quotes Joseph Smith Jr., *History of the Church of Jesus Christ of Latter-day Saints*, 7 vols., eds. James Mulholland, Robert B. Thompson, William W. Phelps, Willard Richards, George A. Smith, and later B. H. Roberts (Salt Lake City: Deseret News Press, 1902–12; 2nd rev. ed., Salt Lake City: Deseret Book, 1951), 4:461.

8. Sydney Ahlstrom, *A Religious History of the American People* (New Haven: Yale University Press, 1972), 504.

9. The year 2000 ended with 60,784 missionaries in the field and 273, 973 converts baptized. *Deseret News*, April 1, 2001.

10. The program was officially sponsored in 1954, largely under the guidance of Spencer W. Kimball, whose ministry was characterized by particular concern for modern-day "Lamanites." Despite its popularity with those Native American families involved, shifting political winds and charges of its "cultural immorality" on the one hand, and improved reservation schools on the other, led to the program's demise in the 1990s. See the overview by James B. Allen, "The Rise and Decline of the LDS Indian Student Placement Program, 1947–1996," in Davis Bitton, ed., *Mormons, Scripture, and the Ancient World: Studies in Honor of John L. Sorenson* (Provo, Utah: FARMS, 1998), 85–119.

11. Truman G. Madsen, "B. H. Roberts and the Book of Mormon," *BYU Studies* 19.4 (summer 1979): 435.

12. For literary examples inspired by the Book of Mormon, see Donald W. Parry, Jeanette W. Miller, and Sandra A. Thorne, *A Comprehensive Annotated Book of Mormon Bibliography* (Provo, Utah: Research Press, 1996). The most accomplished artist in this area was Minerva Teichert, whose paintings are reproduced in John W. Welch and Doris R. Dant, *The Book of Mor-*

mon Paintings of Minerva Teichert (Provo and Salt Lake City: BYU Studies and Bookcraft, 1997).

13. B. H. Roberts, *Comprehensive History of the Church of Jesus Christ of Latter-day Saints* (Provo, Utah: Church of Jesus Christ of Latter-day Saints, 1957), 6:524–26.

14. Richard O. Cowan, *The Church in the Twentieth Century* (Salt Lake City, Utah: Bookcraft, 1985), 168.

15. *LDS Church News, Deseret News,* July 19, 1997.

16. "The Testaments of One Fold and One Shepherd" opened March 24, 2000, and shows nine times daily in a 500-seat theater.

17. John Sorenson, *Images of Ancient America: Visualizing Book of Mormon Life* (Provo, Utah: Research Press, 1998).

18. "An Open Letter to Those Who Are Concerned about 'Plagiarism' in The Memory of Earth." (privately printed, 1993). The series is *Homecoming* (New York: Tor, 1992–96).

19. Nicholas Wolterstorff, "God is Everlasting," in C. Orlebeke and L. Smedes, eds., *God and the Good* (Grand Rapids, Mich.: Eerdmans, 1975), 202.

20. Wolterstorff, "God is Everlasting," 183.

21. The statement, attributed to Charles H. Hull, is cited in *Millennial Star* 89 (1927): 682.

22. Robert N. Hullinger, *Mormon Answer to Skepticism: Why Joseph Smith Wrote the Book of Mormon* (St. Louis: Clayton Publishing House, 1980), xiii.

23. Harold Bloom, *The American Religion: The Emergence of the Post-Christian Nation* (New York: Simon & Schuster, 1992), 80.

24. Richard L. Bushman, "The Secret History of Mormonism," *Sunstone* (March 1996), 66–70. Compare Rodney Stark's criticism of Max Weber: "When Weber wrote that 'We shall understand "prophet" to mean a purely individual bearer of charisma,' he said nothing more than that charismatics have charisma." "A Theory of Revelations," *Journal for the Scientific Study of Religion* 38.2 (1999): 304.

25. Orson Pratt, 13 April 1856, in *Journal of Discourses*, 26 vols., reported by G. D. Watt et al. (Liverpool: F. D. and S. W. Richards et al., 1851–1886; reprint, Salt Lake City: n.p., 1974), 3:347.

26. Oliver Cowdery, *Messenger and Advocate* 1.5 (February 1835): 80.

Index

Abinadi, 200
Abraham, William, 213, 215, 218
Ackerwood, Karl, 101
Adair, James, *History of the American Indians*, 94
Adam
  fall of, 47, 203–4
  taught faith and baptism, 48
Ahlstrom, Sydney, 242
Albright, William Foxwell, 113, 114, 119-20
Alexander, Thomas G., 200, 202, 229
Alma
  as LDS name, 243
  as Semitic name, **140**, 144, 283n
Alma the Younger
  and wordprint studies, 156–57
  as prophet and high priest, 52, 225, 226
  miraculously converted, 133, 172–73
  on mysteries of God, 118
  on atonement, 205–7
  on human nature, 202
  on premortality, 203
  on spiritual knowledge, 223
  on the godhead, 200
  prophesies of Christ, 144, 165, 199
Alter, Robert, 179
Amaleki, 226

Amarna letters, 283n
American Indians
  and LDS student placement program, 308n
  Book of Mormon as history of, 51, 61, 95, 98, 99, 101, 127
  Israelite connection to, 94, 161, 299n
  missionary work among, 65, 70
  origins of, 93–94, 93–94, 115, 143, 148–49, 167
  role in LDS thought, 68, 193, 243
Ammon, 223-24
Anselm of Canterbury, 165
Anthon, Charles, **29**–30, 255n
anthropomorphism
  and heresy, 78, 79, 213, 304n
  and revelation, 215
  in LDS theology, 217–18, 301n, 306n
anti-Catholicism, 164, 290n
apocrypha, 152, 253n
archaeology, 96
  and the Bible, 89–90
  and the Book of Mormon, 96, 98–108, 111–15, 120, 127, 128, 130–32, 141, 142, 145–47, 148–50, 152, 154–55
  of Bible and Book of Mormon compared, 90, 141, 147–48, 177

Armillas, Pedro, 114
Arminianism, 164, 202
Articles of Faith, 197, 247n, 262n
Ashment, Edward, 135, 274n
atonement, 165, 198, 205–7
Augustine, 75, 218

Backman, Milton V., Jr., 31
Baillie, John, 210-13, 215, 223
Bakhtin, Mikhail, 80
Barbour, Ian, 305n
barley, 116, 141, 142, 143
Battle Scroll, 123
Bengel, J. A., 125
Benson, Ezra Taft, 86, 87, 241
Benz, Ernst Wilhelm, 6
Bernhisel, John M., 101
Berry, Wendell, 180
Bickersteth, Edward, 216
    Treatise on Prayer, 304n
Biderman, Shlomo, 4, 87, 226
Bloom, Harold, 5, 6, 170, 246
Boehme, Jacob, 73–75, 76, 79
Boggs, Lilburn, 3
Book of Abraham, 170, 192, 203, 240
Book of Commandments, 135, 192, 240
Book of Mormon
    1830 edition, **59**
    1879 edition, 106
    1920 edition, 108
    anachronisms in, 141–42, 278n
    and doctrine of atonement, 205–7
    and Mesoamerican archaeology,
        100, 99–103
    as biblical plagiarism, 31, 135–38,
        259n
    as sign of second coming, 66–68
    as template for church doctrine,
        197–98
    biblical prophecies of, 43, 63, 95
    boycott threatened, 58–60, 260n
    civilizations of, 96
    compared to Bible, 51, 176–77
    critical text project, 287n
    early media accounts, 50, 58, 91–92
    early reception, 60–61, 157
    geography, **129**, 126–30, 260n

    Hebraisms in, 133–35, 280n
    in early Mormon preaching, 84–85,
        236
    in hymnody, 244
    Jesus Christ in, 47, 48–49, 199–201,
        267n
    limited geography of, 277n
    manuscript described, 31, **57**
    objections addressed to B. H. Rob-
        erts, 109
    on fall of man, 203–5
    partial manuscript lost, 33–34,
        257n
    population issues in, 139–40
    proper names in, 119–20, 140–41,
        144, 274n
    prophesies of three witnesses, 39,
        257n
    rate of translation, 37, 257n
    relationship of to Bible, 189–91
    reputation among archaeologists,
        145–47
    scholarly neglect of, 6, 148–50
    sealed portion, 246
    statistics, 5, 11, 247n, 249n
    structure of, 51–53
    summary of, 44–45
    theological contributions of, 198
    title page described, 268n
    translation order, 257n
    translation process, 32, 30–33,
        255n, 256n
    unity of, 259n
Book of the Bee, 47
Boudinot, Elias, *A Star in the West*, 94
Bradish, Luther, 29
brass plates, 45, 53, 136, 253n
Bridgeman, Peter, 19
Brigham Young University, 5, 112,
    153, 241
Brodie, Fawn, 5, 73, 157, 159, 161,
    163–64, 202
Brooke, John, 5, 170
Brooks, Juanita, 155
brother of Jared, 220, 224, 243, 246
Buber, Martin, 212
Burke, Edmund, 79
Burton, Richard, 85

Bushman, Richard, 9, 72, 143, 153, 174, 236, 237–38, 246
Bushnell, Horace, 214
Byron, Lord (George Gordon), 178

Caiaphas, 89
Calvinism, 164, 202, 205
Cambuslang Revival, 41–42, 79
Campbell, Alexander, 67, 69, 70, 157, 159, 232, 238
  Delusions: An Analysis of the Book of Mormon, 163
Campbellites, 70, 71, 106, 159
Card, Orson Scott, 244
Catherwood, Frederick, 99, **100**
cement, 97, 103, 141, 142
Center for the Preservation of Ancient Religious Texts (CPART), 151–52
Chamberlain, Solomon, 58
Charles, Melodie Moench, 200
Charlesworth, James, 5, 124, 171, 172, 276n
Chase, Willard, 16, 25, 26, 251n, 252n
Chatterton, Thomas, 178
Cheesman, Paul R., Ancient America Speaks, 115
Chesterton, G. K., 155
Chiapas, Mexico, 101, 129, 146
chiasmus, 125, 133, 173, 222
Church of Jesus Christ of Latter-day Saints
  growth of, 11, 250n, 283n
  mortality rates of members, 139, 282n
  names of, 240, 261n
  organized, 36, 260n
  persecution against, 27, 37, 62, 68, 98, 247n, 261n
  statistics, 308n
Clarke, Adam, 23
Cluff expedition, 107–8, 272n
Coe, Michael, 146, 273n, 284n
Coit, T. W., 29
Cole, Abner, 58, 94
Colesville, New York, 19, 21, 260
Coleridge, Samuel T., 75, 214
Copan, 100, 101, 103

Copper Scroll, 123
Corianton, 205, 207, 225, 244
Cotton, John, 232
Couch, "Mr.", 109
Cowdery, Oliver, **40**
  attempts to translate Book of Mormon, 32
  describes resting place of gold plates, 103
  designated First Elder in the Church, 36
  excommunicated, 41
  introduces David Whitmer to Mormonism, 56
  on Book of Mormon, 95
  on Joseph Smith's initial failure to obtain plates, 15
  on sealed portion of Book of Mormon, 246
  one of three witness to gold plates, 39
  receives Aaronic Priesthood from John the Baptist, 36
  sees Holy Interpreters, 22
  serves as scribe to Joseph Smith, 31, 35
  serves mission to Indians, 70
Cross, Frank Moore, 276n
Cross, Whitney, 163

Dam, Cornelius van, 23
Davies, Nigel, 147
Davies, W. D., 191–92, 196, 233, 276n
Dead Sea Scrolls, 47, 123, 126, **140**, 144, 151, 258n
deification, 186, 202, 302n
Deloria, Vine, Jr., 149
del Rio, Antonio, 102
DeVoto, Bernard, 159
Diamond, Jared, 142
diffusionism, 116, 131, 148–49, 285n–86
Dionysius, 76
directors. See Liahona
Doctrine and Covenants, 73, 192, 194, 195, 240
Dulles, Avery, 210-12
Dupaix, Guillermo, 102
Dwight, Timothy, 69

Eichrodt, Walter, 215
Ekholm, Gordon F., 113
Elephantine, Egypt, 140
Elijah, 48
Eliot, John, 94, 299n
Emerson, Ralph Waldo, 76, 77, 78, 217
Enos, 219-20, 234
Ericksen, E. E., 106
Evening and Morning Star, 240

Farrer, Austin, 118
Feast of Tabernacles, 124
Ferguson, Thomas Stuart, 112–15, 145, 147, 285n
Fiedel, Stuart J., 93
Fields, Weston, 151
Finney, Charles, 72
First Vision
    and LDS anthropomorphism, 306n
    as private experience of Joseph Smith, 9, 10, 21, 84, 249n
    different accounts of, 249n
    in LDS thought, 234, 298n
    in Reorganized LDS thought, 296n
    phenomenology of, 37, 38
    publicized, 16, 103
Fisher, James, 42
folkmagic, 17, 168–70, 251n
Follett, King, 202
Forsberg, Clyde, 201, 301n
Foster, Lawrence, 159
Foundation for Ancient Research and Mormon Studies (FARMS)
    appraisal by evangelicals, 143
    founding of, 124–25
    incorporation into Brigham Young University, 5, 153
    participation in Dead Sea Scrolls Project, 150–51
    role in Book of Mormon studies, 142
    scholars of, 276n
Freedman, David Noel, 170, 276n

Gadianton Robbers, 164
Gager, John, 231
Galindo, Juan, 97

Gee, Edward, *Treatise on Prayer*, 216
Gilbert, John H., 31, **60**
glass, 116, 131
gold plates, 14
    ancient parallels, 121, **122**, 123, 253n–54
    description of, 3
    hefted by Martin Harris, 26
    media accounts, 20
    preserved from Willard Chase gang, 25
    seen by Eight Witnesses, 39–40
    seen by Three Witneses, 39
    transcript of, **29**, 279n
Gookin, Daniel, 93
Gordis, Robert, 47
Gordon, Cyrus, 124
Graham, William A., 87
Grandin, Egbert B., 31, 55, 58-59, 60
Grave Creek Stone, 149, 286n
Great Apostasy, 188–89
Griggs, C. Wilfred, 150
Grijalva River, 114, 129
Grossman, Alan, 304n
Guatemala City, 126

Hale, Isaac, 18, 19, 27
Hale, Reuben, 257n
Hamblin, William, 141
Hansen, Klaus, 84
Harmony, Pennsylvania, 16, 18, 20, **27**, 28, 33, 34, 35, 37, 141
Harper, Steven, 84, 238
Harris, Lucy, 33, 34, 256n
Harris, Martin, **28**
    accepts story of gold plates, 26
    aids Joseph and Emma, 26–27, 254n
    excommunicated, 41
    finances publication of Book of Mormon, **31**, 55
    learns of gold plates, 20
    loses 116 pages of manuscript, 33–34
    markets Book of Mormon, 60
    on Book of Mormon translation process, 32
    one of Three Witnesses to gold plates, 39

Harris, Martin (*continued*)
  serves as Book of Mormon scribe, 30
  tests Joseph Smith, 32
  travels to New York to authenti-
    cate Book of Mormon charac-
    ters, 28–30
Hatch, Nathan, 6
Hayden, A. S., 231
Hegel, G. W. F., 213
Helaman, 52, 178, 226, 243
Henning, Paul, 273n
hermeticism, 5, 143, 170
Heschel, Abraham, 221
Heyerdahl, Thor, 113, 285n
Hill Cumorah, **14**, 19, 21, 55, 63, 104,
    244, 260n
Hill Cumorah Pageant, 244
Hill, Marvin, 66, 164, 174, 202
Hinckley, Gordon B., 153, 234
Hittites, 150
Hocking, William Ernest, 212
Hoffman forgeries, 168, 169, 291n–92
horses, 107, 110, 116, 141, 147
Hovey, Joseph, 186
Howe, Eber D., 29, 160, 167
Hullinger, Robert N., 246
Humboldt, Alexander von, 99, 102, 161
Huns, 141
Hunter, Milton R., 113
Hurlbut, Philastus, 160, 167
Hyde, Orson, 157

Indian Student Placement Program,
    244
Ingersoll, Peter, 19
interpreters. *See also* Urim and
    Thummim
  called Urim and Thummim, 23
  revealed with gold plates, 14
Irenaeus, 47, 302n
Isaiah
  and Book of Mormon authenticity,
    135–37
  and Nephite world view, 45
  as Book of Mormon herald, 66, 85,
    95, 151
  authorship question, 136, 166, 172,
    291n

in Ethan Smith's work, 161, 162
  in the Book of Mormon, 32, 45–46,
    52–53, 200
  in the brass plates, 45
  quoted by Joseph Smith, 193
  quoted by Moroni, 13, 64
Isthmus of Tehuantepec, 129
Ivins, Antoine, 112
Ixtlilxóchitl, Alva, 147

Jakeman, M. Wells, 112
James, William, 75, 78, 175
Jaredites, 50, 51, 54, 91, 92, 96, 106,
    119, 131, 146
Jebb, John, 125
Jesus Christ
  "doctrine of", 197
  and extra-biblical predictions, 47
  appears to Joseph Smith, 9
  in Old Testament prophecy, 13, 45
  pervasiveness in Book of Mormon,
    46–47, 199
  pre-mortal appearance of, 220
  visions of, 42, 72
  visits Nephites, 46, 48–49, 65, 137
Johnson, Samuel, 7

Kant, Immanuel, 213
Kenniwick Man, 149
Kidder, Alfred V., 113
Kimball, Spencer W., 194
Kinderhook plates, 105, 271n, 284n
King Benjamin, 123, 124, 173, 199,
    200, 202, 203
Kirtland, Ohio, 71, 98, 99, 193, 250n,
    258n
Knight, Joseph, Jr., 20
Knight, Joseph, Sr., 16, 20–21, 24
Korihor
  as Egyptian name, 119, 140
  Book of Mormon anti-Christ, 243
Kunin, Seth, 6

Laman, 44, 120, 219, 222, 227, 228,
    243
Laban 52, 136, 160, 219, 243
Lamanites
  as Book of Mormon audience, 92,
    241

Lamanites *(continued)*
  connection to American Indians, 99, 109, 128, 243
  history of, 92, 98, 126, 127, 146, 223
  origin of, 44
  war with Nephites, 45, 54, 139, 225
Lamb, M. T., 139
Lane, George, 249n
Larson, Stan, 31, 136-37, 138
Lawrence, Samuel, 20, 21, 25, 26, 252n, 254n
Lee, Ann, 84
Lehi
  as Middle Eastern man, 120–21
  Book of, 33
  landing site of his party, 99, 104, 106
  leads family from Jerusalem, 44
  members of party, 281n
  possible route through desert, 120
Lemuel, 44, 120, 219, 222, 227, 228, 243
Levinas, Emmanuel, 211
Liahona, 15, 22, 39, 53, 225, 243
Lonergan, Bernard, 175

Mace, Wandle, 185, 196
Macpherson, James, 178, 181
MacRae, George, 124
Madsen, Brigham, 178
Madsen, Truman, 152
Magdalena River, 106, 107
Mani, 3
Marriott, J. Willard, 112–13, 114–15
Marsh, Thomas, 56
Martineau, Harriet, 229
Martyr, Justin, 47
Mason, J. Alden, 114
Masonry, 141, 143, 163–64, 170, 246
Mayas, 101, 103, 141, 142, 148
Mayhew, Jonathan, 117
McConkie, Bruce R., 82
McLellin, William, 70, 87
McMurrin, Sterling, 145, 153
Megiddo, 141
Meroitic script, 133
Messenger and Advocate, 43

Metcalfe, Brent Lee, *New Approaches to the Book of Mormon*, 145, 182
Methodists, 187, 230, 238, 249n, 297n
Meyer, Eduard, 159
Michigan Relics, 108
Midgley, Louis, 174, 197
Milgrom, Jacob, 124, 276n
millennialism, 12, 64, 70–71
Miller, William, 67
Millet, Robert, 201
Mitchell, Samuel, 29
Monet, Claude, 4
Morgan, Dale, 155, 162
Morgan, William, 163
Morley, Isaac, 71
Mormon (Book of Mormon prophet), 50, 51, 53–54
Moroni
  admonitions of, 16, 19, 21
  as angel of Revelation, 245
  as writer/abridger of Book of Mormon, 54–55
  description of, 79
  first visitation, 64
  first visitation of, 11–13
  quotes biblical prophecies, 12–13
  travels of, 99
  yearly visitations of, 15–16
Moroni, Captain, 45
Morse, Michael, 35-36
Mosser, Carl, 143, 145, 151, 182
Mother Goose, 43
mounds, 20, 93, 98, 103, 168
Moyle, James H., 112
Mulder, William, 163
Mulekites, 49-50, 127, 289n
mysticism, 76
  distinctness from prophetic calling, 264n

Nag Hammadi library 151, 152, 276n
Nahom, 120, **121**, 147, 275n
naturalism, 166, 172, 174, 176, 182
Nauvoo Expositor, 73, 88, 264n
Nauvoo, Illinois, 48, 62, 85, 99, 105, 153
Nebuchadrezzar, 44, 62
Needham, Rodney, 209

Nephi
    and prophetic fallibility, 182
    becomes Nephite leader, 139
    describes purpose of Book of Mor-
        mon, 188
    prophesies of last days, 165
    quotes Isaiah, 136
    retrieves brass plates of Laban, 136
Nephites, 44
    as Messianic, 199-200
    become secularized, 52
    beliefs of, 45-46
    described by Joseph Smith, 91
    destroyed, 50, 54, 96
    ruins described, 98-99, 104, 271n
    visited by Christ, 48-49, 65, 201
Neum, 136
Neusner, Jacob, 5, 6, 124
New Jerusalem, 68, 67–68, 69, 68–70,
    193, 196, 263n
New Mormon History, 174–75, 293n–
    94
New World Archaeological Founda-
    tion, 113–15, 147
Nibley, Hugh, 96, 118–24, 150, 284n
Norsemen, 115, 116, 130, 131, 141

O'Dea, Thomas, 86, 163
Oepke, Albrecht, 211
Osmond, Donny, 244
Ostler, Blake, 172, 173
Otto, Rudolf, 78
Owen, Paul, 143, 145, 151, 182
Owen, Robert, 238

Palenque, 100, 102, 104, 271n
Palmyra, New York, 8, 9
Parrot, A., 89
Partridge, Edward, 68
Patai, Raphael, 124
Paulsen, David, 290n
Pearl of Great Price, 192, 194
Peterson, Daniel, 151
Peterson, Ziba, 70
Petuchowski, Jakob, J., 212
Phelps, William W., 23, 63
Pinnock, Clark, 211
Plotinus, 76

Popul Vuh, 147
Pratt, Orson
    compares Book of Mormon to
        Bible, 186
    on Book of Mormon geography,
        105, 127
    on Book of Mormon historicity, 103
    on retrieval of gold plates, 103
    on sealed portion of Book of Mor-
        mon, 246
    prepares 1879 edition of Book of
        Mormon, 106
Pratt, Parley P., 70, 71
Pratt, Rey, 111
pre-mortal existence, 48, 203, 297n
Price, John A., 147
Priest, Josiah
    American Antiquities and Discoveries
        in the West, 96
    The Wonders of Nature and Provi-
        dence, 94
pseudepigrapha, 6, 138, 171

qasida, 120
Quellenlieder, 120
Quinn, D. Michael, 5, 169, 292n
Qumran, 47, 123, 137
Qur'an, 182, 191

Raisanen, Heikki, 6
Raish, Martin, 146
Rameumptom, 243
Rebekkah, 305n
Reese, David, 8
reformed Egyptian
    Charles Anthon's assessment of, 29
    historical parallels to, 119, 120, 133
    Joseph Smith on, 80
    meaning of, 132–33
Reorganized Church of Jesus Christ
        of Latter Day Saints, 126, 183–84
revelation
    and rationalism, 117
    as continuing principle, 49, 192,
        195, 198
    as defunct, 86, 218
    Book of Mormon view as dialogic,
        217–24

Reorganized Church of Jesus Christ
    of Latter Day Saints *(continued)*
  Christian models of, 210–13
  in Judaism, 303n
  in LDS thought, 83, 182, 190, 195,
    224–25, 234–35
  in nineteenth-century America,
    229–31
  in social science, 174
  in thought of William James, 176
  LDS version as heretical, 213, 232–
    33
  liberal redefinitions of, 82, 167
  through the Urim and Thummim,
    23, 34, 83–84
  to Emanuel Swedenborg, 78
  to Jacob Boehme, 73–75
  to Joseph Smith, 32, 34, 35, 36, 38,
    64, 73, 87, 98, 105, 189, 192, 195,
    197, 206
Reynolds, George, 106, 271n
Ricks, Stephen D., 124
Rigdon, Sidney, 70
  as Book of Mormon author, 160
  converted to Book of Mormon, 71
  on Book of Mormon, 158
  on miracles, 237
Riley, Woodbridge, 134, 159
Riter, W. E., 109
Roberts, Brigham H., 106–7, 109–11
  on Book of Mormon geography,
    277n
  on Book of Mormon historicity,
    296n
  on Ethan Smith authorship of Book
    of Mormon, 161–62
  writes Hill Cumorah commemora-
    tion, 244
Robinson, John, 8
Robinson, Stephen, 46, 296n
Rosenzweig, Franz, 212
Ryder, Symonds, 183

Sabatier, Auguste, 212
Sachs, Viola, 6
saj^c, 120
Samuel the Lamanite, 46, 244

Sariah
  as Semitic name, 140
  wife of Lehi, 281n
Saussure, Ferdinand de, 62, 210, 261n
Savage, James, 108
Schneider, Sandra M., 215
Scott, Sir Walter, 229
Scott, Walter, 70, 197
scripture. *See also* Standard Works
  as a genre, 294n
  definition, 4, 304n–5
  LDS conceptions of, 195
Second Great Awakening, 8, 9
seer stone, 32
  found by Joseph Smith, 16
  ownership disputed by Willard
    Chase, 25
  use and appearance described, 32
  used to translate Book of Mormon,
    34
Sermon at the Temple, 138
Sermon on the Mount, 48, 137–38,
  200
Shamhozai, 123
Shipps, Jan, 6, 64, 65, 70
Shurtliff, Luman, 236
Shook, Charles, 133
Sidon River, 106, 129, 225
silk, 109, 116, 131, 141, 147
Sjodahl, Janne M., 106, 271n
Skousen, Royal, 31, 32, 134, 135, 137,
  287n
Smith, Alvin, 16
Smith, Emma
  accompanies Joseph to retrieve
    plates, 21
  courtship with Joseph, 18
  marries Joseph, 19
  on Book of Mormon translation
    process, 30, 32
  on Joseph's education, 158
  serves as Book of Mormon scribe,
    30
Smith, Ethan, *View of the Hebrews*, 94,
  110, 161
Smith, James, 139
Smith, Joseph F., 225

Smith, Joseph, Jr., 7, **69**
  and money-digging, **16**–19, 24–25,
    251n
  as modern Moses, 13, 48, 82, 118
  as visionary rather than mystic,
    264n
  boyhood home of, **10**
  character of, 252n
  court trial of, 19
  designated First Elder in the
    Church, 36
  edits *Times and Seasons*, 161
  educational background, 157–58,
    288n
  establishes museum, 105
  Lectures on Faith, 192, 193, 298n
  marries Emma, 19
  moves to Fayette, NY, 37
  on Book of Mormon geography,
    99, 270n
  opposition to, 258n
  relocates in Harmony, PA, 27
  retranslates Bible, 190, 194, 240,
    262n
  retrieves plates, 21
  visited by John the Baptist, 36
  writes Wentworth Letter, 3
Smith, Katharine, 25
Smith, Lucy Mack, 10, 15, 16, 19, 20,
    21, 22, 24, 25, 26, 34, 39, 91, 187,
    237
Smith, Samuel
  as first Mormon missionary, 55, 61
  joins Joseph in Harmony, 35
  preaches Book of Mormon, 85
Smith, Timothy, 186, 193, 230, 233
Smith, Wilfred Cantwell, 3, 87, 89,
    191
Smith, William, 16, 22
Smithsonian
  revised statement on Book of Mor-
    mon, 132
  Sorenson response to Book of Mor-
    mon statement, 130–32
  statement on the Book of Mormon,
    115–16
Soper, Daniel, 108
Sorenson, John, 51, 89, 96–97, 126–32

Southcoate, Joanna, 84
Spaulding, Solomon, 5, 86, 156, 159–
    61, 289n
Stafford, William, 251n, 253n
Standard Works, 194, 195, 249n, 299n
Stark, Rodney, 154, 174, 185, 217, 232
steel, 107, 109, 116, 131, 141
Stendahl, Krister, 6, 138, 150
Stephens, John Lloyd
  *Incidents of Travel in Central
    America, Chiapas, and Yucatan*,
    99–103, 101, 102
  Incidents of Travel in Yucatan, 104
Stillingfleet, Edward, 193
Stowell, Josiah, 16, 19, 21
Swedenborg, Emanuel, 72, 76–78
sword of Laban, 14, 39
Szink, Terrence L., 124

Talmage, James E., 108, 109, 110
Tanner, Jerald and Sandra, 144
Taylor, Thomas, 20, 173
Taves, 85, 267n
Teichert, Minerva, 308n
temple
  complexes in Mesoamerica, 99
  in LDS religion, 48, 170, 245
  Nephite versions of, 44, 48, 96, 123,
    137, 139, 225
  of Solomon, 48
  of Zerubbabel, 171, 253n
Temple Mount, 89
Temple Square, 146
temple text, 138
Temple, William, 209
Theophilanthropist, 232
Thomas, Mark, 165, 179–80, 201
Thompson, Charles, *Evidences in
    Proof of the Book of Mormon*, 65,
    86, 97
Thorowgood, Thomas, *Jews in
    America*, 94
Tiffany's Monthly, 158
Times and Seasons, 65, 80, 97, 102, 104,
    161
Tlatilco seal, **114**
Tov, Emanuel, 151
Toy, Crawford Howell, 82

trinity
  Book of Mormon on, 200–201
  in Christian orthodoxy, 75, 234,
    301n
  Swedenborg on, 77
Tuxtla Mountains, 129
Tvedtnes, John A., 124, 133, 134, 137,
    139, 253n
Twain, Mark, 134
Tyrrell, George, 211

Underhill, Evelyn, 76
Universalism, 164-66, 187, 202
Urim and Thummim, 12
  and "authoritative discourse", 83–
    84
  as hypnotic influence, 159
  described by Lucy Smith, 22
  described by William Smith, 22,
    253n, 255n
  history and meaning of, 22–23, 24,
    253n
  returned to Moroni, 34, 256n
  view promised to three witnesses,
    39

Vatican II, 175
Veracruz, Mexico, 126
visions
  and orthodoxy, 41–42, 265n
  in Puritan era, 264n
  LDS test for authenticity of, 225
  phenomenology of, 37
Vogel, Dan, 165, 166, 167, 187–88

Walker, Ronald, 230
Wardlaw, Gilbert, *Testimony of Scrip-
    ture*, 232–33
Wauchope, Robert, 145, 146
Weber, Max, 309n
Welch, John, 52, 124, 125, 133, 137,
    138, 222
Wentworth Letter, 3, 62, 90–91, 247n
Wesley, John, 233
Whitmer, "Father" Peter
  provides haven for Joseph Smith, 37
  witnesses translation of Book of
    Mormon, 30

Whitmer, Christian, 37, 40, 56
Whitmer, David, 24, **41**
  describes stone box holding plates,
    104
  excommunicated, 41
  one of Three Witnesses to gold
    plates, 39
  relates story of gold plates to
    Oliver Cowdery, 35
Whitmer, Elizabeth Ann, 35-36
Whitmer, Jacob, 40
Whitmer, John, 37, 40
Whitmer, Peter, Jr., 40, 70
Whitney, Orson F., 195
Whittier, John Greenleaf, 239
Widtsoe, John A., 111
  on Book of Mormon archaeology,
    113
Wight, Lyman, 71
Wild, Asa, 72
Wilkinson, Jemima, 72–73
Willey, Gordon R., 113
Williams, Stephen, 146
Wilson, Edmund, 157
Winchell holes, 17, **18**, 251n
Winchester, Benjamin, 66
Wolterstorff, Nicholas, 215, 218, 245
Wood, Gordon, 230
Woodruff, Wilford
  and Moroni's visit to Joseph, 250n
  describes Nephite ruins, 98
  manifesto canonized, 192
  wordprint analysis, 156–57
Wuthenau, Alexander von, 148

Yadin, Yigael, 144
Young, Brigham, 183, 186, 193, 195
Young, Levi Edgar, 111

Zarahemla, 46, 50, 104, 107, 123, 129,
    147, 160
Zeezrom, 200
Zelph, 98, 130
Zenock, 136
Zenos, 136
Zohar, 169
Zosimus, 171–72